CONTENTS

SEVEN MEN

THIS BOOK IS DEDICATED
TO MY FATHER, NICHOLAS METAXAS.

Μέ Αγάπη

Contents

Introduction

As most people would concur, the idea of manhood has fallen into some confusion in the last decades. This book hopes to help correct some of that by asking and answering two vitally important questions: First, *what is a man*? And second, *what makes a man great*?

And you'll forgive me if I begin with John Wayne. "The Duke" is obviously not one of the seven men in this book, but many men of my generation have thought of him as something of an icon of manhood and manliness. We still do. But why? What is it about him? Is it the toughness and the swagger? Is it just that he comes across as big and strong and that most men aspire to those qualities? Well, that all has something to do with it, but I actually think his iconic status is because he usually played roles in which his size and strength were used to protect the weak. He was the good guy. He was always strong and tough but never a bully. Somehow watching him on the silver screen said more to generations of men (and women) about what made a man great than endless discussions on the subject. Sometimes a living picture really *is* worth a thousand words. And what we think of John Wayne is a clue to the secret of the greatness of the men in this book.

So this is a book that doesn't talk *about* manhood—at least not after this introduction, which you may skip if you like, although you've already come this far, so why stop?—but that *shows* it in the actual lives of great men. You can talk about right and wrong and good and bad all day long, but ultimately people need to see it. Seeing and studying the actual lives of people is simply the best way to communicate ideas about how to behave and how *not* to behave. We need heroes and role models.

Now, my own personal *greatest* role model is Jesus. And you may have noticed that he didn't just talk. Of course he said a lot of extraordinary things, but he also lived with his disciples for three years. They saw him eat and sleep and perform miracles. They saw him live life and suffer and die. They saw him interact with all kinds of people, including themselves. He lived among them. That's the main way that he communicated himself to the men who would communicate him to the world. That's how he made disciples—who would make disciples, who would make disciples. So from the gospel stories of Jesus' life, you get the idea that seeing a person's life is at least as important as getting a list of lessons from that person. Yes, sermons are important, but seeing the actual life of the guy who gives the sermon might be even more powerful. And you get the idea that how you live affects others. It teaches *them* how to live.

Historically speaking, role models have always been important. Until recently. The ancient Greeks had *Plutarch's Lives,* and in the sixteenth century we got *Foxe's Book of Martyrs.* The message in these and similar books was that these lives were great and worthy of emulation. Having role models and heroes was historically a vital way of helping a new generation know what it should be aiming at. This is one of the main reasons I wrote biographies of William Wilberforce *(Amazing Grace: William Wilberforce and the Heroic Campaign to End Slavery)* and Dietrich Bonhoeffer *(Bonhoeffer: Pastor, Martyr, Prophet, Spy)*. By the way, one of the last books that Bonhoeffer himself was reading just before he died was *Plutarch's Lives*.

So the idea of having heroes and role models has historically been very important; but as I say, somehow this has changed in recent years. *What happened?*

QUESTION AUTHORITY

Part of what happened is that—since roughly the late 1960s—we've adopted the idea that no one is really in a position to say what's right or wrong. So we're loath to point to anyone as a good role model. "Who am I to judge anyone?" has almost become the mantra of our age.

But how did that happen? Well, it's complicated. But it probably has something to do with the Vietnam War and with Watergate. Without a doubt these events helped accelerate a trend toward suspicion of the "official" version of things and of our leaders. Until Vietnam, all previous wars were generally seen as worthy of fighting, and the overwhelming cultural message was that patriotic Americans must do their duty and pitch in and help defend our country and our freedoms. With Vietnam, all that changed. Ditto with Watergate: for the first time in history—thanks mainly to the taped conversations in the White House—we saw and heard a US president not acting "presidential" at all but acting ignobly and venally and shamefully. We heard him use words we wouldn't want our children to use.

So the authority of that president, Richard Nixon, rightfully came under intense scrutiny. But since then, *all* our leaders have been held in deep suspicion. And we've tended to focus on the negative things about famous people. Every negative sound bite of a TV preacher that can be aired will be heard a thousand times more than the good things he's said. It's hard to have heroes in a climate like that.

We've even extended this idea backward through history, so that much of what we hear about our past presidential heroes is negative.

George Washington is no longer thought of mainly as the heroic "Father of Our Country," but as a wealthy landowner who hypocritically owned slaves. Many of us have forgotten the outrageous and spectacular sacrifices that he made and for which every American ought to be endlessly grateful. This is not only disgraceful; it's profoundly harmful to us as a nation. Columbus isn't held up as a brave and intrepid visionary who risked everything to discover a New World. He's considered a murderer of indigenous peoples. It's true that thoughtless idol worship is never a good thing, but being overly critical of men who are otherwise good can also be tremendously harmful. And it has been.

So the very idea of *legitimate* authority has been damaged. Since I was a kid in the seventies, we have had bumper stickers that said "Question Authority." But this didn't just mean we should question whether authority is legitimate, which would be a good idea. No, it seemed to me to go beyond that. It seemed to say that we should question the very idea of authority itself. So you could say that we've gone all the way from foolishly accepting all authority to foolishly rejecting all authority. We've gone from the extreme of being naive to the other extreme of being cynical. The golden mean, where we would question authority *in order to determine whether it was legitimate*, was passed by entirely. We have fled from one icy pole to the other, missing the equator altogether. We are like the person who was so wounded by a betrayal from a member of the opposite sex that he no longer trusts anyone of that sex. Instead of looking for someone who is trustworthy, we've entirely dispensed with the idea of trustworthiness. No one is trustworthy.

This is a very bad place to end up, and in our culture we are paying a harsh price for it. As I've said, people need heroes and role models. Those of us who take the Bible seriously believe that mankind is fallen and that no one is perfect except Jesus. But we also believe that there are some lives that are good examples and some that are bad examples. Can we really believe that certain lives aren't worthy of emulation?

And that others are cautionary tales? Are we really unwilling to say that we shouldn't try to get our children (and ourselves) to see that Abraham Lincoln is worthy of our emulation and Adolf Hitler and Joseph Stalin are not?

Recently I watched an old rerun of *The Rifleman*, starring Chuck Connors. The series ran from 1958 to 1963 and its audience was largely boys. I was absolutely stunned by how the story was clearly trying to communicate what it means to be a real man, a good man, a heroic and brave man. And it was showing the difference between that and being a coward or a bully. This is vital in raising up young men who aspire to do the right thing. But one look at TV today will tell you that this is entirely gone. This book is for everyone, but in writing a book about these seven men, I've thought that young men especially need role models. If we can't point to anyone in history or in our culture whom they should emulate, then they will emulate *whomever*.

Young men who spend their time watching violent movies and playing video games aren't very easily going to become the men they were meant to become. They will drift. They will lose out on the very reason they were brought into this world: to be great, to be heroes themselves. What could be more tragic than that? They won't understand who they are, and they will have no idea how to relate to women, and they will hurt themselves (and probably some women) along the way. So it is vital that we teach them who they are in God's view, and it's vital that we bring back a sense of the heroic. The men in this book are some of my heroes and I am thrilled to be able to share them with others. I hope they will inspire young men to emulate them.

WHAT IS REAL MANHOOD?

At the beginning of this introduction I said that there was a general confusion about manhood. This confusion relates to the larger idea of authority itself coming under attack, which we've just mentioned. Since the father has traditionally been seen as the leader of the family, it only follows that if we've taken the very idea of authority down, we've taken fatherhood down with it.

Can anyone doubt that the idea of fatherhood has declined dramatically in the last forty or so years? One of the most popular TV shows of the 1950s was called *Father Knows Best*. It was a sweet portrayal of a wonderful and in many ways typical American family. The father, played by Robert Young, was the unquestioned authority, but his authority was never harsh or domineering. His strength was a quiet strength. In fact, he was gentle and wise and kind and giving—so much so that just about everyone watching the show wished their dad could be more like that! But of course today we tend to see fathers depicted in the mainstream media either as dunces or as overbearing fools.

There is something vital in the idea of fatherhood and it gives us a clue to the secret of a great man. But we have to point out that a man needn't be an actual father to bear the traits of every good father. Two of the men in this book, Dietrich Bonhoeffer and John Paul II, never married or had children. Even George Washington, who married, never had children of his own. And yet we Americans call him the father of our country. And in the case of Pope John Paul II, the root word from which we get "pope" is *papa*—father. Being a father is not a biological thing. If we think of the fatherhood of God, we get a picture of someone who is strong and loving and who sacrifices himself for those he loves. That's a picture of real fatherhood and real manhood.

SO WHAT IS GOD'S IDEA FOR MANHOOD?

In a world where all authority is questioned and in which our appreciation of real leadership—and especially fatherhood—has been badly damaged, we end up with very little in the way of the heroic in general. As we've said, the idea of manhood itself has become profoundly confused. And as a result of this, instead of God's idea of authentic manhood, we've ended up with two very distorted ideas about manhood.

The first false idea about manhood is the idea of being macho—of being a big shot and using strength to be domineering and to bully those who are weaker. Obviously this is not God's idea of what a real man is. It's someone who has not grown up emotionally, who might be a man on the outside, but who on the inside is simply an insecure and selfish boy.

The second false choice is to be emasculated—to essentially turn away from your masculinity and to pretend that there is no real difference between men and women. Your strength as a man has no purpose, so being strong isn't even a good thing.

God's idea of manhood is something else entirely. It has nothing to do with the two false ideas of either being macho or being emasculated. The Bible says that God made us in his image, male and female, and it celebrates masculinity and femininity. And it celebrates the differences between them. Those differences were God's idea. For one thing, the Bible says that men are generally stronger than women, and of course Saint Peter famously—or infamously—describes women as "the weaker sex." But God's idea of making men strong was so that they would use that strength to protect women and children and anyone else. There's something heroic in that. Male strength is a gift from God, and like all gifts from God, it's always and everywhere meant to be used to bless others. In Genesis 12:1–3, God tells Abraham that he will bless him *so that Abraham can bless others*. All blessings and every gift—and strength is a gift—are God's gifts, to be used for his purposes, which means to bless others. So men are meant to use their strength to protect and bless those who are weaker. That can mean other men who need help or it can mean women and children. True strength is always strength given over to God's purposes.

But because men have sometimes used their strength selfishly, there has been a backlash against the whole idea of masculine strength. It has been seen—and portrayed—as something negative. If you buy into that idea, then you realize the only way to deal with it is to work against it, to try to weaken men, because whatever strength they have will be used to harm others. This leads to the emasculated idea of men. Strength is denigrated because it can be used for ill. So we live in a culture where strength is feared and where there is a sense that—to protect the weak—strength itself must be weakened. When this happens, the heroic and true nature of strength is much forgotten. It leads to a world of men who aren't really men. Instead they are just two kinds of boys: boasting, loud-mouthed bullies or soft, emasculated pseudo-men. Women feel that they must be "empowered" and must never rely on men for strength. It's a lot like a socialistic idea, where "power" and "strength" are redistributed—taken away from men and given to women, to even things out. Of course it doesn't work that way. Everyone loses.

The knight in shining armor who does all he can to protect others, the gentleman who lays down his cloak or opens a door for a lady—these are Christian ideals of manliness. Jesus said that he who would lead must be the servant of all. It's the biblical idea of servant leadership. The true leader gives himself to the people he leads. The good shepherd lays down his life for his sheep. Jesus washed the feet of the disciples. Jesus died for those he loves. That is God's idea of strength and leadership and blessing. It's something to be used in the service of others. So God's idea of masculine strength gives us the idea of a chivalrous gentleman toward women, not a bully or someone who sees no difference between himself and them.

CHIVALRY AND HEROISM ARE NOT DEAD

Last summer, there was a terrible shooting at a movie theater. Twelve people who had gone to a midnight showing of the most recent Batman movie were senselessly murdered by what can only be described as a madman. But of all the things that have been said about this tragic event, what struck me more than anything was that three young men died protecting their girlfriends from the madman's bullets. Something caused them to risk losing their lives for a young woman. Why did they do that? What does that say about manhood?

In the killer, you have a perfect picture of evil, which is the opposite of love. It is a picture of someone using power (in this case his firearm) to destroy, to harm. But in the three young men, you have a picture of strength expressed as love, which is the opposite of evil. You see men using their power and their strength to protect. In the case of the first you see someone doing something that is unfathomably selfish, someone who seems to see no value in others, and whose actions reflect that judgment. In the second you see three men doing something that is unfathomably selfless. Why did they use their strength and power to help someone else? What was that instinct, and why did they follow it?

The stories in this book are the stories of men who followed that latter path, who seemed to know that at the heart of what it is to be a man is that idea of being selfless, of putting your greatest strength at God's disposal, and of sometimes surrendering something that is yours for a larger purpose—of giving what is yours in the service of others.

HAVING COURAGE MEANS HAVING HEART

I was an English major in college, and now I'm a writer—so I hope you won't mind a brief etymological digression. It doesn't matter if you don't know exactly what that is, but the point I want to make is very important.

We say that the selfless acts of those men in the movie theater— and the selfless acts of most people everywhere—are courageous. Strength in the service of others is courageous. But did you know that the word *courage* comes from the Latin *cor*, which means "heart"? So to have courage simply means to have "heart." Of course the Bible often exhorts people to "take heart" or to "be of good courage." The meaning is effectively the same. So to have heart *means* to have courage. This is God's idea of strength, to have a heart like a lion. A man who has heart can be described as *lionhearted*.

15

You may notice that the false macho idea of manliness sees having "heart" as a weak, soft thing. It misses the true idea of what it is to have heart. Instead, the false macho concept of manhood substitutes having something else. Hint: it starts with a "b." Second hint: the Spanish word is *cojones*. But notice that this concept of manhood reduces God's idea of a noble and heroic man to a sexual level. It puts us in mind of apes and goats, but not of lions. Did you ever read the C. S. Lewis essay titled "Men Without Chests"? Lewis understood that large-hearted men, men "with chests," were real men. It's about having a chest and a heart. Until we realize that God is concerned with the size of our hearts and not that of our genital apparati, we can never understand God's idea of true masculinity.

So what is "heart"? It's courage, but courage to do what? The courage to do the right thing when all else tells you not to do it. The courage to rise above your surroundings and circumstances. The courage to be God's idea of a real man and to give of yourself for others when it costs you to do so and when everything tells you to look out for yourself first.

WHY DID I CHOOSE THESE SEVEN MEN?

Anyone reading this book must wonder why I chose these seven men. Of course this is not a definitive list. There is great subjectivity in these choices. There are many, many more whom I would have liked to include and whom I hope to include in future volumes. But in this first volume I was looking for seven men who had all evinced one particular quality: that of surrendering themselves to a higher purpose, of giving something away that they might have kept. All of them did this in one way or another. Doing this is noble and admirable, and it takes courage and it usually takes faith. Each of the seven men in this book have that quality.

Let me explain briefly what I mean for each of them.

As you'll soon see when you read about him, *George Washington*

(1732–1799) once voluntarily gave up extraordinary power. He actually could have become a king, when being a king really meant something; but he selflessly refused the honor. Such a sacrifice is almost unfathomable to us today. But Washington knew there was something even greater than power. To do the noble thing, the heroic thing, the right thing—for him, that was greater than becoming powerful. He surrendered all that power for the sake of something nobler: he did it for the sake of his new country and for millions yet to be born. If he hadn't done it, that country might not have lasted very long. So anyone who is an American is a direct beneficiary of what this great man did. This is not hyperbole. What he did affected you, personally. He gave up a sure thing to do the right thing, and today he is deservedly regarded to be one of the greatest heroes in the history of the world.

Similarly, *William Wilberforce* (1759–1833) gave up the chance to be prime minister of England. Many have said that he "put principle above party" and gave up becoming prime minister. But for what did he surrender the prize of that office? He gave it up for a cause that to him was far greater than becoming the leader of the greatest empire in the world at that time. He gave up his life for the sake of African slaves, people who could give him nothing in return. But Wilberforce knew that what God had given up for him was far greater, so he did what he did for the Africans he would never meet, and for God.

This man's conversion to the Christian faith changed everything for him. Suddenly he saw everything differently. Suddenly he realized that everything he had been given—wealth and power and influence and connections and intelligence and a gift of oratory—was a gift from God. And he realized that it was a gift to be used for others. The choice was his, of course, but when you really know that God has given you something for others, it's hard not to use it for others. Wilberforce knew that taking everything he had been given and using it to improve the lives of others was the very reason he had been born. And by devoting himself to this for five decades of his life, he became one of the most important human beings who ever lived.

He changed the world in a way that would have been unthinkable at the time.

The 1982 movie *Chariots of Fire* tells the story of *Eric Liddell* (1902–1945) who gave up the acclaim of millions to honor God. It is one of the most extraordinary stories in the history of sports. But it doesn't involve any athletic action. In fact, it involves deliberate athletic *non*-action. It was the historic decision by a devoutly Christian young man to forgo the one thing that everyone said he should want—and deserved—namely, the opportunity to win an Olympic gold medal in the one event in which he was most likely to win it. But God came first, and Liddell surrendered his best chance for Olympic gold. And, as you'll discover, that's only half of his story.

Then there is the brilliant and heroic German pastor and theologian *Dietrich Bonhoeffer* (1906–1945), who courageously defied the Nazis and surrendered his freedom and safety time and time again. He did that most notably in 1939 when he made the fateful decision to leave the safety of America to return to Germany, simply because he felt that was what God wanted him to do. Ultimately, he gave up his life. His willingness to do that has inspired countless people to do the right thing in thousands of situations, and Bonhoeffer's story is inspiring them still.

Jackie Robinson (1919–1972) was given the opportunity to do something historic when he was chosen to be the man who broke the so-called color barrier in professional baseball. But in order to do this, he had to surrender something very few men would have the strength to surrender: he would have to give up the right to fight back against some of the most vicious insults against his race that anyone has ever heard. It must have taken superhuman effort, but with faith in God, and with a desire to bless unknown millions who would have the opportunity to follow in his footsteps, he did just that. He made a great sacrifice for people he would never meet. He thought of his wife and his children, whom he knew, but he also thought of all the others who would benefit from his doing the right thing, and he suffered greatly to do what he did. Because of his courage and heroism, he is in this book of great men.

Karol Wojtyla—whom we know as *Pope John Paul II* (1920–2005)—surrendered his whole life to God in what many would think of as the most typical way: he became a priest and decided to serve God. He became a bishop, an archbishop, a cardinal, and finally, in 1978, the pope. But he was not an ambitious man. He wasn't in it for the power. He gave up his right to himself. He even gave up his right to dignity. When he grew old, he went before the whole world as a picture of a man weakened by Parkinson's disease, but who nonetheless courageously continued to appear before the world, even in that weakened state. As a result, he showed in his own life what he professed with his words, that a human being is sacred in God's eyes. Even in our weakened state, and *especially* in our weakened state, we are children of God. He was a picture of courage and of heroic consistency, a man who practiced what he preached.

The one man in this book I had the privilege to know personally was *Chuck Colson* (1931–2012). In the beginning of his life, Chuck was a man who was not exactly headed for inclusion in a book like this one. He was tremendously ambitious, but he seemed to seek power for its own sake, or for *his* own sake. Eventually he amassed a tremendous amount of it, as special counsel to the president of the United States, Richard Nixon. This was a heady thing for a man not yet forty, and what he did with that power was his great undoing. But when, in the scandal of Watergate, that power was finally stripped from him, Chuck Colson found the real reason for his life and for life in general. And when his role in Watergate threatened to send him to prison, he didn't blink. His faith was so strong that he knew the only thing to do was to trust God so completely that it would look crazy to the rest of the world. And it did look crazy. But he didn't care about what anyone thought—except God. He was playing to the proverbial audience of One and he refused a plea bargain that would have made his life much easier during that time. Then he voluntarily pled guilty when he didn't have to—and went to prison as a result. But he knew that when you give everything to God, only then are you truly free. His is a true picture of greatness for all of us.

THE GREATEST

In my humble estimation, the men in this book are some of the greatest men who have ever lived. So if you get to know their stories, your life will be immeasurably richer. It is my fondest hope that these short biographies would lead you to read longer biographies of these great men. I hope you would want to study these lives—and not just study them but emulate them. It is my prayer that those who read this book would be inspired to become real heroes, to become great men in their own generation.

You may read the seven stories of these seven men in the chronological order in which they appear here, or you might skip around. It doesn't matter. These chapters can stand alone as well as they can stand together.

— Eric Metaxas
New York City
October 2012

ONE

George Washington

1732–99

L et me begin the first biography in this book by saying that even if the seven great men discussed within its pages were not in chronological order, I probably still would have started with George Washington. When it comes to true greatness, Washington's tough to beat. But someone's greatness can sometimes lend him an aura of such outsized fame that we begin to think of him not as a real person but as a cartoon superhero or as a legend. That's often the case with Washington.

As you know, he has a state named after him. (Do I need to say which?) And he has our nation's capital city named after him; he has a soaring obelisk monument in that city; his birthday is a national holiday; and he has a huge bridge named after him right here in my hometown of New York City. And if all these things aren't impressive enough, his face is on the dollar bill! (Perhaps you already knew that.) So who really thinks of him as an actual flesh-and-blood human being who struggled as we all struggle and who put on his breeches one leg at a time? That's the problem with being *that* famous. People often don't really think about you as a person at all.

If you do think of him, you probably think of George Washington as that old guy with the somewhat sour expression on the afore-mentioned dollar bill. In that overfamiliar picture, sporting heavily powdered hair and a lace-trimmed shirt, he looks almost as much like an old woman as an old man.

But what I've discovered is that this famous portrait has given many of us an outrageously false picture of who Washington actually was. It presents him as an elderly man with chronic denture discom-fort, who looks none too happy for it. But the reality is completely different.

What if I told you that in his day, George Washington was consid-ered about the manliest man most people had ever seen? No kidding. Virtually everyone who knew him or saw him seemed to say so. He was tall and powerful. He was also both fearless and graceful. On the field of battle, he had several horses shot out from under him; on the dance floor, he was a much sought-after partner.

There's so much to say about Washington that it's hard to know where to begin. For one thing, he was a man of tremendous contra-dictions. For example, the man who became known as the father of our country never fathered children himself. And he lost his own father when he was a young boy. The man who was viewed as deeply honorable actually told some real whoppers when he was a young man, despite Parson Weems's fictitious episode by the cherry tree: "I cannot tell a lie." More than anyone else, he is responsible for freeing American colonists from the greatest military power on earth—the British Empire—and yet he held some three hundred black men, women, and children in bondage at Mount Vernon.[1]

But here's the biggest contradiction: Washington was an extremely ambitious young man who worked hard to achieve fame, glory, land, and riches—yet at a pivotal moment in American history, he did something so selfless that it's difficult to fully fathom. It's principally because of this one thing that he's included in this book.

So what did he do? In a nutshell, he voluntarily gave up incredible power. When you know the details of his sacrifice, it's hard to believe that he did what he did of his own free will. And yet he did it. The temptation *not* to surrender all that power must have been extraordinary. There were many good reasons not to surrender it, but history records that he somehow did. Somehow he made an impossibly grand sacrifice—and in doing so he dramatically changed the history of the world. Had Washington not been willing to do it, America as we know it almost certainly would not exist. That's not hyperbole.

This is why contemporary memorials to Washington describe him as an American Moses, as someone loaned to Americans from God. He was the right man for his time—arguably the only man who could have successfully birthed the American Experiment. If you wonder whether one person's actions can matter, and if you wonder whether character matters, you needn't look any further than the story of George Washington. So here it is.

◆ ◆ ◆

George Washington was born on February 22, 1732, in what is now Westmoreland County, Virginia, the first son of Mary Ball Washington and tobacco farmer Augustine Washington. George had two older half-brothers, Augustine and Lawrence, and one half sister, Jane, who were children from his father's first marriage. George also had five full younger siblings: Samuel, Elizabeth, John, Charles, and Mildred.

Augustine and Lawrence were sent to England for their educations, but George's father died when George was just eleven, making an English education for him financially impossible. He would regret this deficit in his education throughout his long life. George's brother Lawrence, who was fourteen years older, became a father figure to him, someone whose advice the young George would listen to. In 1751, Lawrence took nineteen-year-old George to Barbados, where Lawrence hoped to be cured of tuberculosis. Alas, George contracted smallpox on this trip. Although the disease was dangerous, it actually turned out to be a hugely fortunate occurrence; George was then inoculated from the disease at an early age, thereby preventing him from future attacks of it when he was a general. During the Revolutionary War, large numbers of soldiers died of disease rather than enemy attacks.

As a boy growing into manhood, George frequently visited Lawrence's home on the Potomac River, which was named Mount Vernon. He also frequently visited Belvoir, owned by Lawrence's in-laws. As one biographer put it, at Mount Vernon and Belvoir, "George discovered a world that he had never known."[2] In particular, Belvoir "was a grand structure, an architectural showcase gracefully adorned with exquisite molding and rich paneling and decorated tastefully with furniture and accessories from England."[3] George "was stirred by the people" in these homes, "people of influence," adults "who were well-read and thoughtful, men who were accustomed to wielding power."[4]

Young George determined to turn himself into one of them—especially someone like Lawrence, who was not only a distinguished war hero but also adjutant general of Virginia, a member of the Virginia legislature, the House of Burgesses, and by marriage, a member of the socially prominent Fairfax family. George threw himself into learning proper etiquette, reading serious books, dressing properly, and improving his character. He also eventually shot up to be roughly six-foot-three, this making him much taller than most of his contemporaries and giving him the heroic, statuesque appearance of a born commander.

Given his future career, it's certainly ironic that George's mother fought his efforts, at age fourteen, to become a commissioned officer in the Royal Navy. She thought such a life would be too harsh for her son, so George decided to learn to become a surveyor. He was fiercely intent on acquiring property and wealth, and a surveying career could lead to quick riches in land and money. By the time he turned twenty, George owned some twenty-five hundred acres of Virginia's frontier land.[5]

But that same year—1752—tragedy struck. George's beloved brother Lawrence lost his battle with tuberculosis. Lawrence's wife and daughter also died within a few years. This meant that George would ultimately inherit Mount Vernon—an estate he would ambitiously enlarge and improve during the next four decades.

When he was twenty-one, George once again turned his attention toward the possibility of a military career. Through the intervention of influential friends, and despite the fact that George had no military experience, Virginia's governor appointed him commander of the southernmost military district of Virginia, a post that gave him the rank of major. This was an unexpected development, and it would not be long before George had an opportunity to test his mettle in a dramatic—and ultimately historic—way.

On the horizon loomed the French and Indian War, in which the French and several tribes of native Americans joined forces against Great Britain (including the Anglo-Americans) for what was then called the Ohio Territory a vast area, much larger than the current US state of Ohio. Both France and Britain claimed this territory, and in 1750, France sent an army there and built Fort Le Boeuf, about fifteen miles from Lake Erie, in what is today the northwestern corner of Pennsylvania. This aggressive move by the French infuriated many Virginians, particularly those who owned territory in the region. What to do? The governor of Virginia, Robert Dinwiddie, consulted Crown officials in London, who advised him to send an emissary to the French, letting them know in no uncertain terms that the territory belonged to the English and that they had better remove their troops posthaste.

When young George Washington learned of the need for a messenger to travel through the mountains and wilderness during that upcoming winter, he immediately put himself forward as the man for the job. Governor Dinwiddie accepted Washington's offer and also gave George a number of other responsibilities. He was to spy out the land and the size of the French force. He was also instructed to consult with the so-called "half-king," the chief of the Seneca tribe, about the possibility of their joining with the British against the French, in the event that war should break out. And he was to attempt to find a good location for building an English fort in the area—something that was an absolute necessity if the Ohio Company, a Virginia land speculation company, were to "gain legal title to the hundreds of thousands of acres it coveted in the Ohio Country."[6]

So twenty-one-year-old George left with the governor's letter and six companions. They spent weeks hiking the many miles from Virginia to Ohio, through the endless terrain of winter snow, headed for Fort Le Boeuf.

When they got close to their destination, a French patrol met them and escorted Washington and his men to the fort. The French treated them civilly, as was the custom. They welcomed them, fed them, received and read the letter George delivered, and then gave George their response to take back to Virginia. But as George suspected from conversations that he overheard, the response was not what the English hoped. The French resolutely declared that the land was theirs. If that was true, the two world powers would soon be at war.

George and his men returned home with the letter—in which the French indeed claimed the land as their own—and he prepared an account of his adventure, which was published in colonial newspapers. His fame also spread through London when his memoir was published in pamphlet form under the title *The Journal of Major George Washington*. It was the first time the British would hear of this valiant young man, and obviously not the last.

Faced with French defiance, the House of Burgesses was forced to take action. The members voted to fund what they named the Virginia Regiment, a three-hundred-man volunteer army. This regiment was to travel to the Ohio Valley to assist in building a fort, which Dinwiddie considered essential to protect British interests. The Virginia Regiment was to be led by an experienced British soldier named Colonel Joshua Fry. The ambitious Washington pressed political friends to promote him to the rank of lieutenant colonel, which they succeeded in doing, and so he joined the regiment with this rank.

But Fry could not immediately leave Virginia, so it was the young Washington himself who was charged with leading 186 men into western Pennsylvania. Upon learning that the French had sent one thousand soldiers to build what they would name Fort Duquesne, Washington was in a quandary. He had far fewer men at his disposal than did the French. He had been urging Indians to join the British, but he had no way of knowing whether they actually would.

He also feared negative repercussions if, in effect, he surrendered before meeting up with French troops. Should he wait for Colonel Fry and reinforcements? Adding to Washington's uneasiness were the stealthy nighttime sounds of men nearby. Were they deserters or French soldiers?

Indian scouts gave Washington a further confusing message. They said that a force of French soldiers was headed in Washington's direction, hoping to meet Washington and attack the English. Washington decided to stay where he was, and two days later he received more news from Christopher Gist, who had traveled with Washington on his previous trip into the Ohio wilderness, that a French party of about fifty men was approaching. These soldiers "had invaded [Gist's] nearby wilderness cabin, vowing to kill his cow and smash 'everything in the house.'"[7]

As one historian notes, the inexperienced Washington made "a crucial decision, and one that violated Dinwiddie's instructions to keep the army within its fortifications."[8] Washington sent half his men ahead and then learned from an Indian ally that the French had been spotted not far away. Washington took forty of his men on a rainy night march, determined to make a surprise attack. What took place the next morning in May 1754 simply boggles the imagination.

On their arrival, Washington discovered thirty-two French soldiers calmly preparing their breakfast. For some unknown reason, Washington ordered his men to open fire, and a dozen of the French were immediately slaughtered. Once the smoke cleared, French ensign Joseph Coulon de Villiers, Sieur de Jumonville, attempted to explain to Washington that his troops were on a diplomatic mission. But at the very moment that "Jumonville read this ultimatum, things got immeasurably worse: the Half-King stepped forward, split open [Jumonville's] head with a hatchet, then dipped his hands into the skull, rinsed them with the victim's brains, and scalped him."[9]

Washington would never forget this unspeakably grotesque scene or the demonic horrors of the chaos that ensued. The Seneca traveling with him now viciously attacked and scalped the wounded French, impaling the head of one man on a stake. "Immobilized either by bloodlust or the awful sights that he was beholding for the first time, Washington made no attempt to stop the carnage," writes biographer John Ferling.[10] It's possible Washington did not want to antagonize the Indians by attempting to stop their atrocities.

After it was all over, Washington wrote to Dinwiddie, claiming the French soldiers were actually "Spyes of the worst sort"[11] who intended to prepare the way for an attack by the French. This may well have been true—the diplomatic message may indeed have been cover—but knowing that his French prisoners would have their own story to tell about what happened, Washington warned Dinwiddie not to believe them.

To be sure, Washington had more to worry about than possible condemnation by Dinwiddie. When French leaders at Fort Duquesne learned of the carnage that had taken place against their men, they would certainly seek revenge. Washington immediately ordered his men to begin construction of what he would call Fort Necessity. But the fort's location was rather ill chosen: forests and hills closely surrounded the fort, which meant that the French would be able to get close to it and shoot the English like fish in the proverbial barrel.

This was precisely what happened. Some nine hundred French and Indian fighters arrived under the command of Louis Coulon de Villiers, who was the brother of Jumonville, and immediately opened fire. After they had killed or wounded a full quarter of Washington's men, Villiers asked Washington if he would like to surrender. Washington agreed to do so and—worse from the standpoint of his record—he signed a document in which he confessed that Jumonville had been murdered.

Washington again sent misleading reports of the battle, falsely claiming that more than three hundred French had become casualties (in reality, they suffered only nineteen) and that the English defeat was due to inexperienced men and dwindling supplies. Washington "never, then or later, admitted to any errors on his part," writes Ferling.[12] Washington also claimed that the man who acted as translator between the French and the English was incompetent and possibly corrupt; otherwise he never would have "confessed" to the murder of Jumonville. Again, it's difficult to know what really happened.

The French and Indian War, as it would henceforth be known, and which these battles launched, would last five years. Despite patently bad decision making, the young Washington's "virtues stood out amid the temporary wreckage of his reputation. With unflagging resolution, he had kept his composure in battle, even when surrounded by piles of corpses. . . . Utterly fearless, he faced down dangers and seemed undeterred by obstacles."[13] In the weeks after the debacle, "condemnation of Washington gradually gave way to widespread acknowledgment that he had confronted terrifying odds at Fort Necessity."[14]

The now twenty-two-year-old Washington, doubtless licking his wounds, retired to Mount Vernon. But it would not be very long before he had a chance to redeem himself.

In 1755, the British sent General Edward Braddock, two infantry regiments, and seven hundred provincial soldiers to take Fort Duquesne from the French. Washington, who was experienced in traveling in the wilderness and in communicating with Indians, was invited to join this expedition and to serve on General Braddock's staff.

On July 9, after fording the Monongahela River, Braddock and an advance force of fourteen hundred men encountered a huge force of French and Indians. The French soldiers, who had learned how to fight Indian-style, raced into the woods, surrounded the British, and rained deadly fire on them, killing or wounding 976 men, including Braddock. It was a tremendous slaughter, "the worst defeat suffered by the British in America prior to the War of Independence."[15] But in this hellish hail of bullets and death, Washington first showed himself as a man of legendary courage and passion on the field of battle. History records that "Washington alone of Braddock's aides emerged unscathed, though his hat and coat were riddled with bullet holes and two horses were shot from beneath him. Washington never ran. He stood and fought with great valor."[16]

It seems genuinely miraculous that Washington survived that day, and the courage involved in staying amidst such gunfire as would put holes in his hat and coat—and not one but two horses—is nothing less than superlatively heroic. As a result of Washington's spectacular gallantry during this battle, Governor Dinwiddie asked him to command Virginia's now much larger army. He would have the rank of colonel. Washington and his men of the Virginia army spent the next several years fighting the Indians, who continued to attack settlements and murder the families living there. Washington often complained about the lack of adequate men, equipment, and Indian allies, along with the fact that they were fighting a defensive rather than an offensive war. And as military leaders often do today, he complained that the civilian leaders who knew little about battlefield tactics were making the wrong decisions.

In 1757, the British government decided that to finally drive the French from Fort Duquesne, it would send three armies to America, one of them under the leadership of Brigadier General John Forbes. Washington now presided over two Virginia regiments of some two thousand men, and Forbes assigned him to lead one of these three brigades. Learning from captured enemy soldiers that Fort Duquesne was lightly garrisoned, Forbes, intent on capturing it, sent twenty-five hundred men under Washington's command to do it. But when they at long last arrived in late 1758, they discovered that the French had fled the fort after burning it. The Americans later learned that the French had become uneasy after their Indian allies left them and decided that their best option was to destroy the fort and leave. There was obviously little glory in Washington's victory, but it was a victory nonetheless. And thus would end the military career of the twenty-six-year-old George Washington—or so he then thought.

Shortly afterward, Washington resigned his commission, to the sorrow of his officers, who had become extremely fond of him. Many of them participated in a moving farewell tribute, noting his commitment to justice, as well as his loyalty, fairness, sincerity, and other positive qualities. Few could question that Washington's disciplined and courageous leadership had inspired them to give their best efforts.

Washington was deeply touched by this farewell. He thanked the men, saying that he did so with "true affection for the honor you have done me, for if I have acquired any reputation, it is from you I derive it."[17] This was typical of the graciousness that would mark him in future years.

But now that he was leaving the military, just what would become of this promising young man?

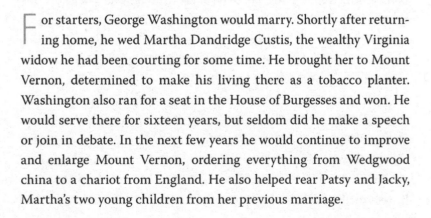

For starters, George Washington would marry. Shortly after returning home, he wed Martha Dandridge Custis, the wealthy Virginia widow he had been courting for some time. He brought her to Mount Vernon, determined to make his living there as a tobacco planter. Washington also ran for a seat in the House of Burgesses and won. He would serve there for sixteen years, but seldom did he make a speech or join in debate. In the next few years he would continue to improve and enlarge Mount Vernon, ordering everything from Wedgwood china to a chariot from England. He also helped rear Patsy and Jacky, Martha's two young children from her previous marriage.

But things were happening in the world beyond Mount Vernon that wouldn't let George Washington remain as he was for long. In 1764, Britain's passage of the Revenue Act, which taxed rum, wine, coffee, tea, molasses, sugar, and tobacco, enraged most Americans, even though the taxes were intended to pay for Britain's defense of America from future attacks by the French or Indians. After all, no American had a seat in Parliament, and taxation without representation was not something they were eager to accept.

When, in 1765, Parliament passed the Stamp Act (a tax on official documents and pamphlets among other things), the outrage against Great Britain increased. For one thing, there were riots. Parliament repealed the Stamp Act in 1766, but it then promptly reinfuriated the Americans by passing the Townshend Acts in 1767, which taxed paper, tea, glass, lead, and paint. American boycotts of many British imports ensued, costing the British much lost income.

In 1770, the Boston Massacre took place, in which British soldiers killed five colonists, further inflaming American feeling against the presence of British troops on their soil. And in 1773, the British imposed the Tea Act, which led to the Boston Tea Party—an act of protest that amuses most Americans today, but that in some of its lesser-known and gruesome details horrified many, including George Washington. Nonetheless, Washington knew that things had come to a point at which something had to be done. Until now he had mostly listened quietly while other members of the Virginia House of Burgesses expressed their wrath at the escalating British abuses. Even he "was prepared for a strident response against Britain's imperial policies, if a majority of colonists were of like mind."[18]

Indeed, they were. The American colonists passionately believed that Parliament had absolutely no legal authority to impose taxes on them. So in August of 1774, Washington was among seven men chosen to represent Virginia in Philadelphia at the newly formed Continental Congress. The Congress decided on a boycott of all British-made goods, to be supported by the thirteen colonies. And the congressmen made plans for activating each colony's militia if the need should arise, which it soon and certainly did.

It was on that now famous date, "the eighteenth of April in '75," that a Boston silversmith named Paul Revere rode through the night to warn his fellow colonists of the imminent arrival of British troops. The British had sent a thousand soldiers to confiscate arms and arrest Revolutionary leaders. The next morning, the curtain rose on that great War of Independence we now call the American Revolution. Most of us know the story of how American fathers and husbands left the warmth of their beds to fiercely resist British troops at Lexington and Concord. The casualties from these historic clashes were shocking at the time, especially given the fact that war had not yet been declared. Nearly three hundred British soldiers and one hundred Massachusetts militiamen were killed or wounded.[19]

Learning of the conflict, Washington memorably mused in a letter to his friend George Fairfax,

> Unhappy it is though to reflect, that a Brother's Sword has been sheathed in a Brother's breast, and that, the once happy and peaceful plains of America are either to be drenched with Blood, or Inhabited by Slaves. Sad alternative! But can a virtuous Man hesitate in his choice?[20]

News of the battles electrified the thirteen colonies; thousands of New England militiamen poured into Boston, besieging the British in an effort not only to trap them within the city but also to force them, through a shortage of food and other supplies, to board their ships and leave, preferably forever.

In what became known as the Battle of Bunker Hill—which the English technically won—the angry Americans, who happened to be very good shots and who broke the rules of military etiquette by targeting officers, forced the British to pay a heavy price: about one thousand

British soldiers were killed or wounded, while the Americans suffered around five hundred casualties.[21]

That May, the Second Continental Congress met. Its members realized that the colonies could not fight independently of one another; the thirteen militias needed to be transformed into a single, national army. But who would lead it? On June 19, 1775, George Washington answered the call. He was forty-three years old.

But we must wonder, what exactly was it about Washington that put him forward as the first choice of the Continental Congress? John Adams joked that he met every qualification: he was tall and handsome, and he moved gracefully—qualities evidently lacking in the other candidates. But there were serious reasons too. For one thing, Washington was rich, so he was considered immune to enemy bribes. That was an important consideration at the time. And he had a sparkling reputation; he seemed to make a grand impression wherever he went. As one Connecticut observer noted, "He seems discreet and virtuous, no harum-scarum, ranting, swearing fellow, but sober, steady, and calm."[22]

Addressing Congress at Philadelphia's State House, Washington— who knew it would take a miracle to beat the British—said with his typical humility: "I do not think myself equal to the command I [am] honored with, [but] as the Congress desire it I will enter upon the momentous duty, & give every power I possess in their service & for the Support of the glorious Cause."[23]

Washington revealed his apprehensions about the militiamen's lack of experience, who were not trained soldiers but farmers and tradespeople. Writing to his brother-in-law shortly after he was given his command, Washington said, "I can answer but for three things: a firm belief in the justice of our cause; close attention in the prosecution of it; and the strictest integrity. If these cannot supply the places of ability and experience, the cause will suffer."[24]

After making final preparations for his new duties and bidding Martha good-bye, Washington fatefully mounted his horse and rode from Philadelphia to Cambridge, Massachusetts.

◆ ◆ ◆

W hat followed, from the summer of 1775 through 1781, were six long years of sporadic fighting from Saratoga to Boston, from Trenton to Long Island; from Moore's Creek Bridge, North Carolina, to Bennington, Vermont; Savannah, Chesapeake Bay, and, finally, Yorktown.

The details of the Revolutionary War have become iconic; the bleak winter of 1777–1778 at Valley Forge, where many of Washington's troops died from sickness. The crossing of the Delaware River that was part of the daring Christmas night attack, surprising hungover Hessian mercenaries and winning a victory when America desperately needed one.

Washington stoically dealt with endless difficulties: constant troop shortages; the disturbing betrayal of a trusted colleague, General Benedict Arnold; attempts at assassination; and efforts to capture him. But somehow—many would say quite miraculously—Washington shaped up a ragtag collection of underfed, underpaid, and underarmed men into the enviable fighting force that (with a little help from the French) vanquished the most powerful military force that had ever existed.

One biographer notes that in the final big battle of the war, in Yorktown, Virginia, "Washington dismounted, stood in the line of fire, and watched."[25] No one disputes that he was tremendously brave. Many times throughout his military career, he fearlessly put himself in harm's way, despite the fact that when the tall general mounted his horse, he provided enemy soldiers with an especially visible and tempting target.

◆ ◆ ◆

M any of us have seen the famous painting of General Washington piously praying on one knee beside his horse. Biographers tell us that there is no record of Washington ever having done anything like this. But there is no doubt that Washington was a deeply religious man and that he relied on his faith to help him when making decisions about the war. So what's depicted in that painting certainly could have taken place.

Washington's nephew, George Lewis, was an inadvertent witness to his uncle's faith. He related what he saw to Washington biographer Jared Sparks, who wrote:

> Mr. Lewis said he had accidentally witnessed [the general's] private devotions in his library both morning and evening; that on these occasions he had seen him in a kneeling position with a Bible open before him and that he believed such to have been his daily practice.[26]

As Ron Chernow relates in *Washington: A Life*, when, during the Revolutionary War, General Robert Porterfield "delivered an urgent message to Washington" he "found him on his knees, engaged in his morning's devotions."[27]

A lifelong churchgoer, Washington served for twenty-two years as a vestryman of Truro Parish and also served as a churchwarden whose duties included assisting the poor. Friends, such as John Marshall, knew Washington to be "a sincere believer in the Christian faith, and a truly devout man."[28] Washington also believed that God had a special purpose for his life, and he spoke of his belief that Providence had saved him from being killed in various early battles precisely because God had a purpose for him.

Washington's charity toward others is also well documented. Before leaving to command the American forces in the Revolutionary War, he made a point of telling his estate manager to continue looking after beggars who showed up at Mount Vernon: "Let the hospitality of the house with respect to the poor be kept up. Let no one go hungry away . . . provided it does not encourage them in idleness."[29]

Chernow notes,

> We know that the Washingtons tried to practice anonymous charity even when it would have been politically expedient to advertise

it loudly. Washington's secretary, Tobias Lear, recorded hundreds of individuals, churches, and other charities that, unbeknownst to the public, benefited from presidential largesse. Even leftovers from the executive mansion were transferred to a prison for needy inmates.[30]

Many of us are familiar with the oft-quoted lines in Washington's Farewell Address in 1796: "Of all the dispositions and habits which lead to political prosperity, religion and morality are indispensable supports." But we're likely less familiar with the rest of the passage, in which Washington warns that "reason and experience both forbid us to expect that national morality can prevail in exclusion of religious principle."[31] As "national morality" is at the heart of self-government, this is an especially important statement.

It says much about Washington's character that, following General Cornwallis's surrender, Washington told his men to treat their defeated foes with respect and to refrain from shouting taunts and insults at them. "It is sufficient for us that we witness their humiliation," he said. "Posterity will huzza for us."[32]

There was something about Washington's heroic, humble, fearless, and fair example that inspired fierce devotion in the men under his leadership. In fact, the respect, admiration, and love his men had for him increased during the years of war. Biographer David Adler writes, "His men followed him barefoot through the snow at Trenton. They wintered with him at Valley Forge without proper clothes, food, or firewood. Surely, they fought not only for independence, but also for Washington."[33]

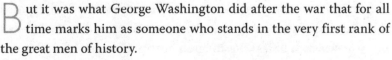

But it was what George Washington did after the war that for all time marks him as someone who stands in the very first rank of the great men of history.

One might well ask: When the heroic struggle for independence was finally won, what next? How should the great man who carried this new nation to its nascent victory be rewarded? How should his epochal triumph be crowned? Some talked of doing so literally, of crowning Washington as King George I of America—or at the very least, of making him into a kinglike figure. Even those who disliked this idea feared that with all Washington had done, it was somehow inevitable: he had simply earned it. And those who bitterly opposed the idea expected Washington to take what he thought belonged to him. They pointed to Washington's desire to maintain a standing army as evidence that he planned a military coup after the war. As they saw it, newly independent America would end up with a military dictatorship, with Washington as dictator in chief.

Yet Washington was that rarest of men on the expansive stage of history because he would have none of it. His attitude toward the idea that he should grab the reins of civilian power is dramatically illustrated in an incident that reveals, as few others do, the singular greatness of George Washington.

It took place in March 1783. The war was over and won, but the mood among the officers of the Continental Army in Newburgh, New York—Washington's headquarters at that time—had turned decidedly ugly. This was mainly because Congress was quite broke and would not likely be able to honor its promise to compensate the soldiers for their years of arduous service to their country. It seemed Congress wasn't even able to provide pensions. This was a tremendously harsh blow to these men who had given so much for their country, and they now complained bitterly.

One officer named Lewis Nicola did more than complain. He took action, circulating an anonymous letter among the men, putting "in writing what many officers were whispering behind the scenes: that the Continental Congress's erratic conduct of the war had exposed the weakness of all republics and the certain disaster that would befall postwar America unless Washington declared himself king."[34] It was a threat: if they did not receive their promised pay and pensions, the officers determined to seize control of the fledgling government. Of course he proposed that Washington should be their leader.

In reply, a horrified Washington told Nicola to "banish these thoughts from your Mind" and "denounced the scheme as 'big with the greatest mischiefs that can befall my Country.' "

The following March saw the arrival of what became known as the Newburgh Conspiracy. As Joseph Ellis writes in *His Excellency, George Washington,* "Scholars who have studied the Newburgh Conspiracy agree that it probably originated in Philadelphia within a group of congressmen, led by Robert Morris, who decided to use the threat of a military coup as a political weapon to gain passage of a revenue bill . . . and perhaps to expand the powers of the Confederation Congress over the states."[35]

An anonymous letter, which later became known as the Newburgh Address, made the rounds in Newburgh. Written by Major John Armstrong Jr., it contained not one but two threats: if Congress did not guarantee back pay and commutation, "the army would disband," even if the war continued (the peace treaty would not be signed until September 3, 1783). And if a peace treaty were signed, well then, the army would simply and absolutely refuse to dissolve. In effect, Armstrong was proposing tyranny and treason both.[36]

When Washington became aware of what was happening, the great man was horrified. And discovering that the leaders of the conspiracy planned to meet on March 11 to plot strategy, Washington stepped in. He "countermanded the order for a meeting [and] . . . scheduled a session for all officers on March 16."[37]

Washington then set about writing the speech of his life. Everything he believed in was at stake. For one thing, his hard-won reputation was in peril, but much more important, the very existence and future of America were threatened. If not for what he then said and did, all he had said and done up to that point might have been for naught: the newly birthed nation might well have been strangled in its cradle.

On March 16, just before noon, the officers were gathered in a newly built hall in Newburgh called the Temple, to await the start of the strategy session, which was to be chaired by General Horatio Gates. At twelve o'clock sharp, General Washington entered the room and strode to the podium. Silence fell over the room as Washington removed his speech from a pocket and began reading in his slow, quiet style.

First, he would rebuke them. "Gentlemen," he began, "by an anonymous summons, an attempt has been made to convene you together; how inconsistent with the rules of propriety, how unmilitary, and how subversive of all order and discipline."[38]

Many of the men present were angry with Washington for not doing enough, in their view, to secure their salaries and pensions. Washington reminded these men that he was one of them:

> If my conduct heretofore has not evinced to you that I have been a faithful friend to the army, my declaration of it at this time would be equally unavailing and improper. But as I was among the first who embarked in the cause of our common country. As I have never left your side one moment, but when called from you on public duty. As I have been the constant companion and witness of your distresses, and not among the last to feel and acknowledge your merits. As I have ever considered my own military reputation as inseparably connected with that of the army. As my heart has ever expanded with joy, when I have heard its praises, and my indignation has arisen, when the mouth of detraction has been opened against it, it can scarcely be supposed, at this late stage of the war, that I am indifferent to its interests."[39]

Washington then got to the main point, referring to the—in his mind scandalous—letter that had been circulated:

> But how are [these interests] to be promoted? The way is plain, says the anonymous addresser. If war continues, remove into the unsettled

country . . . and leave an ungrateful country to defend itself. But who are they to defend? Our wives, our children, our farms, and other property which we leave behind us. Or, in this state of hostile separation, are we to take [our families] to perish in a wilderness, with hunger, cold, and nakedness?

If peace takes place, never sheathe your swords, says he, until you have obtained full and ample justice; this dreadful alternative, of either deserting our country in the extremist hour of her distress or turning our arms against it (which is the apparent object, unless Congress can be compelled into instant compliance), has something so shocking in it that humanity revolts at the idea. My God! What can this writer have in view, by recommending such measures? Can he be a friend to the army? Can he be a friend to this country? Rather, is he not an insidious foe?[40]

Washington then repeated what the soldiers had grown tired of hearing: that they should be patient as the Congress slowly sorted out how and when and how much to pay them. He also pointed out how far their mutiny would reach:

Why, then, should we distrust [the Congress]? And, in consequence of that distrust, adopt measures which may cast a shade over that glory which has been so justly acquired; and tarnish the reputation of an army which is celebrated through all Europe, for its fortitude and patriotism? And for what is this done? To bring the object we seek nearer? No! Most certainly, in my opinion, it will cast it at a greater distance.[41]

The old general then reminded his officers of what they had come to mean to each other:

For myself . . . a grateful sense of the confidence you have ever placed in me, a recollection of the cheerful assistance and prompt obedience I have experienced from you, under every vicissitude of fortune, and the sincere affection I feel for an army I have so long had the honor to command will oblige me to declare . . . that, in the attainment of complete justice for all your toils and dangers, and in the gratification of every wish, so far as may be done consistently with the great duty I owe my country and those powers we are bound to respect, you may freely command my services to the utmost of my abilities.[42]

Washington then gave what to many is the most moving part of his speech:

Let me entreat you, gentlemen, on your part, not to take any measures which, viewed in the calm light of reason, will lessen the dignity and sully the glory you have hitherto maintained. . . . Let me conjure you, in the name of our common country, as you value your own sacred honor, as you respect the rights of humanity, and as you regard the military and national character of America, to express your utmost horror and detestation of the man who wishes, under any specious pretenses, to overthrow the liberties of our country, and who wickedly attempts to open the floodgates of civil discord and deluge our rising empire in blood.[43]

He encouraged his men to look to the future—to imagine what generations yet unborn would think of them and what they had achieved:

By thus determining and thus acting, . . . you will give one more distinguished proof of unexampled patriotism and patient virtue, rising superior to the pressure of the most complicated sufferings. And you will, by the dignity of your conduct, afford occasion for posterity to say, when speaking of the glorious example you have exhibited to mankind, "Had this day been wanting, the world had never seen the last stage of perfection to which human nature is capable of attaining."[44]

Ironically, as magnificent and eloquent as these words are, it was not the words of Washington's speech that turned the tide and saved the American Experiment. Historians tell us that as Washington finished his speech, the room was perfectly silent.

But they differ in their opinions about precisely what happened next. Did Washington plan and rehearse his next move? Or was it a spontaneous act?

Announcing that he had something else to read to the men, Washington now reached into his uniform pocket and slowly pulled out a letter penned by a Virginia congressman. Washington unfolded it and began to read aloud, appearing to stumble over the words. Reaching into his waistcoat pocket, the general produced a pair of wire-rimmed spectacles. His men had never seen them before, although the fifty-one-year-old general had been using them as reading glasses for some time.

Washington apologized for the delay, saying, as he unfolded the spectacles and put them on: "Gentlemen, you must pardon me. I have grown gray in your service and now find myself growing blind."[45]

Somehow, these disarming, humble, and spontaneous words, spoken by the exceptional man standing before them, took everyone by surprise, and in an instant, the mood of the angry, battle-hardened men was utterly changed. Indeed, many of them wept openly as Washington read the letter and then quietly walked out of the room. The powerful temptation to crown Washington king or dictator and to wrest from Congress all control of the fledgling nation had been dealt a death blow—and the Nicola and Armstrong letters were cast upon the ash heap of history.

Who can imagine that the liberty of millions might depend on the character of one man? What was it that gave him the strength to do the right thing when the temptation to do something less noble must have been overwhelming?

In acting as he did that day—and on other occasions when the siren call of power might have overwhelmed a lesser man—Washington "demonstrated that he was as immune to the seductions of dictatorial power as he was to smallpox."[46]

Most of us can hardly fathom just how unusual Washington's decision was. In rejecting power, General Washington became the first famous military leader in the history of the world to win a war and then voluntarily step down instead of seizing and consolidating power. In fact, Washington's sworn enemy, George III of England, could scarcely believe his ears when he heard what Washington had decided to do. If the leader of the army that had defeated the most powerful military force on earth had indeed stepped down, as was being reported, George III declared that man would be "the greatest man in the world."[47]

Whatever else historians say about Washington, all celebrate his willingness to set aside the chance of being crowned King George I of America in favor of going back to being a Virginia farmer. Nor was this a decision he made hastily. Washington had made clear, in the very first year of the conflict, that he was determined not to win the war against King George III only to set himself up as a rival American tyrant once he had won. In a speech to New York leaders, Washington announced that, in becoming a soldier, he "did not lay aside the Citizen"—that is, he recognized civilian authority over the military.[48]

And yet Washington's decision still amazes.

As historian Joseph Ellis describes it,

> his trademark decision to surrender power as commander in chief and then president was not . . . a sign that he had conquered his ambitions, but rather that he fully realized that all ambitions were inherently insatiable and unconquerable. He knew himself well enough to resist the illusion that he transcended his human nature. Unlike Julius Caesar and Oliver Cromwell before him, and Napoleon, Lenin, and Mao after him, he understood that the

greater glory resided in posterity's judgment. If you aspire to live forever in the memory of future generations, you must demonstrate the ultimate self-confidence to leave the final judgment to them. And he did.[49]

◆ ◆ ◆

Of course the preceding events took place years before Washington became president. And yet most of us remember him principally as the first president of the United States. We forget that Washington wasn't simply the first president; he essentially invented the US presidency.

Before him, there was no such thing. He set the precedent for president, so to speak. Specifically, Washington had no model upon which to base such basic decisions as how the president should dress, whom he should meet, how he should make federal appointments, whether people should curtsy or bow to him, or even what he should be called (John Adams provoked much laughter by seriously suggesting that Washington be addressed as "His Elective Majesty" or "His Mightiness"). But let's be clear that what George Washington chose to do became the model for all who followed. Much of what he determined was adopted by virtually every other American president. Perhaps the most important of these decisions was when he refused to serve more than two four-year terms, another humble and selfless decision with incalculable ramifications for the nation's future. Washington also decided where every future president would live when he decided where the nation's capitol should be built.

In his first administration, Washington dealt with the massive debt the country had incurred fighting the war, including money borrowed from France, Spain, and Holland, which somehow had to be repaid. There were numerous conflicts with Indians who, armed by the British, continued to attack white settlements; the British, in defiance of the peace treaty, still kept troops on American soil. The first ten amendments to the Constitution were agreed on and passed into law.

Three more states—Vermont, Kentucky, and Tennessee—were added to the Union.

Actually, Washington wanted to retire at the end of his first term, longing to live at Mount Vernon with his wife and step-grandchildren. He had good reason to think he would be able to do this. As he had hoped and worked for, "a national government existed and was working," and he had "made the presidency into a potent and magisterial office. Already, many of the seemingly intractable economic tribulations of the war years and immediate postwar period had been rectified, and a bright future beckoned."[50]

But the president was pressured by others, including Thomas Jefferson, to stay in office for another term. Jefferson argued, "Your continuance at the head of affairs [is] of the [greatest] importance" because "the confidence of the whole union is centered in you." In addition, a second Washington term would keep "the Monarchial federalists," led by Alexander Hamilton, from "every argument which can be used to alarm & lead the people . . . into violence or secession. North & South will hang together, if they have you to hang on."[51]

Realizing that his country still needed him—especially with the French Revolution in Europe looming—Washington reluctantly agreed to serve a second term.

During the next four years, Washington, over objections by many who remembered how the French had come to America's aid during the war, kept out of the French Revolution, believing it was not in the best interests of the United States to get involved. His prescience in this decision is especially impressive. Washington also negotiated an end to the British practice of attacking and raiding American ships and taking American seamen prisoner. The owner of Mount Vernon, which was home to three hundred slaves, also oversaw the passage of the Fugitive Slave Law, which required all states, even those that had outlawed slavery, to return escaped slaves to their masters. To his sorrow, Washington saw the beginnings of political parties and partisan warfare.[52]

Washington, now sixty-four and exhausted by "those cares [of] which public responsibility is never exempt"[53] and by the increasing personal attacks, adamantly refused to consider a third term. After seeing John Adams inaugurated, Washington joyfully began riding the many miles of his farms again. He entertained the endless parade of guests who came to visit him and spend time with his family. Still, one thing nagged at him: What to do with his slaves?

Washington had wrestled with the slavery issue for much of his adult life, and in July 1799, he finally made an important decision. He rewrote his will, not only freeing his slaves but also ensuring that the young ones would be taught to read, write, and learn a trade, and that the old and infirm ones would be taken care of for the rest of their lives.

Five months later, on December 12, 1799, the sixty-seven-year-old general went out riding, as was his custom, to inspect his farms. The fact that it was storming meant little to him, and when he came in five hours later, he went to dinner in wet clothes. This was because he didn't want to keep his guest waiting. The next day he had the symptoms of a cold but insisted on going out nonetheless. That night he became seriously ill, and the next morning, doctors were summoned.

The medical care that Washington received horrifies us today. He was bled four times—five pints in all. To put this in perspective, that was more than 40 percent of the total amount of blood in his body. The doctors also "blistered" his neck with hot poultices and gave him laxatives. All of these treatments certainly made him weaker. Historians believe he was suffering from "a virulent bacterial infection of the epiglottis,"[54] but the antibiotics that could easily have treated it would not be discovered for more than a century.

Washington died on December 14, 1799, with his beloved Martha at his bedside. When the citizens of Alexandria learned of his passing, bells tolled unceasingly for four days and nights. In France, flags were lowered to half-mast. Out of respect, more than sixty British ships lowered their flags to half-mast as well, in honor of the man who had "out-generaled" them, as one British soldier put it during the war.[55]

◆ ◆ ◆

More than two hundred years after Washington's death, his will-ingness to relinquish power—twice—is the most remarkable thing that we remember about him. These refusals to seize power for himself were the greatest acts of one of history's greatest men.

Despite his human flaws, Washington was inescapably great. He was arguably the only man who could have overseen both the scuttling of the British and the rise of the American republic.

Historian John Ferling concludes that "merely by being there . . . Washington enabled the new nation to hang together and survive its terribly difficult infancy." He "ushered America toward modernity, fashioning the economic system that sustained growth and gradu-ally made the United States a truly independent and powerful nation capable of maintaining its security."[56]

Historian Joseph Ellis writes that Washington led "the continental army to victory against the odds . . . thereby winning American inde-pendence." He secured "the Revolution by overseeing the establishment of a new nation-state during its most fragile and formative phase of development" and embodied "that elusive and still latent thing called 'the American people,' thereby providing the illusion of coherence to what was in fact a messy collage of regional and state allegiances."[57]

Ellis adds, "There was a consensus at the time, since confirmed for all time, that no one else could have performed these elemental tasks as well, and perhaps that no one could have performed them at all."[58]

Washington's successor, John Adams, would have agreed. Days after the general's demise, Adams said, "His example is now complete, and it will teach wisdom and virtue to magistrates, citizens and men, not only in the present age, but in future generations, as long as our history shall be read."[59]

It's a pity that most schoolchildren today think of Washington the way he's pictured on the dollar bill: as that slightly grumpy-looking old man. If I had my way, we'd replace those false images with portraits of the young, vibrant Washington, who can more easily be imagined dreaming big dreams, fighting significant battles, designing America's future—and then riding home to Mount Vernon, happy to have won his battles against power itself—the great temptation that can tempt mortal man. How grateful and how mightily blessed we are that he did.

TWO
William Wilberforce

1759–1833

A lthough the first man in this book lived his whole life in America and the second man in this book lived his in England, both George Washington and William Wilberforce were roughly contemporaries and certainly knew of each other; both were tremendously famous during their lifetimes. You could even argue that Wilberforce was more famous. After his success in abolishing the slave trade and bringing "liberty to the captives,"[1] an Italian statesman described Wilberforce as "the Washington of humanity."[2]

One hundred and fifty years ago, men like Abraham Lincoln and Frederick Douglass spoke of him reverently as the great pioneer and father of the abolitionist movement. But in the last century or so, Wilberforce's name has faded significantly. Only in the last few years has this begun to change, due mainly to the 2007 movie *Amazing Grace*. That movie probably did more to popularize his story than anything else.

Many who saw the movie and perhaps read my biography (also titled *Amazing Grace*) couldn't believe they had never known of the great Wilberforce. One comment I have heard literally scores of times was: "After reading your book about this amazing man, I was ashamed not to have heard about him before!"

But how did *I* hear about Wilberforce?

Like so many others, I first heard about him from my friend Os Guinness. Anyone who didn't learn about Wilberforce from the movie probably heard of him through Os, who did more to keep Wilberforce's memory alive in the years before the film came out than anyone. It's likely the film never would have been made had not Os championed Wilberforce's story far and wide for so many years. But a great story is a great story, and when it's a true great story, it's hard to keep it to yourself. I'm tremendously grateful that Os didn't!

I had also heard about Wilberforce through my hero, Prison Fellowship founder Chuck Colson, the seventh man in this book. I worked for Chuck in the late nineties and learned that Prison Fellowship annually gave out a Wilberforce Award to someone for

> making a significant impact on the social ills of the day through personal effort, skill, and influence; for showing perseverance and selflessness in combating injustice, even to the point of willingness to sacrifice personal comfort, career, and reputation; for making a positive change in the values and character of society—"reforming manners"—through personal witness, example, and education; and for serving as an exemplary witness for Christ.[3]

Just from that glowing description, you couldn't help but wonder who Wilberforce was! But until I wrote my book about him, I really knew very little. I knew that Wilberforce was the member of Parliament who led the battle for the abolition of the slave trade. I knew his faith led him to take on this fight, and I knew that in 1807—after a nearly two-decades-long brutal campaign—he finally succeeded, earning the deserved encomia of the Western world. But that was about it. Actually, how I came to write about him—and learn much more about him—is a funny story.

It happened in 2005, when I wrote a book on apologetics, titled *Everything You Always Wanted to Know About God (but Were Afraid to Ask)*. In the beginning of one of those chapters—it was a chapter about the Bible—I briefly said that William Wilberforce was someone who took the Bible seriously, and as a result of this belief, he literally changed the world. Which is true.

One day in December of that year I found myself on CNN promoting my book. I was expecting the typical hardball questions, such as "How can God be all-powerful and good and yet allow so much horrible evil and suffering in the world?" and "How can an intelligent person believe in science and simultaneously swallow all the medieval nonsense that's in the Bible?" But I didn't get hardball questions. Instead, I got a softball question about William Wilberforce. I almost forgot I'd mentioned him in the book, but the next thing I knew I was talking about him to a national TV audience.

As a result of this interview, a publisher contacted me and asked if I would like to write a full-length biography about Wilberforce. A movie was in production (the aforementioned *Amazing Grace*), and it would make sense for someone to write a biography to appear at the time of the movie's release in February 2007. The movie and the book would commemorate the bicentennial of the 1807 abolition of the slave trade. Since I'd never written a biography before and had no ambition to write one, I had to think about it. But as it turned out, I was interested, and I spent the next year or so writing it.

In the course of my research for the book, I discovered that Wilberforce's leadership in the abolition movement was just a fraction of all that he did. His accomplishments were staggering, almost too many to believe. But I did the research, and the facts were there. I came to see what Os Guinness had long maintained, that Wilberforce was the most successful social reformer in the history of the world.

Wilberforce's story is so fascinating and so inspiring that I thought it important to recount the short version of it in this volume. His life stands as a shining example of what one human being—submitted to God's purposes for his life—is capable of doing.

◆ ◆ ◆

William Wilberforce was born in 1759, the only son of a very prosperous family of merchants in Hull, a large seaport city on the northeast coast of Great Britain. Billy, as he was called at a young age, was only nine when his father died. His mother also became terribly ill at that time, and most thought she would not survive. So she and Wilberforce's grandfather decided to send the boy to live with a very wealthy uncle and aunt at Wimbledon. That he should be raised in the environment of their elite social circle was of great importance to them.

It must be said that the cultural environment in England at that time was not at all Christian, except in the most superficial sense. The general falling away from serious Christianity in eighteenth-century England was due in part to the religious wars of the previous century, which had led to much bloodshed and misery. Most socially respectable people had moved away from any robust expression of the Christian faith and toward what we would today call Enlightenment rationalism or Deism. The "God" that was preached from many pulpits across England in those days was less Jehovah and Jesus, the personal God of Scripture, and more a vague, impersonal energy force.

Wilberforce's mother and grandfather followed this fashion, never taking their religious expression beyond church attendance and looking down on anyone who did otherwise. The Wesleyan revival meetings led by John and Charles Wesley and the evangelistic meetings of George Whitefield were mostly attended by common working-class people. So being "serious" about one's faith was thought of as perhaps acceptable for the lower classes, but to the Wilberforces and most elites, anyone who took God seriously was scorned as a *Methodist* or an *enthusiast*. These were the terms of derision in those days, much as *Holy Roller, Bible-thumper,* and *fundamentalist* have been used more recently.

So what happened to little William during the years he spent with his wealthy aunt and uncle would not have been at all approved by his mother and grandfather. That's because, quite unbeknownst to them, the extremely prosperous couple to whom they had sent little Billy were themselves devoted Methodists. In fact, they were so devoted to their evangelical Christian faith that they used their tremendous wealth to support many endeavors of the Methodist movement. George Whitefield himself often came to their grand home for weeks at a time to do what was called parlor preaching for their wealthy friends and neighbors. Although young William never met Whitefield, who died around that time, many other notable Methodist preachers visited, and the boy seems to have thrived in their company.

One of the most famous and frequent parlor preachers to visit their home was the colorful John Newton, the former slave trade captain who had been converted to the Christian faith and who eventually gave up the slave trade entirely. He became a well-known evangelical preacher, and with his friend, the English poet William Cowper, he wrote many hymns, among them "Amazing Grace." The young Wilberforce came to know Newton very well, almost thinking of him as a father, while Newton, for his part, thought of Wilberforce as a son.

But these happy times were not to last. When Wilberforce was about twelve, his grandfather and his mother were horrified to find out about the Methodism of the aunt and uncle. For them it was all a nightmare, almost worse than if the boy had been captured by Maori cannibals. After all, in their social circles Methodism was far more embarrassing. "If little Billy turns Methodist," his grandfather threatened, "he'll not see a penny of mine!"[4] Everything was at stake, so Wilberforce's mother raced the many miles from Hull to London to rescue her son from the clutches of these pious fanatics.

In the two-and-a-half years that he lived with them, Wilberforce had grown tremendously fond of his aunt and uncle, and they of him. He had come to embrace their faith as well. His sudden departure would be painful for both parties. When Aunt Hannah expressed her fears that Wilberforce might lose his faith if taken from them, Wilberforce's mother retorted, "If it be a work of grace [meaning if it's God's will] it cannot fail."[5] Her lack of seriousness about her own faith makes her statement interesting, to say the least, if not downright prophetic.

So against his wishes and those of his heartbroken aunt and uncle, Wilberforce was returned to life in Hull. His mother and grandfather now undertook to do everything possible to extinguish whatever spark of Methodism was in him, even refusing to allow him to attend their Church of England services, lest the mere liturgical reading of the Scriptures have any ill effects.

The twelve-year-old's faith was quite sincere, and he bravely clung to it with everything he had, even sending secret letters to his aunt and uncle by way of an obliging house servant. But after several years of the decidedly worldly environment, the ardor of his Methodism cooled. The endless parties and the fawning attentions paid to him as a soon-to-be extremely wealthy heir of his grandfather achieved their intended effect; by the time he was sent up to Cambridge, at age sixteen, William had backslid into a perfect picture of sophisticated worldliness. He had become every bit the insouciant young man of the world that his mother and grandfather had always hoped.

When he entered Cambridge, Wilberforce continued the lifestyle of parties and entertainments that he had enjoyed at Hull. Although he was never as terribly bold a sinner as some other students were, there is no question that he had walked away from the faith of his earlier years. He had also drunk the culturally acceptable waters of aloofness and skepticism toward anyone who took Christian faith seriously.

It was during his Cambridge days that he met William Pitt the Younger, who would play a significant role in his future life. Pitt's father, Pitt the Elder, was one of the most famous politicians and statesmen of that day, and he was training his brilliant son to follow in his footsteps. So Pitt the Younger would often travel from Cambridge to London to sit in the gallery of the House of Lords, where he would observe the parliamentary debates of the time and his new friend William Wilberforce often accompanied him.

Although his mother and grandfather expected Wilberforce to take over the family business, his creative, overactive mind and gay temperament were ill-suited to the life of a merchant. When he sat with Pitt watching the spectacular and engaging oratory on the floor of the House of Lords, it seemed that perhaps he should try his hand at politics instead. After all, Wilberforce was a renowned wit, adept at verbal jousting and oratory, talents that were crucial for someone hoping to enter the lists as a political candidate.

During their college years, Wilberforce and Pitt watched Parliament debate many subjects, most notably the fate of the American colonies. After all, it was the late 1770s, and the Revolution was under way. Of course King George III's government was of a mind to crush the colonial rebellion, whose military was led by a certain General Washington, but there were many dissenting voices in Parliament too, among them William Pitt the Elder. Those historic debates must have been intoxicating to the young Wilberforce, and it's no surprise that by the time he graduated Cambridge, he had indeed decided to try for a seat in Parliament.

Once he had made his decision, Wilberforce wasted no time, being elected to Parliament at the earliest allowable age, just two weeks after his twentieth birthday. William Pitt the Younger followed fast on his friend's heels, gaining a seat just a few months afterward. The two young Cambridge graduates soon rocketed through the political ranks to become some of the most powerful members of Parliament of that day.

With his winning personality and fine singing voice, Wilberforce also quickly became an extremely popular and well-known figure in London social circles. He became a member of five exclusive gentlemen's clubs, where he and his friends mixed with the celebrities of the day and were perpetually eating and drinking and singing and gambling until the wee hours of the morning.

Wilberforce's close friendship with Pitt continued, and in the year that both turned twenty-four, the pair and a third friend traveled to France for an extended holiday. Because Wilberforce and Pitt were already famous, all doors were opened to them. During that trip they visited the ill-fated couple, King Louis XVI and his queen, the young Marie Antoinette, who found Wilberforce especially charming. Wilberforce also met the Marquis de Lafayette, who had recently been a tremendous help to Washington and the American cause for freedom.

While he was with Lafayette, Wilberforce also met Benjamin Franklin, then the US minister to France. It's interesting to think that the seventy-seven-year-old Franklin, who was a lonely voice against slavery in the United States, should shake the hand of the twenty-four-year-old Wilberforce, who had yet to take up the battle in Great Britain. But Wilberforce's life was a catalog of meetings with the rich and famous. Many years later—in 1820—when Wilberforce was sixty-one and she only a toddler of eighteen months, Wilberforce had the honor of meeting the future Queen Victoria. It seemed that he met everyone and anyone of importance or celebrity in his lifetime.

At the age of twenty-four, Wilberforce was almost miraculously elected to an extremely significant seat in Parliament. It gave him a dramatic increase in visibility and political power. Around that same time—and also at the tender age of twenty-four—his friend Pitt was elected prime minister of the nation. Even in those days, such extreme youth in a prime minister was far from typical. One newspaper published a mocking verse:

> *A sight to make surrounding nations stare,*
> *A Kingdom entrusted to a school boy's care.*[6]

Pitt and Wilberforce proved up to the task, and Pitt knew that he never could have succeeded without his ally and friend Wilberforce beside him. The two friends were suddenly at the dizziest pinnacle of power and prestige. But it's what happened after this that makes Wilberforce one of the great men in this book of great men.

◆ ◆ ◆

I t all began in 1784—when Wilberforce decided to take a long vacation by traveling to the French and Italian Rivieras. His mother was ill again, and it was thought the trip to a warmer climate might help. She and a young cousin would travel in one coach, while Wilberforce and a companion-to-be-later-named would travel in Wilberforce's personal coach.

To travel there—twelve hundred miles as the crow flies—by the winding roads across the Alps would take many weeks, since the only means of travel was horse-drawn coach. Wilberforce had to choose his companion carefully. He first invited a certain Dr. Burgh to accompany him. Burgh was an Irish doctor whom he knew from York, but as it happened, he was unable to accept the invitation. Wilberforce surely didn't want to travel in his coach alone. The many hours could be passed far more profitably with a suitable travel companion. But whom to choose? Spending what would be hundreds of hours in such close quarters with the wrong companion could be difficult.

It was around this time that Wilberforce found himself at Scarborough, where he bumped into an old friend from childhood, Isaac Milner, who was ten years older than Wilberforce. Milner was the headmaster's brother at Wilberforce's grammar school and had worked at the school when Wilberforce was a student. But in the years since then he had become one of the most fascinating figures of that or any other era. Milner was now the Lucasian Professor at Cambridge, a post once held by Isaac Newton and more recently held by Stephen Hawking. It's no hyperbole to say that whoever holds that academic chair is one of the smartest men on the planet. But Milner was no mere egghead; he was famously jocular and celebrated as a teller of comic tales, often in the broad Yorkshire accent of his youth. He was even said to be the conversational heir to the eminent Dr. Johnson. Adding to his incomparable intellect and powers of entertainment was his nearly unbelievable size: Milner was a giant. Just how big he was is hard to say, but Wilberforce's friend Marianne Thornton once quipped that Milner "was the most enormous man it was ever my fate to see in a drawing room."[7]

So Milner accepted Wilberforce's invitation of an all-expenses-paid trip to the south of France, and the two of them were off. They must have made an odd couple. Wilberforce never grew above five-foot-three, and his chest measured a boyish thirty-three inches. Once, during a period of illness, his weight fell to seventy-six pounds. His green velvet waistcoat—today on display in the Hull museum that was his boyhood home—shows that this extraordinarily great man cut an exceptionally diminutive figure. Nonetheless he and Milner, for all their physical disparity, were well matched in intellect and wit, and their conversation across Europe and back must have sparkled beyond all reckoning.

But something happened during this long coach ride across Europe that would change the course of Wilberforce's life forever. At some point the subject of a certain evangelical pastor came up, and Wilberforce offhandedly remarked that the man in question "took things a bit too far."[8] Like everyone else in his circles, Wilberforce thought that anyone who took God very seriously went too far. But Milner did not agree, staunchly replying, "Not a bit."[9] Was Milner more serious about faith than Wilberforce had been led to believe? Evidently he was, and the conversation continued.

As the miles spooled past them, it became clear to Wilberforce that the effervescent genius with whom he now traveled was something of a closet Methodist. As far as Wilberforce was concerned, this was grievous news. Milner was in no way outwardly religious or off-puttingly aggressive in his views, but neither did he hold them lightly. In latter years Wilberforce admitted that, given his voguish antipathy for such thinking, if he had known beforehand he almost certainly would have chosen another traveling companion. But as the die was cast and they were far from home, Wilberforce was evidently obliged to engage the jumbo savant Milner in serious theological discussion.

To his credit, Wilberforce was intellectually honest, and he didn't shrink from robust debate. The back-and-forth between them continued across the Alps. Milner's intellect and vast learning on the subject were easily able to dispatch most of the objections to the faith that Wilberforce raised, and by the time their trip together had come to an end, Wilberforce was in the unpleasant and difficult spot of believing that he had been quite wrong in his previous views and that Milner had been right.

Wilberforce found to his significant distress that he had come to believe with his whole mind that what he had been sure was false was in fact true: the God of the Bible existed, Jesus existed in history and was the promised Messiah, and the Scriptures were not silly old myths but truth itself. For someone of his social standing and prestige, he was in a curious and uncomfortable position. What to do about it?

By the time Wilberforce returned to London, he was at a serious impasse. He knew that he could not reenter his former life professing the things he had now come to believe. He would be a laughingstock. Already his friends noticed that he was not showing his face at their parties or at any of the five gentlemen's social clubs he had once so hankered to join. For weeks on end, he remained in self-imposed isolation in his grand home, Lauriston House. What he was doing there his friends knew not, but it was soon bruited about that Mr. Wilberforce was "melancholy mad,"[10] which is to say, in a state of depression.

This observation was not far off the mark. Wilberforce simply had no idea how to reconcile what he had come to believe about God with his previous life. And his newfound and growing faith had become so central to him that he thought perhaps he would have to retreat from everything he knew and enter either a monastery or the priesthood. It was all tremendously inconvenient.

Years later, Wilberforce referred to this period of his conversion as

"The Great Change," and he characterized it as a gradual process that took between one and two years. Indeed, there were many changes in his life during this period. Some were superficial, such as the bold decision—executed in the space of a single day—to resign his memberships in all the exclusive gentlemen's clubs.

The activities in these clubs—gambling and drinking and other things inappropriate for a serious Christian—made leaving them a relatively easy decision for Wilberforce. But the question for him beyond this dramatic decision was much more complicated and difficult: Where exactly must one draw the line? Taking God seriously and leaving the so-called "world" meant resigning from these clubs, but what else must it mean? Would he have to leave the dirty world of politics also? On this point he wasn't clear, and for weeks and months the decision twisted in his mind.

It was while he was trying to answer this one question that Wilberforce made the fateful decision to visit his old friend John Newton.

Newton was then sixty and the famous rector of a church at Charles Square in Hoxton, an area of East London. It's unlikely that Newton and Wilberforce had had any contact since Wilberforce was taken away from his aunt and uncle at the age of twelve. Newton had doubtless followed the spectacular career of his brilliant young friend and been praying for him, but as Wilberforce had abandoned his childhood faith and had adopted the more secular attitude of his contemporaries, William might well have been embarrassed by his old sea-captain friend's unapologetic evangelicalism. Now that he had come to faith again, Wilberforce could think of no one better to speak with than this old friend.

But because Wilberforce was so famous, he feared being seen visiting Newton at his rectory, as this might tip people off to what was happening. And so Wilberforce preferred to visit Newton in secret, as Nicodemus had visited Jesus. Finally, one day in early December 1785, with much trepidation, he did so.

Newton was surely overjoyed to welcome his old friend and to know that he had come back to his Christian faith. But Wilberforce was less joyful in the meeting. In fact, he was painfully burdened about what course his life should take. Whether he must leave politics was the particular rub. We often talk today about how dirty politics is, but it was certainly much worse in Wilberforce's day.

But Newton, speaking perhaps prophetically, encouraged his young friend not to leave politics at all. Who knew—his reasoning went—but that Wilberforce had been prepared "for such a time as this"? Who knew but that God would use him mightily in the world of politics, where he was needed more than ever? It's hard to know what's more amazing, that Newton said such things or that Wilberforce accepted them; to remain as a serious Christian in that hostile secular climate was a brave thing indeed. But accept them he did.

And so Wilberforce vowed that he would take his faith into the world of politics and serve God there with his gifts.

◆ ◆ ◆

B ut how, exactly, should he go about it? How would it work out? To what major political objects should Wilberforce turn his attentions? That remained to be seen. But Wilberforce prayed about it and knew that God would lead him.

Less than two years after this historically important decision, Wilberforce wrote twenty words in his diary that would direct the course of the rest of his life. Those words, lived out during his lifetime, would have consequences so far-reaching that they would end in genuinely altering the course of Western civilization. "God Almighty," he wrote, "has set before me two Great Objects: the suppression of the Slave Trade and the Reformation of Manners."[11]

The meaning of these words must be explained. The first "Great Object" to which Wilberforce would dedicate himself mostly explains itself, and it's this first object for which he is principally known. Wilberforce had been aware of the abominable horror called the slave trade for many years. But he would count the cost before he threw himself wholeheartedly into anything, especially in a public way. He did not take lightly his reputation as a politician, and he needed to be sure he knew what he was getting into. He considered a number of issues that might make claims on his attention, and he wanted to be sure that God showed him which to choose.

During this time, a number of abolitionists—the famous Thomas Clarkson and Hannah More among them—realized that they must have a champion in Parliament. They needed a legislator as dedicated as they. And so they settled on Wilberforce and carefully approached him. Wilberforce was at first noncommittal, but in time he came to believe that God himself had called him to this noble task. In the brutal battle for abolition that lay ahead, he would need to know that it was God who had called him.

But what of the second "Great Object," the so-called "Reformation of Manners"? By this term Wilberforce did not mean what we think of when we hear the term *manners* today. He meant the reformation of morality or culture. In other words, he saw that all society was broken and in need of reform. British culture did not have a biblical worldview and did not regard human beings as being made in God's image and therefore worthy of dignity and respect. This unbiblical view led to every kind of evil. The terrible evil of the slave trade was only one— albeit the worst—of the social evils running rampant at that time.

So if the first Great Object was abolishing the slave trade, we might say that the second Great Object referred to addressing every other kind of abuse of human beings beyond the slave trade. Indeed, in Wilberforce's day, wherever one turned one saw abuse and decay and misery. So what Wilberforce called the "Reformation of Manners" was his larger attempt to attack that host of other social problems.

These social evils are worth listing, although it's hard to know just where to start. Child labor was one especially disturbing example. Poor children as young as five and six years old were often employed for ten- or twelve-hour days in horrendous and often dangerous conditions.

Then there was the wider problem of alcoholism, which contributed to almost all the other problems. It was an epidemic of proportions we can hardly imagine today. Everyone seemed to be addicted to alcohol, and there seemed to be nothing to help it. Members of the upper classes were perpetually drunk on claret—in fact, members of Parliament were often drunk during legislative sessions—and the lower classes were drunk on gin. The sexual trafficking of women was another staggering problem, one whose scope is almost inconceivable: fully 25 percent of all single women in London were prostitutes. And their average age was sixteen.[12]

For the entertainment of the perpetually drunken crowds, public displays of extreme animal cruelty such as bullbaiting and bearbaiting were very popular. When these grim spectacles were unavailable, public hangings, which were sometimes followed by ghastly public dissections, fit the bill. People were put to death for the smallest offenses, and the conditions of the prisons were unspeakable. Wherever Wilberforce looked, he saw a world untouched by the good news of Jesus Christ. People used and abused others in a perpetual downward spiral of misery and decay.

But Wilberforce knew that God had called him to do something about it. And since God had called him, he knew that he couldn't do it in his own strength. He would need God's help, and he would need the help of others.

Perhaps the most obvious sign of Wilberforce's conversion to the Christian faith was that it changed the way he looked at everything. Suddenly he saw what he was blind to before: that God was a God of justice and righteousness who would judge us for the way we treated others; that every single human being was made in God's image and therefore worthy of profound respect and kindness; that God was "no respecter of persons" and looked upon the rich and the poor equally.

Once Wilberforce had come to see that God was real and that God loved everyone, everything was different. Suddenly the idea of the slave trade and slavery itself seemed less an economic necessity than merely monstrous and wicked. Suddenly the idea that poor little children should be forced to work in awful conditions for long hours was disturbing and unacceptable. Suddenly the idea that those who had committed minor crimes should be thrown into filthy prisons, where they might die of any number of ailments for lack of treatment, was something that must be remedied. Suddenly the idea that women should sell their bodies so that they could feed themselves or feed their alcohol habit—or the alcohol habit of their pimps—could no longer stand.

For the first time in his life, Wilberforce saw the world through God's eyes. But he was living in a culture where almost no one saw things this way. So the task that lay ahead of him was impossible.

How would he do it?

◆ ◆ ◆

The first thing that must be said in answering this question is that he himself wouldn't do it. Either God would do it, or it wouldn't be done. God might use Wilberforce as his instrument, but apart from God, Wilberforce knew that he really could do very little. In his famous diary entry, Wilberforce wrote that it was "God Almighty" who had set the "two Great Objects" before him.

So Wilberforce didn't leap into the fray in his own strength. He first required a deep sense that God had called him to these things— else he would have been overwhelmed, and the many setbacks would have been a great discouragement. But because he knew that God had set these objects before him, he knew that the battle was God's battle, not his. All he had to do was to be obedient to what God was asking him to do and to know that God brings the victory.

Underscoring this point was a letter that Wilberforce received in 1791 from the great revivalist John Wesley, who was then eighty-seven years old and literally on his deathbed. The letter was written just days before Wesley died, and it seems to have been the last letter he ever wrote. Wesley knew of Wilberforce's heroic efforts against the slave trade, and he wrote to him on that very subject:

Dear Sir,

Unless the divine power has raised you up to be as Athanasius contra mundum [against the world], I see not how you can go through your glorious enterprise in opposing that execrable villainy, which is the scandal of religion, of England, and of human nature. Unless God has raised you up for this very thing, you will be worn out by the opposition of men and devils.

But if God be for you, who can be against you? Are all of them together stronger than God? O be not weary of well doing. Go on, in the name of God and in the power of His might, till even American slavery (the vilest that ever saw the sun) shall vanish away before it.

Reading this morning a tract wrote by a poor African, I was particularly struck by that circumstance, that a man who has a black skin, being wronged or outraged by a white man, can have no redress; it being a law in all our Colonies that the oath of a black against a white goes for nothing. What villainy is this!

That He who has guided you from youth up may continue to strengthen you in this and all things is the prayer of, dear sir,

Your affectionate servant,

John Wesley[13]

It's important to realize that the abominable racial views held by so many people at that time were not held by Wesley, Wilberforce, or most contemporary Methodists. The evangelical Christians of that time generally held God's perspective on this subject, and they stood in stark contrast to the views of people who were not Christians or to those who were cultural Christians and who perhaps attended church for social reasons, but who thought of the Methodists such as Wilberforce and Wesley as "taking things too far."

The main point in quoting Wesley's letter here is to show that this man who had battled a host of social evils for many decades knew better than anyone that without a full reliance on God, the battle could be brutal and all for naught. He felt compelled to warn young Wilberforce that to fight in one's own strength—even and perhaps especially in a noble and godly cause—was insanity; but to rely on God was to be assured of victory, even if one did not get to see it with one's own eyes.

In the battle against the slave trade that lay ahead, Wilberforce would experience a number of crushing defeats. And unless he really knew that God had called him to do what he was doing, it would be too much to bear.

The second point Wesley was making was that it was not merely a political or a cultural battle. It was a spiritual battle. When Wesley wrote, "you will be worn out by the opposition of men and devils," he was not using a colorful metaphor. He meant it literally.

To fight something as wicked as the slave trade was to go against an invisible demonic host. God has the power to fight them, but we do not. That spiritual reality lay behind the political reality, and Wesley wanted to ensure that Wilberforce understood that if he was to be successful in what lay ahead. Great men like Wilberforce and Wesley had the humility and the wisdom to know that whatever strengths they had—and they had many—they could not win without a total reliance on God. At its core, every battle worth fighting is a spiritual battle. Those men were able to succeed only because they humbled themselves and entrusted the battle to God.

But how does one do that?

This brings us to the second way that Wilberforce did what he did. The one-word answer is *prayer*. Wilberforce prayed and read the Scriptures every day, and he prayed with many others over these issues and concerns. He also memorized lots of Scripture. In my book *Amazing Grace*, I relate that he memorized the entirety of Psalm 119. That's hard to believe when you see how long it is, but it's true. Wilberforce would also sometimes walk the two and a half miles from Parliament to his home, and the second half of the walk took him through a portion of Hyde Park. Wilberforce had it timed so that if he began reciting Psalm 119 when he entered the park, he would be finished by the time he got home. It took about twenty minutes to recite the whole thing.

Third, Wilberforce was able to do all he did because of his reliance on a solid community of devout Christian brothers and sisters. Wilberforce was not what we today might call a "Lone Ranger" Christian, keeping his beliefs and prayers to himself. On the contrary, he thrived in the community of his fellow Christians and sought them out for strength and support and advice. The particular Christian community in which Wilberforce spent most of his time is famously known as the Clapham Circle because most of them lived in the London suburb of Clapham. Today Clapham is a bustling part of the city of London—just four miles from Westminster Abbey—but more than two hundred years ago it was a gloriously idyllic village, far from the world of Parliament.

Those who didn't share and were threatened by their religious views often derided members of the circle as the "Clapham Saints" or the "Clapham Sect." Even after he was very famous, most of fashionable society still felt that Wilberforce and his colleagues' religious ideas about things like helping the poor and abolishing slavery were embarrassing. These detractors would end up on the wrong side of history, but at the time, their secular notions were the norm.

It should be said that this Christian community known as the Clapham Circle did not happen by accident. On the contrary, it was the deliberate creation of Wilberforce's dear friend and relative John Thornton, who was extremely wealthy and who chose to buy a huge home at Clapham with twelve bedrooms for the express purpose of luring his friends to live there and share in the community. Thornton then expanded the home and bought others next door, hoping to get his brothers and sisters in Christ to be physically near each other so that they would benefit and be able to help each other in their various causes.

Those who didn't live at Clapham were always welcome to come and stay for weeks or even months at a time. In the mornings they would gather for breakfast and prayer, and whenever an important bill or issue was being worked on, they would pray together for strength and wisdom. Wilberforce would be the first to acknowledge that whatever he did, he did not do alone. First of all, God was the one behind every battle and every victory; and second, the living community of Clapham believers was involved on all levels.

've said that the battles Wilberforce fought were at their core spiritual battles, and this is true of every battle worth fighting. But even once we see that there is a spiritual battle at the center of every battle, we may sometimes think that the main battle in this world is a political one. If only we can elect so-and-so, or if only we can get this law passed or that law repealed, all problems will be solved. But Wilberforce was effective over the course of his lifetime because even though he was a tremendously successful politician, he realized that some battles must be fought in the cultural sphere too.

The battle against the slave trade was largely won when a bill passed both houses of Parliament in 1807, but Wilberforce knew that in order to get the votes he needed to win that particular political battle, he would have to change the hearts and minds of people first— and that was very much a cultural battle. This realization prompted Wilberforce to say that part of his strategy in fighting many of these social evils was to "make goodness fashionable."[14]

He was a legislator and a politician, but he was also an important cultural figure with many influential friends; he had the ability to influence how people thought about things, and he knew that this would have a wide-ranging effect. At the time, goodness was not fashionable at all. To really change things, Wilberforce would have to change the cultural fashions, especially among the elites.

To see one vivid example of just how deeply bad behavior was in vogue, we must only consider the Prince of Wales, a notorious rake who eventually would become King George IV. His father, George III, may have been powerfully misguided in his dealings with the American colonies, but he was an essentially good man who loved his wife and his many children, often reading the Bible to his daughters in the evenings. But his eldest son was quite the opposite. In fact, the Prince of Wales was widely celebrated for having had seven thousand sexual conquests. This and his other myriad indiscretions were well known. If a leading figure in the land is behaving in this fashion, it sets a tone and an example that are powerfully counterproductive to a healthy culture.

Wilberforce used the influence and cultural position that he had to point in another direction. For example, Wilberforce and his wife had six children, and Wilberforce spent every Sunday at home with his family, playing with the children inside and outside their home in Clapham. To us, this behavior sounds rather normal, but in his day it was not the fashion for fathers to spend much time with their children or to observe the Lord's Day as Wilberforce did. He sent a powerful cultural message that family was important, and being a good father and family man meant spending quality time with one's family.

Making goodness fashionable wasn't just setting an example against badness. What Wilberforce wanted to do—and largely succeeded in doing—was to make "doing good" fashionable. It's hard to believe that before Wilberforce the very idea of helping those less fortunate was practically nonexistent. If someone was suffering, the general consensus was that he had brought his difficulties upon himself and he must deal with the consequences of his behavior.

But Wilberforce dared to dream about changing this mind-set. What if people who had money and power and influence would be willing to use those things to do good for their fellow men? What if he could bring a biblical worldview into the culture?

The biblical idea first mentioned in Genesis 12 that we are "blessed to be a blessing" was not at all considered, much less practiced, at that time. Thanks in large part to Wilberforce, most of the Western world today believes that those who are fortunate have some obligation to help those who are less fortunate. But for Wilberforce's contemporaries this idea was quite foreign. Wealthy persons believed they had wealth because God was on their side and they were consequently "blessed." Conversely, they believed that those who did not have wealth deserved their difficulties and were being judged by God. So to help them would be to go against God's purposes. Of course this view is the antithesis of God's view, but it was tremendously widespread. This is really more an Eastern Karmic idea of why people suffer and struggle. In India, a Brahmin would never dream of helping an Untouchable, because their misery was thought to be due to their bad Karma; they deserved their misfortune. One's wealth was thought to be due to one's good Karma, and was therefore deserved. Therefore to help the poor would be to thwart the "divine" plan.

Dramatic as it sounds, Wilberforce's tremendous efforts to change this mind-set over the course of many decades can rightly be seen as one of the most significant accomplishments in history. It was a radical idea, taken by one man from the Gospels into mainstream British culture at a time when the British Empire was huge and tremendously influential. Consequently, these biblical ideas were spread throughout the world, especially throughout Western Europe and the new United States of America.

We in the West have been living with them ever since then, and we've gotten so used to thinking this way that we can hardly imagine a world without them. We assume such ideas were always the norm, but the reality is precisely the opposite. Until Wilberforce and his friends were able to change the culture of elite London and England, these ideas of helping the poor and those less fortunate were essentially unknown.

◆ ◆ ◆

As I have traveled and spoken about Wilberforce over these last years, people have often asked me how Wilberforce did what he did. Although I've noted some of how he did what he did already, it's important to say that Wilberforce wasn't just "religious" but actually had a personal relationship with God. He seems to have been motivated by love—love of God and the love of his fellow man—more than by a simple sense of right and wrong or justice and injustice. This is probably the single most important factor in what he was able to do.

Wilberforce knew the God of the universe as a loving Person who had intervened in his life, so he was filled with gratitude to God for being able to see what he saw and was slow to condemn those who didn't yet see things as he did. Most people, therefore, regarded his humility as authentic.

First of all, Wilberforce was willing to share the credit for all that he did with others, and he knew that he was just one of many working for reform in all these areas. He worked with many friends who were theologically and politically on the same page as he was, most of them in the Clapham Circle.

But second—and even more dramatic—was Wilberforce's ability to work with people with whom he disagreed. For example, he worked with Charles James Fox on the abolition issue, even though Fox was his opponent in many political battles. Fox was also notoriously dissolute and a close friend of the Prince of Wales, but Wilberforce understood that he himself had been saved by grace, and he was not about to pretend to have moral superiority because he disapproved of another's moral or political views. He would show others grace as he had been shown grace, and he would work with them, if possible, toward some common and noble purpose, such as abolishing the slave trade. Wilberforce was clear about what he believed, but he never made agreeing with him on everything a condition of working together. He simply cared about the slaves and about the poor too much for that.

Taking this idea one step further, Wilberforce loved his enemies. He didn't grandstand and fulminate at those who were wrong, even if the subject was the horror of the slave trade. He included himself in the group of those who were guilty. When he gave his maiden speech on abolition on the floor of Parliament, he said, "We have all been guilty."[15] And of course that was true. Wilberforce understood the profoundly important concept that we are all sinners and all fall short of the glory of God. He hated the sin but loved the sinner, and he never demonized his opponents. He fought against them valiantly but always with grace, knowing that he had been part of the problem at one time, too, and knowing that if it weren't for the grace of God, he would still be a part of the problem.

Wilberforce's graciousness in the midst of the battle against the slave trade did a lot to persuade those who were on the fence instead of putting them off and pushing them away. He knew that God had commanded him to love his enemies. It wasn't an option. So he would fight his opponents and try to win, but he would do it God's way, showing love and grace even as he fought with tremendous passion.

His profoundly Christian attitude even helped England beyond the cause of abolition. England was leaning toward the same kind of revolution that was occurring in France. But Wilberforce's statesmanship and measured grace set a tone of such civility that England was somehow able to avoid the bloodbath and misery that took place across the Channel in France.

I n 1807, after eighteen years of heartbreaking effort and many near misses, Wilberforce's dream came true. The much-worked-toward, much-prayed-for dream of the abolition of the slave trade became a reality. He was then forty-eight years old. He had contended with life-threatening illnesses over the years, and he continued to deal with them until the end of his life. Furthermore, opponents of abolition threatened his life numerous times. But the slave trade was finally outlawed.

The battle was not over. Wilberforce spent the remainder of his life working to ensure that the promise of abolition was fulfilled. Enforcement in England and its empire was difficult, since what was illegal remained possible (and highly profitable) for those willing to break the laws. For generations, the British Royal Navy scoured the oceans, searching for and intercepting ships that carried their illegal human cargo.

Also, Wilberforce set out to persuade the other major powers of the world—France, Spain, and Russia, especially—to adopt abolition. He knew that unless these nations and the United States were also determined to root out this evil, his efforts had been mostly for naught. So even after the glorious victory of 1807, the abolitionist battle continued on many fronts.

Only after 1808, when the slave trade was officially ended, did Wilberforce see that abolishing the slave trade alone was not enough. He and others had perhaps naively hoped that by abolishing the trade, slavery would eventually die out. But they quickly realized that was not the case and earnestly set themselves to abolishing slavery altogether. This was itself a decades-long battle. At last, in 1833, just three days before Wilberforce's death, he received a visitor who brought extraordinary news. A young member of the House of Commons told him that earlier that day Parliament had voted to outlaw slavery. Hearing this magnificent news on what turned out to be his last day of consciousness was the fitting coda to a spectacular life, one lived out in obedience to the God who had created him.

The world that Wilberforce left behind was dramatically different from the one he had entered seventy-three years earlier. Not only had the slave trade and then slavery itself been abolished, but the once foreign and strange idea that one should help those less fortunate had taken hold. As a result, much else would change, and those changes have been with the West ever since.

How God used William Wilberforce to change the world is almost unbelievable. One man who gave his talents and time and energies to God's purposes was able to do so much. But we who admire him shouldn't compare ourselves to him directly. We should rather ask ourselves: Am I using what God has given me for his purposes? Do I have a relationship with him so that I know he is leading me? Am I obeying him in all areas of my life—or trying to do so—so that I can know I am in a real relationship with him?

It was in his honestly asking and answering these few questions that lay at the heart of the greatness of the great William Wilberforce.

THREE
Eric Liddell

1902–45

W hen I was a student at Yale in the 1980s, a group of
friends and I went to see the British film *Chariots of Fire*.
It was a box office blockbuster, and everyone was talking about it. In fact it would go on to win the Academy Award for Best
Picture, and it seemed that you couldn't go anywhere without hearing
the music from the sound track. The movie was one of those cultural
milestones that takes over the culture for a while, even to the point of
inspiring spoofs and parodies. But this film was worth all the hoopla;
it's surely one of the most inspiring, well-written, and gorgeously
filmed movies ever made.

To all of us watching it in that theater in New Haven, Connecticut,
the story and its hero were brand new. We certainly had never heard of
the main figure in the film, Eric Liddell, the Scottish runner who electrified the world by winning the 400-meter race during the 1924 Paris
Olympics. And we had never seen a movie about someone whose faith
was at the center of his life. But what made Liddell's story so inspiring
was not just that he won an Olympic gold medal, but that he won it

after refusing to run his best event, the 100 meter. And that was because those heats took place on a Sunday—"the Lord's Day," as he put it.

Even though I wasn't a particularly serious Christian at the time, I found *Chariots of Fire* deeply inspiring. And a few years after graduating from Yale—when I came to faith in a serious way—I recalled the story of Liddell, and I wanted to learn more about him and about the film.

I discovered that although the makers of the movie had taken some liberties with the facts (what filmmaker doesn't?), the gist of the story was accurate. More important, I realized the amazing truth that had Eric Liddell run that 100-meter race, as he was urged to do, he would be largely forgotten today outside of Scotland. If you don't believe me, quick, how many other gold medal winners from the 1924 Olympics can you name? Okay, what about 1928? See?

So Liddell is remembered today for one reason. He was willing to make an almost impossible sacrifice: not only the greatest prize in sports but also the chance to bring honor to his beloved country—not to mention fame, fortune, and glory to himself.

What even Eric Liddell did not know until after the 100-meter race was won by Harold Abrahams was that the God who endowed the young Scot with outstanding athletic ability would bring glory to himself through Liddell's refusal to use these gifts at the very moment the world's eyes were on him.

But there's still so much more to his story. If you know little of Liddell beyond what's in the film—that he won an Olympic gold medal and died in China while serving there as a missionary—I'm confident that you'll appreciate the rest of his amazing story.

◆ ◆ ◆

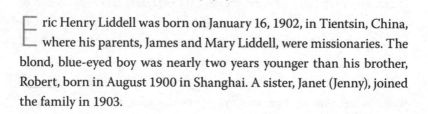

Eric Henry Liddell was born on January 16, 1902, in Tientsin, China, where his parents, James and Mary Liddell, were missionaries. The blond, blue-eyed boy was nearly two years younger than his brother, Robert, born in August 1900 in Shanghai. A sister, Janet (Jenny), joined the family in 1903.

The turn of the twentieth century was a decidedly dangerous time to be a missionary in China. The Boxer Rebellion (1898–1901) was a recent, vivid, and disturbing memory in which nationalist Chinese militants purposed to eliminate all foreign influence, in the process murdering thousands of Chinese Christians and hundreds of Westerners, including missionaries and their families. Warlords competed for power over villages and towns, and bandits kidnapped the well-to-do, holding them for ransom. But the Liddells knew God had called them to China; they would remain there despite the dangers and leave the consequences in the Lord's hands.

Before Eric's first birthday, his parents left Tientsin for Siaochang, where they lived in a newly built house within the compound of the London Missionary Society. There a Chinese nanny, or *amah*, looked after the three Liddell children. Eric was a sickly child, whose mother nursed him through many an illness, but when he was healthy, he and his siblings enjoyed life in the compound. The Liddells were very pious and serious about God, but they also knew how to have fun. At one point, they even allowed the children to adopt a family of goats.

When Eric was five, his parents took the family back to Croftamie, Scotland, on furlough. This was the children's first sight of their family's native land, whose green mountains and sparkling lochs were very different from their dry and dusty Chinese home. Eric and his brother, Robert, explored the village, picked blackberries, and enjoyed being spoiled by the many Liddell relatives who lived there.

At the end of the summer of 1907, just before he and his wife were planning to return to China, James Liddell enrolled his sons in the School for the Sons of Missionaries (later called Eltham College) just outside London. Missionary parents routinely left their children behind for seven years so that they could pursue their educations. The boys' mother, Mary, intended to travel back to China with her husband and young daughter; but just before it was time to go, she changed her mind. She could not bear the thought of leaving her two young sons for so long, so she decided to stay in Great Britain for a year to make sure her boys would be happy at the school, and she moved with Jenny to a house near the campus.

During their years at Eltham, Robert and Eric studied mathematics, languages, science, English, Latin, the classics, geography, and the Scriptures. Outside the classroom, they played touch rugger and looked after a collection of pet birds and lizards. During debates with other boys, Eric was usually quiet, preferring to think about the answers he was hearing rather than entering into the discussions themselves.

In early 1913, the boys received a letter from their mother telling them of the arrival of a third brother—Ernest—in December 1912. When Mary Liddell's ill health and need for surgery brought the Liddells back from China a year earlier than they had planned, Rob and Eric were overjoyed to see their family again.

As Europe was hurtling toward the First World War, both Robert and Eric—then fourteen and twelve, respectively—began excelling in school sports. They played cricket and rugby, and on a school sports day, in the under-thirteen age classification, Eric placed first in the high jump, long jump, and 100-yard dash.

Robert was outgoing and gregarious, joining the debate club and seeking leadership positions. By contrast, Eric grew into a shy, quiet teenager who loved mathematics and science—especially chemistry—and sports.

But his natural diffidence did not stop him from competing ferociously on the playing fields. He had been gifted with a staggering natural talent. In 1918, when he was sixteen, Eric competed in the school championships and took everyone's breath away by placing first in three events: the long jump, the quarter-mile, and the 100-yard dash (tying the school record of 10.8 seconds). Eric also took second place in the hurdle race, the cross-country run, and the high jump. It was a phenomenal performance.

In his senior year, Eric was awarded the coveted Blackheath Cup (an honor given to the best all-around sportsman) and was named the captain of the school's rugby team. Both awards showed that Eric was not just gifted athletically: the gentle young man was also very popular with his classmates.

After Eric's graduation in 1920, he and Robert were again reunited with their mother, sister, and brother Ernest, who had returned to Scotland for another furlough. In February 1921, Eric entered the University of Edinburgh, where he studied physics and chemistry. Amazingly, given his heavy academic schedule, taking part in his beloved sports did not even occur to Eric at this time. But within a few weeks, a fellow classmate wheedled him into participating in the University Athletic Sports Day in late May.

On the day of the competition, Eric's time of 10.4 seconds in the 100-yard dash—which was not his best—won him the race. More important, it won him a place on the university's track team, which would compete against other Scottish schools.

◆ ◆ ◆

If you've seen *Chariots of Fire*, you probably remember the controversy surrounding the decision by Cambridge runner Harold Abrahams to hire a professional trainer. But Eric Liddell had a personal trainer, too, albeit one who worked with him on a volunteer basis. This was to prevent any possibility of Liddell's putting his amateur standing in jeopardy, thus running afoul of the Olympic rules. Under the canny tutelage of Tommy McKerchar, Eric won race after race, competing in the 100- and 220-yard events and quickly attracting the attention of the press, which predicted that a new Olympic contender might be at hand. The public took note of the unusually gracious behavior of the young Scot. Before each race, he always shook hands with his competitors and wished them the best, often lending them his trowel in order to dig their starting blocks, something all sprinters were required to do in those days.

The film accurately captures Eric Liddell's peculiar running style: arms flailing like windmills and knees pumping high. As he approached the finish line, Eric would throw his head back and open his mouth wide. Odd and unorthodox as this style was, McKerchar apparently did not attempt to get Eric to run in a more conventional manner. It was almost as if in throwing his head back, Eric had to rely totally on God to direct him to the finish line, since he couldn't see it himself.

In 1921 Eric joined brother Rob on Edinburgh's rugby team, exhibiting the same ferocious desire to win that he displayed in his running. Two years in a row he was honored to be selected for the Scottish International Team. But in rugby the chances of injury were considerable, so after his second year of play, Eric gave it up and chose to focus on running. Word of his terrific speed eventually earned Liddell the nickname of "The Flying Scotsman," after the well-known express train that connected Edinburgh to London, making the nearly four-hundred-mile journey in just over eight hours.

In April 1923, Eric's growing fame led to the first invitation to speak publicly about his faith. It came from the Glasgow Students' Evangelistic Union, which was engaged, with little success, in an evangelistic rally in a hardscrabble coal-mining town outside Edinburgh. But what if Scotland's fastest sprinter were among the speakers? Perhaps then the men would come and listen. So one of the group's founders, divinity student David Patrick Thomson, agreed to ask Liddell. He traveled all the way to Edinburgh and knocked on the door of the house that Eric shared with his older brother. Eric himself answered, and Thomson put the question to him. Eric thought about it for a few moments and then agreed to do it.

But Eric hated public speaking, and no sooner had he given his assent than he began to regret it. The very next morning he received a letter from his sister, Jenny. At the end, she quoted Isaiah 41:10 (KJV): "Fear thou not; for I am with thee: be not dismayed; for I am thy God: I will strengthen thee; yea, I will help thee; yea, I will uphold thee with the right hand of my righteousness."

Eric felt that those words were God's way of speaking directly to him. Some time later, he said that "those words helped me make my decision, and since then, I have endeavored to do the work of the Master."[1]

When Eric arrived at the meeting, he found some eighty coal miners waiting to hear him. Eric spoke quietly about his faith in Christ, "of what God meant to him," and

> the strength he felt within himself from the sure knowledge of God's love and support. Of how he never questioned anything that happened either to himself or to others. He didn't need explanations from God. He simply believed in Him and accepted whatever came.[2]

Decades later, Eric's daughter Patricia noted, "He felt, 'now who's going to come and listen?' But those times where he went speaking, huge crowds [showed up]."[3] Eric "brought in people who might not have been interested in religion as such, but more into sports: let's see what this sports hero has to say."[4]

Few who heard him speak would have claimed that Eric was a great speaker. His natural shyness kept him from being passionate in his oratory, but somehow his sincerity and self-deprecating humor came through. They certainly did that day. Many of the miners who had come to hear him were deeply moved.

News spread rapidly that the Flying Scotsman had spoken publicly about his faith. Eric soon joined the evangelism group and began speaking with them in town after town, fitting in engagements during school holidays. It gave him great joy to know that God could use his athletic prowess in this way. Years before, Eric had committed himself to serving God in some way, but it seemed he had few talents other than an ability to run like the wind. His heart's desire was to glorify God, and he didn't think that being able to run fast—even as fast as he could run, which was very fast indeed—was of any eternal purpose. Why had God given him this world-class talent? What was the point?

But now he began to see the point, and he was suddenly tremendously grateful for his rare gift.

As he later put it,

> My whole life had been one of keeping out of public duties, but the leading of Christ seemed now to be in the opposite direction, and I shrank from going forward. At this time I finally decided to put it all on Christ—after all if He called me to do it, then He would have to supply the necessary power. In going forward the power was given me.[5]

At this time, Eric became very interested in what came to be known as the Oxford Group—men from Oxford University who urged Christians to surrender completely to God each day and live by the Four Absolutes: absolute honesty, absolute purity, absolute unselfishness, and absolute love. They also urged people to have a daily "quiet time," in which they would read a portion of the Scriptures, pray, and listen quietly for God's leading. Eric would do this for the rest of his life, even during the dark days when he lived in an internment camp in occupied China.

f you've seen the movie, you will probably remember that one of the most unforgettable and dramatic scenes in *Chariots of Fire* involves a quarter-mile race in which Eric is accidentally knocked down by a competitor but against all human odds manages to win anyway. The remarkable event really did happen in July 1923 at Stoke-on-Trent at a so-called Triangular Contest track meet between Scotland, England, and Ireland. Literally right out of the blocks—near the very start of the race—Eric was badly knocked down, and in a quarter-mile race at such a high level of competition, fractions of a second determine the winner. Anyone knocked down is quite simply out of contention. But such accidents are unavoidable in the intense rough-and-tumble crowding of such races.

In this instance, however, despite the fact that he was twenty yards behind, Eric leaped back to the track and madly gave pursuit. That he was twenty yards behind made the attempt to rejoin the relatively short race seem utterly absurd. Nonetheless, Liddell ran at such an astonishing pace that the spectators were goggle-eyed and on their feet, rapt by the unfolding scene before them. Accelerating from far behind, Liddell managed to catch and pass one runner and then another until impossibly, he finally overtook the leader and won the race, at last collapsing onto the cinder track. It was an athletic performance for the ages, and no one who was there would ever forget it.

In 2012, *New York Times* writer David Brooks wrote a column claiming that the charitable aspect of the Christian faith was at odds with the killer instinct needed to win in athletic competition, so that serious faith was a hindrance to victory.[6] But Eric Liddell is the classic example of someone whose faith was not only *not* at odds with the will to win, but also, indeed and on the contrary, was a tremendous boon to it. His competitive instinct, as evinced in this one race, was simply unparalleled. Because he desired to use his athletic gifts to glorify God and because he knew that his winning gave him an opportunity to speak about God to men who otherwise might not be at all interested in the subject, running and winning had an eternal purpose. Because he was not merely running for himself, Liddell was able to summon powers that sometimes seemed miraculous, even to avowed skeptics.

After that famous race, when some of the astonished onlookers asked him how he had managed to win, Liddell again seized the opportunity to publicly glorify God. He reportedly replied, "The first half I ran as fast as I could. The second half I ran faster with God's help."[7]

Although the movie *Chariots of Fire* showed us this dramatic incident, it never told us what happened as a result: Eric had pushed himself so hard to win that he damaged muscle tissue and had severe headaches for days afterward. Those few seconds of superhuman exertion on the track took so much out of him that he didn't even place at a 100-meter race two weeks later, and the 100 was his signature event, one in which he had recently set a record. Indeed, as it turned out, Eric Liddell had given so much in that single performance that he didn't win another race again for the rest of that summer. The 1924 Paris Olympics were just one year away, but even though he did not win any races after that memorable day in Stoke-on-Trent, Liddell was still considered a probable Olympic contender.

To heighten the dramatic effect, *Chariots of Fire* suggests that Eric did not receive the news that the heats for the 100-meter race—his best event—would take place on a Sunday until he was boarding the ship that carried the British team to the Paris Games. But in reality, Eric learned about this in the fall of 1923. This was when, as a prospective Olympic contender, he received the schedule of events from the British Olympic Association.

Still, while deeply regretting that he would not be able to run, Eric did not hesitate making and abiding by his decision. As far as he was concerned, Sunday was the Lord's Day—not a day for playing games—even the Olympic Games. Instead, it was a day for rest and worship. Eric took the Lord's command seriously, that we are to observe the Sabbath day and keep it holy. *Holy* simply means "separated unto God." As he saw it, running in the Olympics on that day was out of the question, and Eric could not compromise on what he believed God had commanded.

While the real Eric Liddell was not confronted by the Prince of Wales and the British Olympic Committee for his decision, as we see depicted in the movie, the scene nonetheless accurately represents the attitude of the British Olympic Committee toward Eric's decision: they were flabbergasted and outraged. And they were not about to let the misguided fanaticism and arrogance of this overly religious young man ruin Scotland's chances for national glory! They would use any means necessary to get this annoyingly headstrong man to run.

First, they tried to convince Liddell that there was no real problem with running on Sunday; after all, his heat wouldn't take place until the afternoon, leaving him more than enough time to attend church services in the morning. Eric didn't buy it. Nor did he buy the argument that he could worship God in the morning and run to God's glory in the afternoon. When, in frustration, a committee member pointed out that the Continental Sabbath lasted only until noon, Eric testily responded, "Mine lasts all day."[8]

When the British Olympic Committee realized that Eric was an immovable object and would not budge, they tried another tack: they would try to budge the International Olympic Committee. They lodged an official appeal to have the heats for the 100-meter race moved to another day in order to accommodate any participants whose religious beliefs prevented them from taking part on the Sabbath. This was a terribly sporting effort on their part: the appeal was denied nonetheless.

The British Olympic Committee was hardly alone in being upset with Liddell's decision not to run in his best event, the one in which he was likely to bring glory to Scotland. When news of his decision became public, many Scots—excited over the chance of Scotland winning its first-ever Olympic gold medal—were aghast at his decision. They felt he had betrayed them. To bow out of the 100 meter at this point was taking things too far. What was it but insanity? As for his chances in the 400 meter, Liddell was a world-class sprinter, not a world-class quarter-miler. It was all an awful mess, but everyone assumed the young man eventually would come to his senses.

But Eric had made up his mind. More important, he felt that he had God's mind on the subject, and that was all that mattered. Eric would obey God, and God would sort out the details of who won what medal. Even if he faced a lifetime of calumny and ignominy for his decision, his desire was to glorify God and to obey God, and the results in these Olympics and in his future life were in God's hands.

So in the end—with just six months to go before the Paris Games—Eric made his decision irrevocable and began training not for the 100-meter race but for the 400-meter event. The 400 is not merely longer than the 100; it is a middle-distance race and requires a completely different strategy. On June 20 of that year, Liddell took part in the Amateur Athletic Association Championships in London. This competition would determine whether he would be tapped for Britain's Olympic Team. Many had their doubts, but the fleet-footed Scotsman nailed his place on the team by finishing second in the 220 and by winning the 440.

◆ ◆ ◆

On Saturday, July 5—roughly two weeks later—the grand opening ceremonies for the 1924 Olympics were held. Two thousand competitors from around the world entered Colombes Stadium in Paris. They watched and listened as the Olympic flag was raised, cannons roared, and thousands of pigeons were released. Eric Liddell was there, snappily dressed in a blue blazer, white flannel pants, and a straw boater, as was the rest of the British team.

The following day—Sunday, July 6—the heats for the 100-meter race were held. Who can imagine what went through Eric's mind that day? But we know what he did. Eric first attended church and then joined his teammates and the Prince of Wales at a ceremony at the Tomb of the Unknown Soldier honoring those who had died in the First World War. Because feelings still ran high over the terrible costs of that war, Germany was not allowed to compete in the Games that year.

The final for the 100 meter was held the next day, Monday, July 7. Eric sat in the stadium watching while his teammate Harold Abrahams, far below on the track, waited tensely for the sound of the starting pistol. When the pistol fired, the runners burst forth, and 10.6 seconds later, Abrahams broke the tape, just ahead of the American, Jackson Scholz. Liddell joined enthusiastically in the roar of delight from British fans, celebrating Great Britain's first-ever win in this event.

The heats for Liddell's two events took place over the next four days. On Wednesday, July 9, Liddell, Abrahams, and four others, including Jackson Scholz, lined up for the final in the 200 meter. British onlookers were hoping for a win by Abrahams. But 21.6 seconds later, it was Scholz who crossed the finish line first, with his teammate Charley Paddock taking silver a tenth of a second later. Liddell, finishing a tenth of a second after Paddock, took home the bronze medal, Scotland's first ever. But this achievement was mostly overlooked in the shock and disappointment over Abrahams's placing not first in this race but dead last.

The 400-meter finals were held the very next day—Thursday, July 10. The overwhelming and sensible view that Eric would not win this event was powerfully confirmed when the American Horatio Fitch shattered the world record in the 400-meter semifinal heat early in the day, with a time of 47.8. Liddell, running in the second heat, managed to finish first, but his time was 48.2—two-fifths of a second behind Fitch's.

And there was more bad news for Liddell. When the six finalists drew lanes for the 400-meter final that evening, Eric drew the outside lane, widely considered the worst possible position. This was because the runner in the outermost lane started the race far in front of his opponents, unable to see them and compare his progress to theirs. Given that this race was hardly his best event, given that Fitch had outperformed him earlier that day with a world record, and given that Liddell had already tired himself in two earlier races that day, Eric's lane position seemed to put the final nail in the coffin on his chances of winning any kind of medal for Scotland.

But Eric was not one to fret. His perspective was quite different from the norm, and his ultimate goal was not to merely win his race or even to compete, but to glorify God. And what the other runners, the crowds, the coaches, and the fans listening to the Games on radios did not know was that Eric had that morning received a reminder of this: as he left his hotel that morning, a British masseur pressed a folded piece of paper into his hand. Liddell thanked the man for it and said he would read the message later.

In his dressing room at the stadium, Liddell unfolded the note and read the following:

It says in the Old Book, "Him that honours me, I will honour."
Wishing you the best of success always.[9]

The "Old Book" to which this referred was, of course, the Bible,
and the quotation was from 1 Samuel 2:30. Receiving that note deeply
touched Eric. As he said a few days later at a dinner in his honor, "It
was perhaps the finest thing I experienced in Paris, a great surprise
and a great pleasure to know there were others who shared my senti-
ments about the Lord's day."[10]

Another man who played a role in encouraging Eric that day was
fellow Scot Philip Christison, the leader of the Queen's Own Cameron
Highlanders. In the moments before Liddell's race began, the regiment's bagpipers played at least part of the rousing "Scotland the
Brave." It was a tune and an instrument that would stir the blood of
any patriotic Scotsman.

As the runners took their places on the track for the race, Eric,
in his typical gentlemanly way, shook the hands of his competitors
and wished them well. Moments later, the starting pistol fired, and
the men were off. In the stands was Harold Abrahams, who knew
something about racing. Abrahams was immediately upset to see that
Liddell, unable to see the other runners, had set a blistering pace, as
though he were running the 100 meter and not the 400. While pacing
was a nonissue in the 100 meter, it was a vital component to the 400
meter. Abrahams could see what Liddell could not, that he had begun
too fast and would not be able to keep up the pace.

But Liddell kept it up longer than Abrahams expected. Halfway
through the race, he was still ahead by three meters. Although it certainly wasn't possible to continue at this blistering pace, somehow Eric
continued.

Back in Edinburgh, seven hundred miles away, Eric's roommate,
George Graham-Cumming, listening to the event on a homemade
radio, jumped up and shouted the announcer's words as he heard
them in his earphones: "They've cleared the last curve. Liddell is still

leading! He's increasing his lead! Increasing and increasing! Oh, what a race!"[11]

Increasing? How could that be? But as the runners entered the last hundred meters of the race, that's precisely what took place. And then in the final stretch, Eric went into his odd, familiar end-of-the-race running style, head thrown back, mouth open, arms pounding the air. Moments later, Eric crossed the finish line. He had won the race. Not only did he win, but he beat his nearest competitor by the unfathomable distance of five meters.

Harold Abrahams and anyone else who knew something about the 400 meter were quite agog at what they had witnessed. The stadium crowd exploded with joy, many of them madly waving Union Jacks. Eric Liddell had just won the gold medal for the UK and for Scotland. A few moments later, his time of 47.6 seconds was announced. It was a new world record. Again the crowd exploded.

Sixty years later, in 1984, the American runner Fitch recalled the event: "I had no idea he would win it. Our coach told me not to worry about Liddell because he was a sprinter and he'd pass out 50 yards from the finish."[12] And Fitch's coach should have been correct. After all, that's what logic dictated must happen. Instead, as Fitch recorded in his Olympic diary, "tho a sprinter by practice, [Liddell] ran the pick of the world's quarter milers off their feet."[13]

Few people remember that the 100-meter race was not the only race from which Eric dropped out because it would have required his participation on a Sunday. He also gave up running in the 4 x 100-meter relay and the 4 x 400-meter relay races. When those events were being run on the following Sunday, July 13, Liddell was nowhere near the Olympic stadium. He was in the pulpit at the Scots Kirk in Paris, preaching to a large and admiring audience.

J ust two days after his return from Paris and the Olympics, the twenty-two-year-old Eric Liddell graduated with his class from the

University of Edinburgh with a bachelor of science degree. But no one there that day was unaware of the national hero in their midst, and his classmates cheered loudly when Liddell stood to receive his degree. That wasn't all. When that part of the graduation was over, a scrum of his classmates triumphantly and giddily carried Eric on their shoulders all the way to Saint Giles's Cathedral, where the commemoration service was to take place.

Here in the coolness of the great cathedral Liddell once again exhibited his characteristic modesty, humility, and grace. Recalling his visit to the United States for a race the previous year, Liddell said,

> Over the entrance to the University of Pennsylvania, there is written this, "In the dust of defeat as well as in the laurel of victory, there is glory to be found if one has done his best." There are many here who have done their best, but have not succeeded in gaining the laurel of victory. To these, there is as much honour due as to those who have received the laurel of victory.[14]

Following his stunning Olympic victory, Liddell stunned the world again when he announced his plans to stop running altogether. He would become a missionary to China, greatly disappointing all those who hoped to see more of his running. But Eric was excited about the great adventure of it all. He planned to teach science, mathematics, and sports at the Anglo-Chinese College in Tientsin, China. The missionary purpose of the college was to bring the gospel to the sons of wealthy families in the hope of influencing China's future leaders.

In preparation, Eric enrolled in the Scottish Congregational College in Edinburgh for the coming year to study theology. During this year, Eric spent every spare moment accepting the deluge of invitations to speak about his faith during evangelistic campaigns across Scotland. He also taught Sunday school and often preached at his church, Morningside Congregational. As was ever the case and now much more so, Eric's willingness to take part in local sporting competitions as part of evangelistic rallies helped bring out people who would likely never otherwise have attended.

It took the Olympic Games to teach Eric that God intended to use his phenomenal athletic ability to bring people to him. And it was Eric's refusal to run on Sunday, sacrificing an almost certain gold medal, that taught the world there was no hypocrisy in this now world-famous Christian follower. Eric also revealed the value he placed on obedience to God: he ranked it above the greatest treasures the world could offer. His decision to forgo earthly glory brings to mind that scene from the Gospels when Jesus is tempted by Satan in the wilderness:

> The devil took him to a very high mountain and showed him all the kingdoms of the world and their splendor. "All this I will give you," he said, "if you will bow down and worship me." Jesus said to him, "Away from me, Satan! For it is written: 'Worship the Lord your God, and serve him only.'" (Matt. 4:8–10 NIV)

So would Eric Liddell have won the 100-meter race if he had violated his conscience? Recalling the race decades later, Eric's daughter, Patricia, put it this way: "The gold [for the 400 meter] was lovely, but not the most important thing. I truly believe that had he run on Sunday [and] sold out his principles, he would not have won. He would not have had the fire. He was running for God."[15]

Chariots of Fire makes this point as well, when a member of the Olympic Committee explains to another member:

> "The 'lad,' as you call him, is a true man of principles and a true athlete. His speed is a mere extension of his life, its force. We sought to sever his running from himself."
> "For his country's sake, yes."
> "No sake is worth that. Least of all a guilty national pride."[16]

◆ ◆ ◆

Anyone who watched *Chariots of Fire* may well believe that the most exciting and significant event of Liddell's life was the moment he crossed the finish line in the Olympic 400 meter. One can hardly blame them; after all, that's where the movie ends. We are told that Eric became a missionary to China and that when he died in 1945, all of Scotland mourned.

But the truth—if we can believe it—is that the second half of Eric's life was even more dramatic than the first, although it's not the sort of story one often sees dramatized in major motion pictures. During his years in Scotland, Eric had publicly told thousands of people of his love for God, but in China this love would blossom into service to everyone he encountered.

Eric arrived in China via the Trans-Siberian Railroad in 1925, one year after his Olympic triumph. His parents, his sister, Jenny, and his brother Ernest were all there waiting, delighted to have Eric back with them at last. But the political situation in China was again tense, with feelings running strong against foreigners. This was in part because of a recent deadly clash between colonial police and some demonstrating Chinese.

The Liddells lived in a large house within the compound of the London Missionary Society, in the British concession of Tientsin, and Eric began teaching at the Tientsin Anglo-Chinese College as he had planned. Thanks to his modesty, good humor, and genuine affection for his charges, he quickly became a popular member of the staff. In addition to teaching science classes, he conducted Bible studies, taught Sunday school, coached soccer, and helped with dramatic productions. And of course he spent considerable time improving his Chinese.

Eric also found time to socialize with other missionary families— and one family in particular: the MacKenzies. As it happened, Hugh and Agnes MacKenzie were the parents of a vivacious, red-headed fifteen-year-old daughter, Florence. Over the next few years, Eric, who was ten years Florence's senior, often found excuses to be around her. He saw her during group activities among the missionary families, helped her study, and regularly popped in for tea at her parents' house.

One evening in November 1929, when Florence had turned eighteen, Eric took her for a walk and proposed. Florence—who somehow had no idea Eric was serious about her—excitedly answered yes. Her father agreed to the marriage on the rather draconian condition that Florence first return to Canada and fulfill her goal of becoming a nurse, which meant a three-year separation for the young couple. It would be the first of many long separations throughout their years together.

In 1931, after he completed his initial four-year commitment to work in China, Eric traveled to Canada where he spent four weeks visiting Florence in Toronto. Afterward, he sailed across the Atlantic to Scotland, where he planned to spend his furlough studying at the Scottish Congregational College. By the time he had to return to the mission field, Eric hoped to become an ordained minister.

But while he was in Scotland, others had plans for him too. The London Missionary Society, which was seriously in debt due to the worldwide economic depression, hoped to exploit Eric's tremendous popularity to bring in both money and recruits. Hundreds of churches and athletic groups were also eager to have him speak. The gracious Liddell—who had difficulty saying no—accepted so many speaking engagements during this time that he became exhausted.

Still, despite the endless calls on his time, Eric was ordained on June 22, 1932. After saying good-bye to his family, who were on furlough once more in Scotland, Eric boarded a ship to Canada for another visit with Florence. After a few joyful weeks together, Eric left his fiancée and returned to China, where he once more plunged into the work of the college and the church.

It would be two full years before Florence and her family came to China. They arrived on March 5, 1934, and three weeks later Eric and Florence were at last married. They set up housekeeping in Tientsin, and Florence assisted Eric in his work. She was especially gifted at entertaining students and the children of missionary families in their home, and many of these students made commitments to follow Christ.

Two years after they were married, Eric and Florence had their first child, Patricia Margaret. The next year another daughter, Heather Jean, was born.

By this time, storm clouds were beginning to gather as Japan engaged in acts of aggression against China. In preparation for a possible conflict, the government demanded that the older students at the college undergo military training. As a result, Eric and his colleagues were forced to accommodate changes in the routine of the college. In the summer of 1937, war came to the Chinese in the same way it would come to Americans a few years later: Japanese planes arrived without warning to bomb Tientsin, causing fires, death, and destruction. Within three days the city had fallen to the Japanese.

Chinese refugees, many of them wounded, flooded into the foreign concessions—which were lands in China governed by the British following the Opium Wars. This included Tientsin. Elsewhere in China, the Japanese army committed atrocities on the civilian population, most infamously in Nanking. Still, despite the chaos all around, the Tientsin school opened that September with 575 students.

In dealing with the problems created by the Japanese, Eric sometimes put his life in danger. Once, attempting to relieve a severe coal shortage, he contracted for sixty tons of hard anthracite, but planned to deliver it personally to Siaochang by barge. Two times on the journey armed thieves attacked and robbed him. He was also detained for a day and a half by the Japanese, and then

> forced by ragtag military groups to pay exorbitant "taxes." With his money exhausted, he left the barge and journeyed back to Tientsin for a fresh supply of currency. After a mutiny by the crew and a half-day's interrogation by members of the Communist army, he and the coal finally reached Siaochang.[17]

On one memorable occasion, Eric took part in a baptism service as the sound of Japanese artillery shells pounded down and soldiers burst into the building, searching for bandits. On another occasion, Eric rescued a man who had been shot and another who had been nearly decapitated during an attempted execution by the Japanese. On at least one trip, he was himself shot at.

In August 1939, Eric and his wife and daughters were able to escape the difficulties of life in China by traveling to Toronto on furlough for a family visit. After that, they hoped to travel to Great Britain. But, Adolf Hitler altered their plans by invading Poland. Of course this led to war between Great Britain, France, and Germany, and everything changed. To cross the Atlantic, now with German U-boats prowling its waters, was not advisable. So Eric and Florence decided it would be best for Florence to remain in Canada with the girls, while Eric traveled alone to England and Scotland. But Florence and the children so missed him that in March 1940, they boarded a ship, safely crossed the Atlantic, and joined Eric in Scotland. The family spent five happy months there. For a time, despite the ravages of war, they could again enjoy family life.

But their return passage to Canada turned out to be even more dangerous than the previous trip to England. Their ship was part of a fifty-ship convoy, which was accompanied by cargo ships; warships of the Royal Navy provided an escort. Hitler's U-boats found them nonetheless, and a German torpedo struck the ship carrying the Liddells. Happily, it was a dud, and the Liddells survived unharmed. Other ships in their convoy were less fortunate. Before the voyage was finished, the Germans had sunk five of them.

The Liddells visited Canada for a few weeks. Their desire to remain there in a safe place must have been extraordinary, but their desire to obey God's call on their lives as missionaries was stronger still. Even with untold dangers and deprivations ahead, they made the return journey to China, but once there, they were unable to remain together. Florence and the children stayed in Tientsin, but Eric went on to Siaochang, a rural outpost where the London Missionary Society had sent him as a village pastor. Eric regretted that he would no longer be teaching. He was also sorry the dangerous conditions in Siaochang made it impossible to have his family with him.

The first thing Eric noticed when he arrived was how busy the Japanese had been. In a letter to Florence, he wrote: "The last few days we have watched rather depressed and dejected men going out on forced labour, to prepare a motor road to pass to the east of Siaochang." He also wrote his wife, "When I am out it is giving, giving, all the time, and trying to get to know the people, and trying to leave them a message of encouragement and peace in a time when there is no external peace at all."[18]

One day, Liddell conducted a wedding ceremony in a village near Siaochang. During the reception, they could hear the sound of big guns firing.

As he bicycled through the region, Eric often encountered gruesome evidence that the Japanese had visited certain villages. The men had been killed, the women had been raped, homes had been set on fire, and many people were suffering from shock. In the midst of these horrors, Liddell continued to minister to whomever he could, and many came to faith in Christ.

Eric visited his family in Tientsin whenever possible, but as conditions worsened, the Liddells had a hard decision to make. Should Florence and the children stay with Eric in China? Or should they travel to Canada, where they would be safe?

After discussing the problem for months and praying about it, the Liddells decided that the two girls and Florence—now pregnant with their third child—should return to Canada to live with Florence's family. Eric expected to join his family within a year or so. The Liddells traveled to Japan and boarded the Japanese ship on which Florence and the children would travel to Canada. Eric hugged his little girls and asked six-year-old Patricia to help her mother when the new baby came. After kissing his wife good-bye, Eric left the ship. Florence and the children went to the upper deck to search for Eric.

Turning to look back, Eric spotted his family and waved a final good-bye before watching the ship steam away. It would be the last time he saw his family.

Back in Tientsin, where he had been temporarily reassigned, Eric resumed his work. He moved into a flat with his friend A. P. Cullen, whose family had also left China. As the war progressed, garbage collection and other services were disrupted, including mail service. It was not until September that Eric received a cable with the welcome news that his beloved Florence had been safely delivered of their third daughter, Maureen.

After the Japanese forces' craven and infamous attack on Pearl Harbor on December 7, 1941, Liddell's life changed dramatically. At precisely the same time as they were bombing Pearl Harbor, the Japanese were busy in Tientsin, rounding up the foreign military forces responsible for guarding the British, French, and American concessions, installing machine gun emplacements, and making it abundantly clear that they were now in charge. They also sent all the college students home, searched the premises (confiscating a radio), and restricted the movement of all foreigners. They ordered all Americans to move to the British concession, terribly crowding the people who already lived there.

Worst of all for Eric Liddell, the missionaries were no longer allowed to do the work for which they had come to China in the first place. As one biographer notes, "they could no longer teach, preach, or practice medicine. . . . They had become missionaries without a mission."[19]

But Eric was not one to sit idle. He felt that God always had something profitable for him to do. So during these chaotic months he found the time to write a devotional guide that he titled *Discipleship*. Each month had a different theme, such as "The Nature of God," "The Character of Jesus," and "The Holy Spirit." The book is still available today.

One cannot help imagining that his decision not to run on Sunday during the 1924 Olympic Games might have been in his mind as he penned the following words:

> Have you learned to hear God's voice saying, "This is the way, walk ye in it?" Have you learned to obey? Do you realize the tremendous issues that may be at stake?[20]

These words reflected not just that one famous decision but the whole direction of his life. Surely the sacrifice of being alone in a war zone—on the other side of the world from loved ones—was a far greater sacrifice than foregoing the glory of an Olympic medal.

Elsewhere, Liddell wrote,

> If I know something to be true, am I prepared to follow it even though it is contrary to what I want[?] . . . Will I follow if it means being laughed at by friend or foe, or if it means personal financial loss or some kind of hardship?[21]

Eric did his best to help the adults, too, such as willingly rising early to do grocery shopping for them when he could.

In March 1943, the final blow was struck: all foreigners—who were now suddenly considered enemy nationals—were to be sent to an internment camp. After parading them through the streets for a mile as an attempt to humiliate them, the Japanese troops ordered the foreigners onto railway cars.

They were sent to Weihsien, an exhausting journey of some three hundred miles. The three hundred captives—among them missionaries, businessmen, tourists, jazz musicians, prostitutes, and opium addicts—finally arrived at their new home. It was a one-block compound built by Presbyterian missionaries. Its four hundred rooms, hospital, and large church had a few new additions: guard towers, searchlights, and machine guns. Japanese soldiers were now using some of the houses. The Japanese had stripped the buildings of water pipes and had stolen much hospital equipment. As a result of the newly non-existent plumbing, the latrines were unspeakably filthy cesspools. Ironically, the compound was named "Courtyard of the Happy Way."

Nonetheless, the captives quickly set to work tidying up the buildings. In a humble and sacrificial display of true Christian love, Catholic priests and nuns, along with the Protestant missionaries, volunteered to clean out the revolting latrines for the others. The internees built furniture and cooked for each other. High-ranking business executives, accustomed to having everything done for them, learned how to pump water, stoke boiler fires, and peel vegetables.

The internees made time for amusements as well, with musical groups performing everything from sacred music for Easter Sunday, to classical pieces, to jazz. Teachers willingly taught academic courses to anyone who was interested, and when the captives were finished with their daily work, they played card games together.

When the winter of 1943 brought severe cold, the internees made fuel by mixing coal dust with mud in order to keep warm. One priest heroically smuggled food into the camp to complement the children's skimpy diet.

Eric, known as "Uncle Eric" to the children of the camp, lived in tight quarters with his friends Edwin Davis and Joseph McChesney-Clark. As he always had, Eric threw himself heart and soul into his work and volunteer activities. He taught in the camp school; organized softball, basketball, cricket, and tennis games; and planned worship services. He organized square dances and played chess with the kids—anything to keep them out of trouble.

Eric took a special interest in the three hundred children who had been taken out of the China Inland Mission School and were now living in the camp without their parents; he thought of his own three girls, so fortunate to be in better circumstances.

Throughout these difficult years, Liddell maintained his belief that Sundays should be reserved for God. But when teenagers got into a fight during a hockey match, Eric—to the astonishment of those who knew of his famous stand at the 1924 Olympics—agreed to referee the game on the following Sabbath.

Joyce Stranks, who was a seventeen-year-old fellow internee, said that Eric

> came to the feeling that a need existed, [and] it was the Christlike thing to do to let them play with the equipment and to be with them . . . because it was more Christlike to do it than to [follow] the letter of the law and let them run amok by themselves. And for me that was very interesting because it was the one thing, of course, everyone remembers about Eric [that he would not run on Sunday because the Sabbath was the Lord's Day].[22]

No matter how busy he was, Eric never neglected his daily time with God. Each morning, Eric and his friend Joe Cotterill woke early and quietly pursued their devotions together by the light of a peanut-oil lamp before beginning a long day of work.

Eric sent monthly Red Cross "letters" to his family, but these messages were limited to an astonishingly terse twenty-five words, and it took many months for these letters to travel back and forth between China and Canada. A year after the internees had been herded into the Courtyard of the Happy Way, Eric wrote a twenty-three-word letter to Florence: "You seem very near today, it is the 10th anniversary of our wedding. Happy loving remembrances, we must celebrate it together next year."[23]

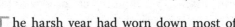

The harsh year had worn down most of the internees, who grew weary of the endless standing in line for everything, from the morning roll call to latrine and shower visits. As the long months wore on, camp residents became less and less concerned about the good of the entire community. Instead, selfishness began to manifest itself. Many began stealing food and other necessities.

Although he deeply missed his family, Eric stayed cheerful for the sake of the others. In a Bible study class, he taught others to love their enemies—including the Japanese guards at their camp—and he exhorted his fellow Christians to pray for them, as the Bible instructed. This one lesson made such an extraordinary impact on Joe Cotterill that he promised God that if he survived the war, he would become a missionary to Japan.

Eric's sincere Christian faith was everywhere on display. Stephen Metcalf, who was seventeen in 1944, remembered one remarkable incident. Metcalf's shoes had completely worn out. One day Eric came to him with something wrapped up in cloth. "Steve," he said, "I see that you have no shoes, and it's winter. Perhaps you can use these." Eric pushed the bundle into Steve's hands. "They were his running shoes," Metcalf says.[24] We can only imagine that Eric had been saving the historic shoes as a memento of his past triumphs, but in the difficult conditions of the internment camp, their practical value to this young man far outweighed their sentimental value to Eric. Others have said that Eric spent much time making peace between various factions of the camp and tried to be a friend to everyone.

I n late 1944, as the internees were about to mark their second full year in the camp, Eric began to experience terrible headaches. Joe Cotterill saw other changes in his friend. He walked and talked more slowly, and his wonderful jokes became a thing of the past. Camp doctors treated him when Eric picked up a flu virus, but the headaches continued nonetheless. Those who knew him best thought he might be suffering from depression, and an old family friend, a Scottish nurse named Annie Buchan, made sure Eric was put back in the hospital where she could keep an eye on him.

Doctors, knowing how hard Eric worked, suggested that he had possibly suffered a nervous breakdown—a diagnosis that deeply disturbed Eric. "I ought to have been able to cast it all on the Lord, and not to have broken down under it," he said bleakly.[25]

On February 11, 1945, Liddell suffered a minor stroke. But just a few days later, he was up and walking around the camp hospital, telling friends he felt much better. The doctors now began to suspect that Eric was suffering from a brain tumor. But without an X-ray machine, they had no way of knowing for sure.

Joyce Stranks visited Eric during breaks from her work in the hospital kitchen, bringing him up to date on what was happening in the camp. On Sunday, February 18, the Salvation Army Band, which played hymns on the Sabbath just outside the hospital, received a special request from Liddell. He wanted them to play "Be Still, My Soul," one of his favorite hymns.

Three days later, Eric typed a letter to his beloved Florence:

> Was carrying too much responsibility. Slight nervous breakdown. Am much better after month's rest in hospital. Doctor suggests changing my work. Giving up teaching and athletics and taking on physical work like baking. A good change. So glad to get your letter of July. . . . Special love to yourself and children.[26]

Joyce Stranks dropped in on Eric as he was finishing up the letter. Sitting beside his bed, she and Eric talked about the need to surrender one's will to God in everything one did, "in our attitudes, not what we wanted to do and felt like doing, but what God wanted us to do," Joyce recalled. "He started to say 'surren—surren'—and then his head went back," she said.[27]

The frightened teenager ran to get the nurse, Annie Buchan, but little could be done. Eric had slipped into a coma, and he died that evening at 9:20. He was forty-three.

When news of his death traveled around the camp the next day, the internees were grief-stricken. "He was known, not because of his Olympic prowess," Metcalf recalled, "but because he was Eric. . . . He was the kind of person who was a friend to everyone. And his funeral bore that out. The church wouldn't hold all the people. . . . The whole camp was closed down. It was a very, very moving occasion."[28]

An autopsy revealed that Eric indeed had an inoperable brain tumor. When his death became known to the outside world, many memorial services were held to honor the man who would not run on Sunday—even at the cost of an Olympic gold medal for his country. The news of his death came as a great shock to his wife and daughters in Canada, who thought Eric's strength and vitality would carry him safely through the war.

Many years later, daughter Patricia talked about her thoughts on the day she learned of her father's death, and of how she wondered why God had seen fit to separate Eric from his family during the last four years of his life. "I have met a lot of the children in the camp—the same age as we were," she said,

and they were put in the camp without their parents. . . . We were safe, and these children did not have their parents, and most of them have done very well. And he made a great influence and steadiness of their lives there. So in that sense, God's hand was there.[29]

Joyce Stranks, who was one of those children to whom Eric was so kind, said, "He made Christ's life so relevant—and made it feel like we who followed Christ must do what He has asked us to do when we are in the situation we are in. You don't get a dispensation because you're in the camp."[30]

Eric's friend A. P. Cullen, who had known Eric most of his life, summed up his friend's life in a camp memorial service on March 3, 1945:

He was literally God-controlled, in his thoughts, judgements, actions, words to an extent I have never seen surpassed, and rarely seen equalled. Every morning he rose early to pray and read the

Bible in silence: talking and listening to God, pondering the day ahead and often smiling as if at a private joke.[31]

◆ ◆ ◆

At Scotland's Morningside Congregational Church, where Eric had taught, and at Dundas Street Congregational Church in Glasgow, thousands of mourners gathered to honor Eric's life. The *Glasgow Evening News* summed up the feelings of the Scottish people regarding the man who had put God before a gold medal and then served so many others in China: Eric Liddell "did [Scotland] proud every hour of his life."

In 1980, fifty-six years after Eric gave up his chance to win the 100-meter dash, another Scot, Allan Wells, won the 100-meter event at the Moscow Olympics. According to the BBC, "When asked by a journalist if he wanted to dedicate his win to Abrahams, who had died eighteen months previously, Wells replied in typically frank fashion: 'No disrespect to anyone else, but I would prefer to dedicate this to Eric Liddell.'"[32]

And sixty-three years after Eric's death, just before the Beijing Olympic Games, the Chinese government revealed something that even Eric's family didn't know: Eric had been included in a prisoner exchange deal between Japan and Britain but had given up his place to a pregnant woman.

Why does the world still remember and love Eric Liddell today, when other athletes from his era have been long forgotten?

Lord Sands, an Edinburgh civil leader, put his finger on the answer during a dinner honoring Eric just after the 1924 Olympic Games. It was not because Eric was the fastest runner in the world that the guests were gathered there that evening, he said. Instead, "it is because this young man put his whole career as a runner in the balance, and deemed it as small dust, compared to remaining true to his principles."[33]

There are greater issues in life than sport, and the greatest of these is loyalty to the great laws of the soul. Here is a young man who considered the commandment to rest and worship high above the fading laurel crown, and who conquered. It was St. Paul, the tent maker of Tarsus, who watched the Olympic Games many centuries ago and wrote, "They who run in a race run all, but one receiveth the prize. So run that ye may obtain."[34]

God had a far greater plan for Eric Liddell's life than a gold medal that would eventually be forgotten, along with the athlete who won it. And he has great plans for each of us. Those plans may include the need to give up something we value highly. But those who give up what we may most desire—if God has demanded it—the Lord will truly honor.

FOUR

Dietrich Bonhoeffer

1906–45

I first heard about Dietrich Bonhoeffer the summer that I turned twenty-five. I was returning to the faith I'd lost at college, and the man who was leading me along that journey gave me a copy of Bonhoeffer's classic book *The Cost of Discipleship*. He asked me if I'd ever heard of Bonhoeffer, and I said that I hadn't. He told me that Bonhoeffer was a German pastor and theologian who, because of his Christian faith, stood up for Germany's Jews and got involved in the plot to assassinate Adolf Hitler. He also said that Bonhoeffer was killed in a concentration camp just three weeks before the end of the war. When I heard all this, I almost couldn't believe it. Was there really a Christian whose faith had led him to heroically stand up against the Nazis at the cost of his own life? It seemed that all the stories I had heard of people taking their faith seriously were negative ones. So this was something new to me, and I instantly wanted to know more about this courageous hero.

One reason I was so interested in Bonhoeffer's story was that I am German. My mother was raised in Germany during the terrible years of Hitler. When she was nine, her father—my grandfather Erich, after whom I'm named—was killed in the war. I always wondered what really happened during that time. How had a great nation of people—of my own people—been drawn down this dark and evil path? My grandmother told me that my grandfather would listen to the BBC with his ear literally pressed against the radio speaker because anyone caught listening to the BBC could be sent to a concentration camp. So I knew that he did not approve of what the Nazis were doing. But he was forced to go to war, like so many men of his generation, and he was killed. My book on Bonhoeffer is dedicated to him.

In many ways, I grew up in the shadow of World War II, and I have always puzzled by the immeasurable evil of the Nazis and the Holocaust. As a result, I've wondered more generally about the question, what is evil and how do we deal with it? The more I know of his life, the more I have come to believe that Bonhoeffer is a powerful role model for us in answering that question.

I remember reading *The Cost of Discipleship* that summer. What Bonhoeffer wrote in that now classic book was every bit as impressive as his amazing life story. His writing had a sparkling clarity and an intensity, and his words bespoke an authentic Christian faith that had no patience for phony religiosity—what Bonhoeffer famously called "cheap grace." As I read that book, I realized that phony religiosity had turned me away from the Christian faith altogether. So it was thrilling to encounter a Christian man who had really lived out his faith, who had put his whole life on the line for what he believed. This was the kind of Christianity that could interest me.

I also learned that this great man of God had somehow felt justified in participating in the plot to assassinate Adolf Hitler. Here was a man who wasn't an armchair theologian, living above the fray. He lived out his faith to the best of his abilities in the real, messy, and often complicated world.

I never intended to write a biography about anyone, much less Dietrich Bonhoeffer. I always say that I'm far too self-centered to want to spend several years thinking about someone else. Nonetheless, I wrote *Amazing Grace*, the biography of William Wilberforce, which came out in 2007, and after that book, people kept asking me, "Who are you going to write about next?" I didn't want to write another biography, but people kept asking the question. Eventually I thought that I might write one more. And there was just one person besides the great William Wilberforce who had captivated my heart and soul and mind such that I would be willing to devote a whole book to him. Needless to say, that man was Dietrich Bonhoeffer. My biography of him came out on the sixty-fifth anniversary of his death.

For a number of reasons, the book struck a chord with many and became a best seller. It has revived interest in Bonhoeffer and his work in a way that I never could have dreamed and that I find deeply gratifying. As a result of writing the book, I've had the honor of meeting two US presidents, and everywhere I go, the message of Bonhoeffer seems to get people talking and debating and thinking. And acting. That's the best part. It's an amazing and profound story that continues to touch and change people's lives, and I'm thrilled to be able to share a short version of it here.

◆ ◆ ◆

Dietrich Bonhoeffer was born in 1906, into what can only be described as an extraordinary family. On both sides of his family were famous ancestors of every stripe, from statesmen and lawyers to painters and theologians. Bonhoeffer's parents were especially impressive. His father, Karl, was a scientific genius who was the most famous psychiatrist in Germany for the first half of the twentieth century. Bonhoeffer's mother, Paula, was also brilliant, earning a teaching degree long before such a thing was widely accepted for women to do and homeschooling all eight of her children. Dietrich was the youngest of the four boys. His twin sister, Sabine, was born ten minutes after he was, something he teased her about his whole life.

All eight children were as remarkable as their parents. Dietrich's eldest brother, Karl Friedrich, went into physics, and at age twenty-three he was involved in splitting the atom with Max Planck and Albert Einstein. Bonhoeffer's middle brother, Klaus, became the head of the legal department at Lufthansa. His sisters were brilliant and married brilliant men. But the way in which they all used their great minds is what made them particularly impressive.

Karl Bonhoeffer taught his children that having a remarkable IQ was of no use if one didn't train one's mind to think clearly and logically. As a scientist, he believed that was of paramount importance. One must learn to follow the evidence and the facts and the logic all the way through to the end. Sloppy thinking of any kind was not tolerated in the Bonhoeffer household. One would surely think twice before opening one's mouth at the dinner table because all statements would immediately be challenged. This early training in how to think was at the core of the Bonhoeffer children's upbringing, and it was one reason that Dietrich grew up to have the tremendous impact on those around him that he did.

Perhaps even more important in the Bonhoeffer family was acting upon what one said one believed. One must not only think clearly but must prove one's thoughts *in action*. If one was unprepared to live out what one claimed to believe, perhaps one didn't believe what one claimed after all! So it was from an early age that Dietrich understood that ideas were never mere ideas but the foundations upon which one built one's actions and ultimately one's life. Ideas and beliefs must be tried and tested because one's life might depend on them. This would hold true in the worlds of science and theology alike.

The Bonhoeffer family was also culturally sophisticated. All of them read great literature and memorized great poems and traveled widely. They were devoted to music, attending operas and concerts whenever possible. Dietrich was a bit of a musical virtuoso. He could play several instruments, was able to sight-read, and was composing and arranging music at an early age. Each Saturday the Bonhoeffer family had a musical evening where they gathered to play instruments or sing. This family tradition continued for many years.

In other ways, Dietrich was a typical boy, sometimes getting into fights in school and needing to be disciplined, but more typically expressing his boyish energies in more positive ways. Later in life, Bonhoeffer loved taking part in athletics; the only movie we have of Bonhoeffer—although it is just a few seconds long—is a home movie of him tossing a ball. You can see this clip in the excellent Bonhoeffer documentary directed by my friend Martin Doblmeier.

As with most Germans of that era, Dietrich was raised in the Lutheran Church. His family members were not big churchgoers, but there was a Christian atmosphere in the home, mainly due to Bonhoeffer's mother. She read the children Bible stories, and the governesses she hired were devout Christians. Bonhoeffer's father seems to have been an agnostic, but he deeply respected his wife's faith. He graciously supported her efforts to raise the children as Christians and always participated in family gatherings where Scriptures were read and hymns were sung.

◆ ◆ ◆

When Dietrich was eight, World War I arrived. Before it ended in 1918, all three of his older brothers were old enough to enlist and proudly did so. The Bonhoeffers were not chest-beating German nationalists, but they had a healthy sense of patriotism and were glad to take part in defending their country, as they saw it. In 1917, Dietrich's brother Walter, the youngest of his three brothers, was called to the front. The whole family saw him off at the station, and his mother ran alongside the train carriage as it pulled away, saying, "It is only space that separates us."[1] Two weeks later the unthinkable happened: Walter was killed. His death was utterly devastating to the family, and Dietrich's mother had what seems to have been a nervous breakdown. For some months she lived with the neighbors, and it was years before she was herself again. Dietrich was deeply affected by it.

About a year later, when Dietrich was thirteen, he made the fateful decision to pursue a career in theology. Not many thirteen-year-olds know what they want to do when they grow up, and those who do rarely decide to become theologians! But the Bonhoeffers took academics very seriously, and the idea of a life in the world of academics seemed perfectly normal. But only up to a point: of all the academic disciplines Dietrich might have chosen, theology was one about which his father had serious reservations. His older brothers were similarly mystified by the choice. So they and Dietrich's older sisters and their friends teased him about it. Yet he was not to be dissuaded. He had thought it through quite thoroughly and met his siblings' needling skepticism with firm resolve.

In his choice of theology, Dietrich was following in the footsteps of his mother's side of the family. Indeed, Dietrich's maternal grandfather was a theologian, as was his maternal great-grandfather, who was quite famous. When Dietrich was a student, his great-grandfather's theological textbooks were still being used, and a statue of him stands today in Jena. So Bonhoeffer's mother likely approved of her youngest son's ambitions.

That same year Dietrich took a confirmation class at the local Lutheran church. At the end of the class, the pastor gave Scripture verses to everyone. Many years later, an old woman who had been in that class with Dietrich Bonhoeffer said she had received the same Scripture verse as Dietrich. It read: "Blessed is the man who remains steadfast under trial, for when he has stood the test, he will receive the crown of life, which God has promised to those who love him."[2]

When he turned seventeen in 1923, Dietrich enrolled at Tübingen University to begin his theological studies. The medieval city of Tübingen is located on the Neckar River, and during his semester there, Bonhoeffer sometimes went skating. One day he slipped and struck his head so hard that he lay unconscious for some time. When his father learned of the accident, he and his wife sped to Tübingen to be with their boy. As a psychiatrist, Karl Bonhoeffer knew a long period of unconsciousness could mean trouble, and after the death of their beloved Walter a few years earlier, the Bonhoeffer parents were understandably anxious to be as close to their children as possible whenever there was any danger or crisis. So they immediately got on a train from Berlin to make sure that everything possible was being done for their son.

To everyone's relief, Dietrich recovered quickly. And as it happened, his parents' unplanned visit coincided with his eighteenth birthday. So what began as an unpleasant emergency ended as a happy celebration. It was during this time that Dietrich had the idea of taking a trip to Rome. He had studied so much about Rome over the years and traveled there in his mind so often that when the idea of actually going there came up, he was giddy with anticipation. His parents weren't thrilled about the idea, but eventually they were willing for him to go if his older brother Klaus accompanied him, and that spring, they went.

Dietrich knew it would probably be extremely enjoyable and educational, but he didn't know that it would be so significant to his future. It was in Rome that, for the first time, Dietrich thought seriously about the question that would dominate his thinking for the rest of his life. That question was: What is the church?

It first came into his mind with real power on Palm Sunday when he was visiting Saint Peter's Basilica. Although not himself a Roman Catholic, Bonhoeffer had great respect for the Catholic Church and attended many Catholic services during his Roman holiday. But that Palm Sunday he saw for the first time in his life people of every race and color celebrating the Eucharist together. This picture struck him with the force of an epiphany. He suddenly saw the church as something universal and eternal, as something that transcended race and nationality and culture, as something that went far beyond Germany and far beyond Lutheranism. He made the intellectual connection that would affect everything going forward: all who called on the name of Jesus Christ were his brothers and sisters, even if they were nothing like him in any other way. This idea would have far-reaching consequences, especially once the Nazis took power. But that would not be for some time.

When Bonhoeffer returned from Rome, he did not go back to Tübingen. Instead he enrolled at Berlin University, which was the most prestigious institution in the world for theological studies in the 1920s. The legendary Friedrich Schleiermacher had taught there in the latter part of the nineteenth century, and the living legend Adolf von Harnack was still teaching there. Bonhoeffer studied with him and knew him very well. They often commuted to the university together on the trolley. Bonhoeffer was not a theological liberal like Harnack, but he respected him and the other theological liberals at Berlin University and learned much from them. Throughout his life, Bonhoeffer was not afraid to learn from those with whom he disagreed.

Bonhoeffer earned his PhD at the startlingly young age of twenty-one. In his postgraduate work, the question he was asking and answering on a high theological and academic level was the same one that had entered his head on that Palm Sunday in Rome: What is the church?

In the course of answering that question, Bonhoeffer discovered that he actually wanted to work in the church as well. He wanted not only to be an academic theologian but also to become an ordained Lutheran minister. But in Germany in those days, one couldn't be ordained until one was twenty-five. So, at age twenty-two, he traveled to Barcelona and served there for a year as an assistant vicar in a German-speaking congregation. Then at age twenty-four, with another year before he could be ordained, he decided to study at Union Theological Seminary in the United States.

◆ ◆ ◆

Since he had earned a PhD in theology from the prestigious Berlin University three years earlier, it can be assumed Bonhoeffer was not principally going to New York for the academic experience. It seems that he was mostly interested in the culturally broadening aspect of a year in America. But what happened to Bonhoeffer during his nine-month sojourn in New York ended up being much more than a culturally broadening experience.

It all began when Bonhoeffer befriended a fellow student named Frank Fisher, an African American from Alabama. The social work component of Fisher's Union studies involved spending time at Abyssinian Baptist Church in Harlem. So one Sunday in the autumn of 1930, Fisher invited Bonhoeffer to join him there. Bonhoeffer was only too eager to go along.

Abyssinian Baptist Church was then the largest church in the United States, and what Bonhoeffer saw there that Sunday staggered him. The vast congregation of African Americans wasn't merely "doing church" or going through the motions; on the contrary, the people in attendance that morning seemed to take their faith very seriously. For most of these people, life was hard, and the God they worshipped was real and personal. He was not a philosophical or theological construct. Bonhoeffer witnessed something that morning more palpable and visceral than anything he had seen in a church before. The worship was more than hymn singing; it was powerful and real; and the preaching was too. The fiery pastor, Adam Clayton Powell Sr., exhorted his hearers not just to have a genuine relationship with Jesus but also to translate that into action in their lives, to care for the poor and do the other things that Jesus urged his followers to do.

The patrician twenty-four-year-old was so moved that morning that he decided to go up to Harlem every Sunday afterward. It was extremely unusual for a blond, bespectacled Berlin academic to be involved in a black church in Harlem, but Bonhoeffer was there often in the months ahead. He even taught a Sunday school class. He became very involved in the lives of the congregation and in the budding issue of civil rights. For perhaps the first time in his life, Bonhoeffer seemed to link the idea of having deep faith in Jesus with taking political and social action. He always knew that real faith in Jesus must lead to action, not just to philosophical and theological thinking; it had to manifest itself in one's life. But the profound faith of the African

Americans in New York, and their struggle for equality, helped him see this in a new way.

Of course Bonhoeffer made the connection to the oppression of the Jews when he returned to Germany, but we don't know whether he made this connection while he was still in New York. On the surface, the Jews of Germany—unlike the African Americans in New York—had enjoyed notable economic and cultural success. It was impossible at that time to imagine the horrors that lay ahead for them. After all, Hitler would not be elected chancellor and president of Germany for several years.

One episode in New York perhaps shows that God knew Bonhoeffer would have an important role in helping Germany's Jews in the years to come. On Easter Day in 1931—the only Easter that Bonhoeffer spent in America—he couldn't get into any of the big mainline Protestant churches. He very much wanted to experience an Easter service in one of them, but he discovered too late that since everyone goes to church on Easter, no seats were available. One literally needed to get a ticket well in advance of the day. So, what did Dietrich do? He went to a synagogue to hear Rabbi Stephen Wise preach. In truth, it wasn't an actual synagogue; it was Carnegie Hall. Rabbi Wise had such a large following that his services couldn't be contained in any of the existing New York synagogues.

The events of the nine months Bonhoeffer spent in America had a profound effect on him, and when he returned to Germany in the summer of 1931, it was clear to his friends that something had changed. He seemed to take his faith much more seriously. Before he had left, his intellect had been in the right place, but somehow now his heart was engaged in a way that it hadn't been before.

Bonhoeffer took a position on the theological faculty of Berlin University and began to teach there. From behind the lectern, he would say things that one did not usually hear in Berlin theological circles.

For example, he referred to the Bible as the *Word of God*, as though God existed and was alive and wanted to speak to us through it. The whole point of studying the text was to get to the God *behind* the text. The experience could not be merely intellectual but must also be personal and real, as it had been for the African American Christians at Abyssinian Baptist Church in New York City. Bonhoeffer also took his students on retreats and taught them how to pray. One of his students said that Bonhoeffer once asked him: "Do you love Jesus?"

Bonhoeffer had changed, but Germany had changed too. Before Bonhoeffer left for New York in 1930, the Nazis had very little political power. They were then the ninth most important political party in the Reichstag, the German parliament. But when he returned in 1931, they had vaulted to being the second most important party and were consolidating more power with each day that passed. Bonhoeffer could see the trouble on the horizon, and he would speak in his classes about it. He was not afraid of saying things like, "For German Christians, there can be only one savior, and that savior is Jesus Christ."[3] That was a brave statement because many Germans were beginning to look toward Hitler as their savior, as the man who would lead them out of the wilderness and suffering of the previous several years.

And who could have guessed what lay ahead under his leadership? Hitler presented himself as a man of moderation and peace, as someone devoted to the German people, and as someone who publicly claimed to be following "God's will." He promised to lead Germany out of the economic hell into which it had fallen, and to lift the deep shame that Germans felt at having lost the First World War.

Hitler fed the idea that they had lost the war because they had been betrayed from within, by Communists and Jews—he often conflated these terms—and he said that the way forward was to purge Germany of these supposed traitors. This idea of treachery from within Germany was known as the *Dolchstoss* (stab-in-the-back) legend, and many accepted it as the main reason that Germany had lost the war.

Hitler also portrayed himself as the one who might lead Germans beyond the humiliation of the Versailles Treaty, through which the victorious Allied powers had imposed unbearable terms on the Germans. The Germans bore deep resentment toward the other European powers, especially France. Hitler brilliantly played upon these various factors. As a result, the average German was only too willing to take a chance on him. After all, what could be worse than what Germany had been enduring?

But Bonhoeffer saw that things could get much worse and likely would. He had an innate sense that the National Socialists would lead Germans into far darker places than they had yet been, and he was one of the very few voices who spoke out against it.

◆ ◆ ◆

Bonhoeffer's first opportunity to speak out on a large stage came shortly after Hitler became chancellor in late January 1933. Just two days later, Bonhoeffer gave a famous speech on the radio in which he dissected the so-called "Führer Principle." This was one of the many half-baked philosophical ideas that had aided Hitler's rise to power.

Führer is the German word for "leader," and the Führer Principle was the idea that Germany needed a strong leader to lead it out of the morass of the Weimar Republic. It all seemed perfectly logical. After all, before their loss in the First World War, Germans had strong leadership under the kaiser, and after they lost the war and the Allies insisted that the kaiser abdicate the throne, everything went sour.

The Allies had imposed a democratic government on Germany, but without a tradition of democracy the Germans simply didn't know how to govern themselves. The Weimar government seemed rudderless, and the results were horrific. There were long bread lines and rampant unemployment and vicious political squabbles. Surely things had been better under the strong leadership of the kaiser! And surely any strong leader would be better than what they now had! The Nazis exploited this idea brilliantly, presenting Hitler as the one-man solution to all of Germany's ills. He would be a strong leader! He would lead Germany back to her glory days under the kaiser!

The only problem was that Hitler's idea of leadership had nothing to do with authentic leadership, and Bonhoeffer made this crystal clear in his radio speech. Bonhoeffer explained that true authority must, by definition, be submitted to a higher authority—which is to say, God—and true leadership must be servant leadership. This notion was precisely the opposite of the idea embodied in the Führer Principle and in Hitler. So, just two days after Hitler became Germany's chancellor, Bonhoeffer was publicly on the record against him and his perverse idea of leadership. Bonhoeffer explained that the idol worship that Hitler was encouraging would make him not a leader but a "misleader." He would mislead the German people, with tragic results.

Somehow Bonhoeffer saw from the very beginning what no one else seemed to see—that Hitler and the philosophy he represented would end tragically, and that Nazi ideology could not coexist with Christianity.

Most Germans had no idea that Hitler in fact despised Christianity. He thought it a weak religion, and he desperately wished that Germany could be rid of it as soon as possible. Of course he could never say this publicly, since most Germans thought of themselves as good Lutheran Christians. So Hitler pretended to be a Christian because he knew that saying what he really believed would erode his political power.

Hitler's goal was to slowly infiltrate the church with Nazi ideology and to take it over from the inside. He wanted to unify all the German churches and create a single state church that submitted to him alone. But he would do it a step at a time to avoid drawing attention to his efforts. And like the proverbial frog in the pot of boiling water, the German people would not realize what was happening until it was too late.

Bonhoeffer tried to warn his fellow Christians of Hitler's intentions. Not only did he have a brilliant mind that had been trained well by his scientist father to think logically and see things through to the end, but Bonhoeffer also seemed to have an uncanny sense of what was happening in Germany. His personal relationship with God and his deep study of the Scriptures helped him see what his mere intellect could not, so he was one of the leading and prophetic voices for the church in his time.

Bonhoeffer knew that true Christians in Germany had to stand against the Nazified state "church" of Adolf Hitler. They had to fight with everything they had while there was still a chance to fight. He devoted a large part of his life trying to wake up the church to what was happening. A slumbering church would be no match for the Nazis, and Bonhoeffer did all he could to get others to recognize that they must prevent the Nazis from imposing their ideology on all German Christians.

The main issue in the battle was the Nazi idea that all things must be seen through a racial lens. According to the Nazis, Germans must be "racially" pure, so they tried to purge the German church of all "Jewish elements." Bonhoeffer regarded this as an absurdity. Jesus was a Jew, as were almost all the early Christians, and Christianity is at its core fundamentally Jewish. To excise all "Jewish elements" from it would destroy the very essence of the Christian faith. Of course that was precisely the Nazis' goal.

One of Bonhoeffer's closest friends, Franz von Hildebrand, was ethnically Jewish, but his family had converted to Christianity and he had been ordained as a Lutheran minister. According to the Nazi idea of what should constitute the German church, all ethnically Jewish men must leave the "German" church. Bonhoeffer knew that the God of Scripture looks on the heart of a person, not at his ethnic background. In the end, a frustrated Bonhoeffer led the way for a number of pastors to leave the increasingly Nazified official German church, and they formed what became known as the Confessing Church.

Bonhoeffer was perhaps the first of his countrymen to see that Christians were obliged to speak out for those who could not, to "be a voice for the voiceless." In the case of Nazi Germany, that meant the Jews. At one point Bonhoeffer made the incendiary statement that "only he who stands up for the Jews may sing Gregorian chants."[4] What he meant was that if we were not heroically and courageously doing what God wanted us to do, God was not interested in our public displays of worship. To sing to God when we were not doing what God called us to do was to be a hypocrite. Many were offended at Bonhoeffer's outspokenness on these issues. But he insisted that Jesus was the "man for others,"[5] and to follow Jesus meant to stand up for the dignity of those others who were different from us.

In some ways the formation of the Confessing Church was a victory for all serious Christians in Germany. But Bonhoeffer was not as encouraged as others were. He seemed to sense that despite the victories they had along the way, it would not end well. He felt that most Christians in Germany—including those within the Confessing Church—did not acknowledge what was really at stake and were unwilling to fight the Nazis with everything they had. They seemed to think that whatever problems existed could be fixed eventually. But Bonhoeffer knew that if the Christians in Germany did not wake up to the radical evil growing in their midst and do all they could to eradicate it, all would soon be lost.

Martin Niemöller, who was Bonhoeffer's friend and colleague in the Confessing Church leadership, was someone who saw what was happening, but when he finally saw it, it was too late. He wrote a famous statement about this:

> First they came for the socialists, and I did not speak out—
>   because I was not a socialist.
> Then they came for the trade unionists, and I did not speak out—
>   because I was not a trade unionist.
> Then they came for the Jews, and I did not speak out—
>   because I was not a Jew.
> Then they came for me—and there was no one left to speak for me.[6]

I n 1935, Bonhoeffer was called upon to lead an illegal seminary in the Confessing Church. There at Finkenwalde he would train seminarians not to be merely Lutheran clerics but true and obedient disciples of Jesus Christ. The years he spent doing this may be thought of as the Golden Age of Bonhoeffer. He wrote about this time in his classic book *Life Together*, telling what it means to live in a Christian community, one that takes the Sermon on the Mount very seriously. He taught the seminarians how to maintain a robust devotional life, praying and studying and meditating on the Scriptures daily.

Some of the more traditional Lutheran leaders were disturbed by what they heard about Bonhoeffer's experiment in living in a community of faith at Finkenwalde. But Bonhoeffer felt that to fight evil, one must train Christians how to pray, how to worship God, and how to actually behave as though these things were true. It was not just about theory and theology. It was about real life. Bonhoeffer was a maverick in that sense. He was helping the young seminarians learn how to live out their faith.

Eventually, the Gestapo shut down Finkenwalde. After all, it was an illegal seminary that had taken a public stand against the policies of the Third Reich. Yet Bonhoeffer continued to teach the young men. He would just have to do it in a clever way, shielded from the prying eyes of the Gestapo. For several years he managed to continue teaching underground. The students lived with pastors in the area and gathered in ways that didn't attract the attention of outsiders. The Gestapo didn't know where the training was happening—sometimes it was in a farmhouse here, and at other times it was in a pastor's vicarage there—so they were unable to stop it for quite some time. But as the Nazis were nothing if not meticulous and relentless, they did stop it eventually.

By the late 1930s, Bonhoeffer's possibilities for openly serving God in Germany were being winnowed down to nothing. The Nazis kept increasing the scope of government with more and more laws and regulations, constricting and choking off the liberties of every German and especially of serious Christians. As the noose tightened, there was less and less that Bonhoeffer could do. After the Nazis forbade him from teaching, they prevented him from speaking publicly. Finally they prevented him from publishing because he had the temerity to write a book on the Psalms. The Nazi ideologues who had tried to purge the German church of all Jewish elements thought that the Psalms and everything in the Old Testament were too Jewish and must be avoided altogether. It may sound absurd and even comical that they would consider such a thing, but for the German Christians at the time it was all deadly serious.

In 1938 and 1939, war clouds were on the horizon. Bonhoeffer knew that when hostilities were declared, his conscience would not allow him to pick up a gun and fight in Hitler's war. Bonhoeffer wasn't a pacifist in our contemporary understanding of that term, but the war that Hitler was bringing to Europe and the world was not a just war in the Christian sense. It was not a war of last resort but a war of pure nationalist aggression. So he prayed earnestly, asking God to show him what to do. It was impossible to declare oneself a conscientious objector in the Third Reich. Nor did he want to take a public stand against fighting in the war, because as a leading figure in the Confessing Church, he could get everyone else in the Confessing Church in trouble. How could he avoid having to fight while not endangering his brethren in the Confessing Church?

Bonhoeffer found a way out: he would go to America, perhaps to teach at Union or elsewhere. If an invitation were proffered and he went to the United States before the outbreak of war, it would be impossible for him to return to Germany. He would be obliged to ride things out across the Atlantic until the war was over. The famous American theologian Reinhold Niebuhr got involved, pulling some strings and wangling an invitation for Bonhoeffer to come back to Union Theological Seminary, where Niebuhr was then teaching. Everything was arranged, and in early June 1939 Dietrich Bonhoeffer once more sailed for America.

But no sooner was he on board the ship than Bonhoeffer began to feel uneasy about his decision. Had he missed God's will? He prayed earnestly, asking God to lead him, to show him what to do. In my book about him I quote at length from Bonhoeffer's copious diary entries and letters during this period. It's a privilege to have this window into his private thoughts as he wrestled with his future at this crucial time. Bonhoeffer obviously expected the Author of the Scriptures to speak to him through those Scriptures, and each day he meditated on the verse of the day, trusting God to guide him.

When Bonhoeffer arrived in New York, the uneasiness did not lift. Indeed, it intensified. He felt terribly lonely and out of place. What was he doing in America when his people were about to undergo such a terrible ordeal? In the end he really believed that God wanted him to go back, to stand with his people, come what may. He knew that danger and possibly death lay ahead, but he went nonetheless.

Bonhoeffer left New York in early July, only twenty-six days after his arrival. The ship steamed out of New York Harbor at midnight, under a full moon. When he arrived in Germany, his friends were shocked to see him. "What are you doing here?" they demanded. "We have arranged things at great difficulty so that you could escape, so that you be spared and be of use to Germany after all of this trouble blows over. Why did you return?" Bonhoeffer was not one to mince words. "I made a mistake," he said.[7] Nonetheless, it didn't answer the pressing question of what exactly he *would* be doing in Germany now.

To understand what he would do, we need to understand that Bonhoeffer's family had been involved in the conspiracy against Hitler for years. They were already having secret conversations about what to do about Hitler in early 1933, just after Hitler had become chancellor. These conversations had continued throughout the decade as Hitler consolidated his power. The Bonhoeffers were exceedingly well connected in elite Berlin circles, and they were also close to a number of the key players in what would emerge as a widespread conspiracy against Hitler. During these years, Dietrich was involved in these conversations, often providing moral support to the conspirators and giving them solid theological reasons to fuel their involvement in their dangerous conspiracy against the German head of state.

Most Germans would not have been comfortable taking any stand or action against their nation's leader. But Bonhoeffer thought the matter through on a much deeper level than most Germans. He believed that to do anything less was to shrink from God's call to act upon one's beliefs. And this included standing up for those who were being persecuted, come what may. To do anything less would be to buy into the idea of "cheap grace" that he had so eloquently written about.

But now that Bonhoeffer had returned and war had broken out, what exactly *would* he do? The time for merely providing moral support to others had passed. For Bonhoeffer, now was the time to get actively involved. But how?

The member of Bonhoeffer's family who was most directly involved in the conspiracy was his sister Christel's husband, Hans von Dohnanyi. Dohnanyi was a leading figure in German military intelligence, called the Abwehr, and the Abwehr was at the very center of the conspiracy against Hitler. His brother-in-law hired Dietrich to work for the Abwehr, ostensibly to use his talents to help the Third Reich during this time of war. But the reality of his role couldn't have been more different. Bonhoeffer had officially joined the conspiracy, and he essentially now had become a double agent.

As an Abwehr agent, Bonhoeffer was able to travel outside Germany to neutral countries such as Sweden and Switzerland. But the real reason he went was to secretly get word to the Allies that there were Germans inside Germany who were working against Adolf Hitler. Bonhoeffer's best friend, Eberhard Bethge, said it was at this point that Bonhoeffer went from "confession to conspiracy."[8] He was openly pretending to be a part of the Third Reich, but in reality he was secretly working to destroy it.

Although he had been officially prohibited from publishing,

Bonhoeffer continued to write. He now worked on his magnum opus, *Ethics*. He never completely finished the work, but Bethge had it published after Bonhoeffer's death.

◆ ◆ ◆

I n 1942, Bonhoeffer was visiting one of his dearest friends and supporters, Ruth von Kleist-Retzow, at her home in Pomerania, when he noticed her eighteen-year-old granddaughter, Maria. Bonhoeffer had known Maria since she was twelve, but because he was eighteen years older than she was, he had always regarded her as a child. A chance meeting that day changed that idea. For many reasons it was an extremely unlikely pairing. But the times were tumultuous for everyone. Maria lost her father and her dearest brother in the war during this year, and she turned toward Bonhoeffer for pastoral comfort. Over the weeks and months the relationship bloomed into something else, and in the spring of 1943, they were engaged.

Although Maria's mother was not pleased with the situation, she eventually came around to accepting it. But no sooner had she agreed to let Dietrich and Maria make their engagement public than Bonhoeffer was arrested. The arrest took place at his parents' home in the Charlottenburg neighborhood of Berlin in April. Bonhoeffer was not then arrested for his role in the plot to kill Hitler because that plot and the wider conspiracy against the Nazi leader had not yet been uncovered. He was arrested for something much less serious, comparatively speaking—for his involvement in a plan to save the lives of seven German Jews.

Leaders of the Gestapo had been suspicious of fishy activity in the Abwehr for some time. For months they kept their eyes on Bonhoeffer, Dohnanyi, and a few others. They had even tapped their telephones. When they discovered a secret plan to get these Jews (the number had grown from seven to fourteen) out of Germany and into neutral Switzerland, the Gestapo had enough information to make an arrest.

Bonhoeffer was taken to Tegel military prison in Berlin, just seven miles from his home. This was not nearly as bad as if he had been taken to the underground Gestapo prison. Bonhoeffer's uncle was the military commandant over Berlin, so while at Tegel, Bonhoeffer was treated reasonably well. It was at Tegel that he wrote most of his now famous *Letters and Papers from Prison* and a number of poems, including his most famous poem, "Who Am I?" Bonhoeffer was by all accounts a picture of peace and quiet joy during his days in prison. Many of his fellow prisoners and even some of the guards later related that he had been a profound comfort to them amidst the uncertainty and dangers of that time.

Bonhoeffer was hopeful that he would eventually be released. He believed that he could probably outfox the prosecutor and prove his innocence when his case came to trial. That was his firm hope, as well as the hope of his fiancée and his family. But Bonhoeffer had two other scenarios in mind that would lead to his release: first, even if his case didn't come to trial, or if it came to trial and he lost, he thought that the Allies might win the war and the Nazis would be removed from power. And second and closer to home, he hoped that the conspirators who hadn't yet been arrested would succeed in killing Hitler and his top lieutenants. That way the whole nightmare would be over. Of course things did not end so well.

What happened instead, fifteen months after his arrest—on July 20, 1944—was that the famous Valkyrie plot went into action. And failed. There were earlier failed attempts to kill Hitler, but in those cases, the bombs had somehow never exploded. The Valkyrie plot was the first time that a bomb actually exploded, yet it failed to kill Hitler. But precisely because it had exploded, the vast conspiracy to assassinate Hitler was for the first time exposed.

Upon learning of the conspiracy, Hitler was beside himself with rage. It put him in mind of the *Dolchstoss* legend from the First World War, which claimed that Germany had been destroyed by traitors within its ranks. This thought was too much for the thin-skinned dictator to bear, so he ordered the arrest and torture of thousands. Names were revealed, and one of those names was Dietrich Bonhoeffer. He was suddenly known to be not just a pastor and academic who had theological difficulties with the Nazi regime; he was now known to be a leader in the conspiracy to kill Adolf Hitler.

At this point, Bonhoeffer knew that his days were probably numbered. In October 1944, he was transferred to the Gestapo's underground high-security prison, where he was threatened with torture. It doesn't seem that he was tortured, but his brother Klaus and brother-in-law Dohnanyi were.

This was now the end of 1944, and the war was winding down. Hitler—increasingly unmoored from reality—believed that history had a grand and noble victory in store for him. But most Germans understood that they were not winning and could not win.

In February 1945, endless squadrons of Allied planes bombed Berlin with such intensity that the Germans decided to transfer all prisoners held at the Gestapo prison to other locations. Bonhoeffer was transferred to the Buchenwald concentration camp where he remained for two months. Then, as April dawned, he was taken on a week-long journey that eventually would take him to Flossenbürg concentration camp, and there, on the direct orders of Hitler, early on the morning of April 9, 1945, he was executed by hanging.

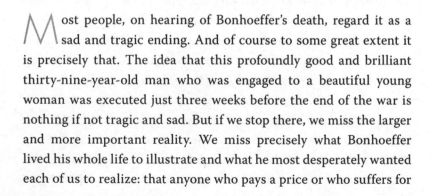

Most people, on hearing of Bonhoeffer's death, regard it as a sad and tragic ending. And of course to some great extent it is precisely that. The idea that this profoundly good and brilliant thirty-nine-year-old man who was engaged to a beautiful young woman was executed just three weeks before the end of the war is nothing if not tragic and sad. But if we stop there, we miss the larger and more important reality. We miss precisely what Bonhoeffer lived his whole life to illustrate and what he most desperately wanted each of us to realize: that anyone who pays a price or who suffers for obeying God's will is worthy of our celebration, not our pity. And if someone goes to his death as a result of obeying God's will, this is even more true.

Bonhoeffer's beliefs about the subject of death in general help us understand how he viewed his own death. We hardly need to speculate, though, since he wrote and delivered a sermon on death in 1933. In that sermon he said, "No one has yet believed in God and the Kingdom of God, no one has yet heard about the realm of the resurrected, and not been homesick from that hour—waiting and looking forward to being released from bodily existence." He continued,

> How do we know that dying is so dreadful? Who knows whether in our human fear and anguish, we are only shivering and shuddering at the most glorious, heavenly blessed event in the world? Death is hell and night and cold, if it is not transformed by our faith. But that is just what is so marvelous, that we can transform death.[9]

In a poem written in the last year of his life, likely knowing that death lay ahead for him, Bonhoeffer called death "the last station on the road to freedom."[10] As a devout Christian, Bonhoeffer worshipped a God who had emphatically conquered death in Jesus Christ through the Crucifixion and the resurrection. Understanding this historical and theological fact—and its far-reaching implications—is unavoidably at the core of the Christian faith, and he went to great lengths to communicate this.

In his 1933 sermon, Bonhoeffer exhorted his hearers to consider this idea, and in the poem he wrote in 1944 he did so again. For him the knowledge that the God of Scripture had actually come to earth and had conquered death changed everything. It gave Bonhoeffer the courage to do all that he did in life, and it gave him the courage to face his own death without fear and trembling. By all accounts, Bonhoeffer faced danger and the gallows with deep peace. What he wrote and said and how he lived and died encourage and inspire us to face our own lives and the evil around us, including the specter of death, with that same deep faith and fearlessness.

◆ ◆ ◆

On the day that Bonhoeffer was executed, the crematorium at Flossenbürg was broken. So Bonhoeffer shared the fate of the innumerable Jews who had recently been killed just as he had been: his body was tossed on a pile and burned. But it seems clear that, for Bonhoeffer, giving his life for the Jews was an honor. The God of the Jews had called him to give his life for the Jews. So it would also have been an honor to have his body disposed of in this way. His ashes mingled with those of the Jews who had died there before him.

Bonhoeffer really believed that obeying God—even unto death— was the only way to live. And it was the only way to defeat evil. In his famous book *The Cost of Discipleship*, he wrote: "When Christ calls a man, he bids him come and die."[11] This was the life of faith in the God of the Scriptures. To accept the God of the Scriptures is to die to self, to embrace his eternal life in place of our own, and to henceforth banish all fear of death. For Bonhoeffer, this was the only way to live.

Jackie Robinson

1919–72

Virtually every American boy is a baseball fan, and I was no exception. I grew up a mile from Shea Stadium and went to my first New York Mets game in 1970, when I was seven.

Many Brooklyn Dodgers fans were looking for a ball club to follow after the Dodgers abandoned Brooklyn for Los Angeles. Many of them became Mets fans.

Not far from Shea Stadium is Jackie Robinson Parkway, named after the great ballplayer who broke the color barrier in major-league base-ball, so from a young age I was aware of Jackie Robinson. But what did I really know about him? Not much beyond the basics. But in 1998, when I was working for Chuck Colson, my colleague Roberto Rivera told me that Robinson was a Christian, and he pointed me to a new biography. I learned not only that Robinson was a Christian but also that his Christian faith was at the very center of his decision to accept Branch Rickey's invitation to play for the all-white Brooklyn Dodgers. I also learned that Branch Rickey himself was a Bible-thumping Methodist whose faith led him to find an African American ballplayer to break the color barrier.

How had I never heard any of this before? How come no one seemed to know this story—that at the center of one of the most important civil rights stories in America lay two men of passionate Christian faith?

◆ ◆ ◆

Jackie Roosevelt Robinson's story begins on January 31, 1919. He was born in Cairo, Georgia, the fifth child of the daughter of a former slave. Robinson's mother, Mallie Robinson, had admired former president Teddy Roosevelt, considering him a great leader, a devout Christian, and a fierce opponent of racism, so she named her son after him. Jackie's mother and his father, Jerry Robinson, were sharecroppers on a plantation owned by James Sasser, a white farmer, at a time when segregation ruled the South.

But the marriage between Jackie's parents was in bad shape by the time he was born, and his father left the family a few months later. Mallie knew that there was no future for her children in the South, and she secretly began to save money to move herself, her five children, and other family members to Pasadena, California. She did it secretly because white southerners often attempted to prevent blacks, who were a cheap source of labor, from leaving. The journey across the continent, in a Jim Crow train, took nine long days.

Mallie found employment as a domestic to a white family, and she worked hard to teach her children the value of "family, education, optimism, self-discipline, and above all, God."[1] She saw to it that her children were in church on Sunday and taught them the value of prayer.

Jackie's childhood years were not easy. The family was poor, his mother was away at work all day, and sometimes there was not enough to eat. As a young boy, Jackie helped the family by mowing lawns and selling hot dogs at ball games. Hostile white Pasadena neighbors tried to buy the Robinsons' house away from them and once even burned a cross in their yard. But Mallie Robinson's dignity, kindness, and hard work eventually won them over. Once, when Jackie and some friends retaliated for a white man's racial slur by spreading tar on his lawn, Mallie forced Jackie to repair the damage, supervising the repairs herself. Mallie believed in what the Bible taught, and the Bible taught that Christians were to bless those who persecuted them.

Jackie's extraordinary athletic talent and fierce competitiveness were apparent from an early age. At John Muir Technical High School, whether the sport was baseball, basketball, football, track and field, or tennis, Jackie excelled, lettering in four sports. At age seventeen, he participated in the Pacific Coast Negro Tennis Tournament, winning the junior boys singles championship.

But Jackie's older brother Mack was an even bigger star. He was such a gifted runner that the United States sent him to the 1936 Berlin Olympics, where he won the silver medal, right behind his teammate Jesse Owens! But on returning home, the triumphant national hero could find a job only as a street sweeper. To be sure, the great country whose Declaration of Independence states that "all men are created equal" was still a long way from any semblance of genuine racial equality.

◆ ◆ ◆

When Jackie enrolled at Pasadena Junior College (PJC) in 1937, his local fame as an athlete grew. Once again, he played football as a quarterback. Entering track and field events, Jackie even broke his famous brother's school broad jump record.

In the spring, baseball beckoned. After making the team, Jackie—who played shortstop and was the team's lead-off batter—made a name for himself by stealing bases.

By the time he left PJC, Jackie had racked up innumerable honors. He and two other black students were the first students of color to be elected to a school service organization called the Lancers. Jackie was elected (by the Kiwanis Clubs of Southern California) to the All-Southland Junior College Team for baseball. In 1938, he also became Pasadena Junior College's Most Valuable Player of the Year.

But racism continued to raise its ugly head during these Depression years. Restaurants and hotels often refused to serve Jackie and black teammates. Again and again Jackie was forced to endure these indignities and injustices, and he often struggled to control his temper.

On January 25, 1938, Jackie was arrested. That evening, he and a friend, Jonathan Nolan, were walking home from the movies when Nolan suddenly burst into song, singing "Flat Foot Floogie." In those days, "flat foot" was a less-than-flattering term for policemen, since most of them walked beats. A passing policeman overheard their tribute and decided to take offense; words were exchanged, and Jackie ended up spending the night in jail. A judge sentenced him to ten days, but because he knew Jackie was a football star, he suspended the sentence on the condition that Robinson avoid skirmishes with the police for two years.

A fellow PJC student named Hank Shatford recalled that the police "didn't regard Jack as a rabble-rouser. It's just that Jack would not take any stuff from them, and they knew it."[2]

One day, Jackie met a Methodist preacher named Karl Downs. Downs had a tremendous ability to inspire young people. He knew that Jackie was a Christian, and taught him that exploding in anger was not the Christian answer to injustice. But he also explained that a life truly dedicated to Christ was not submissive; on the contrary, it was heroic. Jackie's mother had taught her son the same thing, but now, coming from Karl Downs, it struck him in a new way.

Downs eventually led Jackie to a deeper faith in Jesus Christ, and Jackie brought his bad temper and fierce anger at injustices under control. He began to see that the path to justice would be won not with fists and fury but with love and restraint.

By then, Jackie was such a phenomenal baseball player that, had he been white, major-league clubs would have been fighting over him. But the major leagues rigidly enforced the rule against allowing black players on their teams. After leaving Pasadena Junior College without a degree, Jackie began considering college offers, ultimately deciding on UCLA. He was sure that UCLA coaches would use him to actually play instead of allow him to warm the bench as a token black.

But once at UCLA, Jackie decided against playing baseball. He announced he would take part only in football and track, partly because he wanted to concentrate on his studies, and partly because he hoped to follow in his brother Mack's footsteps—literally and figuratively—by being chosen for the US Olympic team.

But in July 1939, tragedy struck. Jackie's beloved brother Frank was killed when a car struck the motorcycle he was riding. A few weeks later, more trouble arrived in the form of a second racially tinged arrest. Jackie was driving his Plymouth home one evening with his friends riding on the running boards, when another car, driven by a white man, pulled up beside them at a stop. Dozens of young blacks crowded around, waiting to see what would happen, causing the white man to leave. When a motorcycle policeman pulled up, most of the crowd left. But suddenly the policeman pulled a gun on Jackie, pressing it into his stomach, and charged him with resisting arrest and hindering traffic. Jackie spent another night in jail, but pleaded not guilty to the charges. He was released on a twenty-five-dollar bond.

When UCLA officials caught wind of the arrest, they leaped into action, but mostly on their own behalf. In Jackie's absence, the judge found him guilty and fined him fifty dollars, which UCLA promptly paid. Jackie received his twenty-five-dollar bail money back, but he was annoyed at the guilty plea, along with the publicity the case received just as he was beginning a promising career at UCLA. Robinson recalled years later that this was his first real experience with vicious bigotry.

On the gridiron that year, "Jackrabbit Jackie Robinson" helped the UCLA football squad win game after game. And in the fall of 1940, Jackie met someone who would change his life: a seventeen-year-old freshman named Rachel Isum. Almost instantly Jackie knew he would marry the beautiful young nursing student, who shared his strong religious beliefs. UCLA's homecoming dance that year was held at the

Biltmore Hotel in Los Angeles. Jackie invited Rachel, and that night they danced to tunes like "Stardust" and "Mood Indigo."

As he and Rachel grew closer, Jackie continued his historic and attention-getting performance in college athletics. He became the first UCLA athlete to letter in four sports: football, baseball, basketball, and track. In 1940, he also won the NCAA Men's Outdoor Track and Field Championship in the long jump competition, leaping twenty-four feet five and a half inches. In basketball, Jackie won the individual league scoring title with 133 points, despite an injury to his hand; but, he was still not named to the All-League Cage Team. The *California Daily Bruin* cried foul in its March 5, 1941, issue, calling the vote a "flagrant bit of prejudice" and a "miscarriage of justice." That it was.

To the chagrin of his mother and Rachel, Jackie dropped out of UCLA just short of graduating, hoping to play professional football. But the black pro teams offered very little money. He then decided to take a job in Atascadero, California, as an athletic director with the National Youth Administration. But as it became increasingly clear that America would likely be joining the war in Europe, the teenagers were all sent home, and the job vanished.

Jackie next joined the Honolulu Bears, a semipro team with the Hawaii Senior Football League. The deal actually included construction work, for which Jackie was grateful, since he was eager to help his mother financially. Jackie played brilliant football, as he always had, but became disenchanted with the team. He also missed his family. On December 5, 1941, he left Hawaii for home aboard the *Lurline*. He left just in time. Two days later, as the ship steamed toward California, the Japanese attacked Pearl Harbor. Jackie was unaware of the attack and wondered why the ship's crew started painting the windows black. The ship, they told the passengers, would do everything possible to avoid enemy submarines.

While the war was bad news generally, in some cases it offered new job opportunities. For example, many African Americans were suddenly hired in defense industries that were previously closed to them. Jackie found a job at Lockheed Aircraft in Burbank, not far from his mother's home.

But the job did not last long. In March 1942, Jackie received his "Order to Report for Induction," and he traveled east to Kansas for basic training at Fort Riley. Jackie Roosevelt Robinson was now a member of Uncle Sam's segregated army. Despite becoming an expert marksman and passing the tests for Officer Candidate School, Jackie was turned down for officer training. The army instead put him in a segregated cavalry unit where he worked as a groom, looking after horses.

Robinson was furious, but the story didn't quite end there. It so happened that the heavyweight boxing champion of the world, Joe Louis himself was also stationed at Fort Riley. The world-famous boxer had enlisted as a soldier to help his country and boost morale. Robinson vented his frustrations to Louis, who decided to use his connections to improve the young man's situation. Louis contacted someone he knew in the White House, who in turn contacted someone else, and Robinson promptly received his officer's commission.

Jackie was appointed as morale officer for the black soldiers at Fort Hood, where he once again pushed the boundaries of segregation. For example, when black soldiers complained about how few stools there were for them at the post soda fountain, he looked into the matter, finding that there were just four for blacks (along the side of the fountain bordering the grill) compared to twelve for white soldiers along the front. Black soldiers and their families had to wait up to an hour to be served, even when seats for whites were empty.

Jackie phoned a Major Hafner to suggest that the number of seats for blacks be raised to six. Hafner, who assumed he was dealing with a white officer, objected; giving black soldiers access to seats in the front opened the possibility that one of them might sit down next to a white soldier or his wife.

"Lieutenant Robinson," Major Hafner said, "let me put it this way. Would you like it if your wife had to sit next to a nigger?"[3]

Robinson exploded into the phone. "I am a Negro officer!" he declared, adding some choice epithets for emphasis. Shortly thereafter, blacks visiting the soda fountain found two additional seats awaiting them.

Racism also showed up in army athletics. Jackie turned out for Fort Hood's baseball team, only to be told he would have to apply to the nonexistent colored team. An enraged Jackie walked off the field. Previously, at Fort Riley, he had been invited to join the football team only to be sent home on leave just prior to a game against the University of Missouri, which, Jackie later learned, refused to play against any team that included black players. An angry Jackie immediately resigned from the team. (But he was allowed to play table tennis, and in 1943 became the US Army's champion player!)

These experiences were minor compared to what the army had in store for Jackie in 1944. That June, Robinson traveled off base for a stay at McCloskey Hospital in Temple, Texas, so that his ankle could be examined. He had injured it during his years playing college football, and doctors were trying to ascertain whether he was fit to be deployed overseas with his unit—if not for combat, then as a morale officer.

On July 6, after spending time at the Negro officers' club, Jackie climbed aboard a Fort Hood bus to return to the hospital. He was heading for the rear of the bus when Jackie spotted Virginia Jones, the light-skinned wife of a fellow Fort Hood officer named Gordon Jones. She was seated four rows from the back.

A few blocks later, the driver noticed that Jackie was not sitting at the back of the bus and, furthermore, was sitting by a woman who appeared to be white. When he hollered back to him, "You got to move back, boy," Jackie refused.

The driver stopped the bus and tried again. He claimed that state law forbade allowing a black man to sit anywhere but the back of the bus, which Jackie knew was nonsense; the army forbade segregation on military buses. Jackie could sit anywhere he wanted. The driver angrily told Robinson that he would make trouble for him when they arrived at the post. Biographer Scott Simon writes: "White voices began to clamor, some telling Robinson to move, others calling for the driver to move on, let the boy be, they had places to go, just drive on and call the police when they stopped at the bus depot."[4]

Among the white riders making a fuss was a post kitchen employee who angrily informed Robinson that she intended to file charges against him. The bus driver asked Jackie for his identification card, which Robinson refused to provide. The driver told the other riders that "this nigger" was making trouble, and eventually the MPs were summoned.

When the military police arrived, they took Jackie to the guard room, where he engaged in several angry clashes with the officer of the day and the commander of the military police, Gerald Bear. Bear declared, "Lt. Robinson's attitude in general was disrespectful and impertinent to his superior officers, and very unbecoming to an officer in the presence of enlisted men."[5]

Jackie objected to this characterization of his behavior, but ultimately he was placed under arrest in quarters and driven back to the hospital. There, a friendly white doctor urged Jackie to undergo a blood test, as he had overheard a plan to accuse Jackie of being drunk and disorderly. Not surprisingly, since Jackie was a teetotaler, the test came back negative.

When Jackie told his senior officer, Lieutenant Colonel Paul Bates, about the incident, he discovered that Bear was planning to court-martial him. Since Colonel Bates refused to go along with this plan, Jackie was transferred to the 758th Tank Battalion, where a more obliging commander agreed to prosecute Robinson.

After his arrest, not trusting military lawyers to adequately represent him, Jackie turned to the National Association for the Advancement of Colored People (NAACP) for help. But the organization declined to assist him at the trial. In the end, Jackie asked that

First Lieutenant Robert Johnson serve as his individual counsel, and he later said that Johnson "did a great job on my behalf."[6]

Jackie was charged with "behaving with disrespect toward Capt. Gerald M. Bear, CMP, his superior officer," and of "willful disobedience of lawful command of Gerald M. Bear, CMP, his superior."[7]

The defense strategy was to "try to show that Robinson had not been insubordinate to Captain Bear but rather that Bear has managed the entire matter poorly," writes biographer Arnold Rampersad.[8] The strategy—which revealed, among other things, how many times Robinson had to listen to himself being described as a "nigger"— worked. Several character witnesses appeared on Jackie's behalf, including Colonel Bates, who told the court that Robinson was not only an outstanding soldier, but that he was also very respected by the enlisted men he worked with. In the end, a relieved Jackie was found not guilty of all charges by a panel made up of whites.

Jackie's deep religious faith helped him through this latest crisis. These difficult experiences may have been God's way of warming up Jackie for what he had planned for him later. They were, in effect, spiritual spring training for the even more difficult episodes that Jackie would face in the not-too-distant future.

Jackie was honorably discharged from the US Army on November 27, 1944. By then, he and Rachel were engaged, but with Jackie jobless, marriage would have to wait.

Although hardly a fan of segregation of any kind, much less in sports, Jackie accepted an offer to play for the Kansas City Monarchs, a Negro National League team. He also fielded an offer from his old friend Karl Downs, now president of the Samuel Huston College in Austin, Texas. Downs invited Jackie to teach physical education at the college, and Jackie accepted, dramatically improving the college's athletic program and becoming a popular figure with students.

As he thought about his future with Rachel and considered what might lie ahead for them, Jackie never could have dreamed of anything close to the reality that was about to occur. His life was soon to change dramatically. A war was then raging in the sports pages around the country about whether major-league baseball should be integrated. And far away from Jackie, in the distant East Coast city of New York, in the borough of Brooklyn, an idea was brewing that would catapult him into the national consciousness—and into American history.

It all began with a colorful sixty-four-year-old figure named Branch Rickey. Rickey was the legendary general manager of the Brooklyn Dodgers team. Rickey was an energetic and relentless innovator whose ideas had already changed baseball in many ways we now take for granted, including use of the batting helmet, batting cages, pitching machines, and statistical analysis. Rickey is even credited with inventing the farm system of the minor leagues and with creating the first spring training facility. But what he was about to do would eclipse all of these things. That's because as far as Branch Rickey was concerned, the national pastime had to be integrated. And he thought that he was the one to bring about the integration. The only questions were, how should he go about it, and who should be the first black player?

Rickey, a devout Christian who refused to play or attend games on Sunday, knew he would have to be very careful as he proceeded. Other baseball owners and managers would be dead set against the idea of integrating baseball, as would many players. But Rickey's deep Christian faith told him that injustice must be fought wherever one found it. As he saw it, the Jim Crow laws that excluded black players from baseball were intolerably unjust. Rickey considered that his past experiences and his position in the game had set him up to do something profoundly important for the sport. Indeed, he saw in all of this "a chance to intervene in the moral history of the nation, as Lincoln had done."[9]

Rickey took seriously Jesus' command that we be "wise as serpents." So, very quietly, he sent scouts to Negro League ball games. To disguise his intentions, Rickey announced that he planned to start a new Negro club to be called the Brooklyn Brown Dodgers. Who could argue with that?

After he reviewed scouting reports, Rickey's attention focused on one particular player, then with the Kansas City Monarchs. According to biographer Scott Simon, Rickey believed that Jackie Robinson had everything he was looking for: Robinson "could run, hit with power, and field with grace. He could steal bases and bunt shrewdly, and he excelled in the game's mental aspects. He was a college man, a veteran, a world-caliber athlete, and a dark, handsome, round-shouldered man with a shy smile."[10]

Perhaps even more important, Rickey saw that Robinson had plenty of experience playing with white players and that—like Rickey—he was a serious Bible-believing Christian with a strong moral character. In the struggle that lay ahead, these characteristics would be crucial. He felt strongly that if the person he chose for this extraordinary task could be goaded into saying the wrong thing or appearing in any way less than noble and dignified, the press would have a field day and the whole project would go up in flames. What was worse, if that were to happen, the whole idea of integrating baseball would likely be set back another ten or fifteen years. Rickey had to be sure he was choosing someone who understood the tremendous import of not fighting back, despite what he would hear—and he would hear plenty. But in the end, he felt he had found the man for the job. It was time for him to meet Jackie Robinson.

That was why, in August 1945, less than three weeks after the explosion of atomic bombs over Hiroshima and Nagasaki effectively ended America's war with Japan, Clyde Sukeforth caught a train to Chicago to talk with Jackie, who was playing with the Monarchs in Comiskey Park. Leaning over the third-base railing, Sukeforth called out to Robinson. He said he was there on behalf of Branch Rickey, who was starting a new team, the Brooklyn Brown Dodgers. Sukeforth asked Jackie to throw a few balls so that he could assess his arm strength. To Jackie it all seemed a bit odd and mysterious.

"Why is Mr. Rickey interested in my arm?" he asked. "Why is he interested in *me*?"[11]

Sukeforth's cryptic response only deepened the mystery: he told Robinson to meet him after the game at the Stevens Hotel. When Jackie arrived, he fired more questions at Sukeforth. The talent scout couldn't say very much—after all, he was on a stealth mission—but his answers were enough to convince Jackie to agree to accompany him to New York and meet Branch Rickey.

A few days later, on August 28, Sukeforth and Jackie met at the Brooklyn Dodgers' headquarters on Montague Street in Brooklyn Heights. Though far from the Jim Crow South, there was still a whites-only elevator in the building. Sukeforth slipped the elevator boy the then princely sum of two dollars to look the other way so that he and Jackie could ride up together to the fourth floor to Rickey's office. Jackie was about to meet the man who would not only change his life but also become like a father to him.

According to Sukeforth, the air in the room when Rickey and Robinson met was electric. At first Rickey and Jackie just stared at each other. Rickey stared because he knew what was at stake and why the moment was potentially historic. The young man before him might well become a historic figure, and this scene might well be written about in future books. For his part, Jackie had no idea what was happening or why Rickey was staring at him. And as Jackie wasn't about to be stared at without staring back, he stared back. What he saw was a pudgy, bespectacled man with bushy eyebrows, a bow tie, and a cigar. The staring continued.

Then Rickey suddenly asked Jackie if he had a girlfriend. It was a bizarre way to start the conversation, Jackie thought, but then again, the whole affair had been strange from the beginning. Rickey made it clear that Jackie might face real challenges ahead, and the love of a good woman—of a good wife—would be very important. Jackie still didn't understand, and his face showed it.

"Do you know why you were brought here?" Rickey asked Robinson.

"Sure," Robinson replied, "to play on the new Brooklyn Brown Dodgers team."

"No," Rickey said. "That isn't it. You were brought here, Jackie, to play for the Brooklyn organization. Perhaps on Montreal to start with, and—"

"Me? Play for Montreal?" Jackie was stunned. The implications were impossible to take in so quickly.

"If you can make it, yes. Later on—also if you can make it—you'll have a chance with the Brooklyn Dodgers."

What Rickey was saying seemed impossible. Jackie was speechless.

Rickey continued to spin out his long-held fantasy. "I want to win the pennant and we need ball players!" he roared, pounding his desk. "Do you think you can do it?"

There was a long pause while Jackie thought it over. Finally he answered: "Yes."

When Rickey asked Jackie if he was up to the job, he wasn't talking only about playing great baseball. He knew Jackie could do that. What he meant, he explained, was that if Jackie were to become major-league baseball's first black player, he would be in for a tremendous amount of abuse, both verbal and physical.

Jackie said he was sure he could face up to whatever came his way. He wasn't afraid of anyone and had been in any number of fistfights over the years when anyone had challenged him.

But Rickey had something else in mind. "I know you're a good ball-player," Rickey said. "What I don't know is whether you have the guts." Rickey knew he meant something dramatically different from what Robinson was thinking, so he continued. "I'm looking," Rickey said, "for a ballplayer with guts enough *not to fight back*."[12]

This was an unexpected wrinkle, to put it mildly.

Rickey then spun out a number of scenarios to convey what he meant, in the form of a dramatic pop quiz. Biographer Arnold Rampersad writes,

Rickey stripped off his coat and enacted out a variety of parts that portrayed examples of an offended Jim Crow. Now he was a white hotel clerk rudely refusing Jack accommodations; now a supercilious white waiter in a restaurant; now a brutish railroad conductor. He became a foul-mouthed opponent, Jack recalled, talking about "my race, my parents, in language that was almost unendurable." Now he was a vengeful base runner, vindictive spikes flashing in the sun, sliding into Jack's black flesh—"How do you like that, nigger boy?"[13]

According to Rickey, not only would Robinson have to tolerate such abuse, but he would need to be almost superhuman and to commit himself to never, ever hit back. This was at the heart of the whole enterprise. If Jackie could promise that, then he and Rickey could make it work. They could open the doors for other black players and change the game forever.

Jackie knew that resisting the urge to fight back really would require a superhuman effort, but he was deeply moved by Rickey's vision. He thought of his mother. He thought of all the black people who deserved someone to break this ground for them, even if it was difficult. He believed God had chosen him for this noble purpose. He believed he *had* to do it—for black kids, for his mother, for his wife, for himself.

Knowing that Jackie shared his Christian faith and wanting to reinforce the spiritual dimensions of what the two men were about to embark on, Rickey brought out a copy of a book titled *Life of Christ* by Giovanni Papini. He flipped to the passage in which Papini discusses the Sermon on the Mount and refers to it as "the most stupefying of [Jesus'] revolutionary teachings." It certainly was revolutionary. In fact, it seemed impossible. In Matthew 5:38–41, Jesus said,

> Ye have heard that it hath been said, An eye for an eye, and a tooth for a tooth: But I say unto you, That ye resist not evil: But whosoever shall smite thee on thy right cheek, turn to him the other also. And

if any man will sue thee at the law, and take away thy coat, let him have thy cloak also. And whosoever shall compel thee to go a mile, go with him twain. (KJV)

Rickey was betting that Jackie Robinson knew what he himself knew: although this was indeed humanly impossible, with God's help it was entirely possible. And Jackie did know it. As a Christian, he knew that if he committed himself to doing this thing—which both men felt was God's will—God would give Jackie the strength to accomplish it.

So Jackie Roosevelt Robinson and Branch Rickey shook hands. And there, in that fourth-floor office in Brooklyn to which Jackie had ridden in a whites-only elevator, under a portrait of Abraham Lincoln, history was made. It was a momentous day not only for baseball but for America.

◆ ◆ ◆

J ackie was now contractually bound to the Brooklyn Dodgers, but this fact had to remain a secret for the present. All who knew of it had to be sworn to secrecy if this noble and daring experiment were to succeed.

Two months later—on October 23—in Montreal, Jackie at last broke his silence and shocked the world by signing a contract to play with the Montreal Royals. When the press besieged him with questions, Jackie answered, "Of course, I can't begin to tell you how happy I am that I am the first member of my race in organized baseball. I realize how much it means to me, my race, and to baseball. I can only say I'll do my very best to come through in every manner."[14]

For his part, Branch Rickey disingenuously insisted that he simply wanted to win pennants. "If an elephant could play center field better than any man I have, I would play the elephant," he claimed.[15]

Some—including New York Giants president Horace Stoneham—applauded Rickey's decision, while others, including many in the press, vehemently attacked it. But it was settled. Next spring, Jackie Robinson would be the first black player in what had been whites-only professional baseball since the 1880s.

In preparation that winter, Jackie went on a ten-week barnstorming tour of Venezuela. Before he began playing for Montreal that spring, Jackie would do something else that was important and momentous. He would marry Rachel. He traveled to California to do just that, and on February 10, 1946, they were married by Jackie's friend Karl Downs in a big traditional wedding at the Independent Church of Christ. The couple honeymooned in San Jose, but the wedding trip was cut short by Jackie's need to begin spring training at the Dodgers' camp in Daytona Beach, Florida. Rachel went with her new husband, and for the first time in her life she witnessed the segregation laws and attitudes of the Jim Crow South. In New Orleans, they were bumped from their next flight and the one after that, too, with no explanation. The couple could not find an airport restaurant to serve them. After spending the night in a filthy hotel room, Jackie and Rachel were finally allowed to fly to Pensacola—where once again they were kept off their next plane, evidently because white passengers wanted their seats. Deciding to take a bus to Jacksonville, the newlyweds were ordered to the uncomfortable seats in the back, where they spent sixteen miserable hours.

"I had a bad few seconds, deciding whether I could continue to endure this humiliation," Robinson wrote later.

The couple were bumped off their flight again in Pensacola, angering Robinson further. But he drew the line at making a scene, because he knew it would only result in newspaper headlines and even possibly arrest for the couple. And giving in to rage might have meant the end of his major-league career even before it began.

In addition, as he and Rachel prepared for the ordeals that would come with Jackie's promotion, they "agreed that I had no right to lose my temper and jeopardize the chances of all the blacks who would follow me if I could help break down the barriers."[16]

Another sixteen-hour bus ride finally brought the couple to Daytona.

Despite a rocky few weeks, by the end of the training camp, Robinson was officially invited to become part of the Royals team, which meant moving to Montreal. Jackie and Rachel had no idea what to expect about racial attitudes there, but they soon discovered to their great surprise that the French-speaking people in their neighborhood could not have been friendlier. By now Rachel was expecting the couple's first baby—Jackie Roosevelt Robinson Jr.—and the neighborhood women brought her advice and ration book coupons so she could buy the healthy food she needed.

Jackie's first game in a Montreal uniform took place on April 18, 1946, at Roosevelt Stadium in Jersey City, New Jersey. That day Jackie officially broke the fabled color line in professional baseball. And his athletic performance could hardly have been better. Jackie got four hits, including a three-run homer, scored four times, and drove in three runs. He even stole two bases. The Royals trounced their opponents 14–1.

To be fair, Jackie's talents on the diamond had never been in question. Far more important was whether he could keep his promise not to respond to the racial ugliness that would surely rear its head in the coming weeks. As Rickey had predicted, Jackie quickly became the regular target of vicious name-calling and race-baiting. But with God's help, Jackie was able to stay above the fray and avoid responding in kind, despite the tremendous temptation to do so.

Throughout that summer, Jackie showed himself to be a man of truly rare character. Anyone with eyes to see could see that Jackie's not fighting back against such filth and injustice was as heroic an accomplishment as anything the sports world had ever witnessed. And if that wasn't enough, his performance on the field continued to stagger the naysayers. That first season he was among the very best players—if not the single best player—in the now-integrated minor league. His batting average was .349, a team record, and he won the league's batting crown, the first Montreal player ever to do so. With Jackie's help, the Royals that season won one hundred games, the most in team history, and they won the pennant by a stunning eighteen and a half games. In every way, Jackie Robinson had magnificently vindicated Branch Rickey's historic decision.

After the season, Jackie returned to Los Angeles to witness the birth of his son. He waited all through the winter for the call he hoped would finally come, inviting him to Brooklyn and, at long last, into baseball's major leagues.

That call came early on April 10, 1947, from Rickey's secretary to Robinson, who was staying in a Manhattan hotel. Could Jackie come immediately to a meeting with Rickey? It all happened with lightning speed. Later that day, while the Dodgers were in the sixth inning of a game, one of Rickey's assistants began handing out press releases to sports reporters in the press box. They announced that the Brooklyn Dodgers had just purchased the contract of Jackie Robinson from the Montreal Royals.

In the Dodgers' dressing room that day, Jackie was given a uniform with the number 42 on the back. Putting it on, he posed and smiled for photographs. The following day, Jackie reported to Ebbets Field to meet with Clyde Sukeforth.

"Robinson, how are you feeling today?"[17]

"Fine," answered Jackie.

"Okay," Sukeforth said, "then you're playing first base for us today against the Yankees."

"I just sorta gulped," Jackie recalled.

Sadly, many opponents of what Robinson and Rickey were trying to achieve showed up at Dodgers' games and loudly expressed their opinions. Worse yet, some of them *played* in Dodgers' games. Just twelve days after the Dodgers signed Jackie, the Dodgers were playing the Philadelphia Phillies at Ebbets Field. During this game, Robinson was subjected to vicious abuse by none other than Phillies manager Ben Chapman, who also encouraged several players to mistreat Robinson.

Jackie remembered the pain many years later in his autobiography. "Starting to the plate in the first inning, I could scarcely believe my ears," he wrote.

Almost as if it had been synchronized by some demonic conductor, hate poured forth from the Phillies dugout.

"Hey, nigger, why don't you go back to the cotton field where you belong?"

"They're waiting for you in the jungles, black boy!"

"Hey, snowflake, which one of those white boys' wives are you dating tonight?"[18]

The next day was just as bad. It was profoundly ugly. In fact, much of what was said was much worse, and is unprintable here. Of course, when he heard all of this, Jackie was strongly tempted to go back on his word to Branch Rickey. But he held his tongue and his temper. Instead, he stoically walked to the plate without favoring the Philadelphia bench with so much as a glance.

Ironically, the flood of filth from Chapman had an unexpectedly positive result: it so infuriated Jackie's teammates that it put all of them on Robinson's side, once and for all. Until that point, a number of the Dodgers players had been none too keen about playing alongside a black man. But what they saw that day changed everything forever. Second-baseman Eddie Stanky spoke for the whole team when he shouted at the opposing dugout: "Listen, you yellow-bellied cowards, why don't you yell at somebody who can answer back?"[19]

Branch Rickey was delighted with the team's response. Chapman's evil intentions had, he said, "solidified and unified thirty men, not one of whom was willing to sit by and see someone kick around a man who had his hands tied behind his back."[20]

Yet the abuse continued from other sources. On the road, hotels and restaurants refused service to Jackie, forcing him to eat and sleep away from the team. Letters arrived, containing death threats. Players on other teams kicked Jackie, stepped on his feet, struck him on the head with pitches, and even slashed painfully at his leg with their spikes, one time creating a seven-inch gash in his leg. Despite all of it, Jackie kept his cool—and his promise to Rickey. And he kept his reliance on God, getting down on his knees every night to pray for strength.

That season, Jackie played in 151 games and somehow he got through all of them without a single incident of retaliation. By the end of the 1947 season, Jackie Robinson had become one of the most famous men in America. And once again, his performance on the field spoke as loudly as anything. He was voted 1947 Rookie of the Year. His batting average was .297; he had amassed an amazing 175 hits and had scored 125 runs; and he had even led the league in sacrifices and stolen bases.[21]

His numbers the following year were again spectacular. But the abuse continued. At one game in Cincinnati, when spectators in the stands were shouting racist comments at Robinson, his teammate Pee Wee Reese pointedly walked over to him and put his arm around him, as though to say to the bigots in the crowd, "if you are against him, you're against all of us." It was a signature moment, and a statue commemorating it stands today in Brooklyn's minor-league KeySpan Park.

In 1949, Jackie exceeded everyone's already high expectations by putting up a batting average of .342, with 124 RBIs, 122 runs scored, and 37 stolen bases. He even started at second base during that year's All-Star Game. At the end of the season, he won the National League's MVP Award. Anyone who doubted whether this man was a great baseball player had to put those doubts aside. And anyone who ever doubted whether he could withstand the torrent of abuse that came against him had to do the same. Branch Rickey knew that his difficult and noble experiment had been a resounding success.

I n 1948, several other black players were invited to play in the major leagues, taking some of the pressure off Jackie. Gradually the level of invective tailed off, and Jackie could concentrate on simply being a spectacular baseball player. His 1949 stats were so impressive that the Dodgers raised his salary to $35,000, at the time a grand sum and the highest salary ever paid to any player in the franchise. Jackie's fame was now such that Count Basie recorded a hit song titled "Did You See Jackie Robinson Hit That Ball?" and in 1950 Hollywood produced the feature film *The Jackie Robinson Story*. As was often done in biopics of that period, Jackie was hired to play himself in the film.

Business opportunities began to come his way, and Jackie got involved with many charitable groups, especially those that helped children of both races. During these years as a player for the Dodgers, Robinson began to challenge hotels and restaurants that still discriminated against black ballplayers, with the result that a number of them dropped their segregationist policies.

And his success as a ballplayer continued. In 1950, Robinson led the league in double plays for a second baseman, and in 1951, he did it again. That year, his outstanding talents as a player almost carried the Dodgers into the World Series, but the crushing defeat of Bobby Thompson's famous "Shot Heard 'Round the World" home run took them out of contention. The next year, 1952, Jackie and the Dodgers brought victory—and bedlam—to Brooklyn when they won the National League pennant, although they eventually lost in the World Series to the Yankees in seven games. In 1953, Jackie batted .329 and led Brooklyn to another National League pennant, but the Dodgers again lost the World Series to the Yankees, this time in six games. In 1954 the team didn't win the pennant; but at last, in 1955, the Dodgers won the pennant again and then went on to take the World Series in seven games from their Bronx rivals.

Winning the World Series was a high-water mark for Robinson. But age was beginning to take its toll on his performance: his average that year dipped to a career low of .256.

The following year marked Jackie's tenth anniversary as a Dodger. It was also the year he began exhibiting the effects of undiagnosed diabetes, and at the end of the season, the Dodgers opted to trade him to the New York Giants.

With his body wearing down, the thirty-eight-year-old baseball legend had already decided he'd had enough baseball and announced his retirement from the game. Even before the Dodgers traded him, he had decided to take a job with the Chock Full O'Nuts company, where he would serve as vice president for personnel. He would never play for the archrival Giants.

In an article he wrote for *Look* magazine, Jackie said: "I'll miss the excitement of baseball, but now I'll be able to spend more time with my family." His three children, Jackie, Sharon, and David, would now "have a real father they can play with and talk to in the evening and every weekend. They won't have to look for him on TV."[22]

Always interested in helping the poor, Jackie now formed the Jackie Robinson Construction Company, dedicated to building low-income housing. He regularly bought food for the needy, leaving it at food banks for distribution. He visited sick children in hospitals and crusaded against drug use, which his son Jackie had struggled with. He also became deeply involved in the burgeoning civil rights movement, working with Martin Luther King Jr. and traveling to the Deep South in an effort to bring about full freedom for the descendants of slaves. Robinson also became the first black analyst for ABC's *Major League Baseball Game of the Week* program and became a board member of the NAACP.

In 1962, the forty-three-year-old icon was voted into the Baseball Hall of Fame—the first black player to be so honored. Almost unbelievably, it had been just fifteen years since blacks had been allowed to play in the major leagues. Yet in that same year, as Robinson sadly noted in an essay, University of Mississippi students rioted as African American James Meredith attempted to enroll at Ole Miss. To use a phrase from Winston Churchill, Jackie's admission to baseball's Hall of Fame was not the beginning of the end of America's toxic racial battles, "but merely the end of the beginning."

I n more and more ways, Jackie's body began letting him down. He suffered severe pains in his legs and feet, the legacy of the years spent playing football, basketball, and baseball. He suffered mild heart attacks in 1968 and 1970 and was diagnosed with diabetes and hypertension. Blood vessels ruptured in his eyes, which led to the loss of much of his vision.

In June 1971, Robinson's troubled older son, Jackie Jr., was killed in a car accident at the age of twenty-four. Those who knew Jackie felt that after all he had been through over the years, this was the hardest blow of all.

On October 15, 1972, just one week before his death, Jackie Robinson and his family gathered at Riverfront Stadium in Cincinnati where Jackie threw out the first ceremonial pitch during Game Two of the World Series. As tens of thousands of Pirates and Reds fans watched, the baseball icon graciously accepted a plaque marking the twenty-fifth anniversary of his debut with the Dodgers, and then, his voice shaking with the emotion of the day, the man who'd broken baseball's color barrier said, "I'd like to live to see a black manager, I'd like to live to see the day when there is a black man coaching at third base."[23]

There were still civil rights battles to be fought, but Jackie would not live to see them waged and won. On the morning of October 24, 1972, Rachel was fixing breakfast when Jackie raced from the bedroom to the kitchen. Putting his arms around his wife of twenty-six years, Jackie said, "I love you," and collapsed. He died of a heart attack in an ambulance headed to the hospital. He was just fifty-three.

A few days later, Jackie's funeral took place at New York's Riverside Church before twenty-five hundred mourners. Tens of thousands of people lined the streets as Jackie was taken to Cypress Hills Cemetery, where he was buried next to his son and namesake.

The intervening years have brought even greater recognition not only of what Jackie Robinson did but also of who he was: a man of character and courage, dignity and faith. In 1984, President Ronald Reagan posthumously awarded Jackie the Medal of Freedom, America's highest civilian honor. In April 1997, President Bill Clinton joined fifty-four thousand Mets fans at Shea Stadium to celebrate the fiftieth anniversary of Jackie's breaking the color barrier in the major leagues. Robinson's grandson Jesse threw out the ceremonial pitch, and Baseball Commissioner Bud Selig announced that major-league baseball would retire Robinson's number. "Number 42 belongs to Jackie Robinson for the ages," he said, and the crowd roared.[24]

In 1999, twenty-seven years after his death, Robinson was named to major-league baseball's All-Century Team.

Usually, when considering the life and career of a baseball player, we tote up his statistics and compare them to the statistics of those who have gone before. But how can we tally what an achievement it was to endure what Jackie Robinson endured those first few years? It was an incalculable and heroic sacrifice that can never be reckoned or understood by any conventional standards. Robinson did what he agreed to do when he met that day with Branch Rickey, and he changed the game forever. It was a singular feat of such great moral strength that all athletic strength must pale in comparison. With God's help, one man lifted up a whole people and pulled a whole nation into the future.

January 31, 2019, will mark Jackie Robinson's one hundredth birthday. There will surely be many memorials around the world. But I hope the world will not forget the heart of the Jackie Robinson story, that he changed America by successfully living out, both on and off the baseball field, the revolutionary and world-changing words of Jesus:

> Ye have heard that it hath been said, An eye for an eye, and a tooth for a tooth: But I say unto you, That ye resist not evil: But whosoever shall smite thee on thy right cheek, turn to him the other also. And if any man will sue thee at the law, and take away thy coat, let him have thy cloak also. And whosoever shall compel thee to go a mile, go with him twain.

SIX
Pope John Paul II

1920–2005

The new pope was the subject of the news everywhere during the last week of August in 1978. I was a fifteen-year-old, about to enter my junior year in high school in Danbury, Connecticut. Although I had many Catholic friends, I was raised Greek Orthodox, so I took little real interest in anything having to do with who was or wasn't the pope. But it was impossible to be unaware of the events transpiring in Rome at that time. It was very big news, and I could understand why, since there were almost a billion Catholics around the world.

Besides, there was never a new pope. As far back as I could remember, the pope had always been Pope Paul VI. This was a given, and not something I thought could ever change, in the same way that the Queen of England was always Queen Elizabeth and, as I write this book, is still Queen Elizabeth. Not many things transcend election cycles, but popes and English monarchs are two that do. So until that fall, when the news was awash with this monumental change, I didn't think change was possible. I remembered once hearing about the pope before Pope Paul. His name was Pope John, but that papacy ended before I was born and, as far as I was concerned, might as well have been during the Middle Ages. So for me, there was only one pope in the world. And suddenly all that changed.

The new pope, Albino Luciani of Venice, took the name Pope John Paul, and since he was the first pope in two thousand years who had the name John Paul, he was officially Pope John Paul I. So that was settled. But no sooner had the news about the new pope died down than there was new news that the newly named pope had died. This was on September 28, just thirty-three days after he had become pope. And so, one month after a pope had died and the College of Cardinals had elected a new pope once more, that new pope died, and they would have to elect a second new pope. It was all quite out of the ordinary, to say the least. Once again the world focused its attention on what was happening in the Vatican. In a way you began to hope that whomever they picked would be reasonably young and healthy.

As it turned out, he was. The man who was now chosen by the College of Cardinals was named Karol Wojtyla, and amazingly he was only fifty-eight years old, practically a teenager by historical papal standards. What's more, he was said to be especially youthful and athletic for his age. And oh, yes, he was from Poland. To almost everyone, the idea of a non-Italian pope was a bit surprising, almost as surprising as if the cardinals had chosen a Protestant. It had been 456 years since the last non-Italian pope began his papacy. A Dutchman, Adrian VI, was elected in 1522. So yes, it had been a while. To put things in perspective, Pope Adrian was a rough contemporary of Christopher Columbus.

This was all very big news on many levels. And there was more. This new pope was said to speak twelve languages and to have written plays and poetry and to have studied philosophy. He was an avid sportsman, who loved soccer and who hiked, weight-trained, swam, and jogged. Had I heard that correctly? A pope who weight-trained and jogged? Even in the 1970s, when it seemed that everyone was jogging, the idea of a pope doing such a thing was almost unthinkable.

Out of respect to his short-lived predecessor, John Paul I, the new pope chose the name John Paul II, which occasionally came to be abbreviated as JP2. Even that seemed young and contemporary. And the more one saw and heard of him, the more extraordinary it all seemed. There was a friendliness, a sunniness, and an optimism to this man that were tremendously refreshing. How was it that his election could somehow stir even non-Catholics? What was it about him that seemed to represent hope? He was supremely serious about God, but he didn't come across as dour or "religious" in the negative sense. He seemed fun and full of life.

So yes, the election of this new pope was big news in a few ways, even to a non-Catholic teenager.

But as the years passed I realized that this pope was more than merely young and non-Italian. He was different in many ways. Before the attempt on his life and before Parkinson's disease slowed him down, he was extraordinarily active and vigorous, traveling the world almost constantly, eventually visiting some 129 countries, beaming at crowds, and drawing vast numbers of young people to the faith.

He was even brave and heroic, traveling to Poland, where he publicly stood up to the Communists there and encouraged the fledgling Solidarity movement. And we cannot forget that he was shot by an assassin and almost died—and later met with the man who tried to kill him and forgave him. It was all like something out of a movie.

So who was this spectacularly gifted man, suddenly now the supreme pontiff? Who was this heroic figure who had once acted in plays, but who would play a lead role in a compelling real-life drama in modern history, the battle between freedom and communism?

Of all the great men in this book, there is only one who has come to be called "the Great." John Paul the Great. Let's find out who he was.

The man who became Pope John Paul II was born Karol Wojtyla on May 18, 1920, in Wadowice, Poland. (The name Karol is another form of the English Charles.) The boy's father, Karol Sr., was an army clerk, and his mother, Emilia, was a part-time seamstress and former teacher. The family lived close to the local church, and as both parents were devout Catholics, little Karol—or Lolek, as he was nicknamed— was there every day.

Lolek was the youngest of three children born to his parents. Edmund was fourteen years older, but Lolek's sister died before Lolek was born. Lolek's mother was quite sickly throughout his childhood, suffering from heart and kidney disease, so the bulk of the parenting fell to his father, Karol Sr. In their book *John Paul II: A Tribute in Words and Pictures*, Monsignor Virgilio Levi and Christine Allison write:

> The Wojtylas were like most Catholic Poles; their home contained the symbols of their faith—crucifixes, a painting of the Blessed Mary, and holy water in a vessel by the door. Lolek wore the scapular he received at First Communion every single day. . . . But faith in the Wojtyla home went deeper: it was embodied in the human heart. Karol Sr. lived a life of simple Christian humility. "Almost all of the memories of childhood are connected with my father," Lolek would write, years later, as pope. "His example alone was sufficient to inculcate discipline and a sense of duty."

The image of his father on his knees in prayer would never leave Karol Wojtyla. And the world would often see him in precisely this pose, too, whether kissing the soil as he landed in a foreign country or at his more usual place of prayer at Saint Peter's in Rome.

When Lolek was just eight, his mother died. It was only the beginning of a number of tragedies that would befall the boy. Four years later, when Lolek was twelve, his beloved brother, Edmund, died of scarlet fever. Despite their differences in age, Edmund and Lolek were close, and young Lolek was devastated by the loss. Years later he wrote, "My mother's death made a deep impression . . . and my brother's perhaps a still deeper one because of the dramatic circumstances in which it occurred and because I was more mature."[1] His brother's death forced him to grow up quickly, and without question it drove him closer to God. The quiet, devout boy now became even more devout, spending more of his time in church and in prayer.

Lolek had a brilliant mind and did very well in school. But despite his serious devotion to God and his studiousness, he was a rather typical teenager of his time. For one thing, he was athletic and an avid soccer player. During his high school years, he was passionate about the theater, acting in and even directing and producing plays presented by the Wadowice Theater Circle.

As valedictorian of his high school class, Lolek delivered a speech at the commencement exercises. The archbishop of Krakow, Adam Sapieha, was present that day as the primary speaker. The brilliant young teenager's speech so impressed the visiting cleric that he took the opportunity to inquire whether Karol was considering attending seminary. When the young man replied that he was not, the archbishop was deeply disappointed.

After high school, Karol enrolled in the Jagiellonian University in Krakow. Established in 1364, this was one of the world's oldest universities, and there Karol continued to excel, studying philology and numerous languages. He was also a volunteer librarian and was active in the theater, both as an actor and as a playwright.

Despite all his activities, Karol kept up his daily church attendance and devotions. In this way he was certainly atypical of other students with whom he spent much of his time, and it's hard to know what they made of their profoundly Christian friend and classmate. In his book *Great Souls: Six Who Changed the Century*, David Aikman tells us that "on one occasion, as a practical joke, his classmates placed a note on his desk that read, 'Karol Wojtyla, Apprentice Saint'."[2]

During these years in Poland, the culture around Karol was in a state of turmoil. For one thing, anti-Semitism, which had already reached monstrous levels in Germany under Hitler, was now making its way into Poland as well. But Karol's upbringing would set him in serious opposition to all of it. His hometown, Wadowice, was one-third Jewish, and the Catholic and Jewish communities there coexisted amicably. The Wojtyla family had always had many Jewish friends with whom their lives were intertwined. One close Jewish friend of Karol's was Jerzy Kluger. In fact, Kluger and Karol remained lifelong friends. When many years later Kluger settled in Rome as an adult, his family treated their old friend—then living in Rome as Pope John Paul II—as one of their own.

Despite this growing anti-Semitism in Krakow, young Karol stood up for the Jews whenever he could. Yet like most Poles then—indeed, like most Europeans—he failed to grasp the seriousness of the worsening situation, even when Jewish friends were forced to leave the country.

Regardless of the turmoil, this period represented a calm and mostly studious time in the life of Karol Wojtyla. That calm was shattered dramatically, however, on September 1, 1939, the day the Nazis attacked Poland. All that terrible month, Hitler's Luftwaffe rained hell from the skies while ruthless SS troops murdered Polish soldiers and civilians alike on the ground. By November the country called Poland had officially ceased to exist and—thanks to the Hitler-Stalin pact—it was occupied by both the Nazis and the Soviets. What happened to the Polish people during this era has been much written about, and it is among the saddest periods in the history of any nation. Millions of Poles would be killed in the months and years ahead. Among those rounded up and deported as the Nazis took over were 186 professors from Jagiellonian University, which soon shut its doors.

Doing his best to cope with his circumstances, Karol found work first as a delivery boy and then as a quarry worker to support himself and his father, who was living with him in Krakow. He was later transferred to the Solvay chemical plant. Throughout those years, Karol kept his mind and soul fed through reading, having religious discussions and debates with coworkers, participating in clandestine theatrical activities, and praying. In his magisterial biography, *Witness to Hope*, George Weigel writes:

Fellow workers . . . remember Karol Wojtyla praying on his knees at the Borek Falecki plant, unafraid of ridicule and seemingly able to tune out the racket around him to concentrate on his conversation with God. On his way home . . . he frequently stopped at the parish in Podgorze run by the Redemptorist priests, to pray or to attend early morning Mass after completing the night shift. "From here," he recalled thirty years later, "I gained the strength to last through the difficult times of the years of Occupation."[3]

Karol was greatly helped and guided during these years by an unassuming man named Jan Leopold Tyranowski, whom Karol met at his parish church. Tyranowski was a tailor, not a clergyman, but he was a deeply spiritual layman who participated in a discipleship program called the Living Rosary, created to help Polish youth remain dedicated to their faith during the war years. Meeting with young men both in groups and individually, Tyranowski was a spiritual director who had a significant impact on their lives.

Karol would always remember Tyranowski's teachings on suffering and how it can draw us closer to God. After becoming pope, he recalled the humble tailor as "one of those unknown saints, hidden like a marvelous light at the bottom of life, at a depth where night usually reigns." In him young Karol had seen "the beauty of the soul opened up by grace."[4]

The years of occupation and the manual labor they brought with them taught him something else besides. They "introduced him," as Weigel puts it, "to a world he had never known before, the world of the industrial laborer."[5] In this world he learned new lessons about the dignity of labor and of those who performed it. The lessons would serve him well in the years to come.

In the meantime, one of the greatest blows yet was about to befall the young Karol. One night he arrived home with food and medicine for his father, only to discover that the sixty-two-year-old man had died. The son was devastated and spent the whole night in prayer beside his father's body. Though a friend had come to stay with him, he later said of that night, "I never felt so alone."[6] His mother, his brother, and now his father were gone; at the age of twenty, he felt all alone in the world.

But in part as a result of these sufferings, a new life was beginning to call to him. Throughout his twenty years, various teachers and friends suggested that he might be meant for the priesthood, but until that point, he had never taken the idea seriously. Now he began to see the events of his life as leading him irrevocably in that direction and Karol Wojtyla began to form an idea that would exist at the very center of his life for all the decades ahead. It was that God's hand was always at work, and there was no such thing as coincidence, certainly not in his own life. Every incident, every person he had met, every talent he had been given were helping him along the path God had planned for him.

It must be said that to become a priest in Poland at that time required an extra measure of commitment. Indeed, it was nothing less than a life-or-death decision. The seminary that Karol would now begin attending had to be kept secret from the Nazi occupiers. Anyone rumored to be involved with it—much less attending it—could be sent to a concentration camp or put to death by firing squad.

Between keeping up with his work at the chemical factory and his theatrical involvement, Karol also found time to study and attend secret lectures, for the teachers in this underground seminary did not dare to hold actual classes. In charge of Karol's training was Archbishop Sapieha, the man who had seen his potential as a priest several years before.

Despite the careful precautions taken by the seminarians, Karol's life was twice endangered before the end of the war. One incident occurred purely by accident: when walking back from work one day in February 1944, he was hit by a speeding German truck and knocked down, hitting his head. Both a passing Polish woman and a German officer stopped to help him, and he was rushed to the hospital. Karol suffered a bad concussion and had to stay in the hospital for a couple of weeks, but he recovered completely (and managed to find and thank the Polish woman who had helped him).

In August of that same year, he faced a very different kind of threat. The Nazi occupiers were simultaneously being driven back by the invading Russians and dealing with Polish uprisings. The Nazi response to any form of local resistance had always been crushing and brutal, and this would be no different. They conducted a typically thorough security sweep through Krakow, rounding up and marching off all the young men and boys they could find, to what fate one can only imagine. As they came nearer and nearer to the basement apartment that Karol was sharing with friends, the young man prostrated himself on the floor in his room and prayed.

The Nazis came closer and closer—and then passed them by. Whether they didn't see the apartment door or simply forgot about it, no one can say, but the young seminary student and his friends were spared.

After this miraculous delivery, Karol and the other six students at the seminary moved to the archbishop's episcopal residence for safety. They would remain there until the final German retreat from the city in 1945.

When the Jagiellonian University was once again able to reopen, Karol became an assistant instructor in theology there while finishing his studies for the priesthood. One class in particular, a moral theological study of the right to life, would have a profound effect on Karol's personal philosophy in the years ahead.

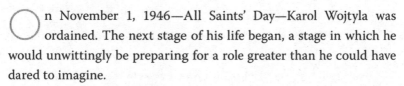

On November 1, 1946—All Saints' Day—Karol Wojtyla was ordained. The next stage of his life began, a stage in which he would unwittingly be preparing for a role greater than he could have dared to imagine.

Yet again, Sapieha played a key role. He had been promoted from archbishop to cardinal early in 1946, and he now sent the young priest to Rome to work toward his doctorate in sacred theology at the Pontifical Angelicum University.

In what was turning out to be a recurring pattern in his life, Karol would have the opportunity to taste several lifestyles at once. At the university, he worked hard on his dissertation about Saint John of the Cross. In his daily life in Rome, he encountered a level of economic prosperity unheard of in Poland, still recovering from the war and also beginning to experience the full force of Soviet tyranny. And on his summer vacation, he traveled to France and Belgium in order to study the new worker-priest movement—a movement that inspired the young student to pronounce: "Catholic intellectual creativity alone will not transform the society."[7]

In Western Europe, Karol for the first time noticed that material wealth often went hand in hand with spiritual poverty. Compared to Poland and those countries behind what would come to be called the Iron Curtain, the Western nations were prosperous, awash in material goods. Yet many of their churches were empty. Well aware of the economic crisis back home and the spiritual crisis surrounding him, he was simultaneously developing his opposition to communism and his critiques of unfettered capitalism.

When he returned to Poland in 1948, Karol became a parish priest, first in a rural parish and then in a more urban one. He continued to teach and to study—he earned a second doctorate, this time in philosophy—and he continued to write plays and poetry but under a pseudonym. He also developed a ministry to youth, marked by his strong empathy and understanding of their needs and struggles. David Aikman writes:

> Karol began conducting hiking trips for young people around the region's mountains and lakes, talking to them in great detail about the challenges they were facing in their lives. Priests were not permitted by the Communists to conduct church meetings outside of their parishes,

so Karol traveled in mufti [civilian dress] with his young charges, men and women, hearing them speak with a frankness unusual in the presence of a priest about sexual temptations and about the struggles of being spiritual in a harshly materialistic and highly controlled society. They talked, joked, and sang deep into the night around campfires, and Karol conducted Mass each morning.

He also took his students to the theater, played chess with them, and had them bring their parents to church-organized functions.[8]

In 1960, at the age of forty, Karol published his first book, *Love and Responsibility*, which had grown out of his work with young adults, especially engaged couples and newlyweds. In it he tackled some of the most contentious issues of the era. The Catholic Church's positions on marriage, sexuality, and family life were under direct assault by the Communist government, and Karol, in his pastoral work, was dealing with the fallout. Poland's Communist government even encouraged young people to have premarital sex, specifically to cause them to break from the church.

Karol argued in his book that sexual love, in order to be all that it was meant to be, must be expressed in the context of responsibility to God and to another person. The sexual ethic of the church, as he framed it, was the way to find true sexual freedom because it helped us learn how to genuinely love others instead of merely using them for our own pleasure. In this book we see an early expression of the sexual ethic he would promote so strongly and consistently during his papacy.

But he expressed that ethic in positive rather than negative terms. Instead of rattling off a list of dos and don'ts, he spoke of a higher good, of real love and real freedom. Weigel points out an often overlooked aspect of Wojtyla's theology here:

Rather than asserting that either the begetting of children or the communion of spouses was the "primary end" of marriage, Wojtyla's sexual ethic taught that love was the norm of marriage, a love in which both the procreative and unitive dimensions of human sexuality reached their full moral value.[9]

His years as a parish priest were among some of the most important and formative years of his life, and crucial to the development of his theology. But eventually he would leave that life behind as his teaching duties increased and he began work on his second doctoral dissertation. It was then that the hardworking priest, educator, and author began to be noticed by influential people within the church hierarchy. In 1958, when he was only thirty-eight, Karol Wojtyla had been named suffragan (subordinate) bishop of Krakow. This appointment was the start of a meteoric rise through the ranks of the Catholic Church—a rise that would bring the largely apolitical priest into unforeseen conflict with Communist government authorities.

To handle this conflict, Wojtyla had to use all his diplomatic skills. He learned to stand up for the church's rights and to promote its presence in Polish society, while at the same time avoiding a direct challenge to the political authorities. His approach helped explain why they regarded him as no significant threat, even as he continued to rise to prominence.

During this period (1962–65), the famous and historic church council that would come to be known as Vatican II was held, and Karol Wojtyla started becoming broadly known in the larger church. Some developments for which he was a strong advocate in that council included the promotion of religious freedom for all, not just for the Catholic Church, and the absolution of the Jewish people as a whole for the Crucifixion of Christ. He argued that "religious freedom . . . touched the heart of the dialogue between the Church and the world, because religious freedom had to do with how the Church thought about the human condition."[10] Though he warned against the potential misuse of freedom, he nonetheless believed it was a crucial and fundamental value, one that the church must consistently advocate for all human beings.

While all this was going on, Wojtyla was made archbishop of Krakow in 1964, and just three years later, Pope Paul VI would make him a cardinal. It was a truly rapid and remarkable rise for a priest who had never involved himself more than he could help with either religious or secular politics (though, when the need arose, he handled it with shrewdness and skill).

A friendship began to grow between him and Pope Paul, who increasingly sought the brilliant and deep-thinking Polish cardinal's advice. Some of Wojtyla's ideas on artificial contraception—namely, his ideas on the dignity and worth of the human person as a creature created and loved by God—would turn up in *Humanae Vitae*, Paul VI's encyclical reiterating the church's opposition to such contraception. Among church leaders, Wojtyla's intellectual vigor and spiritual strength were a powerful and energizing force.

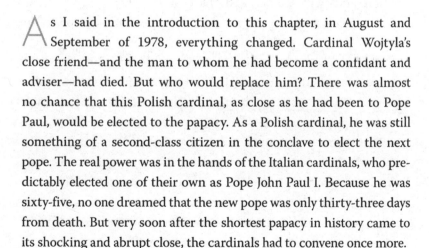

As I said in the introduction to this chapter, in August and September of 1978, everything changed. Cardinal Wojtyla's close friend—and the man to whom he had become a confidant and adviser—had died. But who would replace him? There was almost no chance that this Polish cardinal, as close as he had been to Pope Paul, would be elected to the papacy. As a Polish cardinal, he was still something of a second-class citizen in the conclave to elect the next pope. The real power was in the hands of the Italian cardinals, who predictably elected one of their own as Pope John Paul I. Because he was sixty-five, no one dreamed that the new pope was only thirty-three days from death. But very soon after the shortest papacy in history came to its shocking and abrupt close, the cardinals had to convene once more.

David Aikman sets the scene:

> This time, the mood was tense not simply because of the crisis of such a short papal reign, but because there was no longer any consensus on another candidate. The options seemed so wide open that, for the first time, the assembled prelates took the possibility of a foreign pope seriously.[11]

As the conclave went on, the one foreign candidate they began seriously considering was none other than Karol Wojtyla. The diversity of his views attracted a similarly diverse coalition of backers. And it must be that after Pope John Paul I's unexpected demise, the idea of athleticism and youthful vigor forcefully entered the list of things to be considered in a viable candidate.

At last, he was chosen.

During the process, Karol had been seen to turn red and lower his head into his hands. Says George Weigel, "Jerzy Turowicz later wrote that, at the moment of his election, Karol Wojtyla was as alone as a man can be. For to be elected Pope meant 'a clear cut off from one's previous life, with no possible return.'"[12] But when formally asked for his response, he did not hesitate.

"It is God's will," Karol stated. "I accept."

The moment had arrived for the new pope's introduction to the world.

This time, when the name of their new leader was announced, the response of the faithful gathered in Saint Peter's Square was somewhat confused. Usually there is unbridled jubilation. Screams of joy mingle with triumphant shouts of *"Habemus Papam!"* (Latin for "We have a pope!") Flags are waved, and hats soar into the sky. But on this day, the two hundred thousand persons who had gathered—again—were more baffled than anything else. Was it because what was usually a rare occurrence had just happened some weeks before? Or was it simply because no one had ever heard of Karol Wojtyla? Who was this man? And could it really be true that he wasn't Italian?

Part of the reason for the confusion among the faithful that day was that Karol Wojtyla was mostly unknown beyond the leadership of the church itself. Those leaders deeply respected him for his tremendous intellectual and pastoral gifts, but in the wider world he was quite unheard of. Of course all that was about to change in dramatic fashion. But for the moment, it was a fact.

The mood of the crowd began to change as the new pope addressed them directly. This was contrary to precedent, but in the years ahead, he would do much that was contrary to precedent. He now spoke with both humility and contagious confidence. And though a Pole himself, he even spoke in Italian. With a smile, he began, "Jesus Christ be praised!" and then went on:

> Dear brothers and sisters, we are still grieved after the death of our most beloved John Paul I. And now the most eminent cardinals have called a new bishop of Rome from a far-off land; far yet so near through the communion of faith and in the Christian tradition.

He paused at one point to note: "I don't know if I express myself in your—our—Italian language well enough. If I make a mistake, you will correct me."[13]

His openness, vulnerability, and humor drew laughter and applause from the crowd. By the time the extemporaneous speech drew to a close, a remarkable thing had happened: the crowd that was surprised and confused before was now wholeheartedly on John Paul II's side. The observers in Saint Peter's Square—and observers around the world—were with him.

Part of the greatness of this man was his extraordinary ability to communicate humbly and humorously and clearly. There can be no other word for it: he was charming. Like a great politician, but without a hint of guile, he managed to connect with his audiences in a way that delighted them. He would do it many times in the years ahead, but that day in Saint Peter's Square was the first time he did it. And after he had delivered this inaugural speech, he did something else that politicians do, but that popes did not: he waded into the crowd. Aikman writes:

> Wielding his crosier over the crowds in the sign of blessing as though it were a two-edged sword, he kissed babies, embraced worshipers in wheelchairs, and acted as though he had prepared all his life for

a starring role in one of the greatest historical dramas of the twentieth century.[14]

It was a tremendously promising beginning. But who could ever continue along these lines? Yet, a promising beginning was not enough. He must continue as he had begun. At the papal coronation a few days later, he gave every sign of doing just that. His inspiring words rang out above the crowd:

> Be not afraid to welcome Christ and accept his power. Help the Pope and all those who wish to serve Christ and with Christ's power to serve the human person and the whole of mankind.
>
> Be not afraid. Open wide the doors for Christ. To his saving power open the boundaries of states, economic and political systems, the vast fields of culture, civilization, and development.
>
> Be not afraid. Christ knows "what is in man." He alone knows it.[15]

The words of the new pope reflected a lifetime of devotion, trust, humility, and service—the qualities that had equipped him to be one of the greatest leaders of the twentieth century.

But if the man was extraordinary, so, too, were the times in which he was appointed to serve and the tremendously difficult task set for him. Ever since the Second Vatican Council, held in the previous decade, the Catholic Church had been in a state of transition. Wojtyla, then the archbishop of Krakow, participated in that council, designed in large part to help the church adapt to the needs and requirements of the modern world, and he advocated many of its reforms. It was largely because of this that many tended to think of him as a progressive church leader rather than a traditionalist.

People would often make that mistake about the man who became Pope John Paul II. His willingness to embrace change where he believed it was needed and to work across party lines, along with his disarming personality, misled many to think that his inner convictions might be as flexible as his outward manner. Those who believed this were soon disillusioned.

The interesting twist was that even from the disillusioned ones who would have preferred a more progressive pope, John Paul II commanded a mysterious, almost unwilling respect. This was perhaps due to the varied experiences of his life that combined to produce a man who was simultaneously broad-minded in his views and strict in his orthodoxy. But how could this be? A generous broad-mindedness and a serious theological orthodoxy were not two characteristics that one often saw together. It was a baffling blend that both attracted and repelled many observers.

David Aikman quotes one reporter and "liberal Catholic," Jennifer Bradley, as typical of many who weren't quite sure what to make of this man. Writing in the *New Republic*, she said that she was initially "unexcited about the pope," but after attending an outdoor mass celebrated by him in 1995, her perceptions changed: "Now my skepticism will have to share space with awe and, oddly, gratitude."[16]

They felt it as an inherent contradiction, not realizing that John Paul II's views as a whole, including the ones they approved and the ones they disliked, came from the same source: the pope's fervent, long-held belief that we are created in God's image, that we are his beloved children, and that all of our rights, freedoms, and responsibilities come to us from him. That underlying belief drove everything from his stand on sexuality, contraception, and abortion, to his ongoing fight against communism. It was all there, in the writings and teachings of his lifetime, and yet for some reason few of his ideological opponents seemed to figure it out, or fully comprehend it if they did.

◆ ◆ ◆

As he settled into his new role, John Paul II's focus continued to be where it had always been: with, in Jesus' words, "the least of these," the weak and the needy. "When he went out into crowds," according to Levi and Allison, "he was a security nightmare, shaking hands, blessing babies, embracing the elderly and infirm. If he wanted to visit a friend, he just did."[17] At his installation as pope, he made sure that space was reserved in the front row to allow the sick to attend and participate.

The pope also reached out to people of other traditions and faiths, especially Protestants and Jews, in an attempt to reconcile age-old differences and disputes wherever possible. Among Christians, his desire was to further the cause of ecumenism, as he firmly believed that it was God's will; among Jews, he wanted to help heal wounds that had been caused by the church. Wherever he thought it necessary—and this included areas ranging from the Inquisition to the Holocaust—he offered apologies for the church's past conduct.

One emphatic testimony to the effect of what the pope was doing came from the writer and Holocaust survivor Elie Wiesel. After the pope visited the Wailing Wall and put his request for Jewish forgiveness into a chink in the wall, Wiesel told a newspaper, "When I was a child, I was always afraid of walking by a church. Now all of that has changed."[18]

As always, the pope continued to reach out to young people, and they responded with enthusiasm and affection—drawn by his gentle good humor, his openness, his compassion, and above all his unwavering faith.

Levi and Allison note,

> John Paul II's papacy would continue just as it began: as a surprise. He would surprise the papal staff, who frankly could not keep up with him. He would surprise liberals by tightening discipline on the clergy of the Church. He would surprise conservatives with his heartfelt pacifism and ecumenism. He would surprise the Romans by being a more hands-on bishop than any Italian in recent memory.[19]

On May 13, 1981, another surprise was in store. As the pope was entering Saint Peter's Square in Rome, a Turkish assassin named Mehmet Ali Agca pulled out a 9mm semiautomatic pistol and shot the sixty-one-year-old pontiff four times, twice in the abdomen. The pope lost nearly three-quarters of his blood and came near death. But somehow he survived, spending weeks in the hospital recovering. This brush with death brought his priorities into even sharper focus. His friend Cardinal Stanislaw Dziwisz recalls, "He thanked God not only for saving his life but also for allowing him to join the community of the sick who were suffering in the hospital."[20] It was a strange thing to be thankful for, unless one took seriously the words of the Bible about giving thanks in all circumstances, and took seriously the idea of identifying with the weak as Christ had. But of course he did.

So it had always been throughout his life. This man seemed to know the true secret of greatness. He had not sought greatness and had not sought power, but both had come to him as he focused his attention and energy, as Christ taught, on those who were least able to reciprocate. As pope, he did not always accomplish what he set out to accomplish, but there were times when his mere presence seemed to inspire change. For instance, reflecting on one aspect of the pope's opposition to communism and its effect on his native country, David Aikman notes:

> Some have denied any connection between the sense of exultation created in Poles by John Paul's visit in June 1979 and the sudden emergence of the Solidarity free trade union in Gdansk in August of the following year. Certainly there would have been labor troubles in Poland no matter who had been pope at the time. But would the results have been anything like what they turned out to be if John Paul had not carefully nurtured the events in his own country throughout the 1980's decade? It doesn't seem likely.[21]

Again, without adopting a confrontational style, the man whom Polish Communist authorities had once regarded as relatively harmless became one of the key figures in the collapse of communism across Europe. Though he clashed at times with US leaders over the use of military force, which he deplored, in his own way he worked in tandem with them to defeat the Soviet regime, standing up for human rights and giving aid and comfort to foes of communism, such as Solidarity leader Lech Walesa, even as he avoided direct conflict with Communist leaders.

◆ ◆ ◆

I n his demanding and multifaceted role, the pope's relative youth and his exuberant health sustained him for a long time. Stories were told of unsuspecting skiers who were surprised to catch sight of the head of the Catholic Church enjoying himself on the slopes. But as the twentieth century drew to a close, his health slowly started to fail. He began to show clear symptoms of Parkinson's disease.

And so Pope John Paul II began to live out the last great paradox of his life: in suffering and weakness, he would show God's strength. As a man once known for his athleticism and vigor, he was uncomfortable appearing in public when his health was obviously failing. But that failure, many believed, helped him identify more strongly with the sufferings of Christ on the cross and, by extension, with the sufferings of people everywhere.

He also used his disease to call attention to the need for a cure for Parkinson's and to publicly draw the distinction, as so few were willing to draw it at that time, between ethical and unethical methods of research. In accordance with his beliefs about the sacredness of all human life, the pope took an unyielding stand against the use of human embryonic stem cells in medical research.

The press seldom acknowledged the remarkable courage and self-lessness of his stand. Many members of the US mainstream media, for instance, fervently supported embryonic stem cell research and were far more apt to make heroes of those with Parkinson's and other disabilities, such as Michael J. Fox and Christopher Reeve, who fought to advance it. Ironically, in doing so, the media missed a truly heroic story of the man who took a firm stand against what appeared, at the time, to be in his own self-interest. (As it happens, later developments in the research brought into question the effectiveness of treatment with embryonic stem cells. But just a few years ago, the popular narrative was more or less that the use of these cells would be the cure to end all cures.)

One typical article, on CNN's website, reported on John Paul's meeting with George W. Bush, in which the pope strongly urged the president not to fund such research. The article covered the Vatican's uncompromising stand on the issue, the president's dilemma, and various other related issues. And then, in the very last paragraph:

> Scientists believe research using stem cells might unlock cures for diseases including Alzheimer's, Parkinson's and diabetes, as well as spinal cord injuries. The pope himself suffers from symptoms of Parkinson's disease.[22]

It would be hard to surpass that for understatement.

Once again, the pope was identifying with some of the weakest and most helpless members of society: in this case the unborn. And though it received scant notice, no statement on their behalf could have been more powerful than his unwillingness to sacrifice these helpless ones to benefit himself.

One of the most memorable images of Pope John Paul II from these last years of his life—perhaps one of the most memorable images ever taken of him at all—was taken in 2005 during the *Via Crucis*, the Good Friday marking of the Stations of the Cross. For the first time that year, John Paul II was too ill to lead the walk. But as George Weigel observes in his book *The End and the Beginning: Pope John Paul II—The Victory of Freedom, the Last Years, the Legacy*, in effect he still did lead it, albeit in a different way:

> As Cardinal Ratzinger led the solemn procession through the ruins of antiquity, John Paul II prayed the *Via Crucis* while watching the ceremony at the Colosseum on a television set that had been placed

in the chapel of the papal apartment. A television camera at the door of the chapel showed the world John Paul's prayer. He was seated, and grasped in his arms a large crucifix, as he prayed through the fourteen stations with the congregation near the Roman Forum. Those watching at the Colosseum and on television could see only John Paul's back; his face was never shown. Contrary to press speculations, however, he was not hiding his pain or the ravages of weeks of illness. Rather, he was doing what he had always done, which was not to say, "Look at me," but rather, "Look to Christ."[23]

Whereas once he was known as a physically vigorous and strong man, he was now seen as a man who was forced to rely more fully than ever on Christ for all things, in the physical as well as in the spiritual realm. And he was loved all the more for it.

He would not live much longer; less than a week after that vigil in the chapel, he developed septic shock following a urinary tract infection. Deathly ill, he tried to bless the Easter crowd in Saint Peter's Square but was unable to speak and could only make the sign of the cross over them three times before withdrawing. On April 2, as he lay dying, he conveyed to those around him that he had a message for the young people gathered outside his window, still faithful to the leader they loved: "I have sought you out. Now you have come to me. I thank you."[24] A few hours later, he was gone.

As Dr. Jean Bethke Elshtain of the University of Chicago recalled at one of our Socrates in the City events in New York City (the transcript is available in *Socrates in the City: Conversations on "Life, God, and Other Small Topics"*), the pope's funeral produced "an outpouring of humanity that took the media utterly by surprise." She added:

By then, it shouldn't have taken them by surprise, because it happened every time he did anything. But what struck me were the millions of young people who turned up and stayed there under these very difficult conditions for days, in order that they could be present.

Something was calling to them. He somehow spoke to them, even in his infirm old age, with the Parkinson's and all the rest. If we could think this through with you—it would be a very interesting exercise considering what that embodied and what hope that represented—we could see some possible sparks for a certain kind of renewal of our humanity more fully understood.

Such a renewal was indeed the legacy of Pope John Paul II. In his strengths and weaknesses alike, he demonstrated charity and compassion born out of his belief that every human being is a beloved child of God. George Weigel, a Catholic, acknowledges that Pope John Paul II at times made serious errors in judgment, but that even these were usually connected to his "profound disinclination to humiliate, or make a spectacle of, someone else; his intense dislike of gossip; his occasional tendency to project his own virtues onto others; and his determination to find something good in another's actions or words."[25] But the strength of his beliefs, Weigel adds, was that they sustained him in "radical self-giving . . . only possible through the grace of God in Christ."[26]

From a Protestant point of view, David Aikman quotes Billy Graham's statement that Pope John Paul II was "the strong conscience of the whole Christian world," and then Aikman reflects:

> I am not a Roman Catholic, and I certainly share many of the Protestant reservations about some aspects of Catholic doctrine and some forms of Catholic devotionalism. Yet it is my view that Pope John Paul II, in his profound spiritual depth, his prayer life, his enormous intellectual universe, his compassion and sympathy for the oppressed, and above all in his vision of how Christians collectively are supposed to live, is the greatest single Christian leader of the twentieth century.[27]

There is much to be said for that view. Through the paradoxes of his life—achieving strength through weakness, power through humility, generosity and broad-mindedness through orthodoxy—Pope John Paul II exemplified Christ's radical and revolutionary teaching that whoever loses his life shall find it. In his judicious exercise of power and his identification with the powerless, he was a Christian leader of a theological and moral stature that we have seldom seen in our lifetimes.

Charles W. Colson

1931–2012

H is memorial service took place at Washington National Cathedral on a beautiful spring day, May 16, 2012. Familiar faces were everywhere.

Journalists Brit Hume, Fred Barnes, and Cal Thomas were there. So were human-rights advocates Michael Horowitz, Joni Eareckson Tada, and former congressman Jim Ryun, who in 1964 had been the first high schooler to break the four-minute mile. I also saw the writer Joe Loconte. The gifted gospel singer Wintley Phipps was there, too, and sang "Amazing Grace."

President Reagan's attorney general, Ed Meese, was there. President Clinton's special counsel, Lanny Davis, was there. President George W. Bush's chief speechwriter, Michael Gerson, was there.

They were all present to honor the man who had worked hard, in his younger years, for President Richard Nixon—the most powerful man on earth, but who spent the second half of his life working even harder for the King of kings.

I was there to honor a man I loved, whose life had been a powerful inspiration to me, and whom I had been privileged to know and work for and call a friend.

I would have been astonished had I known, as a ten-year-old reading the newspapers in 1973, that I would one day befriend the notorious Watergate hatchet man, Charles W. Colson. He was one of that crew—H. R. Haldeman, John Erlichman, and G. Gordon Liddy— whose disregard for truth in their blind service of power brought a great nation to the edge of ruin.

After I came to faith in 1988, I heard Chuck Colson's name again, this time identifying him as the founder of Prison Fellowship Ministries. Not long afterward, a friend turned me on to his books.

Those books! Reading them was a revelation. First, I read his autobiography, *Born Again*, and then I read *Loving God* and *Kingdoms in Conflict*. They were a tremendous education for someone hungry to learn about his new faith.

A few years later I heard that Chuck was speaking at Yale Law School in New Haven, and I practically raced there to hear him. I even wrote a long letter to him, introducing myself and gushing about how much his work had meant to me, and I placed it inside a children's book I had written *(Uncle Mugsy and the Terrible Twins of Christmas)*, which I inscribed to his grandchildren. When he came off the stage, I shook his hand and handed him the book and letter. Not much more than a week later, I got a letter in return. I was staggered. The letter said something about how much my letter meant to him, and it added that he would keep it in his files, that perhaps we might work together someday. I almost couldn't believe my eyes, but I chalked it up as probably a well-meaning but unrealistic sentiment.

Of course, I didn't know Chuck Colson very well at that point, but about a year later I got a phone call from his office. The caller said they were in need of a writer and editor for *BreakPoint*, the daily radio commentary that Chuck had been doing for a few years. Was I interested in applying for the job? I was amazed that Chuck, who probably wrote thousands of letters every year, remembered our correspondence. But I applied and got the job, and suddenly I was working with my hero, Chuck Colson. Working for Chuck was deeply gratifying, but it was tough too; he may have been a redeemed marine, but he was still a marine. After two years I was exhausted enough to decide to take a different kind of job, working for VeggieTales. Bob the Tomato was a much less demanding boss and had never been in the marines. But Chuck and I kept in touch.

A few years later I was able to get Chuck to agree to speak at a forum I founded in New York City called Socrates in the City. He spoke for us twice. The first time was at the Union League Club in Manhattan in 2006. The room was packed with 350 people, and when Chuck finished, the audience exploded into powerful applause. As the applause continued, Chuck walked down the center aisle triumphantly, shaking hands left and right. Everyone there said that it was as though he had just given the State of the Union address.

The second time Chuck came to speak at Socrates in the City was in December 2010 for our Christmas gala. Again, it was a tremendous event.

I was there the day Chuck fell ill during his final speaking engagement in Virginia on March 30, 2012. In fact, I introduced him for what would become his last speech. Toward the end of it, he couldn't continue, and a doctor was summoned. As he was lying on a gurney, waiting to be put into the ambulance, I put my arm on his shoulder and just stood there, wanting him to feel the comfort of a human touch. Then I said, half-joking, not knowing if he was able to take it in: "Is there anything you want me to tell the crowd, Chuck?"

But he did get it. "Just tell them that I'm so sorry to have ruined everyone's evening!" And those were the last words I would ever hear from this great man and friend. How I miss him. But I take real comfort in knowing that I'll see him again.

Like all the stories in this book, it's the story of an inspiring and a great man. May it inspire you to greatness.

◆ ◆ ◆

Charles Wendell Colson was first born during the Great Depression, on October 16, 1931, in North Boston to Inez "Dizzy" and Wendell Colson. I say "first born" because Chuck would be born again many years later, but let's not get ahead of ourselves. Chuck's father worked as a bookkeeper at a meatpacking plant, and eventually, by attending night school, he earned a law degree.

Chuck was one of those children born with extraordinary gifts of drive and intelligence. In his book *The Good Life*, Chuck tells the story of how as an eleven-year-old boy during World War II, he led a successful drive to raise money for a jeep for the American armed forces.

But Chuck's parents were ambitious, too, and they made many sacrifices so their only child could attend the prestigious Browne and Nichols School in Cambridge, Massachusetts. It was one of those schools whose *raison d'etre* seemed to be getting its students into the Ivy League. In Chuck's case, it succeeded. In fact Chuck was offered two full college scholarships: one to Harvard and another, a Navy ROTC scholarship, to Brown. In what happened next, we see an early instance of Chuck's pride revealing itself.

"As a boy I used to stand on the pebbly beach looking across the gray-green waters of the harbor at the city then run by the Brahmins, the Beacon Hill establishment which traced its ancestry through generations of Harvard classes back to the *Mayflower*," Chuck recalled.

> We were neither the new ethnics—Italians, Irish Catholics just seizing political power in the wards of Boston—nor old stock. "Swamp Yankees," we were called. Acceptance was what we were denied—and what we most fervently sought. Now in this one moment, I had it—admission to the elite. And in my pride I believed I had something better still—the chance to turn them down.[1]

Chuck turned down Harvard, choosing to attend Brown instead. He graduated with honors in 1953, and not long afterward, he married

Nancy Billings of Boston. In the next few years the couple became the parents of three children: two boys—Wendell and Christian—and a daughter named Emily.

In the same year that he graduated and got married, Chuck received his commission in the Marine Corps, serving in Korea just after the end of major US involvement there. With his typical drive and ambition, Chuck rose quickly in the marine's ranks to become the youngest captain in their long and fabled history. It was during his time with the marines that Chuck, who had been raised in the Episcopal Church, had his first serious thoughts about God.

During the summer of 1954, Chuck and his battalion were sent to the coast of Guatemala, where Communists were engaged in an uprising. The US Marines had been summoned to protect the lives of the Americans living there.

Standing on the deck of the USS *Mellette* on a hot, dark night, Chuck—a bit fearful of what might happen in the days ahead—looked up at the millions of stars sparkling in the inky sky. "That night I suddenly became as certain as I had ever been about anything in my life that out there in that great starlit beyond was God," Chuck writes in *Born Again*. "I was convinced that He ruled over the universe, that to Him there were no mysteries, that He somehow kept it all miraculously in order. In my own fumbling way, I prayed, knowing that He was there, questioning only whether He had time to hear me."[2]

Guatemala's pro-US regime dealt with the Communists on its own, and not long afterward, Chuck resigned his commission and entered George Washington University Law School, taking classes at night and working during the day. He graduated—again with honors—in 1959. Throughout the 1950s, Chuck also had become involved in politics. In fact back in 1948, when he was just seventeen, he had volunteered with the campaign of Massachusetts governor Robert F. Bradford, and there he learned his first lessons in campaign dirty tricks, from planting fake news stories to spying on the opposition. So now, when he was called upon to manage the 1960 reelection campaign of Massachusetts senator Leverett Saltonstall, he would employ all the dirty tricks he had learned in 1948, and invented a few of his own. Saltonstall won.

Following this victory, Chuck and his friend Charlie Morin opened their own law firm, which became highly successful. His personal life was far less so. Chuck writes that his obsession with politics, which his wife did not share, was driving them apart. The couple eventually divorced, and in 1964, Chuck married the woman who would be his wife for the next forty-eight years: Patty Hughes.

◆ ◆ ◆

Chuck's unprincipled rise to giddy heights of power and his spectacular fall from those heights are the proverbial stuff of legend. Despite the career-induced failure of his marriage, Chuck's drive to the top continued, unabated and without course correction.

He became involved in the 1968 presidential campaign, working hard to elect Richard Nixon. The long hours and hard work paid off: Nixon won. But they would pay off in an even greater way: in 1969 Nixon appointed Chuck to be his special counsel. For Chuck Colson, it was the ultimate prize. At age thirty-eight, he had the ear and the confidence of the most powerful human being on the planet.

Chuck's gung-ho nature, coupled with his brilliance and a strong desire to please the president, quickly made him Nixon's go-to guy in every situation. He would do virtually anything for the president, and before long Nixon was egging him on to cut corners and make things happen, no matter the cost.

Those who knew him at the time saw that a certain ruthlessness had overtaken Chuck. In his own mind, of course, it was all for a good cause. He viewed his actions in comparison to the actions of others; so it was always the other guy who started the fight. It was always the other guy who had behaved ruthlessly first. What else could he do, Chuck reasoned, but return fire?

Of course this sort of moral reasoning—or lack of moral reasoning—will soon lead anyone into a swamp of self-deceit. In the case of

Chuck Colson and many others in the Nixon administration, that self-deceit led to the historic political meltdown known as Watergate.

Watergate was such a game-changing scandal in the history of American politics that almost every political scandal since has had the -gate suffix attached to it. And although it all hinged on a ridiculous burglary in the Watergate Hotel, it was part of something much bigger. That burglary was just the symptom of the ugly atmosphere that had taken over the Nixon White House, and Chuck Colson was at the center of it.

In the fall of 1972, Nixon was reelected in a landslide, in some large part due to Chuck's brilliant—and sometimes underhanded—political maneuverings. But in the dark, pragmatic, and ungrateful world of the Nixon White House, such values as loyalty didn't count for much. As the Watergate scandal mushroomed, it became evident to Nixon and his aides Haldeman and Erlichman that Chuck, despite all he had done, was a political liability. So they decided to make him a scapegoat. Not long after the November victory, the president made it clear that Chuck had to go. Chuck wasn't happy, but in the rough-and-tumble world of politics, this sort of thing happened. There was nothing he could do.

And so, taking up his post-White House life, Chuck began to rebuild his law practice. One of the biggest clients he hoped to land was that of the Raytheon Company, located in Massachusetts. In mid-March 1973, Chuck found himself in the offices of Tom Phillips, Raytheon's CEO.

But something had happened to the successful titan of industry in the previous week: Phillips had accepted Christ at a Billy Graham Crusade. At the end of his meeting with Chuck, Phillips said, "I'd like to tell you the whole story someday of how I came to Christ. I had gotten to the point where I didn't think my life was worth anything. Now I have committed my life to him, everything has changed—attitude, values, the whole bit. If you'd like to hear more, give me a call."[3]

Chuck was uncomfortable with such talk and didn't intend to

continue the conversation. But Phillips had a feeling that Chuck was more interested than he realized and waited to hear from him.

Meanwhile, the Watergate scandal was growing. On July 16, 1973, a bombshell exploded when a lower-level White House aide revealed that Nixon had secretly taped most of his Oval Office conversations. This news reinvigorated those who were out to get Nixon, and in the hue and cry that followed, Chuck cringed to think about some of the things he had said in the false privacy of the Oval Office—words that were almost certainly on those tapes.

News reporters and cameras were now stationed outside Chuck's home, and three times the FBI was called to investigate bomb threats. It was madness. Chuck escaped the gathering storm by taking a trip that August to the Maine seacoast, stopping en route to visit his parents in Massachusetts. While he was there, he decided to visit Tom Phillips at his home in Weston wanting to know more about why Phillips had considered his life empty despite having achieved such success in business. The brewing troubles of Watergate were bringing about a newfound introspection in Chuck, so that now, if only to himself, he grudgingly began to acknowledge that he, too, felt an emptiness inside, despite all his remarkable achievements.

At Phillips's home, Chuck asked what had happened to alter him so dramatically.

"I would go to the office each day and do my job," Phillips recalled, "striving all the time to make the company succeed, but there was a big hole in my life. I began to read the scriptures, looking for answers. Something made me realize I needed a personal relationship with God."[4]

Chuck was skeptical of the whole thing. It all sounded too simple and to some extent ridiculous.

But as the conversation turned back to Watergate, and Chuck began trying to justify his actions in the whole mess—pointing the blame at Nixon's enemies—Phillips pushed back. He saw it was pride that had led Chuck and the other Nixonites to do what they did. He pulled out a paperback copy of C. S. Lewis's famous book *Mere Christianity*, and there on the screened porch, he read aloud from chapter 8, "The Great Sin: Pride."

As Phillips read about how pride corrupts us, Chuck cringed, but not because he was embarrassed. It was because he began to recognize himself in the description. He knew that Lewis's words applied to him in particular. It was indeed his own pride that had corrupted him, twisted his thinking, and led to the frightening circumstances in which he now found himself. As Chuck recalled some of the prideful ways he had behaved over the course of his life, and most recently as Nixon's special counsel, he felt an agony of shame.

Yet when Phillips stopped reading and asked Chuck for his response to what he'd heard, Chuck made it clear that he wasn't ready to accept Christ into his life; the deep skepticism toward religious conversion remained. Phillips pressed ahead, reading aloud from Psalm 37. "Do not fret," it said. "Trust in the LORD and do good. . . . Delight yourself in the LORD and he will give you the desires of your heart. Commit your way to the LORD; trust in him and he will do this."[5] It all sounded powerfully inviting to Chuck in his hour of need.

Then Phillips read the third chapter of John's gospel, where Jesus tells Nicodemus that he must be born again. He then asked Chuck if he could pray for him. Chuck was not expecting this question and hardly knew what to say, but he was in enough turmoil that he wasn't about to refuse. He allowed Phillips to proceed.

"As Tom prayed, something began to flow into me—a kind of energy," Chuck recalls in *Born Again*. "Then came a wave of emotion which nearly brought tears. I fought them back. It sounded as if Tom were speaking directly and personally to God, almost as if he were sitting beside us."[6]

Phillips gave Chuck his copy of *Mere Christianity* and some other reading material and said that a friend of his named Doug Coe might be in touch with him to continue the conversation. That was it. Chuck bade his friend good-bye and walked out into the August night.

Then the floodgates opened. Sitting alone in his car, Chuck, the marine, take-no-prisoners tough guy, began to sob. Filled with emotion, he realized that he should go back into Phillips's house and pray with his friend. But now when he glanced at the house, he saw the lights being switched off. It was too late.

Chuck drove toward home, but he realized that he was weeping so copiously he could scarcely see the road. Afraid he might crash into an oncoming car, he pulled over. And there, alone in the night, by the side of a road, Chuck Colson gave his heart to God.

"God, I don't know how to find you," he prayed, "but I'm going to try! I'm not much the way I am now, but somehow I want to give myself over to you."[7]

Over and over as he sat there in the car, Chuck asked God to receive him. It was a humble prayer by a man the world knew as anything but humble. As Chuck relates in *Born Again*,

> I had not "accepted" Christ—I still didn't know who He was. My mind told me it was important to find that out first, to be sure that I knew what I was doing. . . . Only that night something inside me was urging me to surrender—to what or to whom I did not know. I stayed there in the car, wet-eyed, praying, thinking for perhaps half an hour, perhaps longer, alone in the dark of the quiet night. Yet for the first time in my life I was not alone at all.[8]

How many drivers in cars passing on that strip of roadway that evening wondered why that car was parked there on the side of the road? Who could have guessed that inside it there was a famous man, a national figure, weeping and humbling himself before the God of the universe? Little did they know that a holy transaction was taking place, one that would affect the lives of millions in the decades to come.

Chuck told no one about what happened that night except Patty. His wife had been a churchgoing Catholic for her entire life, but she wasn't conversant in the terminology of evangelical Christianity. So when Chuck asked her if she knew what a conversion experience was, her answer was a short no.

Chuck told her that he had experienced one. Patty might not have known what a conversion experience was, but she could tell that whatever happened to her husband, it was good.

As with all true mysteries, the mystery of conversion cannot be dissected very effectively. Does conversion take place in a single moment? Or is it a process? What happens in such a conversion? In the case of Chuck Colson, as with William Wilberforce and so many others, there was no way to say. All Chuck knew was that at one moment he had asked God into his heart in a simple way and that the desire to do so had come out of his brokenness. After it happened, he had a strong desire to learn more. He said yes to something with his whole being, but he still had a strong desire to find out just what he said yes to.

In the following week, as he and Patty enjoyed their time on the Maine coast, Chuck went to work. He had brought along *Mere Christianity* and a raft of yellow legal pads. In his sometimes comically thorough and deliberate way, Chuck made notes and followed the arguments like the brilliant lawyer that he was. He wasn't about to accept something without thinking it through.

At first, the idea that he had to accept not just God, but Jesus, was confusing. How could he logically accept a two-thousand-year-old historical figure from Palestine as the God of the universe? It seemed absurd. Then he read the famous passage in Lewis's book where Lewis lays out the three alternatives in no uncertain terms, saying that Jesus was either Lord, liar, or lunatic. The alternative not open to us is to think of Jesus merely as a powerful moral teacher. It was clear and it was discomfiting. Chuck knew that in his encounter with the mind of C. S. Lewis, he had met his match. The man's logic was irrefutable.

"There was my choice as simple, stark and frightening as that," Chuck later recalled. "No fine shadings, no gradations, no compromises. No one had ever thrust this truth at me in such a direct and unsettling way."[9]

Chuck was afraid that in his desperate state he might make an illogical leap, so he continued to wrestle with the arguments. But on his sixth day with Patty in that Maine cottage, he knew his mind was made up, and he prayed a simple prayer, asking Jesus to come into his life.

◆ ◆ ◆

Returning to Washington, Chuck resumed the process of building up his post-White House law practice. But Watergate kept intruding. Every day there was some fresh humiliation. The media savaged Chuck, reveling in the downfall of the so-called White House hatchet man who—in their eyes and in the eyes of many others—was finally getting his just deserts.

As a brand-new Christian, Chuck had no idea how his newfound faith related to the hell through which he was now going.

"I was about as stressed out as a guy can possibly be," he recalled.

> Every night I would have at least three or four large scotch and sodas in the hope of drowning it all out. I was waking up in the morning as tired as when I had gone to bed the night before. In the middle of the night I was waking up, sometimes to think about prison but more often to get angry about things being said about me that were untrue. . . . My greatest agony in this period was hearing something or seeing something written about me that was completely wrong. So I'd try and correct it by testifying or by writing a letter, only to find out that nobody would believe me. It was excruciating torture.[10]

Besides Patty, Chuck's most consistent solace in the midst of this unending storm was a small group of men who had invited him into their circle of Christian fellowship in Washington, DC. They were part of the Fellowship, a fiercely bipartisan group of Christians who met regularly for prayer. The leader of this group was Doug Coe, who had begun the National Prayer Breakfast during the Eisenhower administration. Once Coe learned from Tom Phillips that Chuck had turned his life over to God, he invited himself into Chuck's life and dragged him into the group of men who eventually became his closest friends.

One of them was the ferociously liberal Iowa senator Harold Hughes. Hughes was one of the most well-known enemies of the Nixon White House, and Chuck couldn't believe that such a man would have anything to do with him. But once Chuck told Hughes that he had accepted Jesus, Hughes embraced him in a bear hug and told him that all was forgiven. "I love you now as my brother in Christ. I will stand with you, defend you anywhere, and trust you with anything I have," Hughes promised.[11]

Chuck had never experienced anything like this. Could it be for real? He was quickly amazed to learn that it was. Hughes and the other men of the Fellowship became his closest allies during the painful months to come. They went far out of their way to emphasize bipartisanship, teaching Chuck that a relationship with Jesus should never be used as a political tool. Chuck knew that his newfound faith would baffle as many on the political right, who had been his allies, as on the left, who hated him.

This understanding established in Chuck a desire to remain above the political fray whenever possible. The four-decades-long advocacy for prisoners that would become his life's chief legacy would be the principal example of this view.

As the months passed, the pressures of the metastasizing Watergate scandal were getting worse. Chuck's aggressive, no-holds-barred public defense of Nixon in the past year would now bite back. After Nixon himself, Special Prosecutor Leon Jaworski most wanted Colson. Viciousness and ruthlessness had characterized the way Chuck had dealt with his political enemies, and it would now characterize how Jaworski dealt with him. He was reaping what he had sown.

Chuck was in a terrible spot, and he knew it. The fear of going to prison was very real for him. He had heard about the grotesque reality of prison rape, and he knew that there was a very palpable possibility of other kinds of violence against him. It was an indisputable fact that some prisoners, convinced that their lives were hell because of government officials, would have liked nothing better than to get revenge on a high-profile White House figure like Chuck Colson.

Realizing that he could put the screws to Colson, Jaworski offered him a plea bargain, asking Chuck to plead guilty to the misdemeanor charge of conspiring to break into the offices of Daniel Ellsberg's psychiatrist. Chuck had engaged in many dirty tricks, but this simply was not one of them. Yet to save his own skin and be allowed to continue to practice as a lawyer and feed his family, he would have to lie. It would have been a prudent thing to do, and Chuck's lawyer made it clear that refusing this deal would be sheer insanity. He must take it and move on with his life.

But as a new Christian, Chuck felt deeply uncomfortable with the thought of lying, even to save his own skin. He was no longer a man of mere pragmatism. He believed he had to honor God with everything he said and did, to the best of his abilities. Stating that he had done something he had not actually done seemed wrong.

What did his family think? Chuck consulted with them, and their response bolstered him in his decision. It was settled. Chuck then gave the hard news to his lawyer, who exploded with fury. But Chuck felt confident that if he honored God in this matter, God would honor him.

Chuck soon discovered that God doesn't always honor us in the way we think he should. Chuck refused the deal, and the prosecutors promptly indicted him on felony charges.

Thus the media circus surrounding the Watergate scandal continued, with new revelations emerging almost daily. A group of Nixon's secret tapes were then released to the public. Could it get any worse? They painted a picture of deviousness, lying, and just plain nastiness inside the White House, and it was painful for Chuck to realize he had been part of it all.

Chuck had been no idle bystander. He knew in his heart that he had contributed to the amoral—and often deeply immoral—atmosphere in the White House. He knew that even if he wasn't guilty of what he was being accused of, he was certainly guilty in other ways. In the eyes of God, which was the only judgment that really counted, he was terribly guilty.

The pugnacious side of Colson was not dead yet, though. It was very much alive and kicking, as twenty million viewers discovered when he made his now famous appearance on CBS's *60 Minutes*. Although Chuck had become a devout Christian, he was also the defendant in an important case, and he had to figure out how to reconcile these two elements. How could he defend himself while knowing his guilt in so many other matters?

During the interview, Chuck saw that he was trying to have things both ways, vigorously defending himself before the court of public opinion while trying to be an outspoken Christian. It wouldn't work. His pugnacious side could not coexist with his new life in Christ.

Chuck decided that the only way to go forward was one that made no sense to anyone except his handful of Christian friends. In fact, it would make refusing the plea bargain seem like child's play. He decided to voluntarily confess to something that he *had* done and trust God with the outcome. He might have to go to prison, but if he did, he knew that God would go with him. To many, the idea sounded insane. Why would anyone do such a thing?

Even Patty was skeptical, but Chuck assured her that this really was the only way forward, the only way that things would get better. Chuck would be putting everything in God's hands. He knew he could trust God with the whole thing and that somehow it would be okay. Of course, Chuck's lawyer did not see it that way. In fact, his reaction to hearing this proposed course of action is unprintable. But Chuck wouldn't back down.

He had decided to plead guilty to "disseminating derogatory information to the press about Daniel Ellsberg while he was a criminal defendant."[12] This was true, and although many didn't think it constituted an actual obstruction of justice, Chuck figured the judge would accept it as such and would probably be inclined to show at least a little mercy.

And so Chuck Colson pled guilty to this act. But Judge Gerhard Gesell didn't show one iota of mercy. He didn't seem to care that Chuck had done this purely voluntarily. He threw the book at him anyway, stunning witnesses by imposing a sentence of one to three years. Patty, who was in the courtroom, was the most horrified of anyone.

After the sentencing, Chuck had to face the media on the courthouse steps. What he said there was not what the assembled members of the Fourth Estate were expecting. It was not what anyone was expecting to hear. In fact, what he said was as staggering as the harsh sentence. "What happened in court today," Chuck said, "was the court's will and the Lord's will. I have committed my life to Jesus Christ and I can work for him in prison as well as out." What Chuck said was quite true, but he didn't know at the time that this extraordinary statement would prove to be prophetic.[13]

Of course the press had a field day with Chuck's conversion. The *Los Angeles Times* published a cartoon by the famous political cartoonist Pat Oliphant featuring Chuck dressed as a medieval monk, painting the word *Repent* on the gates of the White House. Another cartoon showed him walking past a shocked Nixon while carrying a placard that said, "The End Is Nigh."

The media—whose members tend to be more secular than not— could not get their minds around what was happening to Chuck Colson. He was being transformed, but in their world, this sort of thing simply didn't occur. Nasty people like Chuck Colson didn't change overnight and start being kind to others. Chuck had to be making a Machiavellian maneuver, designed to garner sympathy from the prosecutor or at least from the world of public opinion.

Just as the apostle Paul had once been a zealous persecutor of Christians and had been literally blinded by the Light and transformed into the most zealous Christian of them all, Chuck Colson really was a changed man. But some observers could not accept it, and some would never accept it. Even at the end of his life—after nearly forty years of serving God and prisoners in prisons and beyond—some people refused to believe he had ever changed.

◆ ◆ ◆

On July 8, 1974, Chuck entered the US prison system, becoming prisoner number 23226. After a short time at Holabird detention center in Baltimore, he was transferred to Maxwell Federal Prison Camp in Alabama. He endured the typical humiliations and indignities of prison life, trading in his Brooks Brothers suit for an ugly brown uniform and underwear that had been worn by previous prisoners. There were rats and roaches to deal with, as well as racial tension. One day a friendly prisoner told Chuck that he had overheard someone talk about "killing Colson," and he said that it didn't sound like an idle boast.

Chuck was determined to show that he wasn't someone special—or that he didn't think of himself as someone special—so he volunteered for a number of menial chores, such as mopping floors. One day an African American man asked him, "How you like living with the scum after having all those servants in the White House?"[14] But seeing the man was young, Chuck replied that he'd been doing things like this years before the younger man had been born, and that he'd served in the marines while the other man had still been in diapers.

Somehow this seemed to do the trick. Word spread that Colson was okay.

While Chuck worked in the prison laundry, he would leave his Bible out, hoping someone might notice and start a conversation about it. No one did. The prison atmosphere was closed to anything having to do with God.

But now that he was in prison, Chuck was even more interested in learning what the Bible had to say, and he undertook a serious Bible study. One day he read Hebrews 2:11: "For the one who makes men holy and the men who are made holy share a common humanity. So that [Jesus] is not ashamed to call them his brothers" (PHILLIPS).

Something about this passage got to Chuck. In reading those words he suddenly understood why he was in prison. If Jesus, who was God in the flesh, was not ashamed to call human beings his brothers, perhaps the high-and-mighty Chuck Colson, who had had an office next to the president of the United States, was put here to do the same thing—to empty his pride and call his fellow prisoners his brothers and to know that they really were his brothers.

For Chuck, it was nothing less than a divine revelation, an epiphany. He saw that his prison sentence and his suffering were part of a grand and holy scheme. God had humbled him and brought him there precisely so that Chuck could help these men. Chuck now knew that his life had not been destroyed by coming to prison; instead, prison was part of God's greater purposes. It was the beginning of something wonderful and new. With that, everything changed.

Suddenly, Chuck was zealous to make an impact for God right there in the prison. The first thing he would do was try to recreate something of the fellowship he had on the outside with members of the Fellowship. It wouldn't be easy. Even the one prisoner who told Chuck that he had "accepted the Lord" wasn't interested. He was afraid of the abuse he'd have to take if someone saw him getting involved in a Bible study. It just wasn't the thing to do. Better to keep your head down and not draw attention to yourself, he advised.

Then one day Chuck met a passionate Christian named Tex. Chuck overheard him talking about a fellow prisoner named Bob Ferguson, who had five kids and desperately needed the parole board to let him out. The odds were strongly against his being released, but it was such a desperate situation that Tex said they should pray with Ferguson. They needed a real miracle. That's all Chuck needed to hear, and he leaped in, offering to join them. The pair found Ferguson, and both men prayed for him. The small group of inmates who surrounded them were impressed by Chuck's prayer.

And the next day the miracle actually happened. Ferguson got his parole. Almost instantly, four or five men were interested in joining Chuck's prayer and Bible study group.

Chuck now began to help prisoners in other ways too. One inmate who was unable to read or write asked Chuck to help him write a letter to the judge who could grant him parole. Such needs broke his heart. Although he'd been advised not to use his legal expertise to help other inmates, "I could not refuse those who needed help," Chuck said. "These were my brothers. The Lord had shown the way and now I was following."[15]

Over time, Chuck saw that God had brought him to Maxwell not only to teach him that his fellow prisoners were his brothers in Christ but also so that he could identify with them and see the world from their perspective. Only after he had done this would he be able to effectively help them. Chuck didn't know what lay ahead, but he knew that he wanted to fulfill God's purpose for his life, so he continued doing what he was doing. He was confident the Lord would reveal his plan in his own time.

One weekend, Chuck had a visit from an old friend, Fred "Dusty" Rhodes, who had been a committed Christian for many years. The little group Chuck had gathered at Maxwell impressed Dusty, and he was affected by Chuck's vision for prison ministry. Fred was close to retirement as the chairman of the US Postal Rate Commission, and as he listened to Chuck talk, he was profoundly touched. He believed that God was calling him to help, even if that meant doing so in a full-time capacity.

Chuck continued to study his Bible and read voraciously. He was especially impressed by Dietrich Bonhoeffer's *Letters and Papers from Prison*, which the German pastor and theologian had written during the two years he was imprisoned by the Nazis. This book began for Chuck a lifelong appreciation of Bonhoeffer and his writings. He realized that if Bonhoeffer hadn't been in prison, he never would have written those letters. This was part of how God showed Chuck that

"God causes all things to work together for good to those who love God, to those who are called according to His purpose" (Romans 8:28 NASB). Even prison.

◆ ◆ ◆

As January 1975 dawned, Chuck was filled with hope that he might be released early. Three other Watergate conspirators—John Dean, Jeb Magruder, and Herb Kalmbach—were being released early on the orders of US district judge John Sirica. But the gruff Judge Gerhard Gesell, who had jurisdiction over Chuck's case, did not feel inclined to follow Sirica's kindly lead. Colson, he decreed, would remain behind bars.

After having his and Patty's hopes raised so high by the release of the other three Watergate figures, the news came as a brutal blow. Life behind bars could be hard, even for someone filled with the peace, love, and joy of Jesus Christ, and it was agony to face the reality that he might have to spend another two years and five months in prison.

It was especially hard for Chuck, knowing that his innocent wife and children were suffering because of his misdeeds, forced to live their lives without him. The days following Gesell's decision were the toughest time of all for Chuck, and there was more bad news to come. On January 20, 1975, Chuck learned that the Virginia Supreme Court voted to disbar him from practicing law again. And there was still one more piece of bad news to come.

Chuck received word that his son Chris had been arrested for drug possession. To be unable to be there for his son at such an important time was heartbreaking. But this experience only deepened Chuck's empathy for his fellow prisoners, many of whom were going through similar situations. He took comfort in knowing that after he was released, he would remember the pain he was enduring now, and it would fire him up to help people facing similar trials.

On January 29, when Chuck was perhaps at his lowest ebb, his friend Harold Hughes came to visit. Chuck's four Fellowship friends had been regular visitors during his incarceration. But today Hughes saw that his friend had hit bottom. Hughes exhorted Chuck to practice what they all preached and to turn all his problems over to God. It sounded so simple, but doing it was not so easy. Nevertheless Chuck took his friend's advice, and that night in his cell, he prayed, giving everything to God. "Lord," he prayed,

> if this is what this is all about, then I thank you. I praise you for leaving me in prison, for letting them take away my license to practice law—yes, even for my son being arrested. I praise you for giving me your love through these men, for being God, for just letting me walk with Jesus.[16]

Somehow, that prayer changed everything; Chuck could feel it. Amidst his difficulties he experienced a joy that had been absent before. As Chuck recalled later, "This was the real mountaintop experience. Above and around me the world was filled with love and beauty. For the first time I felt truly free."[17]

What Chuck didn't know then was that outside the prison walls, his lawyer was talking to Judge Gesell again, asking whether he would at least give Chuck a ten-day furlough to be with his son, Chris, who badly needed his father. Gesell, who had been a hard-nosed and unpleasant judge and had proved he was not the sort to be budged, was somehow moved by all that he heard. He decided to rule in a way that no one could have anticipated. He wouldn't give Chuck a ten-day furlough. He decided to release Chuck permanently. In a moment, without a hint that this was a possibility, Chuck Colson was a free man. Was it a coincidence that after he had really turned everything over to God and felt truly free that this happened—that he was literally freed? Chuck didn't think so.

Not long afterward, Chuck arrived home to the same media glare he had left. He was disoriented by his sudden release, and whatever he managed to say was reduced to the following headline in the next day's *Washington Post*:

"Gesell Frees Colson. Colson Thanks the Lord."

Chuck's homecoming, with many friends and family there to greet him, was a warm one. Retiring to bed that night, he was alone with his thoughts for the first time in a long time. Finally falling asleep, he had a nightmare about being back at Maxwell. He dreamed that several prisoners were playing cards when one of them, a heavily tattooed six-foot-six inmate named Archie, menacingly confronted Chuck:

"You'll be out of here soon. What are you going to do for us?!"

Chuck somewhat lamely responded that he would help in some way.

"I'll never forget you guys, or this stinking place," he promised.

Archie wasn't buying it. He had heard promises like this before.

"There ain't nobody cares about us. Nobody!"

"I'll care," Chuck said. "I'll remember."[18]

Archie shouted back angrily with an expletive and underscored the word with an obscene gesture.

But Chuck's dream was not the product of his imagination; it was the memory of a real-life conversation with an inmate named Archie. The question was, why had he dreamed it? And what would he do about the promise he'd made?

His first priority had to be his family. Four days after arriving home, Chuck and Patty flew to visit Chris in Columbia, South Carolina. Instead of speaking sternly to his son, as he had planned, Chuck wrapped his arms around him and told him that everything would be all right. During their tearful reunion, Chuck realized that one of the most important things he would have to do, now that he was free and no longer had White House responsibilities, was to spend more time with his children, whom he had neglected during his rise to power.

After visiting Chris, Chuck flew to Maxwell Prison Camp for a reunion with old friends. That Chuck willingly entered the prison just a few days after he was released was a sign of things to come.

———— ◆ ◆ ◆ ————

With all that had happened and was still happening, Chuck and Patty badly needed to get away, so shortly after visiting Maxwell, they decided to fly to Spain for a real vacation. When they returned home, Chuck was still unclear about what to do next.

He couldn't practice law in Virginia, but there was a good possibility that he could do so in Massachusetts. He received lucrative business offers and endless speaking requests, many from Doug Coe and the brothers at the Fellowship. They wanted Chuck to speak publicly about how he came to faith in Jesus. But Chuck was still unsure of what he should be doing.

Then one day in April 1975, while staring at himself in the bathroom mirror, Chuck had a vision of what God wanted him to do with his life.

"As I stared at my reflection, a startling series of images flashed across my mind," Chuck later said.

I saw men in prison gray moving about. Classes. Discussions. Prayers. The pictures became more sharply focused—of smiling men and women streaming out of prisons, of Bibles, and study groups around tables. These mental images lasted but a few seconds, then they were gone. I had never experienced anything like it before or since.[19]

Chuck was not the sort of Christian who would then or in the future talk much about mystical experiences. He was an extremely rational man. But he could not deny that this vision had occurred. What did it mean?

Then Chuck heard an almost audible voice, telling him, "Take the prisoners out, teach them, return them to prisons to build Christian fellowships. Spread these fellowships through every penitentiary in America."[20] Was he going crazy, or was God speaking to him?

Chuck immediately called his friend Harold Hughes. Surely Hughes would be able to make sense of it. Hughes drove over to Chuck's house, and they talked it over. Now the usually wide-eyed Hughes played the role of sober realist. There was no way to get prisoners out of prisons, he said.

But Chuck had never been one to let stubborn facts get in the way. He became convinced there was a way to turn this dream into a reality. After all, if God had given him this idea, surely God would find a way to achieve it, wouldn't he?

In June, Chuck and Harold met with the director of the Federal Bureau of Prisons, Norman Carlson. During their conversation, Carlson mentioned that he had been at a service in a California prison when a prisoner had prayed a spontaneous prayer for him and his wife. Why, Carlson asked Chuck, would that man pray for the very person who was keeping him behind bars?

"Mr. Carlson," Chuck replied, "that man prayed for you because he loves you."[21]

The answer clearly made an impression because Carlson unexpectedly told Chuck and Hughes that he would issue the order to bring Chuck's vision to America's prisons.

The Bureau of Prisons approved a proposal, brought to them by Chuck and Hughes, to allow the Fellowship Foundation to select federal prison inmates to attend a two-week retreat in the Washington DC area, at which the inmates would engage in Bible study and leadership training.

The results were exciting. Inmates from the first group offered to visit Arlington County Jail and Lorton Reformatory, both in Virginia, to talk to prisoners about God and his plan for their lives. After finishing their retreats, inmates returned to their prisons to begin prison fellowships—discipling their fellow inmates and finding ways to serve God behind bars. It worked, and it continued to work. The bold idea that God had given to Chuck Colson had become a reality.

As with everything that Chuck ever got involved with doing, he did it all the way. Within three years Prison Fellowship Ministries, as it was named, grew to employ one hundred employees in twenty-three states. Nearly seven thousand volunteers worked with inmates who had finished in-prison seminars in six hundred prisons. It was a remarkable achievement, making prison ministry a front-burner issue in many churches, many of which had forgotten that Jesus commands his followers to visit those in prison. Prison Fellowship International was also started, first in Great Britain and eventually in more than one hundred other countries.

◆ ◆ ◆

In 1976, Chuck wrote his first book, *Born Again*, which exploded onto the best-seller lists, and the term *born again* entered the popular lexicon as a description of someone who had a life-changing experience with God. Chuck soon made the commitment to devote himself full-time, for the rest of his life, to serving God in America's prisons. He also began deepening his knowledge of Christian teachings, meeting with Christian intellectuals and philosophers, such as Richard Mouw, Nicholas Wolterstorff, Stephen Monsma, R. C. Sproul, Dr. Carl Henry, Francis Schaeffer, Os Guinness, and Richard Lovelace. He read the writings of Luther, Zwingli, and Calvin, Abraham Kuyper, Paul Johnson, and fellow prisoners Alexander Solzhenitsyn and Dietrich Bonhoeffer. Chuck became convinced that it was absolutely necessary to develop a Christian worldview—a comprehensive framework regarding every aspect of life, from science to literature to film to politics.

One question that Chuck now explored was why people committed crimes in the first place. Some experts blamed poverty; others blamed race. But Chuck, studying the writings of sociologist James Q. Wilson, knew the real answer: crime is a moral problem that demands a moral solution. He was to hammer home this theme again and again. Commenting on a tragic school shooting in 1998, Chuck said:

What's happening to our children? The first thing we must understand is that only a biblical worldview of human nature can make sense of these murders. The Bible makes two things clear about humanity. First, we are created in the *imago Dei*, the image of God, and knowledge of right and wrong is implanted on the human heart. But we're also warned that we live in a fallen world—and that the human heart is desperately wicked. These two facts require any civilized society to make the moral training of its young its number one priority. . . . The great criminologist James Q. Wilson says all of his studies have led to the same conclusion: Crime begins when children are not given adequate moral training, when they do not develop internal restraints on impulsive behavior.[22]

Chuck's deep interest in worldview, and the need to teach it to the faithful, resulted in the radio program *BreakPoint*, which rapidly grew until some eight million people were listening to it every day. Later, wanting to influence the culture even more deeply, Chuck established the Centurions Program, which accepts one hundred serious Christians each year into a yearlong distance-learning class in which participants learn about worldviews—the Christian one and those that compete against it—and develop a project in which to teach what they've learned to their neighbors.

As the years passed, Chuck embraced other ways of ministering to prisoners and their families. A former bank robber named Mary Kay Beard convinced him to start a ministry called Angel Tree; ordinary people purchase Christmas gifts for the children of prison inmates and give them on behalf of a parent in prison who has no means of giving gifts to his or her children personally.

In 1983, Chuck set up Justice Fellowship as a wing of Prison Fellowship, devoted to criminal justice reform. He successfully fought for a law that would do much to prevent prison rape. He fought for the religious rights of prisoners—rights that were endangered by a Supreme Court decision in the 1990s.

He wrote more books: *How Now Shall We Live?, Loving God, The Good Life, The Body, The Faith*, and many others.

In 1993, Chuck was awarded the one-million-dollar Templeton Prize for Progress in Religion. He donated the prize money to Prison Fellowship.

Each year, Chuck seemed to become busier and busier: magazine columns, speaking engagements, radio, prison visits, trips overseas to visit some of the most infamous gulags in the world.

Chuck so admired William Wilberforce that he set up the Wilberforce Award, given annually to a Christian who confronted social injustice, often related to human slavery. Winners include Philippine leader Benigno S. Aquino Jr., Bishop Macram Max Gassis, and Baroness Cox of Queensberry.

He also provoked intense controversy when he and Father Richard John Neuhaus set up a theological study group (and later wrote a document) they called "Evangelicals and Catholics Together"; its goal was to "minimize hostility and maximize cooperation between these two polarized pillars of the Christian world in the mission field." ECT also attempted to reconcile theological differences between the two groups.

In 1999, with the help of then Governor George W. Bush, Prison Fellowship took over a wing of a Texas prison for the InnerChange Freedom Initiative, a program in which prisoners volunteer for a tough, Bible-based program of activities that prepare them for successful reentry into society when they finish their sentences.

Chuck constantly fought the culture of death, especially when his friend President George W. Bush was in the White House, encouraging the president, with considerable success, to get behind efforts to fight human trafficking, end the civil war in Sudan, combat the global spread of AIDS, and protect persecuted Christians in the Middle East. In the process, Chuck helped to change the image of Christianity in the minds of many secular observers, earning the admiration of those who had previously disdained what Christians stood for.

Chuck's biggest fault, as those who knew him will attest, was that he was always trying to do too much. In the last two or three years of his life, this human tornado seemed to be conscious that time was running out for him. His two last big projects began in 2009, when he was seventy-seven years old. The first was establishing the Chuck Colson Center for Christian Worldview, which promotes worldview teaching, and the second was helping write the Manhattan Declaration, which calls for the church to defend the sanctity of human life, traditional marriage, and freedom of religion.

In the weeks before his death at age eighty, Chuck was planning yet another big project, "perhaps the biggest of all," writes former *BreakPoint* managing editor James Tonkowich. "A movement of Christians to reform education—public, charter, private and Christian—from Kindergarten through university. This is a vast undertaking for someone half his age, but then again, [Chuck] never thought that way."[23]

◆ ◆ ◆

Chuck truly was a Wilberforce for our times. Like Wilberforce, he came to genuine faith in adulthood. Like Wilberforce, he wanted to help those in society who suffer; he wanted to right wrongs and teach people to think. Like Wilberforce, he refused to give up, even if it took decades to solve entrenched social problems. Chuck's motto might have been borrowed from Winston Churchill: "Never give in—never, never, never, never—in nothing great or small, large or petty—never give in except to convictions of honour and good sense."[24] He didn't let the rest of us give up, either.

Throughout his ministry, Chuck loved to say that no matter what, Christians must be at their posts, doing their duty. And that message—stay at your posts—was on the pins that mourners were given at the Washington National Cathedral memorial service, attended by the great and the powerful of the land, who sat side by side with those who, like Chuck, had once been locked away behind bars. People Chuck had loved and served, dined with and prayed with.

Chuck's message to stay at your posts was echoed by his daughter, Emily, who told mourners,

Today is a celebration of my father's life, but today is also about us— you and me. What will we do in the shadow of such an extraordinary role model?

There is work to be done. I encourage you to continue the work God has begun through my father's life. Do the right thing, seek the truth, defend the weak, live courageous lives.[25]

Chuck's last words to us, which he left with his family, were a final witness to the God he served. "I want my funeral services to be joyful," he wrote. "I don't want people to be sad because I believe with every ounce of conviction in my body that death is but a homecoming, and that we'll be in the presence of God. It's the culmination of life. It's a celebration."[26]

Do you believe that? It's true.

Notes

CHAPTER 1: GEORGE WASHINGTON

1. Henry Wiencek, *An Imperfect God: George Washington, His Slaves, and the Creation of America* (Reprint, New York: Farrar, Straus and Giroux, 2004), 46.
2. John Ferling, *The Ascent of George Washington* (New York: Bloomsbury Press, 2010), 10.
3. Ibid.
4. Ibid., 10–11.
5. Ibid., 13.
6. Ibid., 16.
7. Edward G. Lengel, *General George Washington: A Military Life* (New York: Random House Trade Paperbacks, 2007), 35.
8. Ferling, *The Ascent of George Washington*, 21.
9. Ron Chernow, *Washington: A Life* (New York: The Penguin Press, 2010), 42.
10. Ferling, *The Ascent of George Washington*, 21.
11. Ibid., 22.
12. Ibid., 24.
13. Chernow, *Washington: A Life*, 42.
14. Ibid., 50.
15. Ferling, *The Ascent of George Washington*, 29.
16. Ibid.
17. Chernow, *Washington: A Life*, 92.
18. Ferling, *The Ascent of George Washington*, 75.

19. David A. Adler, *George Washington: An Illustrated Biography* (New York: Holiday House, 2004), 94.
20. *The Papers of George Washington,* accessed November 26, 2012, http://gwpapers.virginia.edu/documents/revolution/letters/gfairfax2.html.
21. "Battle of Bunker Hill" http://en.wikipedia.org/wiki/Battle_of_Bunker_Hill.
22. Chernow, *Washington: A Life,* 186.
23. Ibid., 187.
24. Ibid., 189.
25. Adler, *George Washington: An Illustrated Biography,* 149.
26. Chernow, *Washington: A Life,* 133.
27. Ibid., 132.
28. Ibid., 131.
29. Ibid., 133.
30. Ibid.
31. "Washington's Farewell Address, 1976," accessed November 26, 2012, http://avalon.law.yale.edu/18th_century/washing.asp.
32. Adler, *George Washington: An Illustrated Biography,* 150.
33. Ibid., 152.
34. Joseph J. Ellis, *His Excellency George Washington* (London: Vintage, 2005), 139.
35. Ibid., 141.
36. Ferling, *The Ascent of George Washington,* 232.
37. Ellis, *His Excellency George Washington,* 142.
38. "George Washington Prevents the Revolt of his Officers," accessed November 26, 2012, http://www.historyplace.com/speeches/washington.htm.
39. Ibid.
40. Ibid.
41. Ibid.
42. Ibid.
43. Ibid.
44. Ibid.
45. Chernow, *Washington: A Life,* 435–436.
46. Ellis, *His Excellency George Washington,* 141.
47. Ibid., 139.
48. "The American Revolution, 1763–1783," accessed November 26, 2012, http://www.loc.gov/teachers/classroommaterials/presentationsandactivities/presentations/timeline/amrev/contarmy/newyork.html.
49. Ellis, *His Excellency George Washington,* 274–275.
50. Ferling, *The Ascent of George Washington,* 306.
51. Ibid.
52. "The American Revolution, 1763–1783," accessed November 26, 2012, http://www.loc.gov/teachers/classroommaterials/presentationsandactivities/presentations/timeline/amrev/contarmy/newyork.html.
53. George Washington, *Washington on Washington* (Lexington, KY: The University Press of Kentucky, 2003), 138.

54. Ellis, *His Excellency George Washington*, 268.
55. Barnes Historical Series, *A Brief History of the United States* (Whitefish, MT: Kessinger Publishing, 2004), 101.
56. Ferling, *The Ascent of George Washington*, 370–371.
57. Ellis, *His Excellency George Washington*, 270.
58. Ibid., 270–271.
59. Adler, *George Washington: An Illustrated Biography*, 206.

CHAPTER 2: WILLIAM WILBERFORCE

1. Isaiah 61:1, Luke 4:18 NKJV.
2. Robert Isaac Wilberforce and Samuel Wilberforce, *The Life of William Wilberforce*, vol. 4 (London: John Murray, 1838), 373.
3. *Joni Eareckson Tada 2012 Wilberforce Award Recipient*, http://www .breakpoint.org/wilberforce-weekend-2012/wilberforce-award.
4. Robert Isaac Wilberforce and Samuel Wilberforce, *The Life of William Wilberforce*, vol. 1 (London: John Murray, 1838), 7.
5. Ibid.
6. Earl Philip Henry Stanhope, *Life of the Right Honourable William Pitt*, vol. 1, (London: John Murray, 1862), 283.
7. E. M. Forster, *Marianne Thornton: A Domestic Biography* (London: Hodder and Stoughton, 1956), 43.
8. Wilberforce and Wilberforce, *The Life of William Wilberforce*, vol. 1, 75.
9. Ibid.
10. John S. Harford, *Recollections of William Wilberforce During Nearly Thirty Years* (London: Longman, Green, Longman, Roberts and Green, 1864), 216.
11. William Wilberforce, "Journal, Sunday, October 28, 1787," quoted in Wilberforce and Wilberforce, *The Life of William Wilberforce*, vol. 1, 149.
12. Wilfrid Prest, *Albion Ascendant: English History, 1660–1815* (Oxford: Oxford University Press, 1998).
13. John Wesley, "Letter to William Wilberforce, London, February 24, 1791," in Thomas Jackson, ed., *The Works of John Wesley*, 14 vols. (Franklin, TN: Providence House, 1994), CD-ROM, 13:153.
14. John Charles Pollock, *Wilberforce* (London: Constable, 1977), 64.
15. William Wilberforce, in "Debate on Mr. Wilberforce's Resolutions respecting the Slave Trade," in William Cobbett, *The Parliamentary History of England. From the Norman Conquest in 1066 to the year 1803*, vol. 28 (1789–91), (London: T. Curson Hansard, 1806–1820), cols 42–68.

CHAPTER 3: ERIC LIDDELL

1. *Eric Liddell: Champion of Conviction* (Dolby DVD, January 2008).
2. Catherine Swift, *Eric Liddell* (Ada, MI: Bethany House Publishers, 1990), 78.
3. *Eric Liddell: Champion of Conviction*.
4. Ibid.

5. RBC Ministries, *Our Daily Bread*, "Life-Changing Choices," accessed January 17, 2013, http://mobi.rbc.org/odb/2012-08-04.html.
6. David Brooks, "The Jeremy Lin Problem," *New York Times*, February 16, 2012, http://www.nytimes.com/2012/02/17 /opinion/brooks-the-jeremy-lin-problem.html.
7. Swift, *Eric Liddell*, 86.
8. David McCasland, *Eric Liddell: Pure Gold* (Grand Rapids, MI: Discovery House Publishers, 2001), 80.
9. C. S. Lewis Institute, Joel S. Woodruff, Ed.D., "Eric Liddell: Muscular Discipline and Olympic Champion," Summer 2012, http://www .cslewisinstitute.org/webfm_send/1386.
10. McCasland, *Eric Liddell: Pure Gold*, 103.
11. Ibid., 96.
12. http://en.wikipedia.org/wiki/Horatio_Fitch.
13. McCasland, *Eric Liddell: Pure Gold*, 98.
14. Ibid., 101.
15. *Eric Liddell: Champion of Conviction*.
16. Hugh Hudson, *Chariots of Fire* (Dolby DVD, January 2004).
17. McCasland, *Eric Liddell: Pure Gold*, 210.
18. Ibid., 223.
19. Ibid.
20. Eric Liddell, *Disciplines of the Christian Life* (eChristian Books, Kindle Edition, January 2011).
21. *Eric Liddell: Champion of Conviction*.
22. McCasland, *Eric Liddell: Pure Gold*, 268.
23. Ibid., 269.
24. *Eric Liddell: Champion of Conviction*.
25. McCasland, *Eric Liddell: Pure Gold*, 279.
26. Ibid., 280.
27. *Eric Liddell: Champion of Conviction*.
28. Ibid.
29. Ibid.
30. Ibid.
31. *From the Ends of the Earth*, "Marinating in the Word," June 17, 2012, http://bencarswell.blogspot.com/2012/06/marinating-in-word.html.
32. BBC, "Golden Scots," June 25, 2012, http://www .bbc.co.uk/sport/0/scotland/18534527.
33. McCasland, *Eric Liddell: Pure Gold*, 105.
34. James H. Taylor, III, Weihsien Paintings, accessed January 10, 2013, http:// www.weihsien-paintings.org/NormanCliff/people/individuals/Eric01 /PureGold/txt_foreword.htm.

NOTES

CHAPTER 4: DIETRICH BONHOEFFER

1. Liebholz-Bonhoeffer, Sabine, *The Bonhoeffers: Portrait of a Family* (New York: St. Martin's, 1971), 21–22.
2. James 1:12 ESV.
3. "Inge Karding interviewed by Martin Doblmeier," *Bonhoeffer*, directed by Martin Doblmeier (First Run Features, 2003), DVD.
4. This statement has been "traced to 1933, though never recorded in writing" according to Stephen R. Haynes, *The Bonhoeffer Legacy: Post-Holocaust Perspectives* (Minneapolis: Fortress Press, 2006), 32–33.
5. "Outline for a Book," August 8, 1944, in John W. De Gruchy, ed., *Letters and Papers from Prison*, vol. 8, *Dietrich Bonhoeffer Works* (Minneapolis: Augsburg Fortress, 2010), 501.
6. The famous "First they came . . ." statement by Martin Niemöller was delivered in diverse variations during his many postwar speaking engagements. This most definitive version was published by Franklin Littell, who knew Niemöller. Franklin H. Littell, "First They Came for the Jews," *Christian Ethics Today* issue 9, vol. 3, no. 1 (February 1997), 29.
7. Wolf-Dieter Zimmermann and Ronald G. Smith, eds., *I Knew Dietrich Bonhoeffer*, Käthe G. Smith, trans, (New York: Harper and Row, 1966), 158–160.
8. Michael Robert Marrus, *The Nazi Holocaust. Part 8: Bystanders to the Holocaust*, vol. 1 (Munich: KG Saur Verlag, 1989), 1401, citing Eberhard Bethge, *Dietrich Bonhoeffer: A Biography*, Victoria J. Barnett, ed. (Minneapolis: Fortress, 1967–2000).
9. Keith Clements, ed., *London: 1933–1935*, vol. 13, *Dietrich Bonhoeffer Work* (New York: Fortress, 2007), 331.
10. John W. De Gruchy, ed., *Letters and Papers from Prison*, vol. 8, *Dietrich Bonhoeffer Works* (Minneapolis: Augsburg Fortress, 2010), 370–372.
11. Dietrich Bonhoeffer, *The Cost of Discipleship* (London: SCM, 1959), 99.

CHAPTER 5: JACKIE ROBINSON

1. Arnold Rampersad, *Jackie Robinson* (New York: Ballantine Books, 1998), 24.
2. Ibid., 51.
3. Ibid., 96.
4. Scott Simon, *Jackie Robinson and the Integration of Baseball* (Hoboken, NJ: John Wiley & Sons, Inc., 2007), 19.
5. Rampersad, *Jackie Robinson*, 103.
6. Ibid., 106.
7. Ibid.
8. Ibid., 107.
9. Ibid., 122.
10. Simon, *Jackie Robinson and the Integration of Baseball*, 63.
11. Rampersad, *Jackie Robinson*, 125.
12. Ibid., 126.

13. Ibid., 127.
14. Ibid., 129.
15. Murrey Polner, *Branch Rickey, A Biography* (Jefferson, NC: McFarland & Company, 2007), 176.
16. Jackie Robinson, Alfred Duckett, *I Never Had It Made: An Autobiography of Jackie Robinson* (New York: Harper Perennial, 2003), 41.
17. Rampersad, *Jackie Robinson*, 167.
18. Robinson, Duckett, *I Never Had It Made*, 58.
19. Rampersad, *Jackie Robinson*, 173.
20. Simon, *Jackie Robinson and the Integration of Baseball*, 122.
21. Jonathan Eig, *Opening Day: The Story of Jackie Robinson's First Season* (New York: Simon & Schuster, 2007), 224.
22. Sharon Robinson, *Jackie's Nine: Jackie Robinson's Values to Live By* (New York: Scholastic Inc., 2002), 89.
23. Rachel Robinson, *Jackie Robinson: An Intimate Portrait* (New York: Abradale /Abrams, 1998), 216.
24. ESPN's 100 Most Memorable Moments, "93: Baseball retires Jackie Robinson's No. 42," accessed November 26, 2012, http://sports.espn.go.com/espn/espn25 /story?page=moments/93.

CHAPTER 6: POPE JOHN PAUL II

1. Monsignor Virgilio Levi and Christine Allison, *John Paul II: A Tribute in Words and Pictures* (New York: William Morrow & Company, 1999).
2. David Aikman, *Great Souls: Six Who Changed a Century* (Lanham, MD: Lexington Books, 2003), 272.
3. George Weigel, *Witness to Hope* (New York: HarperCollins, 2001), 56–57.
4. Aikman, *Great Souls: Six Who Changed a Century*, 277.
5. Weigel, *Witness to Hope*, 57.
6. Ibid., 68.
7. Aikman, *Great Souls: Six Who Changed a Century*, 283.
8. Ibid., 285.
9. Weigel, *Witness to Hope*, 142.
10. Ibid., 164.
11. Aikman, *Great Souls: Six Who Changed a Century*, 296.
12. Weigel, *Witness to Hope*, 254.
13. Gunther Simmermacher, "The Southern Cross," October 15–21, 2003, http:// www.mail-archive.com/pope-john-paul-ii@yahoogroups.com/msg00008.html.
14. Aikman, *Great Souls: Six Who Changed a Century*, 253.
15. Ibid., 262.
16. Ibid., 255.
17. Monsignor Virgilio Levi and Christine Allison, *John Paul II: A Tribute in Words and Pictures*, 113–116.
18. Stanislaw Dziwisz, *A Life with Karol: My Forty-Year Friendship with the Man Who Became Pope* (New York: Doubleday, 2008), 237.

19. Levi and Allison, *John Paul II: A Tribute in Words and Pictures*, 116.
20. Dziwisz, *A Life with Karol*, 249.
21. Aikman, *Great Souls: Six Who Changed a Century*, 301–2.
22. CNN World, "Vatican Reasserts Stem Cell Stand," CNN.com, July 25, 2001.
23. George Weigel, *The End and the Beginning: Pope John Paul II—The Victory of Freedom, the Last Years, the Legacy* (New York: Image, 2011), 370–371.
24. Ibid., 385.
25. Ibid., 418.
26. Ibid., 429.
27. Aikman, *Great Souls: Six Who Changed a Century*, 307.

CHAPTER 7: CHARLES W. COLSON

1. Charles W. Colson, *Born Again* (Ada, MI: Chosen Books, 1976), 24.
2. Ibid., 26–27.
3. Jonathan Aitken, *Charles W. Colson: A Life Redeemed* (Colorado Springs, CO: Waterbrook Press, 2005), 194.
4. Colson, *Born Again*, 109.
5. Psalm 37:1, 3–5 NIV.
6. Colson, *Born Again*, 115–116.
7. Ibid., 117.
8. Ibid.
9. Ibid., 125.
10. Aitken, *Charles W. Colson: A Life Redeemed*, 220.
11. Colson, *Born Again*, 150.
12. Aitken, *Charles W. Colson: A Life Redeemed*, 241.
13. Ibid., 248.
14. Ibid., 254–255.
15. Ibid., 258.
16. Ibid., 278.
17. Ibid.
18. Ibid., 271.
19. Ibid., 274.
20. Ibid., 276.
21. Ibid.
22. Chuck Colson, "Kids Who Kill," BreakPoint.org, March 30, 1998.
23. Jim Tonkowich, "The Wideness of Worldview: Remembering Chuck Colson," April 23, 2012, http://www.religiontoday.com/news /wideness-of-worldview-remembering-chuck-colson.html.
24. Winston Churchill, speech at Harrow School, October 29, 1941, http://www.winstonchurchill.org/learn/speeches /speeches-of-winston-churchill/103-never-give-in.
25. As remembered by the author.
26. Ibid.vv

SEVEN WOMEN

FOR SUSANNE

Contents

Introduction

B
efore I wrote this book, I wrote two long biographies, one about Dietrich Bonhoeffer[1] and one about William Wilberforce.[2] I was overwhelmed at the response to these books. It was clear that these stories had deeply impacted and inspired many readers, and though I knew the stories of many other extraordinary and inspiring figures, I didn't plan to write any more long biographies. But then I realized that I could write shorter ones—and so I wrote *Seven Men*.[3] The response to this book was also beyond what I had expected or hoped and further confirmed my belief that there is a great hunger for heroes in our culture.

Although I was never sure whether I would write a book that included the biographies of seven women, people kept asking me about it, and the more I thought about it, the more I knew that I must do it. I've always admired the women in this book and realized that many people didn't know their stories. To be clear, in neither *Seven Men* nor this book is the list of seven persons in any way definitive. There are many other inspiring men and women I might have included. For each book I simply chose seven people whose stories I found most compelling and inspiring—and there's no doubt that the stories of the seven great women in this book are hugely inspiring, and not just to women. I hope men will read these stories and not deny themselves the inspiration of these truly extraordinary lives. For the many men whose view of women has been twisted and dented by our cultural assumptions, these lives will be inspiring and encouraging news.

But whose stories should I tell? I began asking friends for suggestions and soliciting their thoughts. In doing so I encountered an assumption about women's greatness that wasn't surprising, but that is worth mentioning here. Many people suggested women who were the first ones to do something that men had already done. Amelia Earhart, who was the first woman to fly solo across the Atlantic in 1932, was mentioned, as was Sally Ride, who was the first American woman in space. No one mentioned Shirley "Cha Cha" Muldowney, who was the first female Top Fuel dragster champion, but I'm sure she would have come up eventually. But what these women had accomplished didn't exemplify the kind of greatness I had in mind—neither for men nor women. If it had, in writing *Seven Men* I would have replaced Wilberforce and Bonhoeffer with John Glenn and Charles Lindbergh—and might have replaced Pope John Paul II with Don "Big Daddy" Garlits or perhaps even Don "The Snake" Prudhomme, two of the greatest drag racers in history.

What struck me as wrong about these suggestions was that they presumed women should somehow be compared to men. But it seemed wrong to view great women in that way. The great men in *Seven Men* were not measured against women, so why should the women in *Seven Women* be measured against men? I wondered what was behind this way of seeing things, that women should be defined against men? Or that men and women should even be compared to each other?

Two interrelated attitudes seemed at play. First, men and women are in some ways interchangeable, that what one does the other should do. Second, women are in some kind of competition with men, and for women to progress they need to compete with men. This thinking pretends to put men and women on equal footing, but it actually only pits them against each other in a kind of zero-sum competition in which they usually tear each other down.

When I consider the seven women I chose, I see that most of them were great for reasons that derive precisely from their being women, not in spite of it; and what made them great has nothing to do with their being measured against or competing with men. In other words, their accomplishments are not gender-neutral but are rooted in their singularity as women. All of them existed and thrived as women and stand quite apart from anything touching the kind of thinking I encountered.

The first woman I chose, Joan of Arc, is a good example. She is sometimes thought of as great because she did what men do—she donned armor and became a warrior—but that is far off the mark. Joan of Arc was no fierce amazon. Far from it. There was nothing even slightly "manly" about her. On the contrary, it was her youth, innocence, purity, and holiness that made it possible for her to do what she did. Only just past girlhood she was deeply affected by the suffering she saw in the battles around her, never becoming inured to the carnage and agonies of war, as a male soldier typically will do. It was precisely her vulnerability and womanly virtue that stunned and inspired the rough soldiers in a way that no man ever could do. It was because of these qualities that they were in awe of her and respected her. Though her spirit was as large as anyone's who has ever lived, she herself was neither big nor strong. In other words, there could never be a male Joan of Arc. The very idea is a laughable oxymoron.

Similarly, Rosa Parks was specifically chosen to do what she did because she was a woman. Those who wanted to make a federal case out of her arrest knew they must have the right person, and they knew it must be a woman. Her feminine dignity was vital to the case, so there never could have been a male Rosa Parks. Obviously Susanna Wesley—who bore nineteen children and raised the surviving ten—could not have been a man; and Saint Maria of Paris wanted to be a mother to all she encountered and positively exuded motherhood.

Hannah More was considered a model of femininity by those who knew her, and because of this she was especially valued and respected by the many men whom she called friends. She was nothing like their male friends, and so the cultural influence she wielded was not a result of her being "one of the boys." Quite the contrary. Corrie ten Boom exudes an unmistakably feminine warmth; and who can doubt that it was Mother Teresa's femaleness that flummoxed and disarmed and charmed those with whom she dealt? Can we as easily imagine a man doing what she did?

So the stories of these great women show us that men and women are not interchangeable. There are things men can and should do that women cannot, and there are things that women can and should do that men cannot. So comparing men and women is something like comparing apples and oranges, except apples and oranges are actually far more like each other than are men and women. Apples and oranges can exist without each other, but men and women cannot. Men and women were deliberately designed to be different. Indeed we are specifically created as complements to each other, as different halves of a whole, and that whole reflects the glory of God. It's patently obvious that we were physically created to fit together, and of course if that weren't the case, we could not create life. So when men cease to be such or when women deny their uniqueness, they make that complementarity impossible, and the whole, as it were, suffers. There's much to be said on that subject, but the point to make here is that we are meant to be different and God wants us to celebrate and rejoice in our differences, never to suppress them or denigrate them.

'm privileged to be friends with someone whose husband was born in 1889. For context, that's the year Vincent van Gogh painted *Starry Night*, Jefferson Davis died, and Adolph Hitler was born. Alice von Hildebrand—her friends call her Lily—is a delight, so much so that I've now twice had her as my guest at Socrates in the City,[4] a forum that encourages busy and successful professionals in thinking about the bigger questions in life. Her age (ninety-one as I write this) gives her a great measure of authority, but it hasn't dimmed her fire even slightly. It would not be inaccurate to describe her as a pistol. I mention her now because she has written two books that deal with the issue of men and women. One is *The Privilege of Being a Woman*,[5] and the other is *Man and Woman: A Divine Invention*.[6] As she fiercely declared in my most recent interview with her,[7] she is tremendously pro-woman—and she was that evening we spoke—but she also makes it abundantly clear that it is precisely for this reason that she is a devoted and lifelong opponent of feminism. She firmly believes feminism to be anti-woman because it pressures women to become more like men. Everyone who heard her speak that evening was surprised, but we were sternly schooled by Dame von Hildebrand on this subject.

The lesson in all this is that to pit women against men is a form of denigration of women, as though their measure must be determined by masculine standards. The worst standards of masculine value—power usually at the top of those long lists—become the very things that some women are told they must aspire to meet. How ironic that modern culture, by so often intimating power as the highest good, should force women to accept what amounts to nothing less than patriarchal thinking, in the most pejorative sense of that adjective.

Of course this is entirely understandable. Some men have misused their power and strength to harm women. As I say in the introduction to *Seven Men*, whatever God gives us is meant for us to use to bless others, and God gives men strength and power, generally speaking, only so they will use it to bless those who do not have it. But when men fail to do so, women who are victims of the worst expressions of manhood—in fact, abrogations of real manhood—feel that the only way to deal with this is to wrest that power from men. So the idea of "female empowerment" arose, until it became another ubiquitous and thought-free cliché. But the problem with this idea is that it presupposes the tremendously harmful and distorting idea of a competition for power.

That idea was famously popularized in 1973 in the so-called "Battle of the Sexes," the much-heralded and nationally televised tennis match between Billy Jean King, a woman, and Bobby Riggs, a man. The cultural climate at the time was that there were two ways of seeing the world. One was the bigoted "Male Chauvinist Pig" way, and the other was the enlightened "I Am Woman (Hear Me Roar)" way. In this scenario women and men were pitted against each other as bitter adversaries, and the only way for women to lift themselves up was to denounce men as sexists and cavemen.

Billie Jean King was then in her prime, twenty-six years younger than Bobby Riggs, who had been a tennis champion in the 1940s. That she prevailed was no great surprise to anyone paying attention, but the way the match was publicized made it out to be an epochal event. The most important and terrible thing was that it portrayed the relationship between men and women as a zero-sum game. If one won, the other lost. In this view of the relationship between the sexes, there can be no equity, no mutual admiration, no mutual encouragement, and of course, no real love. That night it was this view writ large: the only way for one to win was for the other to lose. It made for great television ratings, but this idea is a pernicious lie, one that has hurt men and women terribly.

Whether we like it or not, men and women are inextricably intertwined. Because the Bible says that we are made in God's image—"male and female He created them" (Gen. 1:27)—the fortunes of one are so linked to the fortunes of the other that there is no way to lift one without lifting the other and no way to degrade one without degrading the other. So whenever men have used their positions of authority or their power to denigrate women, they have denigrated themselves and have denied themselves the fullness of manhood God intended for them. When women have tried to ape the behavior of power-hungry men, they have degraded themselves and denied themselves the dignity of being above that vulgar fray.

It is all the more noteworthy that the great women in this volume stood on their own as women, but not in a defiant stance that pitted them against men. On the contrary, they were large-hearted enough and secure enough in who they were to show remarkable magnanimity toward men, with whom they had notably warm relationships. Joan of Arc's relationships with the soldiers who served under her is nothing less than moving; Susanna Wesley's love for her sons and their reverence for her speak volumes; Hannah More's relationships with her four sisters were at the very heart of her life, but she also had a pronounced capacity for friendship with men, including David Garrick, Horace Walpole, Dr. Samuel Johnson, and William Wilberforce. Maria Skobtsova's (Saint Maria of Paris) love for her son and relationship with Father Dimitri Klepinin tell us everything about her, as does Corrie ten Boom's relationship with her father. Mother Teresa's friendship with Pope John Paul II was well known, and it is clear that Rosa Parks's relationship with her husband was at the center of her life and accomplishments.

Perhaps the best thing about biographies is that they enable us to slip the strictures of time and provide a bracing corrective to our tendency to see everything in the dark glass of our own era, with all its blind spots, motes, beams, and distortions. We must be honest enough to recognize that each era cannot help having a pinched, parochial view of things, and of course the largest part of that parochialism is that each era thinks it is not parochial at all. Each era has the fatal hubris to believe that it has once and for all climbed to the top of the mountain and can see everything as it is, from the highest and most objective vantage point possible. But to assert that ours is the only blinker-less view of things is to blither fatuousness. We need to delve into the past to know that we have not progressed to any point of perfection and objectivity, and in examining the lives of these seven women, we are doing just that. We see that our view of many things, not least our view of how women can be great, is fatally tinged by our own cultural assumptions. The Bible says we are to humble ourselves, and in reading the stories of great men and women from the past, we inevitably do just that. But in humbling ourselves in that way we ironically gain a far greater objectivity and a far better vantage point from which to see things.

May the true stories of these seven great women help you to see yourself and your own time and world all the more clearly.

— Eric Metaxas
New York City
July 2014

ONE

Joan of Arc

1412–1431

E ven to those who know it well, the story of the woman called
Joan of Arc is an enigma. I knew little about her until I saw the
landmark silent film *The Passion of Joan of Arc*[1] some years ago.
But after seeing the film and reading more about her, I quickly understood that her character and her exploits were so extraordinary as to
be almost beyond belief. They are certainly without equal. But what
are we to make of this woman? Those who would make her out to be
an early feminist, or a religious fanatic, or a lunatic subject to strange
delusions may be forgiven their confusion, because—although she was
none of those things—her life stands well apart from all others. She
was so pure and so brave and so singular in her faith and obedience to
God that, perhaps like Francis of Assisi or even like Jesus himself, she
challenges many of our deepest assumptions about what a life can be.

To get a sense of who Joan of Arc was, imagine a teenage farm girl
entering the halls of the Pentagon in Washington, DC, and forcefully

235

demanding to see the secretary of defense, saying that God had given her a plan to end all terrorism aimed at the United States and her allies, and all she required was an army of soldiers with weapons. Most people would sensibly assume such a young woman was mentally ill or perhaps simply extremely naive. The last thing we would imagine is that she was actually sent by God, and that everything she said was true and would come to pass precisely as she said it would. But this was approximately the scenario that faced French military and political figures in 1429, when a humble, uneducated seventeen-year-old girl from a small village appeared before them.

In order to appreciate what this girl was proposing, we have to understand the situation in France at that time. The war that came to be known as the Hundred Years War had been raging on and off since 1337. The English, having taken over vast tracts of France by 1429, were winning, and they now hoped to literally crown their efforts by putting an English king on the French throne. At the time, this practically seemed a *fait accompli*. But Joan innocently and forcefully explained to French officials that she had been sent by God to drive the English out of the great city of Orléans. What's more, she claimed that she would ensure that the proper Frenchman—Charles VII—was crowned king of France! Taking her seriously was out of the question; and yet somehow, in the end, the befuddled and desperate leaders of France did just that. They had run out of sensible options and knew they had nothing to lose. But far less bizarre than their taking her seriously is the fact that she would actually succeed in everything she said she would do. It is preposterous to consider, and yet history records that it happened.

◆ ◆ ◆

Jeanne d'Arc—or Joan of Arc, as she is called in English—was called Jeanette by her parents. She was born in 1412 into a peasant family in Domrémy, a village in northeastern France. With her parents and four siblings, she lived in a simple stone house next to the village church.

Like most peasant girls of that time, when she was old enough Joan helped her father, Jacques, in the fields. She also took care of the family's animals, weeded the vegetable garden, and helped her mother in the house. She is said to have especially enjoyed weaving and spinning. Joan was never taught to read or write, but she had a passionate interest in the church and in God. At an early age, she prayed frequently and fervently. Long after her death her childhood companions remembered how they had teased their friend for her piety.

Life was precarious for the citizens of France. The Hundred Years War had been the agonizing backdrop of their lives for as long as anyone could remember. The English firmly believed that France should be part of England, and because of much intermarrying between the royal families of England and France, the line of succession was unclear.

The confusion started around 1392, when the French began hearing rumors that the man they considered the rightful king of France, Charles VI, was suffering bouts of madness. His uncle, Philip the Good (so-called), seized the reins of the kingdom. He and Charles's unpleasant wife, Queen Isabeau, were attempting to end the war in a way that was handsomely profitable to themselves and to England, but decidedly detrimental to France.

Philip was also the powerful Duke of Burgundy, whose lands—constituting a considerable portion of France—were under English control. He wanted France to give in to English demands in order to stop the endless fighting. Queen Isabeau went along with this plan and wheedled her mentally compromised husband into signing the Treaty of Troyes. This treaty gave Charles VI the right to rule France during his lifetime, but upon his death, Henry V of England would rule both countries. To make the provisions of the treaty more palatable, Henry V married Princess Catherine, the daughter of Charles VI and Queen Isabeau, so any children they had would be half-French.

It all might have worked, but for one person: Princess Catherine's younger brother, the crown prince Charles—or the Dauphin, as the French called him—who was intent on remaining in the line of succession. In 1422, to complicate things further, King Charles VI died. But the Duke of Burgundy and Queen Isabeau's plans to have England's Henry V succeed him were no longer possible because Henry himself had died two months earlier. Who then would become the next king of France? That was the question that burned in the hearts of every Frenchman—and that burned in the heart of the inhabitants of Joan's village, Domrémy.

There were two principal contenders: the Dauphin (Charles VII) and Henry VI, the infant son of Henry V and Catherine. The English and their allies, the Burgundians, who controlled northern France, predictably supported Henry VI, while those in southern France supported the Dauphin. So the war raged on, and now the French were fighting not only the English but each other as well.

Most of the Hundred Years War had been fought on French soil, and the French had not won any significant victories in decades. By 1429, when Joan was seventeen, the English had managed to conquer a good deal of France's northern territory, and sections of southwestern France were under the control of the Anglo-allied Burgundians. The French populace had suffered greatly during the bubonic plague pandemic (the Black Death) that first spread from China to Europe in the 1340s. French merchants were cut off from foreign markets, and the French economy was in shambles.

Joan and her fellow Domrémy villagers strongly supported the Dauphin and considered the English a foul enemy, in part because it was not unusual for English soldiers to march into French villages, killing civilians, burning homes, and stealing crops and cattle. But what could they do to ensure that the Dauphin would become king? It was not something that anyone would have thought probable. But around the time Joan was twelve, something began happening that would catapult her into the center of these events and make her the principal player in leading France to victory and making the Dauphin her rightful king: she began hearing voices and seeing visions. Joan said that messengers from heaven were visiting her in her father's garden. She believed them to be the archangel Michael, Saint Catherine, and Saint Margaret. At first they didn't say anything about France or her role in saving France from the English; they just encouraged Joan in her already deep faith.

Joan looked forward to and loved her interactions with these heavenly visitors, but over time their words to her became quite specific and serious. They informed her that she had a great mission to perform. She was to rescue France from the English and take the Dauphin to the city of Reims to be crowned. Like Mary, the mother of Jesus, Joan was amazed at what these heavenly visitors told her. Who was she to lead an army? She hardly knew how to mount a horse, much less how to lead soldiers into battle. But as she was a girl of deep faith, she did not doubt that these messengers were indeed from heaven and must be taken seriously.

Joan was not the only person in the family to be troubled by things difficult to understand. One night her father dreamed that his pretty, adolescent daughter would run away with soldiers. Misunderstanding its meaning, he dramatically instructed his sons to drown their sister if she ever did such a thing. He also preemptively began to plan for Joan's marriage to a local swain. Unbeknownst to her father, however, Joan had made a private vow to God never to marry. So when the time came, she refused to go through with the ceremony, despite the fact that her so-called fiancé went to court over the broken arrangement.

When Joan was about sixteen, her "voices," as she called them, told her that her time had come at last. They gave her specific instructions to travel to the town of Vaucouleurs. Once there, she was to ask Governor Robert de Baudricourt to provide her with an armed escort to the castle of Chinon, where the Dauphin and his court lived. Knowing how her parents would react, Joan told them she wished to visit her married cousin, Jeanne Laxart, who lived a short distance from Vaucouleurs. They allowed their daughter to go.

She did visit her cousin but then talked her cousin's husband, Durand, into taking her to see Baudricourt. The governor patiently listened to Joan describe how God had instructed her to lead an army in driving the English out of France and then to oversee the crowning of the Dauphin as king of France. But what was the esteemed and dignified governor to make of this simple girl's outrageous story? He did what anyone else likely would have done: he told Durand to send her home immediately but not before boxing her ears for all the trouble she was causing.

The frustrated Joan returned home, but no sooner had she arrived than the horrors of the war finally came to her own doorstep. Burgundian soldiers swept into Domrémy and cruelly laid waste to the entire village by fire. She and her fellow villagers fled to a nearby fortified town. Then, a few months later came worse news: the English had surrounded the great French city of Orléans and were laying siege to it. Joan's voices gave her an urgent new message: God intended for her to rescue Orléans.

Joan, now seventeen, returned to Vaucouleurs and spent the next six weeks attempting to see the governor again. While waiting, she spoke openly to all who would listen about her God-given mission. The Vaucouleurs townspeople remembered a famous prophecy that France would one day be lost by a woman and then restored by a maiden—a virgin. They came to assume that the woman who would lose France was the despicable Queen Isabeau and that the maiden who would restore their country might well be Joan. As for the governor, he was less encouraging and again dismissed her and her preposterous ideas.

But Joan did not take his rebuffs to heart. "I must be at the King's side," she insisted. "There will be no help if not from me. Although I would rather have remained spinning at my mother's side . . . yet must I go and must I do this thing, for my Lord wills that I do so."[2]

There's little doubt that Joan really did wish to remain at home with her family, doing the things she had grown up doing. But she knew that God himself was calling her to the task at hand. She would not disobey, and she would not relent until she had done what God called her to do.

Baudricourt agreed to see the persistent farm girl again, but this time, Joan told him something remarkable, something she had no way of knowing. In Mark Twain's fictional account of Joan's life, which he researched and wrote for twenty years, the outspoken religious skeptic presented this account of Joan's meeting with Baudricourt:

> "In God's name, Robert de Baudricourt, you are too slow about send- ing me, and have caused damage thereby, for this day the Dauphin's cause has lost a battle near Orléans, and will suffer yet greater injury if you do not send me to him soon."
>
> The governor was perplexed by this speech, and said:
>
> "To-day, child, to-day? How can you know what has happened in that region to-day? It would take eight or ten days for the word to come."
>
> "My voices have brought the word to me, and it is true. A battle was lost to-day, and you are in fault to delay me so."
>
> The governor walked the floor a while, talking within himself, but letting a great oath fall outside now and then; and finally he said:
>
> "Harkye! go in peace, and wait. If it shall turn out as you say, I will give you the letter and send you to the King, and not otherwise."
>
> Joan said with fervor: "Now God be thanked, these waiting days are almost done."[3]

Word arrived that the French had indeed lost the battle. The gov- ernor was flabbergasted and finally convinced.

Orléans, located along the Loire River, was the final obstacle to an assault on the rest of France and therefore of tremendous strategic importance. Given the unlikelihood that Orléans could long endure a lengthy siege, rescue of the city was essential if France were ever to rule itself again. But to see the Dauphin, Joan would have to travel to Chinon, where the royal court had relocated from Bourges.

Joan began working out practical details of her 350-mile journey. It was for her own safety when traveling across enemy territory that she decided to cut her hair short and dress as a man. The citizens of Vaucouleurs clearly saw the sense in this and provided her with masculine clothing—a tunic, hose, boots, and spurs. They also provided her with a horse, and Baudricourt himself gave Joan her first sword.

On a cold February night, Joan—who now simply called herself "La Pucelle," which translates to "the Maid," or "the Maiden," meaning a young woman or a virgin—swung herself atop her horse and began the long journey to Chinon, accompanied by six male escorts. They had agreed to travel by night and sleep by day in order to avoid enemy soldiers, whom they might otherwise encounter, as they rode through hostile Burgundian lands.

Eleven days later Joan and her escorts stopped in Fierbois, a three-hour ride from Chinon. There Joan dictated a letter to the Dauphin, asking to meet with him. The Dauphin agreed, and soon the little band clattered onto the cobblestoned streets of Chinon. Joan was met by many curious stares, for stories of the virgin who claimed she would save France had preceded her.

Like Robert de Baudricourt, the Dauphin had prepared a test for Joan. She had hinted in a letter that, although she had never met him, she would be able to identify the Dauphin. So Louis de Bourbon, Count of Vendôme, led Joan through a stone passage opening into the castle's grand hall, where she found herself in the company of hundreds of gorgeously dressed and bejeweled guests. After looking around for a moment, Joan walked straight toward the Dauphin and knelt before him. "God give you life, gentle king," she said.[4]

"I am not the king," the Dauphin replied. "There is the king!" he said, pointing to another man.

Joan responded, "In God's name, Sir, you *are* the King, and no other! Give me the troops wherewith to succour Orléans and to guard you to Rheims to be anointed and crowned. For it is the will of God."[5]

Still not quite convinced, the Dauphin took Joan aside to speak privately. In an effort to prove she had been sent by God, she told him about something he had done in private: he had prayed that God would reveal to him whether or not he was actually the son of Charles VI. His mother, hardly a virtuous woman, had claimed he was not. If he were not the son of the late king, the Dauphin prayed that God would take away his desire to rule.

The Dauphin was overjoyed when Joan told him that he was, indeed, of royal blood; she said that she knew this because her voices had told her. He then gave Joan a room in Chinon Castle's Tower of Coudray, along with a household staff, including a young page, who, all his long life afterward, recalled Joan's "prayers and her fervor."[6] She was also given a knight, John d'Aulon, and a chaplain, John Pasquerel, who later wrote a lively biography of her. Among the men who met with Joan was Jean d'Alençon, the celebrated Duke of Alençon and a cousin to the king, of whom Joan became fond, calling him her "handsome duke."

But not all the king's men were impressed with Joan. Georges de La Trémoille, Count of de Guînes, who had substantial influence over the Dauphin, said that he "found it absurd . . . that so young a girl of low birth, unlettered, lately come from nothingness, should play the leader."[7]

It was he and other advisers who urged the Dauphin to investigate Joan's background and claims and determine whether these voices of hers came from heaven or hell. Additional precious weeks passed as Joan was thoroughly investigated. She was required to travel to Poitiers, a university town, where the council of church scholars examined her. These men insisted she perform a miracle, which she refused to do. She might have told them about the miracle of her knowing the Dauphin's secret worries about his legitimacy, which he had confirmed, but she chose not to embarrass him by doing so.

The Dauphin's advisers remained skeptical. But Joan had no doubt about what God had told her and had grown impatient. "In the name of God," she replied, "I came not here to Poitiers to work miracles. At

Orléans you will see miracle enough. With a few men or with many, to Orléans will I go."[8]

Joan then prophesied to them that four events would take place. She said, "Orléans I shall relieve. The Dauphin I shall crown in Rheims. Paris will come back to its true king. The Duke of Orléans, captive in the Tower of London, will return home."[9]

In the end they agreed that the Dauphin would accept Joan's help. By then, as biographers Regine Pernoud and Véronique Clin put it, Joan "had come to personify hope, the type of hope that (according to the witnesses of her time) the distressed kingdom no longer maintained—that is, the hope of divine assistance."[10] She was given a military retinue consisting of a steward, pages, two heralds, messengers, and her brothers, John and Peter, along with the equipment she would need as the leader of an army. She was fitted out with a specially designed suit of armor, and the Dauphin himself gave her a magnificent horse.

Joan also required a standard. This flag was necessary so that soldiers would have a way of recognizing their commander when his—or her—visor was down, as it must be during the fighting. Joan explained that the voices had described to her just how it should appear. It should be made of "fine white linen, with the lilies of the realm scattered on it and sewn, and there was to be painted on it the figure of Our Lord with the world in His hand, and on either side two angels adoring, with the motto: 'Jesus, Mary.'" On Joan's blue shield was painted a white dove holding in its beak a scroll, upon which were written the words "By command of the King of Heaven."[11]

Joan already had a sword. Nonetheless she sent a letter to the priests of the shrine of Saint Catherine de Fierbois, the place where she had prayed while waiting to travel to Chinon. She told them to dig behind the altar, where they would discover a rusted sword that was engraved with five crosses. Her voices had told her the sword was there, and *mirabile dictu*—indeed it was. The priests dug and found it, removed the rust, and then sent it to Joan. The Maid did not intend to ever harm anyone with the sword. It was, she said, intended merely to be a symbol of command.

Joan began giving commands to her soldiers, instructions that probably astonished these rough men. She made it clear that the army she commanded would be God's army in every way. She told the men that they must not swear and must confess their sins. They also were to be just in everything they did. And although they would indeed be conquerors, they must not do what soldiers in those days almost always did: loot the villagers' homes and burn them. Joan personally chased "immoral women" from the camp. Her army also included priests, who morning and evening were assembled to sing hymns to the Virgin Mary.

Having a female leader, and a young one at that, was a new and challenging experience for the French soldiers. An eyewitness to the attitudes of the soldiers who fought under Joan's command, Gobert Thibault, described the phenomenon of an innocent young girl living among virile men: "I heard many of those closest to her say that they had never had any desire for her; that is to say, they sometimes felt a certain carnal urge but never dared to let themselves go with her, and they believed that it was not possible to desire her; I have questioned several of those who sometimes slept the night in Joan's company about this, and they answered as I have, adding that they had never felt any carnal desire when they saw her."[12]

Before engaging in the Battle of Orléans, Joan sent a letter to English leaders during Holy Week of 1429, urging them to "surrender to the Maid, who is sent here from God, the King of Heaven, the keys to all of the good cities that you have taken and violated in France. . . . She is entirely ready to make peace," it read, "if you are willing to settle accounts with her, provided that you give up France and pay for having occupied her."[13]

In the letter she ordered English troops to leave France and warned, "If you do not do so, I am commander of the armies, and in whatever place I shall meet your French allies, I shall make them leave it, whether they wish to or not; and if they will not obey, I shall have them all killed. . . . If you do not wish to believe this message from God through the Maid, then wherever we find you we will strike you there, and make a great uproar greater than any made in France for a thousand years."[14]

The English were not impressed. They warned Joan that if they caught her, they would burn her at the stake. Joan and her troops likely assembled at the Blois fortress on the Loire, about halfway between Tours and Orléans. Both Tours and Blois were controlled by the French. The English controlled the Loire's right bank, upriver. Joan's confessor, John Pasquerel, described this moment: "They marched out on the side of the Solonge [the south bank of the Loire] . . . camped in the fields that night and the following day as well. On the third day, they arrived near Orléans, where the English had set up their siege along the bank of the Loire. And the king's soldiers came so close to the English that Englishmen and Frenchmen could see one another within easy reach."[15]

Joan was about to meet the man who would become her great ally: Jean d'Orléans, the Count of Dunois, known throughout his life as the Bastard of Orléans because he was the illegitimate half brother of the Duke of Orléans. But this Bastard, alas, believing he knew far more about battle tactics than a teenage girl, had deceived Joan. He was now in charge of Orléans troops (because his half brother, the duke, was being held prisoner in London). He arranged for Joan's soldiers to make a long detour, causing them to come in "well arrayed up to the banks of the Loire on the Sologne side."[16] He had decided on this detour in order to keep clear of the English, who had staked out positions in the vicinity of Orléans. But Joan, eager to begin fighting, discovered that she and her men had been duped and had in fact bypassed Orléans.

Joan was livid and gave the Bastard a tongue-lashing he would never forget. Approaching him on horseback, she asked, "Are you the one who gave orders for me to come here, on this side of the river, so that I could not go directly to [General John] Talbot and the English?"

As the Bastard recalled later, "I answered that I, and others, including the wisest men around me, had given this advice, believing it best and safest."

"In God's name," Joan replied, "the counsel of Our Lord God is wiser and safer than yours. You thought that you could fool me, and instead you fooled yourself; I bring you better help than ever came to you from any soldier to any city: It is the help of the King of Heaven."[17]

The English soldiers had camped mainly along the Loire outside the western gate of Orléans. Joan said the English would not come out from their forts or their camp, and she was right. Their strength was insufficient, so for the time being they stayed with their guns, waiting for reinforcements to arrive. If she had gone there when she had wanted to, her forces would have had the advantage.

Joan at last made a triumphal entry into the besieged city on the evening of April 29, 1429, accompanied by the Bastard and many other noblemen and men at arms. The crowds, holding torches high, cheered and reached up to touch her as she made her way from the Burgundy Gate across the city to the home of Jacques Boucher, today the Maison de Jeanne d'Arc. Seeing the famous Maid gave the people tremendous hope. She was wise beyond her years and yet innocent; she was strong and vulnerable; she was bold and humble. She was all these things at once, and she seemed to embody France itself, and hope itself too.

Joan lodged at Boucher's home and spent the next nine days impatiently waiting to go into battle. The Bastard had convinced her to wait until reinforcements arrived from the Dauphin. She twice went out to stand on the bridge of Orléans and trade insults with the English; she urged them to surrender or be slaughtered. The English in turn called her a cow-herd and insulted her soldiers with crude epithets.

In the meantime, the Bastard had ridden out to meet the French reinforcements, and when he returned he had news: a new English army, commanded by the famous captain John Fastolf, had been sent to Orléans to lead the battle against them. Joan was delighted that at last the battle would begin, but she took no chances that the Bastard might again deceive her. Turning to him, she warned, "Bastard, O

Bastard, in God's name, I order you, as soon as you know of Fastolf's coming, to let me know it!"[18] He promised that he would.

But when the first short skirmish occurred, Joan was asleep, and nobody thought to wake her. The Bastard took the army to attack the fortress at Saint-Loup. Joan suddenly awoke, telling her steward, Jean d'Aulon, that her voices had told her to "go against the English,"[19] but she was unsure whether this meant she should attack their fortifications or Fastolf, who was coming to resupply them.

After lashing out at her page for neglecting to wake her while French blood was being spilled, Joan shouted for her horse to be readied and her standard brought while she dressed quickly. She then rode to the Burgundy Gate, where a battle was raging. As soon as the French forces saw Joan, their spirits soared. They raised a shout and managed to take both the *bastide* (fortified town) and the fortress itself. In terms of territory, the victory was rather insignificant, but the revitalizing effect it had on French forces was extraordinary.

The brutal reality of war, however, which Joan had never before seen, greatly disturbed her, and when she saw the many wounded and dead French soldiers, she wept. Joan went to confession afterward and urged her fellow soldiers to "confess their sins publicly and to give thanks to God for the victory that He had granted."[20]

Two days later Joan was readying herself for combat when she ran into Raoul de Gaucourt, the governor of Orléans, who told her he would not allow her to make an attack that day because the captains did not want her to do so. But Joan was defiant. "[W]hether you wish it or not," she told him, "the men-at-arms will come and gain what they gained the other day."[21]

So Joan and her soldiers crossed the Loire. The Maid led her troops to the left bank, where the English had erected another bastide. But then she saw that it was deserted. The English had escaped up river to a second bastide, one that was stronger. The English withdrawal made a French advance more dangerous, but Joan rode toward them nonetheless. An eyewitness, Jean d'Aulon, noted:

When they perceived that the enemy was coming out of the Bastide of the Augustinians to rush upon them, the Maid and La Hire, who were always in front of their men to protect them, immediately couched their lances and led the attack upon the enemy. Everyone followed them, and they began to strike the enemy in such a manner that they constrained them by sheer force to withdraw and to return to the Bastide. . . . With great diligence, they assailed that bastide from all directions so that they seized it and took it by assault quickly. The greater part of the enemy were killed or captured.[22]

Joan had again won a tremendous victory, but once more the Dauphin and his counselors dithered about what to do next. They complained that there were too few French and too many English. The city of Les Tourelles was well provisioned with food, they said, so why not simply guard it while waiting for the king's help?

Joan would have none of it. She ordered Pasquerel to rise early the next day, May 7, 1430, and prepare for battle. They would attack the fortress of Les Tourelles. She prophesied that she would be wounded in the fighting above the left breast, but that the wound would not be fatal, and the French would take Les Tourelles. This was precisely what happened.

The great Anglo-French writer and historian Hilaire Belloc described the battle: "The stone walls of the rampart swarmed with the scaling ladders full of men hurled down [under an assault of arrows] and assault upon assault repelled, and the Maid in the midst with her banner; when, at noon, a shaft struck right through the white shoulder plate over her left breast and she fell."[23] .

Joan bravely pulled the arrow out herself, had the wound treated with olive oil, rested awhile, and then leapt back into the fray. By nightfall the soldiers had spent thirteen exhausting hours in battle. The English were certain of victory, especially when they heard the Bastard's trumpets sounding retreat. But Joan had no doubt that the French would win. After going away for a time of prayer while her exhausted men rested and had something to eat, Joan convinced the Bastard to make one final assault. Holding her standard high so that her men could see it in the fading light, she shouted, "When the flag touches the stone, all is yours!"[24] The weary soldiers rose to the occasion magnificently, breaking down the English defenses and pouring over the walls.

The English ran for their lives toward a wooden drawbridge, but the French had torched a boat and sent it floating beneath the bridge. It caught fire. As the English raced across it, a portion collapsed. All those soldiers who fell into the water in their heavy armor drowned. The citizens of Orléans came forward to patch the bridge with ladders and planks then rushed across the structure "to attack the fort from the rear, setting it on fire with flaming arrows."[25] At last the towers fell, and everyone within the fortress was killed or taken prisoner.

It was a tremendous victory, so great that today, nearly six hundred years later, the French still celebrate it every May 7. Despite her injury Joan visited the bridge that night to see the rejoicing of the citizens of newly freed Orléans. From his position on the far side of the river, the English general, Lord Talbot, heard bells of celebration ringing through the night. He pulled his troops out of the remaining forts that surrounded Orléans.

Orléans was relieved, just as Joan had prophesied. Now she must crown France's rightful king at Reims. The following day she and the Bastard rode to the castle of Loches to meet the Dauphin, who was overjoyed to see her. She urged him to travel immediately to Reims, the traditional place for crowning French kings. But again the Dauphin's counselors were unwilling to act quickly. They would spend nearly two weeks debating what should be done next. She continued to press the Dauphin to act. Her voices had told her that she would have only a year to achieve her goals. "Dauphin, noble Dauphin," she said, "linger not here in council with many words, but come to Reims and be crowned! For the voice calls to me: 'Go forward, Daughter of God; I am with you. Go! Go!'"[26]

In the end the Dauphin was finally convinced, and the army set out to clear the towns for his unimpeded passage to Reims. The objective of the Loire campaign, commanded by the Duke of Alençon, "was to dislodge the enemy from their entrenched positions on the banks of the Loire River and in the plains to the north, in order to protect the rear of the army when it departed for Reims."[27]

But Reims was roughly twice as far away as Paris and deep within enemy territory, so the idea that the Maid and her soldiers would travel there was unthinkable to the English. They assumed the French would do the sensible thing and attack Normandy or attempt to recapture Paris.

It was a stunning campaign, taking just one week. First, the French captured Jargeau, the town to which the English had fled following their rout at Orléans. Joan "stood to see the firing of the great gun brought from Orléans, and when . . . a tower fell, [the Duke of] Alençon dreaded the breach, thinking it not wide enough yet and too high piled with stone; but she said to him. 'To the Breach and fear nothing! This is the hour of God's pleasure; and do you not remember how I told your wife in Tours that I would bring you home?'"[28]

Joan was injured during this battle when she attempted to scale a ladder. A stone struck her helmet, causing her to tumble to the ground. But she quickly recovered and shouted to her men: "On, friends, on! Hearts high! We have them in this hour!"[29]

Once again inspired by the Maid, her soldiers captured the town. Many English lost their lives, and the English leader, the Duke of Suffolk, was captured. Then Joan and the Duke of Alençon rode triumphantly back to Orléans. By now, her reputation was such that English-held towns simply opened their gates to her. With no effort, her soldiers took the towns of Meung-sur-Loire and Beaugency.

But at last the army of Sir John Fastolf had arrived, and Lord Talbot would have help. Their combined forces marched confidently toward the French in what would be remembered as the Battle of Patay. The French victory on June 18 was a rout, one of inconceivable and absurd proportions. History records that the French lost three men, while the casualties on the English side numbered more than four thousand.

When Joan and her army returned victorious to Orléans, the citizens erupted with jubilation. She would at last travel with the Dauphin to Reims to crown him king. But again his court wrung their hands and delayed his departure. There were still some walled cities held by the Burgundians, they said, so they did not think the Dauphin should make the trip. She went to him and urged him to go to Reims immediately. He must be crowned king, she said, and soon! The Dauphin thanked her for her victories on his behalf but suggested she first rest before they make the journey. She knew this would be a mistake and persisted. Finally the Dauphin relented, and in late June, Joan and her men set out for Reims, with the Dauphin following two days later.

Upon the Dauphin's arrival in Reims on July 16, the citizens cheered themselves hoarse for joy. Even Joan's father and mother had traveled there to witness the great, almost incredible accomplishment of their daughter. Two of her brothers had come as well. But even in the midst of this long-sought climax, she was already looking forward to what lay ahead. The following morning, as preparations went forward for the coronation, she dictated a letter to the Duke of Burgundy, demanding that he make a "firm and lasting peace with the king of France."

"You two must pardon one another fully with a sincere heart, as loyal Christians should," she added. "I must make known to you from the King of Heaven, my rightful and sovereign Lord, for your good and for your honor and upon your life, that you will win no more battles against loyal Frenchmen."[30]

Later that day, to shouts of acclamation, the Dauphin rode his horse into the Cathedral of Reims itself, there to be crowned king. And standing beside the Dauphin was the humble Maid whose faith and fire had brought it all to pass. As the crown was set upon the Dauphin's head, Joan knelt beside the man who now, in this moment, was officially King Charles VII. With tears running down her face, she said, "High-born King, now is the will of God accomplished. For He it was who ordained that I should free Orléans and bring you here to this city of Reims for your sacring, to blazon it forth that you are Rightful Lord. And now the Realm of France is yours."[31]

As a reward for her services to him, King Charles granted Joan's wish that her home village of Domrémy be forever exempt from paying taxes. That was all she had asked, and this promise was kept for four centuries.

Tragically, however, this weak monarch would in a very short time betray the noble woman who had done so much to place the crown of France upon his head.

◆ ◆ ◆

The crowning of Charles would have significant consequences. Cities that had been under the control of the English-allied Burgundians were now prepared to recognize Charles as their rightful ruler. And Joan's army, under the command of the Duke of Alençon, was eager to take back Paris—just as she had prophesied—and not only that, but to drive the English out of all of France once and for all.

Joan had not once failed in her advice to the king; all she had said had, in fact, come to pass. Nonetheless, Charles and his advisers didn't trust her instincts. They had ideas of winning the war in other, easier ways. They hoped to persuade the Duke of Burgundy to break his alliance with the English and to join the French side. They did not tell Joan that the king had agreed to a fifteen-day truce with the Duke of Burgundy, wherein the duke had promised to surrender Paris at the conclusion of that time. In truth, the deceptive duke would double-cross them. He had only bought time with his lie and was awaiting the arrival of reinforcements from England—some thirty-five hundred of them.

When Joan became aware of the truce, she was immediately suspicious, so on August 5, she wrote to the citizens of Reims:

It's true that the King has made a truce with the Duke of Burgundy lasting fifteen days, by which he [Burgundy] must turn over the city of Paris peaceably at the end of fifteen days. However, do not be surprised if I don't enter it [Paris] so quickly. I am not at all content with truces made like this, and I don't know if I will uphold them; but if I do uphold them it will only be in order to protect the honor of the King; also, they [the Burgundians] will not cheat the Royal family, for I will maintain and keep the King's army together so as to be ready at the end of these fifteen days if they don't make peace.[32]

In the meantime Joan and the French army marched through towns near Paris, in each case not having to fight but accepting a peaceful surrender.

Joan knew that attacking Paris would be difficult, much more so than the Battle of Orléans. Paris was well fortified and even surrounded by a moat. But she was undeterred. As she had always done before attacking, she shouted to the English to surrender or die; and as they had before previous battles, they vowed to fight.

On September 8, the French forces under Joan's leadership began the attack. At one point, she decided that she herself would determine the depth of the moat. But just as she was dipping her lance into the moat's water, an arrow from an English crossbow struck her in the thigh, in the very place where her armor did not protect her. Lying on the ground in pain, she urged her soldiers to leave her where she was and continue the battle, but the Raoul de Gaucourt and others came to her and carried her off, ending the assault.

It is worth noting that Joan had not received any instructions from her voices regarding this battle and was now acting on her own initiative. She was never to receive their advice again regarding battle tactics.

The next day brought terrible news. King Charles himself had ordered that they cease the assault on Paris altogether. Once again the timorous, irresolute Charles had been influenced to take this stand by his advisers—particularly Grand Chamberlain Georges de la Trémoille, who disliked Joan.

The Maid's brief but remarkable military career was now nearing its end. Her voices had warned her in June that she would soon be captured, that she should "take it favorably,"[33] and that God would aid her.

In October Joan's army captured Saint-Pierre-le-Moûtier but failed to take La Charité-sur-Loire. King Charles had signed a truce with England, leaving a frustrated Joan idle—until the truce ended the following spring. In May 1430 English and Burgundian forces attacked Compiègne, and Joan traveled there with a small force of four hundred men to take part in the city's defense.

During the May 23 battle the French, seeing six thousand Burgundian reinforcements approaching and fearing that they would be overwhelmed, rushed onto the bridge of boats that Guillaume de Flavy had strung out across the Oise. Joan, who never withdrew without regret, protected their retreat. Perceval de Cagney later described what happened: "During that time, the captain of the place, seeing the great multitude of Burgundians and Englishmen ready to get on the bridge, out of fear that he would lose his position, raised the drawbridge of the city and closed the gate. So the Maid remained outside and only a few of her men were with her."[34] Joan fought the enemy bravely until one of them yanked her off her horse and threw her to the ground.

Biographers have their doubts about this description. Pernoud and Clin, for example, noted that it was not "the main gate of the city that had been closed but a gate in the curtain wall, which was not vital to the defense of the city proper and which presumably cut off the combatants' retreat. This is why—though reasonable skepticism persists—some believe that Joan's fear of betrayal was fulfilled."[35]

Joan now became a prisoner of Lionel of Wandomme, a lieutenant of John of Luxembourg, who was, in turn, under the Duke of Burgundy's control. Lionel transported her to Margny-lès-Compiègne, where she was kept under guard in a tower at Beaurevoir Castle until November.

The English, who had come to believe they would never win glory on the field of battle while the Maid lived, rejoiced at her capture and immediately began pressuring the Duke of Burgundy to hand her over to them. The duke eventually agreed, accepting a ransom of ten thousand francs, in addition to six thousand francs for the soldiers who had actually captured the Maid.

Joan far preferred death to being given over to the English, and while these negotiations regarding her fate took place, she seems to have wished to end her life, leaping from the seventy-foot-high tower in which she was being held. But somehow she survived, landing on a patch of soft earth. She was discovered unconscious hours later and returned to her cell, having escaped not only death, but injury. This was one of several efforts she made to escape. But now one of her voices—she said it was Saint Catherine—told Joan to "confess myself and ask pardon from God for having jumped."[36]

King Charles had initially promised vengeance for the capture of Joan. After all, it was her fearless obedience to God that had brought him the French crown. But, in fact, he did nothing to help her during this time.

Joan was then taken to Rouen, the seat of the English occupation government, where she was put in chains in a castle dungeon to await trial. There, five male guards mocked and insulted her and made efforts to violate her. Fear of rape led Joan to continue wearing her masculine attire, which offered more protection than a dress.

In January 1431 it was announced that a church court would try Joan for heresy, blasphemy, and witchcraft. She pointed out that if this were the case, she ought to be held in a church prison and attended by nuns. But this ecclesiastical rule, like many others, was flouted.

Her trial began on January 9, 1431, and lasted five miserable months. The main judge in this sham court was Pierre Cauchon, whose appointment to this position was no coincidence. Cauchon despised Joan for humiliating him and damaging his career. Under his leadership as rector of the University of Paris, the university had thrown its support behind the Burgundians and developed the "double monarchy" theory—the idea that an English king should rule both England and France. But thanks to Joan, he and his theory were out of favor. Just before the coronation, he had been living in Reims. He was forced to flee from that city to Beavais. Then when that town welcomed Charles VII, he had to flee again. If during this trial Joan could be proved a heretic, Cauchon might have his revenge. He would see his "double monarchy" theory again viewed with the admiration it had once enjoyed.

Many witnesses were called in the trial, including bishops, abbots, and specialists in church law, but witnesses on Joan's behalf were not allowed to take part. Clerical notary Nicolas Bailly, commissioned to collect testimony against Joan, could find no adverse evidence, so legally speaking, there ought not to have been a trial at all. Her adversaries denied her the right to legal counsel and made certain that the tribunal sitting in judgment upon her was made up entirely of pro-English clergy. Documents were falsified, and any authorities who protested her treatment had their lives threatened. Such threats—and the domination of this trial by the secular English government—made the trial a mockery of justice. They were clear violations of the church's rules about such trials, which must be held without any interference from secular entities.

Still the trial took place, and it is one of the remarkable facts of history that the transcript of it survives. It reveals how bafflingly well this simple peasant girl performed against her highly educated, hostile English adversaries. Those who questioned her behaved much as attorneys do today, hoping to confuse her by jumping around in their questioning. They also repeated questions in an effort to get her to contradict herself. But to their chagrin and astonishment, she performed brilliantly.

At one point the members of the tribunal were so frustrated that they considered torturing Joan, but in the end they decided against it. In March she made a prediction, telling her goggle-eyed inquisitors,

"Within seven years the English will lose a greater prize than Orléans, and then, all France."[37] They hardly knew what to make of this, but she would be proved correct in 1450, when the English were finally driven from Paris and then lost the Battle of Formigny, in which they sacrificed some twenty-five hundred men—about 50 percent of their force. As a result, the French were able to retake much of their territory.

But Joan's most impressive moment came when she was asked a trick question: "Are you in a state of grace?" If she answered yes, she would have been charged with heresy, because the church taught that no one can know with certainty that he or she is in a state of grace. But if she answered no, it would be tantamount to acknowledging her own guilt. She cleverly replied, "If I am not, may God put me there; and if I am, may God so keep me."[38] According to a witness, her interrogators were astonished.

Joan also announced that her voices had told her that in three months she would be free. Whether she knew her freedom would come in the form of death we cannot know.

Exactly one year to the day of her capture, a priest arrived to exhort Joan "in loyalty to God . . . to accept authority and to submit."[39] It is possible he believed that Joan suffered from delusions and wished to save her from the terrible death that awaited her if she did not repent.

On May 14 Cauchon received a letter from the rector of the University of Paris to announce that, after various consultations and deliberations, they had reached unanimous consensus that the time had come to act. It declared that Joan was "an apostate, a liar, a schismatic, and a heretic."[40] Cauchon lost no time in sharing these conclusions with Joan's inquisitors. On May 23 they gave her their final and formal admonition.

Her reply was characteristically defiant and guileless. "If I were already judged and saw the fire lit," she said, "and the bundles of sticks ready and the executioners ready to light the fire, and even if I were within the fire, I would nevertheless not say anything other. I would maintain unto death what I have said in this trial."[41]

The following day Cauchon, intent on creating a dramatic spectacle, set up platforms in the abbey of Saint-Ouen's cemetery, one for Joan and additional ones for her judges. She was forced to listen to a sermon by the canon of Rouen, Guillaume Erard. Following the sermon, Erard ordered her: "Behold my Lords your Judges, who, at divers times, have summoned and required you to submit yourself, your words and deeds, to Our Holy Church, showing you that there did exist in your words and deeds many things which, as it did seem to the Clergy, are not good either to say or maintain."[42]

Joan was then handed a letter of abjuration, an oath of repudiation. Jean Massieu, an usher, urged her to sign it, so that her life might be spared. Twenty-five years later, Massieu reported it was clear to him that she did not seem to understand the document. The illiterate Maid asked that the letter "be inspected by the clerks, and that they should give her counsel." But Erard ordered Joan to sign the document immediately, "otherwise you will end your days by fire."[43]

And so, with the help of Laurence Calot, Joan signed the document by drawing a circle and a cross.

What did that document actually say, and what did Joan's peculiar "signature" signify? After all, she had signed documents before by writing her name. According to Pernoud and Clin, the document "was said to contain a promise that Joan would no longer wear men's clothes. According to the testimony of Guillaume Manchon, who in his capacity as a notary should have been aware of the meaning of this scene, Joan laughed. We may ask if the cross that she had just drawn in place of a signature . . . might not have been a reference to the cross she had sometimes put on military messages, as a previously agreed signal indicating that whoever received that letter should consider it null and void."[44]

The crowd of Englishmen were angry because their dearest wish— that Joan be condemned and executed—had not taken place. After serving a term as a heretic, she might well be allowed to return home. The Earl of Warwick complained, but Cauchon quietly reassured him: "My Lord, do not worry; we will catch her again."[45]

Afterward, Joan again asked to be placed into a church prison but was instead taken back to her dank castle cell. This decision was more crucial than it may appear. If convicted heretics relapsed, religious authorities could condemn them to death and hand them over to civil authorities, who would then carry out the sentence. As Pernoud and Clin explain, Cauchon "had succeeded only in making men's clothes the symbol of Joan's refusal to submit to the church."[46] She had promised not to wear them. But once back in her cell, she was again threatened with rape by her guards.

One witness said that three days later, she resumed wearing men's clothing, because they provided a better defense against sexual assault. Another witness said she resumed wearing them because her guards had removed her feminine clothing while she slept and thrown a bag filled with men's attire into her cell.

Regardless of the reason, when Cauchon discovered that Joan was once again wearing men's clothing, he quickly went to the castle prison. With him were Jean Lemaitre, the vice-inquisitor, and several others. Why, they demanded to know, had Joan resumed wearing men's clothing? She replied:

> I did it on my own will . . . because it was more lawful and convenient than to have women's clothes because I am with men; I began to wear them again because what was promised me was not observed, to wit that I should go to mass and receive the body of Christ and be freed from these irons. I would rather die than stay in these irons; but if it is permitted for me to go to mass, and if I could be freed of these irons, and if I could be put in a decent prison and if I could have a woman to help me, I would be good and do what the church wishes.[47]

Joan was then asked if she had heard from her voices. Yes, she replied; they had told her of God's "great sorrow that I did a very wicked thing to which I consented in abjuring and making a revocation, and said that I was damning myself to save my life."[48]

That was all Cauchon needed to hear. He left the prison, immediately went to the castle court, and told the Earl of Warwick: "Make good cheer. It is done."[49]

On May 30 two priests came to Joan and told her she would die at the stake that very morning. She burst into tears. When Cauchon visited her later, she lashed out at him, saying, "Bishop, it is by you that I die!"

The bishop condescendingly explained that Joan was to be executed because she did not keep her promise to refrain from wearing men's clothing. Enraged, Joan answered, "Had you put me in the Church's prison with women to guard me as was of right, this would not have been. I summon you before God the great Judge."[50]

Once more Cauchon violated procedural rules, which called for Joan to be taken to a hall where a secular bailiff could hear her case and pronounce a secular sentence. But he was taking no chances that she would escape the punishment he had marked out for her. Two hundred guards escorted her to the Old Marketplace, where the stake had been prepared atop a huge pile of wood. She was forced to wear a paper miter emblazoned with the words *"Heretique, Relapse, Apostat, Idolatre"* (Heretic, Relapsed, Apostate, Idolator).

The English soldiers helped her climb the wood piled around the stake and tied her to it with chains. She then asked for a cross. A sympathetic English soldier devised one of sticks and gave it to her. She kissed it and pushed it inside her clothing, and then she publicly forgave her enemies. Friar Isambart de la Pierre, intent on finding her a crucifix, located one in the Saint-Laurent church. But when he returned he saw that a torch already had been put to the wood beneath the Maid. As the flames crackled and Joan burned, he held the crucifix aloft so that she could look upon it.

According to witnesses, she continued "to praise God and the saints while lamenting devoutly; the last word she cried in a high voice as she died was: 'Jesus!'"[51]

Many in the English crowd that day—and there were hundreds—wept in pity for the girl. Joan's own cries deeply disturbed her executioner, who told a friar "that he had sinned gravely and that he repented what he had done against Joan, whom he now took to be a holy woman; for as it seemed to him, this Englishman had himself seen, at the moment that Joan gave up her spirit, a white dove emerge from her and take flight toward France."[52]

Jean Tressart, secretary to England's king, having seen Joan burn, lamented, "We are all ruined, for a good and holy person was burned."[53]

In order to prevent the collection of relics, English soldiers dug through the coals to expose her burned body. Concerned that people would claim that she had escaped death by fire, they then set fire to her body twice more; nothing now remained but ashes.

Her remains were then cast into the Seine. Thus ended the mortal life of Joan of Arc, the savior of France.

But that is not the end of her story. In 1449, eighteen years after Joan's death, King Charles VII, along with Joan's mother and Inquisitor-General Jean Bréhal, asked Pope Callixtus III to authorize posthumously a "nullification trial" to determine whether Joan's original trial had been just, according to canon law. The pope agreed. Empaneled theologians called 115 witnesses and examined their testimony. In 1456 Bréhal issued a final summary. It was an utter repudiation of the previous verdict. Joan, he declared, was innocent. He further decreed that not only had she been killed unjustly but she had suffered a martyr's death.

Cauchon had Joan executed because she had supposedly violated biblical teachings about the proper clothing for men and women, but that conviction was reversed "in part because the condemnation proceeding had failed to consider the doctrinal exceptions to that stricture."[54]

But there was more to come. The vile Cauchon, who had convicted and executed the innocent Joan for personal reasons, was now himself denounced by the court as a heretic. It was poetic justice, marred only by the fact that Cauchon had died years before.

Nearly five hundred years after her death, in 1909, Joan of Arc was beatified; and in 1920, she was canonized as a saint in the Catholic Church.

TWO
Susanna Wesley

1669–1742

W hile writing my book about William Wilberforce,[1] I first came to appreciate the historic and cultural earthquake known as the Wesleyan Revival. Most of the dramatic social advances of the nineteenth century—including all that Wilberforce and his friend Hannah More were able to accomplish—were a direct result of that unprecedented outpouring of faith. It can be said without exaggeration that John and Charles Wesley's efforts—their evangelism and service to the poor, the disenfranchised, and the hopeless—changed the world. It also can be said without exaggeration that who these great men were and all they did in their lives had everything to do with the extraordinary woman who raised them.

◆ ◆ ◆

S usanna Annesley Wesley came into the world in 1669, the twenty-fifth of twenty-five children born to her parents, the Rev. Samuel Annesley and his wife, Mary. Bitter religious controversies raged in England at that time. At the center of them all was the battle between the Church of England and the Puritans. King Charles I represented the Church of England, and Oliver Cromwell led the Puritans.

Having gained the upper hand in 1649, Cromwell and the Puritans had King Charles I imprisoned and then beheaded. Cromwell ruled England until his death in 1658, at which point the Royalists returned to power, making Charles I's son, Charles II, the new king. In 1662, in an attempt to wipe out Puritanism for good, Parliament passed the Act of Uniformity, decreeing that all religious leaders must follow the teachings of the Church of England.[2] But at the risk of their lives, two thousand ministers bravely refused to do this. One of them was Susanna's father, Samuel Annesley. As a result he lost his position, causing considerable hardship for his large family. In 1672, ten years after the act was passed, Charles II softened it, and most of the two thousand ministers immediately went back to their preaching.

Susanna Wesley was remarkably intelligent. While still a young girl her brilliant, curious mind absorbed and analyzed what was happening around her, especially since her own father and family were directly affected by it. Her childhood home was often filled with the intelligent and well-read friends of her father—including Daniel Defoe, the author of *Robinson Crusoe*—who vigorously debated theological issues. We don't know whether she attended a local school or was taught by older family members, but there can be little doubt she read many of the volumes in her father's library. Years later, as a mother teaching her own children, Susanna displayed, according to biographer Arnold A. Dallimore, "a theological knowledge superior to that of many ministers of that day."[3]

Given what her father suffered at the hands of the Royalists, it is quite remarkable that Susanna, at the age of twelve, made up her mind to become a member of the Church of England. Perhaps more remarkable yet is that her father gave her the liberty to do so. Her own account of her decision underscores her precocity. "Because I had been educated among the Dissenters," she wrote, "and there being something remarkable in my leaving them at so early an age, not being full thirteen, I had drawn up an account of the whole transaction, under which I included in the main of the controversy between them and the Established Church, as far as it had come to my knowledge."[4]

At her sister Elizabeth's wedding the following year, the brilliant thirteen-year-old met her future husband, nineteen-year-old Samuel Wesley. Samuel's father—another Dissenter—had died in prison, where he was serving time for preaching the Puritan way. Thanks to the generosity of his father's friends, Samuel had attended a Dissenting academy, where he focused on classical studies.

Despite his father's imprisonment and death at the hands of the established church, Samuel, like Susanna, had decided to join the Church of England. It's possible this was in part because he saw within the church's leadership structure a better chance of promotion through the ranks than with the Dissenters. In 1683 he began his studies at Oxford's Exeter College, supporting himself through publishing poetry, tutoring other students, and doing translations for Oxford's Bodleian Library. He took his bachelor of arts degree in 1688 and soon afterward was ordained and given a curacy, at which point he felt free to marry. He and Susanna had stayed in touch since their meeting six years earlier. They married on November 11, 1688. He was twenty-six, and she, nineteen.

Until their marriage, the couple had known each other almost exclusively through the letters they exchanged, but after they were married, they discovered to their dismay that, beyond their shared enthusiasm for the Church of England, they had less in common with each other than they might have hoped. One other thing they did have in common was a certain stubbornness, which would cause them difficulties in the years ahead.

Samuel could be impulsive too. For example, he had been in his curacy for only a few months when he decided to accept a position as a chaplain aboard a navy ship. It was true that the position offered more than twice what he had made as a curate, but a few months after the chaplaincy had begun, he gave that up as well, claiming he was mistreated and that the food was terrible. Things got so bad financially that Susanna, who was now pregnant, was obliged to live in a boarding house until he returned, after which they went to stay with her parents to await the baby's arrival.

On February 10, 1690, Susanna gave birth to the couple's first son, Samuel. The new father again found work as a curate and supplemented his meager pay with writing. But the rector of the church disapproved of his curate doing other work and promptly fired him. So the small family returned to the boarding house. Samuel was then offered a position as rector of St. Leonard's Church, located on the Isle of Axholme, a river-island in the northwest corner of Lincolnshire. He accepted the post, again supplementing his income with literary endeavors.

He soon found himself indebted to a number of people from whom he had borrowed money to furnish the rectory and to purchase farming implements. Sadly, the interest on and repayment of these sums would remain a burden for the remainder of his life.

More children followed in quick succession. A girl, named Susanna for her mother, was born in 1694; another daughter, Emelia, was born within the year but died some months after. In 1695 the Wesleys lost twin boys, who were just a few weeks old.

Susanna's father, Samuel Annesley, died in 1696, and for reasons no one can know, he left all his money to his other children. It is likely this was due in part to her decision to become a member of the Church of England. Nevertheless, she grieved greatly for her father.

Three more daughters—Susanna (nicknamed Sukey), Mary, and Mehetabel (nicknamed Hetty)—were born, followed by another set of twins, a boy and a girl, who both died shortly after their birth in 1701.

Daughters Anne and Martha followed a few years later, while John and Charles, brothers whose world-changing ministry would carry the Wesley name into the history books, came into the world in 1703 and 1707.

In 1697, following the death of King James II, William and Mary arrived from Holland to rule as king and queen of England. (Mary was King James's daughter.) Samuel Wesley had dedicated his book, *Life of Christ*, to her, and he now found himself invited by King William himself to become rector of a parish in Epworth, which paid far more than what he was receiving at St. Leonard's. So the family promptly packed up and moved to the three-story rectory. Epworth was located in a rural backwater about as remote from civilization and its benefits as one can imagine.

Writing to her brother, Susanna laments that this was hardly the ideal situation for the erudite man of letters who was her husband: "And did I not know that Almighty Wisdom hath views and ends in fixing the bounds of our habitation, which are out of our ken, I should think it a thousand pities that a man of his brightness and rare endowments of learning and useful knowledge in relation to the church of God should be confined to an obscure corner of the country, where his talents are buried, and he determined to a way of life for which he is not so well qualified as I could wish."[5]

◆ ◆ ◆

But the distance from literary society was not the principal difficulty. Not long after moving to Epworth, Samuel Wesley's renown had the odd result of adding to the family's growing debts. He was invited to preach the Visitation Sermon in Gainsborough and to speak before the Society for the Reformation of Manners. These were great honors, but the humble man of God was expected to pay his own traveling expenses. In addition his position as a proctor of the Lincoln diocese was also unpaid.

Samuel decided to try his hand at farming to supplement his

income. He worked hard, but still the debts increased. In 1700 Samuel appealed to the Archbishop of York, Dr. John Sharpe, listing all his expenses—including rebuilding a barn and supporting his elderly mother—which had led to his falling three hundred pounds into debt, an astounding sum, considering his annual salary was just two hundred pounds. The archbishop was moved to help Samuel financially and even prevailed upon others to do so. But his financial difficulties continued. He was overwhelmed by it all, especially given the increasing number of children he had to support. He fell into a depression, terribly disappointed that he had not made more of a success of his life.

It was during this time that he made a desperate and irresponsible decision: he abandoned his wife, his children, and his congregation. The reason he gave for leaving had nothing to do with his finances. Many years later, his son John described the grim situation: "The year before King William died my father observed my mother did not say amen to the prayer for the king. She said she could not, for she did not believe that the Prince of Orange was king. He vowed he would not cohabit with her till she did. He then took horse and rode away; nor did she hear anything of him for a twelvemonth."[6]

Susanna was hardly alone in refusing to view King William III, Prince of Orange—who was Dutch—as England's true king. Many shared her view. King William's claim to the throne came through his wife, Queen Mary II. She was the daughter of James II, and she and William served as co-regents of England, Scotland, and Ireland while James was exiled during the religious wars. They were crowned in 1689. But it's hard for us to fathom how something like this could cause such problems in the Wesley marriage.

Precisely why Susanna wouldn't mutter an "amen" to assuage her distressed and sensitive husband's feelings, or conversely why something so seemingly small could be the excuse for a man to abandon his family, causing them to suffer tremendously, is a great mystery to us, three centuries hence. Here is a window into Susanna's thinking in a letter to her friend, Lady Yarborough.

You advise me to continue with my husband, and God knows how gladly I would do it, but there, there is my supreme affliction, he will not live with me. . . . [Since] I'm willing to let him quietly enjoy his opinions, he ought not to deprive me of my little liberty of conscience.[7]

Susanna also confided in Suffragan Bishop George Hickes:

My master will not be persuaded he has no power over the conscience of his Wife. . . . He is now for referring the whole to the Archbishop of York and Bishop of Lincoln, and says if I will not be determined by them, he will do anything rather than live with a person that is the declared enemy of his country.[8]

After Samuel had been absent for a year, however, fate intervened. The house in which Susanna and her children were living caught fire, nearly killing one of her small daughters and destroying most of the house and all their belongings. Upon hearing this news, Samuel returned to his family and set about rebuilding the house. And since Queen Anne had ascended the English throne during this time, the Dutch-born source of the couple's conflict had been removed.

As her husband rebuilt their home, Susanna turned her attention to the education of her children, a job she would continue for twenty years as additional offspring arrived. It was not at all customary to educate girls in that time, so it is remarkable that Susanna wanted not just her three sons, but all her children to be able to read, write, and reason well. Nor did her ideas about education end with letters and logic. She also knew that above all she must teach her children to love God.

As far as she was concerned, the state of their souls formed the focus of her education. Much of what she taught them was for the purpose of helping them see through—and therefore be able to resist—the secular doctrines of that time. So she may be regarded not only as the inventor of homeschooling, but also of what today is sometimes called "worldview teaching," something modern Christian parents in the West have begun embracing as they raise their children in an increasingly post-Christian culture.

Susanna's dedication to educating her children is simply staggering. "Though the education of so many children must create abundance of trouble," she wrote,

and will perpetually keep the mind employed as well as the body; yet consider 'tis no small honour to be entrusted with the care of so many souls. . . . [I]t will be certainly no little accession to the future glory to stand forth at the last day and say, "Lord, here are the children which Thou hast given me, of whom I have lost none by my ill example, nor by neglecting to instill in their minds, in their early years, the principles of Thy true religion and virtue!"[9]

Each child's formal education began at age five, but much earlier than that, Susanna taught them that there "was a Supreme Being to whom their gratitude and homage must be reverently rendered."[10] She taught them to treat both their siblings and the servants with great courtesy. Even before they could walk or talk, they were "taught to ask a blessing upon their food by appropriate signs; thus learning, at the very beginning, to recognize their dependence upon" God.[11] Susanna helped them memorize short prayers and had them say the Lord's Prayer upon rising and retiring.

When Susanna failed to find textbooks that met her exacting standards, she decided to write her own. The first textbook took on arguments about the nature of the universe and how it pointed to God as the creator. The book invited her children to use reason and intellect to evaluate the teachings of their faith critically. She wanted to equip them with the tools to analyze the objections to faith that were so prevalent in the "Age of Reason."

Susanna's second textbook was her own exposition of the Apostles' Creed. A remarkably sophisticated piece of writing, the book is written simply enough for children to understand. Her third explored the teachings of the Ten Commandments, which she used to teach her children the fundamentals of divine moral law and to show that God's moral law was universal, for all human beings in all times.

Clearly, Susanna could not have taught her children so well had she herself not been encouraged as a child to read deeply, to listen to the debates of her elders, and to join in theological conversations.

The children's daily routine was rigorous. Susanna required them to study for three hours each morning and three each afternoon, six days a week. They began and closed each academic day by singing a psalm and reading from the Bible. Most of her children learned the entire alphabet on their first day of school. Discipline was the order of the day, which the children were accustomed to. They had been subjected to Susanna's notions of discipline from birth.

The "Mother of Methodism," as she was called later, was manifestly methodical in raising her children. Her babies were fed on a schedule, rather than being fed on demand, as is the preferred method today. But that was just the beginning. "The children were always put into a regular method of living," she wrote, "in such things as they were capable of, from their birth; as in dressing and undressing, changing their linen, etc. . . ." When they turned a year old (and some before) they were taught "to fear the rod."[12] To raise them otherwise, she felt, would have been selfish and cruel. "[B]y this means," she wrote, "they escaped abundance of correction they might otherwise have had."[13]

She was not strict for its own sake. "In the esteem of the world," she wrote, "they pass for kind and indulgent, whom I call cruel, parents, who permit their children to get habits which they know must be afterward broken."[14]

Her belief that girls should be educated ran so deep that she refused to teach her daughters to work until they could first read excellently. She said that parents who did not enforce this rule were "the very reason why so few women can read fit to be heard."[15]

After her small children finished their supper and had their baths, they were put to bed awake, "for there was no such thing allowed of in our house as sitting by a child until it fell asleep."[16] Of course, this sounds much less harsh when we remember how many children she had to bring up.

"When the will of a child is totally subdued, and it is brought to revere and stand in awe of the parents," she wrote in a letter to her son John, "then a great many childish follies, and inadvertencies may be passed by. Some should be overlooked and taken no notice of, and others mildly reproved; no willful transgression ought ever to be forgiven children, without chastisement, less or more, as the nature and circumstances of the offense require."[17]

So "childish follies" could be overlooked, but not willful disobedience. In the same letter to John, Susanna explained the spiritual basis for all this discipline: "I insist upon conquering the will of children betimes [early] because this is the only strong and rational foundation of a religious education, without which both precept and example will be ineffectual. But when this is thoroughly done, then a child is capable of being governed by the reason and piety of its parents till its own understanding comes to maturity, and the principles of religion have taken root in the mind."[18]

No one can doubt that Susanna's methods of child rearing resulted in children who grew to show tremendous strength of character. And strict attention to the children's behavior meant that "taking God's name in vain, cursing and swearing, profanity, obscenity, rude ill-bred names, were never heard among them."[19] While her children did their schoolwork, Susanna sewed, went over household accounts, wrote letters, and nursed the latest baby. At night before bed the children played games, sang psalms, and read books from their father's library. Samuel Wesley also took part in educating his children, teaching his sons Greek, Latin, and classical literature in order to prepare them for additional, formal schooling at boarding schools, to which all of the boys were subsequently sent.

One of the most dramatic examples of how busy and crowded the house often was is that as a signal to her children to be quiet, Susanna would sometimes sit down and pull her apron over her head so that she could pray in peace. When she was thus accoutered, the children knew not to interrupt her.

In 1705, something else happened that would add to the family's woes. During an election campaign, Samuel came out in support of two of the four men running—one Tory and one Whig. But when he discovered that the Whig position on the church and royalty differed from his own, he withdrew his support, causing the Whig candidate's supporters to publicly attack Samuel. And then the real troubles began. Samuel wrote a letter about it to Archbishop Sharpe.

"The election began on Wednesday, 30th," he wrote. "A great part of the night our Isle people kept drumming, shouting, and firing of pistols and guns under the window where my wife lay, who had been brought to bed [to recover from childbearing] not three weeks. I had put the child to nurse [the nurse lived nearby]; . . . the noise kept his nurse waking till one or two in the morning. Then they left off, and the nurse, being heavy to sleep, overlaid the child," suffocating him.[20] Frightened servants threw the dead child into the arms of a barely awake Susanna.

What this must have been like for her can only be imagined. Later, Samuel was told by friends that some of the local men intended to kill him. When he arrived home, "they sent the drum and mob, with guns etc., to compliment me till after midnight. One of them, passing by on Friday evening and seeing my children in the yard cried out, 'O ye devils! We will come and turn ye all out of doors a-begging shortly.'"[21]

The vicious harassment continued for some time, and what they suffered seems unimaginable. Villagers stabbed several of the family's cattle, wounded their dog, and set fire to their crops. Then one of the men to whom Samuel was indebted, furious over his change of mind in the election, had Samuel tossed into debtors' prison, where he languished for some time. At one point, Susanna sent him her wedding rings so that he might sell them and pay off his debt, but he would not hear of it and sent the rings back.

Of course, with Samuel behind bars, Susanna found it more difficult than ever to feed her large family. The vile characters behind such attacks were attempting "to starve my poor family in my absence," Samuel wrote, "my cows being all dried up by it, which was their chief subsistence,"[22] because the cows provided milk, butter, and cheese for the Wesleys. Friends eventually sent enough money to pay off Samuel's debt, allowing him to return home, where he bravely continued his parish work.

But in 1709 the most terrifying event yet to affect the Wesley family took place when the family's home burned a second time. Susanna described the event to her nineteen-year-old son, Samuel, then away at school:

> The fire broke out about eleven or twelve o'clock, we being all in bed, nor did we perceive it till the roof of the corn chamber . . . fell upon your sister Hetty's bed. . . .
>
> We had no time to take our clothes. . . . When I was in the yard I looked about for your father and the children; but seeing none, concluded 'em all lost. But thank God, I was mistaken! Your father carried sister Emily, Suky, and Patty into the garden; then, missing Jacky [John], he ran back into the house, to see if he could save him. He heard him miserably crying out in the nursery and attempted several times to get upstairs, but was beat back by the flame; then he thought him lost and commended his soul to God and went to look after the rest. The child climbed up to the window, and called out

to them in the yard; they got up to the casement and pulled him out just as the roof fell into the chamber.[23]

Another servant, Harry, saved Mary and Hetty by breaking the glass in the parlor window and throwing them out to safety.

This time the house burned to the ground completely, along with everything they owned. Having suffered thus twice, Samuel would now rebuild the house with brick. It is certainly possible that Samuel's enemies started the fire. In any event the terrifying event was life-altering and contributed to Susanna's many difficulties. As she wrote to her brother years later, "Mr. Wesley rebuilt his house in less than a year; but nearly thirteen years are elapsed since it was burned, yet it is not half furnished, nor his wife and children half clothed to this day."[24]

A month after the fire, Samuel and Susanna's nineteenth and last child, Kezia, came into the world. Nine of the Wesley children had died in infancy; those who survived were three sons—Samuel, John, and Charles—and seven daughters: Emelia, Susanna, Mary, Hetty, Anne, Martha, and Kezia.

◆ ◆ ◆

The fire not only threatened the lives of the Wesley children but also had an adverse effect on their characters as well and, Susanna feared, their very souls. During the many months it took to rebuild the rectory, the children lived in the homes of friends and relatives as far away as London. Susanna lamented: "Never were children better disposed to piety . . . till that fatal dispersion of them, after the fire, into several families. In those they were left at full liberty . . . to run abroad, and play with any children, good or bad. They soon learned to neglect a strict observation of the Sabbath, and got knowledge of several songs and bad things. . . . A clownish accent, and many rude ways, were learned, which were not reformed without some difficulty."[25]

When the children were finally home again, Susanna supplemented the classroom teaching with weekly visits with each child, helping them to understand how wicked their new habits were and how to behave in a way more pleasing to God, not to mention their parents.

The highly organized way Susanna reared and educated her children had the strongest influence on her son, John. In fact, while studying at Oxford he was mocked by other students for the highly organized way he approached the practice of his faith. He led a club of Oxford students who assiduously prayed, fasted, and performed acts of charity. Because their fellow students thought them so especially methodical, they took to calling the group he formed the "Methodists." John decided to take this insulting term as a compliment, adopting it with pride. It eventually became the name of the movement that swept first across England and then across the American colonies, changing the world in ways that are still felt today, more than two centuries later.

◆ ◆ ◆

Susanna's influence extended well beyond her own children. In 1712 a curate named Inman came to assist Samuel, so on the Sundays that Samuel was out of town, Inman preached the sermon. He had a mysterious predilection for preaching on the evils of debt, which the congregation did not find terribly compelling. Susanna was displeased that her children were not getting better spiritual food, so she decided to gather them in the kitchen each Sunday afternoon and read aloud printed sermons that her father or husband had written.

At first only her children and the servants were present, but soon others began to ask if they could attend. Before long the house was crammed with scores of people wanting to hear Susanna read the sermons—more people than were attending church each week. In fact, the morning church services eventually dwindled to almost nothing. Whenever Inman was preaching, most parishioners skipped church in the morning and showed up at the Wesley home in the afternoon.

Inman was predictably outraged and promptly fired off a letter to

Samuel in London, accusing Susanna of conducting an "illegal meeting." Samuel then wrote his wife, suggesting she allow a man to read the sermons aloud, inasmuch as it was then considered improper for women to preach. But she responded that few if any of her listeners could read well enough to carry out the project. Nor was she actually preaching, but only reading.

When Samuel persisted in criticizing her, she erupted with the righteous exactitude for which she was so well-known: "If you do, after all, think fit to dissolve this assembly, do not tell me that you desire me to do it, for that will not satisfy my conscience; but send me your positive command, in such full and express terms, as may absolve me from guilt and punishment for neglecting this opportunity of doing good, when you and I shall appear before the great and awful tribunal of our Lord Jesus Christ."[26]

Samuel was not willing to go that far, and the Sunday afternoon sermon reading continued. When he returned home, he discovered that, thanks to his wife's "illegal" efforts, his congregation had swelled considerably, and relations between the Wesleys and their neighbors were greatly improved.

◆ ◆ ◆

Susanna rarely failed to keep her evening appointment with God. Her fierce commitment to a fixed schedule, especially in her devotional life, is what we would expect from the "Mother of Methodism," but sometimes it is almost comical in its impressiveness. "For many years," her son John wrote, "my mother was employed in an abundance of temporal business. Yet she never suffered anything to break in upon her stated hours of retirement, which she sacredly observed from the age of 17 or 18 to 72."[27]

Susanna's devotional writings give us an insight into her piety, as well as into the varying and seemingly constant difficulties she faced. Like many busy wives and mothers, she appears sometimes to have felt overwhelmed. "O God, I find it most difficult to preserve a devout and serious temper of mind in the midst of much worldly business," she wrote. "Were I permitted to choose a state of life, or positively to ask of Thee anything in this world, I would humbly choose and beg that I might be placed in such a station wherein I might have daily bread with moderate care and that I might have more leisure to retire from the world without injuring those dependent on me."[28]

The woman who twice endured the loss of her home by fire wrote: "Help me, O Lord, to make a true use of all disappointments and calamities in this life, in such a way that they may unite my heart more closely with thee."[29]

In her difficulties, she was likely tempted to be jealous of her neighbors. She sought guidance in this matter as well: "May I give way to no direct murmurings, no repinings at the prosperity of others. . . . Save me from thinking severely or unjustly of others: from being too much dejected or disposed to peevishness, covetousness, or negligence in affairs."[30]

Spending twenty years teaching her children at home may have led to loneliness too. She wrote, "Enable me to live so as to deserve a friend, and if I never have one on earth, be Thou my friend, for in having Thee I shall have all that is dear and valuable in friendship."[31]

The persistent financial difficulties must have been especially hard to bear, and she wrote prayers asking for help in learning to accept them: "May I learn by practice to love Thee above all things, that so I may be out of the power of the world and my earthly circumstances give me no uneasiness, I would have my wealth to be Thy favor."[32]

If life was not difficult enough for Susanna, bizarre supernatural events began taking place at the Epworth rectory. They began on a cold December night in 1715: odd knockings with no discoverable source; the distinct sound of footsteps going up and down stairs;

sudden winds blowing *inside* the house; doors flying open of their own accord; and mysterious shrieks in the night. The family hardly knew what to make of it. Had demonic forces been assigned to frustrate the work of these diligent servants of God?

The first to experience the strange happenings was a maid named Nanny Marshal, who told the family of hearing sounds "like the dismal groans of a man in the pains of dying." Then one by one, Sukey, Anne, Emelia, and a young servant boy began noticing strange noises as well.

Susanna assumed that rats were responsible for the noises, until one night she went into her daughter Emelia's room and heard strange noises coming from beneath the bed. Suddenly, a small animal, which the eminently sober-thinking Susanna said she thought to be a "headless badger,"[33] ran across the room and then disappeared.

In the superstition of that day, a ghost often portended a death in the family, so Susanna told Samuel what was going on. Samuel himself believed in ghosts and apparitions but adamantly refused to believe his own house was being haunted. "Sukey," he told his wife sternly, "I am ashamed of you. These boys and girls frighten one another; but you are a woman of sense and should know better. Let me hear of it no more."[34]

But he would hear of it again, and not from his wife. One night Samuel himself was awakened by the sound of knocks. Some nights later the knocks returned, this time so loud the Wesleys were unable to sleep. Samuel and Susanna searched the house together but kept hearing sounds that seemed to emanate from the room they had just inspected. Samuel actually wondered whether his daughters or their male admirers might be playing tricks on the family.

But after he invited another minister, Joseph Hoole, to witness the disturbances, he changed his mind. Walking through the house that night, both men heard the strange tappings and saw Samuel's daughters trembling in their beds. Angered, Samuel prepared to shoot a pistol in the direction of the noises, stopping only when Hoole reminded him that no earthly missile could harm a spirit.

The irritated Samuel finally threw out a challenge: "Thou deaf and dumb devil, why doest thou frighten children that cannot answer thee? Come to me in my study that am a man!"[35]

On Christmas Day, the spirit made its presence known to the entire family. As Susanna later wrote, "There was such a noise in the room over our heads, as if several people were walking, then running up and down stairs . . . that we thought the children would be frightened." As she and Samuel searched the house, the spirit kept up its "rattling and thundering in every room, and even blowing an invisible horn at deafening decibels."[36]

For nearly a month following this yuletide cacophony, the family heard nothing. But then the spirit returned with a vengeance. During their evening devotion, the family heard knocks as they prayed for the king, and upon reaching the "amen," they heard a load thump. The spirit seemed to delight in harassing Samuel. As daughter Susanna wrote to her brother Samuel, "Last Sunday, to my father's no small amazement, his trencher [wooden plate] danced upon the table a pretty while, without anybody's stirring the table."[37] The spirit also pushed Samuel forcefully against his desk several times.

When concerned clergymen friends urged Samuel to abandon the rectory, he answered, "No; let the devil flee from me; I will not flee from him."[38]

The antics of the spirit stopped abruptly in early February 1716, three months after they had begun. With the single exception of Hetty, every one of the Wesleys living at the rectory when the spirit made his presence known wrote about their experiences. Susanna described the strange events in a letter to her son John, then away at the Charterhouse School in London, and tried to determine just why the apparition had appeared:

> I do not doubt the fact, but I cannot understand why these apparitions are permitted. If they were allowed to speak to us, and we had strength to bear such converse, if they had commission to inform us

of anything relating to their invisible world that would be of any use to us in this, if they would instruct us how to avoid danger, or put us in a way of being wiser and better, there would be sense in it; but to appear for no end that we know of, unless to frighten people almost out of their wits, seems altogether unreasonable.[39]

Given the theological sophistication of Susanna, it is odd that demonic disturbance did not occur to her as the simplest explanation.

❖ ❖ ❖

With her sons away at London schools, Susanna continued teaching them in the form of long letters. She took particular pains to warn them of the temptations common to young men away from home for the first time. Regarding the consumption of alcoholic beverages, Susanna warned Samuel, "Two glasses cannot hurt you, provided they contain no more than those commonly used. . . . Have a care; stay at the third glass; I consider you have an obligation to strict temperance, which all have not—I mean your designation for holy orders."[1] She also wrote to John about "the dangers of human love" and passion.[2]

Samuel wrote his sons too. One letter in particular reveals that he had learned to value his wife:

You know what you owe to one of the best of mothers . . . often reflect on the tender and peculiar love your dear mother has always expressed towards you, the deep affliction both of body and mind which she underwent for you both before and after your birth; the particular care she took of your education when she struggled with so many pains and infirmities; and, above all, the wholesome and sweet motherly advice and counsel which she has often given you to fear God, to take care of your soul, as well as your learning, to shun all vicious practices and bad examples. . . . You will not forget to evidence this by supporting and comforting her in her age. . . . In short, reverence and love her as much as you will.[3]

Given such kind words, Samuel's behavior toward his wife is puzzling. By all accounts, he allowed her and his daughters to live in poverty, spending whatever money he had on the best education that England had to offer for his three sons. When his own brother, Matthew, condemned him for this, Samuel's response was that God would take care of his family after he was gone. For her part, Susanna—and her children—shared Matthew's view that they were being forced to suffer because of Samuel's poor financial decisions. One daughter later wrote feelingly on the "scandalous want of necessaries,"[4] blaming them for the many illnesses her mother suffered.

The growing Wesley daughters were now attracting the attention of young men. They lived in the hope that Susanna's brother, Samuel Annesley, who had made a fortune in India, would soon return and keep a promise he had made to help his nieces financially. The family was still quite poor, and the girls had to help take care of the farm animals and assist with the housework. Daughter Emelia worked as a teacher in Lincoln, some distance from home.

Annesley wrote his brother-in-law, asking if he would like to manage his business affairs in London. Susanna expressed doubts about her husband's ability to do so, but Samuel took the job and in short order proved his wife's judgment correct. His annoyed brother-in-law fired him and announced that he was now having second thoughts about assisting the Wesley daughters as he had promised. Once again, Samuel Wesley's actions had spoiled things.

This was a crushing disappointment to the girls—so much so that in 1721, Sukey felt compelled to rush into marriage with a wealthy man of base character named Richard Ellison. Susanna upbraided her brother for Sukey's unhappiness, writing, "When, by your last unkind letters, she perceived that all her hopes in you were frustrated, rashly threw herself upon a man (if a man he maybe called who is little inferior to the apostate angels in wickedness) that is not only her plague, but a constant affliction to the family."[5] Years later, Sukey left her husband to live with her four grown children.

Susanna also gave a lively defense of her husband, whom Annesley had apparently accused of dishonesty. Brother and sister apparently made up their quarrel, and when Annesley returned to England, Susanna traveled to London to watch his ship dock. But to her great dismay and bafflement, her brother was not on the boat, though his possessions were. The ship's crew did not know what had happened to him: Had he fallen overboard, or had he been murdered and his body thrown to the sharks? His loss was a heavy burden for Susanna to bear. But even worse was to come.

Perhaps the brightest, loveliest, and liveliest of Susanna's daughters was auburn-haired Hetty. Following the fire that destroyed her home, Hetty, then aged twelve, and her fourteen-year-old sister, Sukey, were sent to live in London with their uncle Matthew, a well-to-do doctor and apothecary, and his wife for more than a year. In London the girls not only had the freedom they did not enjoy at home, but they also became accustomed to greater luxury and the entertainments London provided.

Once they returned home the girls were bored, and the shortage of eligible young suitors frustrated them. Whenever they did enjoy the company of young men, their father considered the men beneath his daughters. At the age of twenty-seven, Hetty was, as biographer Sir Arthur Quiller-Couch described her, "a queen in a country smock and cobbled shoes, a woman made for love, and growing toward love, though repressed and thwarted."[6]

Given the youthful age at which young women married in those days, it is curious that the beautiful Hetty, now approaching thirty, was still unmarried. Were the young men who courted her truly beneath her, or was her father behaving unwisely yet again by refusing to allow Hetty to find a mate? While Hetty loved her mother, she resented her father.

Her resentment surely increased when her father insisted she break off her romance with a young schoolteacher named John Romley. Samuel had become angry, and probably embarrassed, when Romley sang a song before a group of people that, according to Dallimore, "was a stinging parody of the changes made by Samuel Wesley in his endeavours to gain preferment."[7] An outraged Samuel ordered Romley out of his house, and told Hetty to have nothing more to do with him. Defiantly, Hetty secretly exchanged letters with Romley, and when her father discovered this, he sent Hetty to a nearby village to serve as a companion to a wealthy woman, Mrs. Grantham.

Not surprisingly Hetty hated her new life, and she soon left the position. It is not known where Hetty went or what she did in the months after leaving Mrs. Grantham, but some months later, she returned to the family home and, to her parents' horror, was five months pregnant.

Hetty hoped she might be allowed to marry the child's father, whom she loved, but Samuel would not hear of it. He had for some reason determined that Hetty should instead marry a journeyman plumber and glazier named William Wright, an illiterate man who lacked manners and was too fond of alcohol. The plumber was delighted to be given such a prize as the beautiful Hetty, but her mother, sisters, and brothers were outraged and could not fathom how Samuel could condemn his bright, educated daughter to such a fate.

Daughter Mary stood up to him, saying, "Oh, sir, you are a good man! But you are seldom kind and rarely just. . . . You are a tyrant to those you love, and now in your tyranny you are going to do what even in your tyranny you have never done before—a downright wickedness!"[1] Her brother John even preached a sermon, "Showing Charity to Sinners," before his father, hoping to get him to change his mind, but the stubborn Samuel became even more determined to proceed with his plans. Less than two weeks after her return home, Hetty was married to Wright, and the pair moved in with Wright's father, himself an unpleasant man.

The child arrived in February 1726 but soon died, and a devastated Hetty interpreted the loss of her child as a sign of God's judgment. Then, Hetty's uncle Matthew Annesley came to her rescue, giving the couple a gift of five hundred pounds, which allowed them to move to London and start a new business. After Hetty lost two more babies, her husband began drinking heavily, and Uncle Matthew again took pity on her, taking her to Bristol for a break, where she could meet people of her own kind. In time, Susanna forgave her daughter the great shame she had brought to the family, and the two became close. But Hetty's father never forgave her.

In 1749, twenty-four years after her forced marriage, fifty-two-year-old Hetty began not only attending her brother John's religious services in London, but also actively assisting him. She died in 1753 at the age of fifty-five.

Several other of the Wesley children also endured unhappy marriages. Emelia twice fell in love, but both times her brothers advised her against marrying the man—one, because his character was not what they felt it should be, and the other because he was a Quaker. Now in her forties, two decades beyond the age at which women married at that time, Emelia made a desperate choice. She married an apothecary who was a bad businessman and who took whatever money Emelia made from her work at a school for girls. The man proved to be heartless and by all accounts made Emelia's life miserable.

Martha fell in love with Westley Hall, a clergyman who proved to be of ignoble character. Soon after their engagement, he met Martha's younger sister Kezia, who knew nothing of the engagement, and his ardent attentions caused Kezia to fall in love with him. Eventually, Hall claimed that God had told him to go back to Martha, and the couple were wed. Some years later, Hall seduced a young seamstress, who became pregnant, and afterward fathered a second illegitimate child. Eventually he declared himself an atheist and abandoned Martha altogether.

Not all the sisters married unhappily. Anne married John Lambert, a land surveyor, and the marriage turned out well; and Mary, at the advanced age of thirty-eight, wed a curate. The couple was very happy, but Mary died in childbirth before the pair had celebrated their first anniversary. She was the first of three adult children Susanna would lose.

Kezia, the youngest and most delicate daughter, seems never to have recovered from having her heart broken by Westley Hall. She died when she was just thirty-two.

As for the Wesley brothers, John jumped impulsively—though he was forty-eight—into marriage with a widow named Mary Vazeille. The couple was deeply unhappy, and when after fifteen years his wife left, the great man confided to his journal, "I did not forsake her, I did not dismiss her, I will not recall her."[2]

Charles was happily married to Sarah Gwynne, and Samuel was happily married to Ursala Berry, the daughter of a vicar. To Susanna's great grief, Samuel, her favorite child, died in 1739, aged forty-nine.

◆ ◆ ◆

By the time her son John was ordained a deacon in 1725, Susanna was fifty-six, and she and Samuel were beginning to suffer the symptoms of old age. Samuel had a stroke that left him with a paralyzed right hand. Unable to write, he made use of his daughters for both his correspondence and a commentary he was writing on the book of Job. That their arduous life might have given him something to say on the subject is no surprise. Susanna, who had over the years suffered episodes of gout and rheumatism, now had what her husband described in a letter to John and Charles as "little convulsions."[3]

After surviving several accidents Samuel was ill for six months and then died in April 1735. He was seventy-three, and predictably he left behind numerous and significant debts.

And inasmuch as the vicarage must now be vacated for the new vicar, Susanna found herself again homeless. Worse yet, those to whom Samuel owed money now put pressure on her, in one case even having her arrested. Her sons quickly stepped forward with financial help, and Susanna moved in with daughter Emelia, who lived at the school where she was employed. John and Charles had at this time decided to sail to America as missionaries, leaving their mother with no notion of when they would return. Susanna afterward went to live with her oldest son, Samuel, and his wife and then one year later to the home of her daughter Martha and her husband, Westley Hall. This was of course before Hall abandoned his wife.

After John and Charles returned from America, they famously underwent a great spiritual transformation when they heard their friend the evangelist George Whitefield preach the electrifying message: "You must be born again." For them, it would change everything. The pair also came in contact with evangelical Moravians, from whom they understood that although one must indeed work out one's salvation "with fear and trembling," salvation was nonetheless not by one's good works, but by faith. At a Moravian meeting in London on May 24, 1738, John heard a reading of Martin Luther's preface to the Epistle to the Romans. It was after this that he penned his now famous words: "I felt my heart strangely warmed."[4]

Just a few weeks later he preached a sermon on the subject of salvation by faith and soon thereafter preached another sermon on the doctrine of grace, which he described as "free in all, and free for all."[5]

Charles also experienced this new understanding of salvation. It happened three days before his brother's conversion, on May 21, 1738. This led him to write his famous hymn, "And Can It Be." It is one of the most popular of the six thousand he wrote.

The Wesley brothers shared their views with their mother, who had taught her children, as she put it in a letter to Samuel when he was a teenager, to "carefully 'work out your salvation with fear and trembling,' lest you should finally miscarry."[6]

In another letter to Charles, Susanna wrote, "Blessed be God, who showed you the necessity you were in of a Savior to deliver you from the power of sin and Satan (for Christ will be no Saviour to such as see not their need of one), and directed you by faith to lay hold of that stupendous mercy offered us by redeeming love. . . . Blessed be God, he is an all-sufficient Saviour; and blessed be his holy name that thou hast found him a Savior to thee, my son!"[7]

In 1739 Susanna went to live with her son John, who had purchased a building called the Foundry. While most of it was converted into meeting space, John turned a portion of it into an apartment for himself and his mother, where she was able to live comfortably for the final three years of her life. In a communion service at the Foundry in 1740, Susanna for some reason found herself deeply affected by the words from *The Book of Common Prayer*, "The blood of our Lord Jesus Christ which was given for me." "These words struck through my heart," she wrote, "and I knew that God for Christ's sake had forgiven me all my sins."[8]

In 1742, Susanna, now aged seventy-three, began to fail. Her remaining five daughters—Susanna, Anne, Emelia, Hetty, and Martha—and John and Charles—gathered around her. Charles was forced to leave but hoped his mother would linger until his return. On July 20, John wrote, "I found my mother on the borders of eternity; but she has no doubt or fear, nor any desire but (as soon as God should call) 'to depart and be with Christ.'"[9] Susanna died the following day. But according to her children, who witnessed it, she awoke twelve hours before her death, and declared: "My dear Saviour! Are you come to help me in my extremity at last?"[10] As Susanna had requested, her children, to whom she had devoted so much of her time, energy, and love, sang a psalm of praise to God at her death.

Few human beings have influenced the world as Susanna Wesley did. The manner in which she taught her children greatly influenced the work of her son, John, and the Methodist movement he founded led to world-changing revival and to such an array of social reforms as can never be calculated. The abolition of the slave trade and slavery are at the top of a long list that includes penal reform, the end of child labor in England, laws against cruelty to animals, and the establishment of countless private societies and organizations dedicated to caring for the poor and suffering. The denomination he founded today claims eighty million members around the world, along with many Methodist hospitals, colleges, and orphanages.

More than 375 years after her death, we sing the hymns Susanna's son Charles wrote—including "Hark! The Herald Angels Sing," the Easter hymn "Christ the Lord Is Risen Today," and the Christmas song "Come Thou Long Expected Jesus." Despite tremendous trials, each of Susanna's children passionately embraced faith in God and lived out that faith to the end of their days.

Anyone believing that the life of a woman dedicated to her family must be less than optimal cannot know the story of Susanna Wesley. Despite poverty, illness, a difficult marriage, and heartbreak in endless forms, she used her intellect, creativity, time, energies, and will in such a way that can hardly be reckoned. The world in which we live owes much of the goodness in it to her life.

THREE

Hannah More

1745–1833

One of the great joys of writing *Amazing Grace: William Wilberforce and the Heroic Campaign to End Slavery* was that in learning about the extraordinary Wilberforce I also got to know a number of his brilliant and eccentric friends, Granville Sharp[11] and Isaac Milner[12] being two of the most colorful. But the third figure in the superlative triumvirate of geniuses I discovered while researching Wilberforce was the incomparable Hannah More.

More was nothing less than the most influential woman of her time. She was already a well-known figure when Wilberforce met her in 1787: a best-selling playwright and author, whose works at the time outsold Jane Austen's ten to one, and a woman of such boundless wit and charm that everyone wished to be in her society. She was close with Samuel Johnson, David Garrick, Horace Walpole, and every other bold-faced name of that day, but it was her friendship with Wilberforce that fueled their collaborations against the slave trade and a host of other social evils. Between them, they would quite literally change the world.

When I stumbled across Hannah More, I almost could not believe she existed. It was as though I had discovered a gurgling Bernini fountain in the midst of a desert. When I came to fathom the crucial role she played in the history of abolition and the so-called Reformation of Manners, I was positively disturbed at the outrageous ellipsis. So to remedy it in the tiniest way, I crammed all I could about her into my Wilberforce book—without putting in so much that it would betray that my affection for her had temporarily eclipsed that of my affection for Wilberforce himself (my affection for them is now equal, but different)—and I desperately hoped that someone would write a full popular biography of her as soon as possible.

I'm thrilled to say my friend Karen Swallow Prior has done just that, and I vigorously commend to the reader her excellent and entertaining book *Fierce Convictions: The Extraordinary Life of Hannah More—Poet, Reformer, Abolitionist* from which I gather much of the information in this chapter. But until you have that estimable volume in your hands, I offer this sketch.

◆ ◆ ◆

Hannah More was born in the reign of King George II, on February 2, 1745, the fourth of five daughters born to Jacob and Mary More in a small four-room cottage in Stapleton in Gloucestershire. Jacob More was the schoolmaster at a charity school at Fishponds, the village where they lived. But Jacob and Mary educated their four girls at home, giving them an education far superior to what most girls received at that time. Indeed girls in those days did not get much by way of education at all.

All the girls were bright, but from the earliest age Hannah was recognized as especially so. At age three she widened the eyes of the local vicar by reciting her catechism at church and took home a sixpence for the performance. By four she could read and write, and her love for writing grew apace. Every year as her birthday approached, Hannah requested paper, something scarce and expensive at that time. She was endlessly writing poems and essays.

From the earliest age, she was known for her sharp tongue and quick wit as well as for a remarkable memory. But she was also known for having a distinctly moral bent, often imbuing her writings with particular lessons, a penchant that would follow her throughout her life. Hannah was also a somewhat sickly child, and the family used it as an excuse to dote on her.

Jacob and Mary hoped their five daughters would open a school of their own someday, and Jacob More steered their home education in that direction. In 1758 Hannah's eldest sister, Mary, then twenty, fulfilled her parents' expectations and opened a girls boarding school in Bristol. Hannah was thirteen and enrolled as a student, but at age sixteen she joined her older sisters—Mary, Betty, and Sally—in teaching at the school.

The school was aimed at the growing middle class in the economically thriving city. Following in their father's advanced footsteps, Hannah and her sisters thought women's education should not be significantly different from that offered to men. Throughout her life Hannah was an outspoken advocate of educational reforms for women. She was also a believer in engaging the imagination in education, something that was considered unorthodox at that time. Years later she wrote that teachers should avoid "mere verbal rituals and dry systems."[13] She considered it crucial to communicate lessons as lively and invitingly as possible.

Living in the cultural and social swirl of Bristol must have been exhilarating to a young woman of Hannah's talents and affinities. The city's prosperous economy drew the noble, smart, and fashionable, and the events and opportunities on offer stood in starkest comparison to life at Fishponds. When she was sixteen the charming and vivacious Hannah befriended the renowned Scottish astronomer, globe maker, and portraitist James Ferguson, who was in town delivering lectures on experimental philosophy. Two years later, in 1763, she attended a lecture by Thomas Sheridan, who was the godson of Jonathan Swift and the father of the great poet and playwright Richard Sheridan. Hannah struck up a friendship with Sheridan after he read one of her poems, and he encouraged her in her writing. Her talent at winning the trust and friendship of notable people followed her through life.

That same year, the eighteen-year-old Hannah wrote her first play, titled *The Search After Happiness*, a pastoral drama in verse, intended to be performed by the girls at the school. Like much of what she would write the years ahead, it was greatly entertaining, but it also had a moral sensibility, something sorely lacking in similar plays of the time. It was this lack that prompted her to write the play in the first place, as the often off-color content of what was available was certainly not appropriate for the girls Hannah was teaching.

The Theatre Royal opened in Bristol to great fanfare a few years later in 1766. Many of the school's students had ties to the theater, and frequent student outings to dramatic performances became a regular part of the school's offering. This held great appeal for parents wishing to expose their daughters to culture. Hannah became close friends with theater manager William Powell, toast of the London stage.

In 1767 Hannah visited the nearby estate of William Turner, who was cousin to two students at the Mores' school. Turner was in every way a gentleman, possessing excellent character, education, breeding, and taste. He was wealthy too. His estate, called Belmont, was only a few miles from Bristol, so when his two younger cousins came to spend their holidays, Hannah and her younger sister, Patty, accompanied them. Though Hannah was two decades his junior, she always seemed beyond her years, and the two shared many overlapping affinities. Within the year he proposed marriage, and Hannah gladly accepted.

The new and glamorous life that now lay ahead would be dramatically different from what she had known as a teacher or as a child growing up in her parents' humble cottage. She immediately began preparations for her future as the Lady of Belmont: she gave up her share in her sisters' school and began spending much time and money buying clothes suited to the life she would soon be leading. But not that soon. The engagement lasted six years, during which time Hannah visited Turner often and appropriately played the role of wife-to-be, consulting with her future husband on everything, including the landscaping and design of the gardens that adorned Belmont's impressive grounds. Turner had some of More's poems engraved and posted on plaques around the estate and even gave her a cottage to use as a place to write, naming it after her.

In time, quite as expected, a date was set for their wedding, and preparations made. But suddenly Turner had a change of mind. He did not wish to end their engagement, only to postpone it. So another date was set, but Turner suffered cold feet again. A third date was set, and—in typical fashion—Turner postponed it once more. But for the very patient Hannah, this was the end. Though Turner earnestly begged her to forgive him and not to end the engagement, saying she could pick the wedding date herself and he would promise to stick to it, Hannah was adamant that it must now be broken once and for all. Her sisters strongly encouraged her in this decision.

As was common in those days, Turner arranged to provide Hannah with the considerable annual sum of two hundred pounds in recompense. She staunchly refused, but her sisters would not have it. They forced her to change her mind and accept. It would be this money that enabled her to do much of her writing in the years to come.

In the meantime, however, the discord was more than Hannah could bear, and she suffered some sort of nervous breakdown. While recovering in Weston-super-Mare, about twenty miles from Bristol, she met and befriended Dr. James Langhorne, the vicar of Blagdon. He was a translator and, like herself, a poet. Their friendship soon blossomed, and Langhorne—who had lost two wives in childbirth—proposed marriage. But Hannah refused. Why she did so we can never know, but she remained good friends with Langhorne for the rest of her life. Twenty years later, she even resumed her friendship with William Turner, who never overcame letting her slip away.

But it was now, after Hannah had rejected the idea of marriage, that the world of London opened to her, and with London, all else besides.

◆ ◆ ◆

Hannah visited the great city for the first time in 1774, at the age of twenty-nine. She took in the famous historical and literary sites and befriended David Garrick, then the best-known actor in London and manager of London's Theatre Royal. James Stonhouse, a longtime family friend who wished to support Hannah in her literary ambitions, had forwarded a manuscript of her play, *The Inflexible Captive*, to Garrick. The play had already been staged in Bristol to rave reviews. But it was not until her second trip to the city that the opportunity arose to meet Garrick. When they met at his home in London's Westminster section, the actor and his wife hit it off with Hannah immediately. That one meeting commenced the strongest friendship of all their lives.

Garrick flung open the bronze doors of the city's sanctum sanctorum and introduced his new friend to a veritable who's who of late eighteenth-century London. She was soon enjoying the company of the great cultural figures of that day, including the playwright Richard Sheridan; the conservative parliamentarian Edmund Burke; the famous portraitist Sir Joshua Reynolds; and the celebrated Edward Gibbon, author of the epic *History of the Decline and Fall of the Roman Empire*, and whose work Hannah once characterized as "fine, but insidious." [14] If this weren't enough, she soon became friends with none other than the renowned and everywhere-celebrated Dr. Samuel Johnson.

Hannah's introduction to the man, who two decades before had created the first dictionary in the English language, could not have been better scripted. Joshua Reynolds warned her of Johnson's foul moods, but Johnson entered with a dazzling parrot perched on his hand and a line from Hannah's poetry on his lips. Their friendship was off to a roaring start and never flagged. They entertained each other and were so fond of each other that, though they were separated by thirty-five years, people often teased them about their affections for one another.

In a letter to one of her sisters, Hannah wrote, "I had the happiness to [walk] Dr. Johnson home from Hill Street, though Mrs. Montagu publicly declared she did not think it prudent to trust us together, with such a declared affection on both sides. She said she was afraid of a Scotch elopement."[15] The law requiring an announcement three weeks before a wedding did not apply in Scotland. Montague, convener of the exclusive literary and intellectual circle to which Hannah was a frequent guest, was worried the pair might get carried away and slip up north.

Because of her humble beginnings, Hannah often felt she must be dreaming to find herself in this vaunted cultural and social Elysium. At times she wore a social insecurity about her, and those who disliked her or who, like Johnson's celebrated biographer James Boswell, were jealous of her, often took base swipes at her in print. But all who knew her for the wit and charm would never believe she thought herself unworthy of their company. Johnson's opinion of her was perhaps the highest of all. He called her "the most powerful versificatrix" in the English language.[16] When someone mentioned poetry at a gathering, Johnson interrupted: "Hush, hush. It is dangerous to say a word of poetry before her. It is talking of the art of war before Hannibal."[17]

In the *Nine Living Muses*, Richard Samuel's painting that today hangs in London's National Gallery, Hannah is pictured as Melpomene, the Muse of Tragedy. But Garrick and his wife sometimes called their friend by the pet nickname "Nine," meaning they thought her to be the very embodiment of all the muses combined.

Hannah quickly grew so close to the Garricks that she became their semi-permanent house guest. Garrick's wife, Eva Marie, was a celebrated beauty who had danced in the courts of Europe, and the childless couple adopted the charming spinster as an intimate member of their small family. Hannah returned to London for six or more weeks each year and lived with them. Hannah was David Garrick's greatest fan and boasted of once seeing him on stage twenty-seven times in a season. But he admired her writing every bit as much as she admired his acting, and he once made the present to her of an inkstand carved from the wood of a mulberry tree that belonged to Shakespeare.

In 1774 Hannah's play, *The Inflexible Captive*, was published by Thomas Caddell. A year later he published two more volumes, *Sir Eldred and the Bower* and *The Ballad of Bleeding Rock*. Hannah's pen never stopped nor seemed even to slow for very long. Caddell cashed in and became her publisher for the next forty years.[18]

In 1777 the Covent Garden Theater produced Hannah's play *Percy*, a tragedy. This was a tremendous honor, but perhaps greater yet was that Garrick wrote both the play's prologue and epilogue. She attended the premier with the Garricks and was overwhelmed at the "bursts of applause" it drew.[19] It proved to be a smash success. Indeed, it was literally the most acclaimed play of that era. The printers blew through four thousand copies in the span of two weeks. Productions were mounted across England and then in France and Austria too.

Hannah's Christian faith and moral bent were less pronounced now than they would eventually become, but they were nonetheless an important part of how she saw the world and what she wrote. Garrick was by no means a serious Christian, but he was greatly respectful of Hannah's faith. It is in her ready acceptance and love of those who did not share her faith that we see an important aspect of Hannah More. She did not let the indifference or even the irreligiosity of most in these circles dissuade her from enjoying their company. Like her future friend Wilberforce, she did not lose her wit when she found God.

The success of *Percy* led Garrick to urge Hannah to write another play, which she did. It was titled *The Fatal Falsehood*, and its principal theme was self-restraint, or "self-conquest," to use Hannah's phrase:

> *[I]f to govern realms belong to few,*
> *Yet all who live have passions to subdue.*
> *Self-conquest is the lesson books should preach,*
> *Self-conquest is the theme the stages should teach.*[20]

Garrick himself helped guide Hannah in her writing of the play, but in January 1779, a month before his sixty-second birthday, he died. He was so beloved by the nation that he was accorded the honor of being the first actor to be buried in the Poets' Corner at Westminster Abbey. "I am disappointed by that stroke of death," Johnson wrote, "which has eclipsed the gaiety of nations, and impoverished the public stock of harmless pleasure."[21] Hannah continued to live with Garrick's widow, Eva Marie, who was her dearest friend, but their grief at his loss was considerable.

A few months later Hannah took the play she had written to Covent Garden. It was produced almost immediately, but Hannah was too sick to attend when the curtain on it rose in May. It's just as well that she was absent. During the second night of the performance, Hannah Cowley, a dramatist and poet in attendance, shot up in her seat. "That's mine!" she yelled. "That's mine!" Garrick had mentored Cowley as well. Was there some overlap in his direction? Hannah was mortified and denied any wrongdoing. Indeed, the supposed plagiarism would prove unfounded, but Hannah was so bruised by the incident that she decided the play was no longer the thing and thenceforth abandoned writing for the stage.

❖ ❖ ❖

That an unmarried woman via her own talents and efforts could rise from humble circumstances to eventual fame and great wealth was an idea far ahead of its time. Social mobility of any kind was not the norm in the late eighteenth and early nineteenth centuries, so a poor schoolmaster's daughter mixing with London's elites was remarkable. Perhaps more remarkable yet is her acceptance as an equal by many of the most prominent men of her era.

Hannah's idea that a large part of women's education should be to make them better companions in marriage may seem backward today, but it was forward-thinking for the time. "Indeed," says Karen Swallow Prior, "the companionate marriage—rather than the politically or economically expedient one that had been the norm for all of human history—was an idea advanced by evangelicals, including Hannah, who understood marriage to be an institution established to advance the kingdom of God, not property."[22] Hannah was no feminist, but her Christian understanding of the spiritual equality between men and women was far ahead of its time and did much to advance women toward a greater role in public life. She participated in some social circles that had been the exclusive precinct of men. In fact, one weekly men's meeting—calling itself the "Sour-crout Party" from its regular menu—always opened its doors to her.

But with the death of Garrick and the misfortune over *The Fatal Falsehood*, Hannah began a slow withdrawal from London and the exciting life she had lived over the previous five years. They were now days of transition. The social swirl that had once been so appealing became less so, and the Christian faith that had always been a part of the background of her life began to move into the foreground. Prior writes: "More became increasingly disenchanted with the trappings of high society and turned more fully toward the Christian faith she had assumed all her life but not embraced with full intention."[23]

The principal catalyst for this was John Newton's book *Cardiphonia*, which More read in 1780. Newton was the former slave ship captain who embraced Christian faith and gave up the trade, eventually becoming a minister in the Church of England and writing the famous hymn, "Amazing Grace." Embracing much of the new evangelical message of George Whitefield and John Wesley, Newton was no run-of-the-mill Anglican. In a letter to one of her sisters about *Cardiphonia*, Hannah wrote, "There is in it much vital religion, and much of the experience of a good Christian, who feels and laments his own imperfections and weaknesses."[24] Hannah recommended the book to everyone she knew. "I like it prodigiously," she said.[25]

That same year she befriended that "sacriligeous charmer," Horace Walpole. Walpole was a celebrated cynic and rake who had an early homosexual affair with the poet Thomas Gray, invented the Gothic novel, wrote a definitive, though extremely catty memoir of the Georgian period, and coined the word *serendipity*.

Hannah and Walpole would remain lifelong friends, but the dissonance between what she believed and what he and most of her other friends in London society believed had begun to concern her. Writing to Newton, she said, "I know that many people whom I hear say a thousand brilliant and agreeable things disbelieve, or at least disregard, those truths on which I found my everlasting hopes."[26] She felt herself being pulled between two worlds. Much like Wilberforce, who thought getting serious about God might mean leaving the world behind, including politics, so Hannah More thought she might need to leave London and its elite cultural circles, along with status as their much-sought-after darling. Hannah would indeed leave London, but it was her ability to be friends with these people with whom she disagreed that set her apart from many Methodists and pietists and that would make her singularly effective as an agent of cultural change.

In the meantime, however, she was still working these things out and feeling uncomfortable. To turn her back on the theater was no small thing, but she now could not help feeling the pointlessness of much of what passed for life in London society. For example, women's obsession with fashion—which at that time expressed itself in increasingly outrageous hats—suddenly seemed too much to bother with. But neither did she wish to openly buck the fashion trends, lest in being unfashionable it appear she were trying to draw attention to herself! It was a conundrum.

Hannah's growing objections to the stage did not extend to her views on literature in general. Indeed, her writings during the period following Garrick's death "saw no inconsistency between the devout-est piety and the cultivation of elegant literature and taste," as her biographer Henry Thompson put it.[27] Hannah knew the power of dramatic literature and was drawn to employing that influence toward didactic ends. In 1782 she publicly signaled her growing faith when she published *Sacred Dramas*, dramatizations of various Bible stories in verse. Hannah More understood that the culture in which one lived was as much or more influenced by the arts than by legislation, and she undertook to use her gifts in God's service. She did not wish to retreat from culture into a religious sphere, but rather to advance with the wisdom and truth of religion into the cultural sphere.

But as it is today with Christians trying to accomplish similar things, atheists and secularists were not her only trouble. Pietistic Christians took umbrage at the idea of mixing the things of the Bible and God with the things of the world. Hannah saw the folly in such thinking and stood firmly against it. "I hope the poets and painters will at last bring the Bible into fashion," she wrote, "and that people will get to like it from taste, though they are insensible to its spirits, and afraid of its doctrines."[28] She was a pioneer and, like all pioneers, took grief from those she was leaving behind and those she encountered as she blazed her new trails. As Prior puts it, "Neither the literary elite nor the strict religionists were pleased."[29]

Even her friend Samuel Johnson took the "religious" line of that day and spoke against dramatizing or touching the stories in the Bible. "All amplification is frivolous and vain," he said. "All addition to that which is already sufficient for the purpose of religion, seems not only useless, but in some degree profane." He felt that the events of the Bible, inasmuch as God himself scripted them, were "above the power of human genius to dignify."[30] When a decade later it was announced that someone planned to produce a stage production of one of the stories from *Sacred Dramas*, it was not angry atheists who were up in arms, but the town's religious conservatives.

Though she adored Johnson, Hannah would disagree with him on something else during this period. He had famously quipped that to be tired of London was to be tired of life. Hannah was not tired of life, but she had surely grown tired of London. In a way it was Johnson's own death that confirmed her desire to leave the fabled city for new pastures. For Hannah, David Garrick and Samuel Johnson were the very best of London, and after the latter's death in 1784, both of them were gone and, with them, most of what tied her to life in the city. So in 1785 Hannah set up house at Cowslip Green, a cottage in Somerset's Mendip Hills. There she could spend her hours gardening.

It was a dramatic change from big-city life, but an even greater change was underway by 1787. That was the year she met both John Newton and William Wilberforce and joined them in the great battle for the abolition of the slave trade.

Newton had as storied a life as one can imagine. He was an exceedingly rough man who became a slave ship captain, but who in the midst of a life-threatening storm at sea surrendered his life to God. He eventually left the slave trade and became a minister in the Church of England, though he avoided the skim milk of French Enlightenment rationalism preached from most Church of England pulpits and ardently embraced a "vital Christianity" as Methodist as it was Anglican.

While in his forties he often did what was called "parlour preaching" in the homes of wealthy people, and at the home of John Thornton he met the nine-year-old William Wilberforce. During the next two years Newton became something of a father figure to the boy. But Wilberforce's mother was horrified when she caught wind of his being exposed to Methodism and dragged him back to Hull, where he was forbidden even from attending church, lest he have his incipient faith rekindled. In time, Wilberforce lost what faith he had, but at age twenty-six, on a journey to the French and Italian Rivieras, he found it again.

That year, 1785, he visited his old friend John Newton—then sixty—and Newton encouraged him to stay in politics, so that God could use him there. But how would God use him? "God almighty has set before me two great objects," Wilberforce wrote in his diary two years later, "the suppression of the slave trade and the reformation of manners." This was the great calling to which Wilberforce would devote himself for the rest of his life. And it was none other than Hannah More who would be his closest collaborator in both of these "great objects."

Though Hannah had maintained a correspondence with Newton, she had never met him in person. But in 1787 she made a pilgrimage to his church, St. Mary Woolnoth in London. She attended service and afterward spent an hour speaking with this great man who had already so influenced her. It was principally her friendship with Newton that turned Hannah toward a more evangelical faith.

That same year she met William Wilberforce in Bath. "That young man's character is one of the most extraordinary I have ever known for talent, virtue, and piety," she told her sisters. "It is difficult not to grow better and wiser every time one converses with him."[31] Their relationship was immediate and magnetic, and it was one of the most enduring and significant of her life. How Wilberforce came to be the chief champion of abolition—and how he was able to succeed in ending the slave trade in Great Britain in 1807, after twenty years of battling—has everything to do with Hannah More.

The story began nine years earlier, in 1776, when Hannah met Sir Charles and Margaret Middleton, who had an estate in Teston. Their clergyman was a certain James Ramsay, who had seen the unspeakable horrors of the slave trade firsthand and who succeeded in influencing the Middletons that something must be done. Lady Middleton became especially passionate about the topic and had many dinner parties at which the issue was discussed. Thus was Hannah drawn into the fray. But they eventually realized that abolition must have a champion in Parliament, and they soon settled on Wilberforce, inviting him to consider it. After some prayer and reflection, Wilberforce accepted the role: he would lead the charge against the slave trade in Parliament. But just as Hannah and her friends needed someone in politics to help them, so Wilberforce desperately needed someone in the world of culture to help him, and Hannah was that person.

So when in 1788 Wilberforce decided it was time to bring to Parliament his bill abolishing the slave trade, Hannah began work on "Slavery," a poem designed to help sway public opinion on the slave trade, and specifically to influence the voting on Wilberforce's bill. "I am now busily engaged on a poem, to be called 'Slavery,'" she wrote her sister: "I grieve I did not set about it sooner; as it must now be done in such a hurry as no poem should ever be written in, to be properly correct; but, good or bad, if it does not come out at the particular moment when the discussion comes on in parliament, it will not be worth a straw."[32]

For all her protestations, it was an excellent poem. No less than the poet William Cowper thought it so admirable that he scotched his own plans to compose one along similar lines.

The genius of the abolitionists—and the likely reason for their ultimate success—is that they understood that their battle was not merely political and went to great lengths to make the cultural case against slavery and the trade as well. Josiah Wedgwood created a famous image of a slave in chains with the motto "Am I Not a Man and a Brother?" that was reproduced everywhere, and a poster was created that showed how tightly packed the slaves were on the slave ships. These and other things touched people's hearts and contributed to turning the popular tide against slavery. But it was Hannah's pen that did the most.

Her role in the war against slavery can hardly be overstated. She helped the average Briton see the humanity of the African slaves for the first time—as mothers, fathers, and children little different from their white, British counterparts. Most of Hannah's readers had never even seen an African and thought of slavery as an abstract economic necessity. But with her great poetic powers, Hannah helped them see that the slave trade caused tremendous suffering, that to support slavery meant supporting a practice that tore infants from the breasts of their mothers. Her words pricked the consciences of millions, who came to feel that their country—which called itself a Christian country—must have no part in such an evil. Eventually hundreds of thousands of Britons signed petitions against the slave trade, which were brought by Wilberforce into Parliament and swayed its members toward abolition.

Another important figure who was friends with Hannah More was Beilby Porteus, whose role in abolition and other social reforms is rarely fully appreciated. Porteus was an evangelical who in 1787 was made bishop of London. "I rejoice for many reasons," Hannah wrote on hearing the news, "but for none more than that his ecclesiastical jurisdiction, extending to the West Indies, will make him of infinite usefulness in the great object I have so much at heart—the project to abolish the slave-trade in Africa."[33] Porteus would indeed do all he could to help Hannah and her friends in their battles for abolition and the other social evils of that day, and he could do a lot. He was also the one Hannah credited as having influenced her toward using her literary gifts for God's purposes—specifically for Wilberforce's two "great objects." And what of the second?

I n 1788, in addition to writing "Slavery," Hannah undertook a second major writing project. She knew that many of the social evils of that day—especially the slave trade—stemmed from the worldview of most Britons, who thought of themselves as Christians, but who were in reality and in practice pagans and agnostics. They might have attended church, but it was a mere formality, and their lives did not exhibit anything like the robust—the word in those days was "vital"— faith that Hannah had experienced and knew possible for all. So she now wrote a book titled *Thoughts on the Importance of the Manners of the Great to General Society.*

Hannah More and Wilberforce both knew that it was the elites who set the fashion not just in clothing, but in people's behavior too. And in general the immorality and irreligiosity of the upper classes at that time can hardly be believed. For example, the Prince of Wales, who would become King George IV, was a notorious ne'er-do-well who racked up astronomical gambling debts—which were paid by the taxpayers from the national treasury—and who was rumored to have bedded thousands of women over the serpentine course of his dissolute life. The effect of these practices on the middle and lower classes was powerful, so Wilberforce determined that they, as John Pollock memorably put it, would "make goodness fashionable."[34] Legislation was not enough, so he and Hannah worked hard to influence the cultural elites directly. But events of the next year would make this job even harder than it would otherwise be.

The French Revolution erupted in 1789, causing major changes in the political and cultural climate in England. The radical ideas that were causing the streets to run with blood in Paris were alive in London, too, and that the violence and revolution did not leap across the Channel and rout the British way of life is in large part once again due to the pen of Hannah More.

Hannah was persuaded by friends that she must use her gifts to counter the destructive ideas being put forward by Thomas Paine in the cheap pamphlets that were so popular in those days. In a letter to the Earl of Oxford, Hannah wrote, "I happened to know of a good many of the religious people, both in the church and among the different sects, whose fondness for French politics entirely blinds them to the horrors of French impiety."[35] So she wrote a pamphlet much like the ones that Paine was producing, but which exposed the deep anti-clericalism that lay behind most of the French radicalism. She titled it *Village Politics* and published it under the pseudonym "Will Chip." To divert suspicions of her authorship, she sent the manuscript to a different publisher than Caddell—the ruse worked for a while.

There had never been anything like it, and the hunger for *Village Politics* was stunning. She addressed the pamphlet to "The Mechanics, Journeymen, and Labourers, in Great Britain," but it seemed as if everyone wanted a copy.[36] Hundreds of thousands circulated in London and beyond, including Scotland and Ireland. Patriotic citizens printed reams at their own expense. But the wild success meant the author could not hide behind her *nom de plume* for long. Eventually Hannah's identity was out in the open, and she was soon credited by many with preventing revolution on English soil.

In August of that same year, Wilberforce and his sister paid a visit to Hannah and her sisters at Cowslip Green. While there, he decided to take an excursion. Nearby Cheddar Gorge was known for its beauty, but Wilberforce was caught off guard by the poverty of the villagers there. When he returned to Cowslip Green, he was clearly upset, so much so that he skipped the evening meal to be alone in his room. When he later emerged, the sensitive and generous Wilberforce told Hannah More and her sister Patty what he had seen and what he proposed as a solution. He said that if they "would be at the trouble" to help those poor people, he would "be at the expense."[37]

This launched one of the greatest successes of Hannah More's life, the so-called Sunday schools of that region, which were not church schools for religious instruction, as Sunday schools are today, but actual schools that were open on Sunday, when workers had the day off. The idea behind these schools was, as she explained, "to train up the lower classes to habits of industry and piety."[38]

Hannah's initial and ongoing efforts to educate the poor of the Cheddar region of Somerset were simply heroic, even Herculean. But she knew what was at stake. Education, specifically in religion, would go a long way toward lifting these people out of the morass of hopelessness and criminality so rampant among them. At first, she worked hard simply to persuade the poor to send their children to these schools, but it was often the wealthy and influential people of a region who were most opposed to her. Part of this has to do with the fact that education is an equalizing force, one thought by many to be destabilizing and therefore to be discouraged at all costs. But many of the wealthy also thought religion itself was the problem.

One of Hannah's letters to Wilberforce provides a startling example. "I was told we should meet with great opposition if I did not try to propitiate the chief despot of the village, who is very rich and very brutal, so I ventured to the den of this monster," she wrote. The man informed her that religion was "the worst thing in the world for the poor, for it made them lazy and useless."[39] She did all she could to persuade the man, but failed nonetheless. As a result, Hannah became discouraged. Was enlisting the wealthy even worth the trouble? She knew the schools could never succeed without the local gentry on her side—or at least not fighting her. So she continued, making eleven more visits to unpleasant and disagreeable souls in their large houses. She wrote to Wilberforce of her efforts:

> Miss Wilberforce would have been shocked, had she seen the petty tyrants whose insolence I stroked and tamed, the ugly children I praised, the pointers and spaniels I caressed, the cider I commended, and the wine I swallowed. . . . [T]hey are as ignorant as the beasts that perish, intoxicated every day before dinner, and plunged in such vices as make me begin to think London a virtuous place.[40]

The poverty, ignorance, and immorality of many in these villages was truly shocking, but Hannah and Patty More waded in fearlessly, even though they were often warned not to venture into these wretched areas for the sake of their own safety. The Church of England had abandoned most of these villages, leaving their inhabitants to live under the despotism of the chief landowners and farmers and in complete igno-rance of the Christian faith.

In a letter to John Newton, Hannah wrote, "One great benefit which I have found to result from our projects, is the removal of that great gulf which has divided the rich and poor in these country parishes, by making them meet together; whereas before, they hardly thought they were children of one common [F]ather."[41] But it was this very whiff of egalitarianism that caused many to oppose her work, assuming it would lead to the kind of rebellion as was raging across France.

Still, the effort was a glorious success. Before long there were three hundred children attending the school in Cheddar, and within a decade, Hannah and Patty had set up twelve schools in the neighbor-ing villages. They built on these successes by adding evening classes for adults and weekday classes for girls. By the 1850s, 75 percent of all laboring-class children between five and fifteen were enrolled in Sunday schools.

Perhaps one of the reasons Hannah More is regarded as the most influential woman of her time is that she had the singular abil-ity to use her writing skills to influence both the educated wealthy as well as the uneducated poor. She and Wilberforce knew that this two-pronged approach was necessary to bring about change in the culture of that time.

In 1791 Hannah once more focused her writing on those in the upper classes. She published a book that was essentially a sequel to *Thoughts on the Importance of the Manners of the Great to General Society*. It was titled *An Estimate of the Religion of the Fashionable World*. In the book, she wanted to speak about those of the "more decent class" who "acknowledge their belief of its truth by a public profession, and are not inattentive to any of its forms, yet exhibit little of its spirit in their gen-eral temper and conduct."[42] She went so far as to compare these people to Christ's betrayer, Judas, right in the introduction. She made the case, and it struck a chord. Because of her deft genius as a writer, and because of the great esteem in which she was held as a result, Hannah could say strong things in a way that was generally accepted, even by those on the receiving end of such strong words.

But in 1795 she would turn her writing skills back toward the poorer and less educated. The wild success of *Village Politics* encouraged Hannah to continue writing similar tracts, which in 1795 she began to produce at the prodigious rate of three per month. The anti-religious tracts of Thomas Paine continued to be all the rage. Roberts writes that they worked "to undermine, not only religious establishments, but good government, by the alluring vehicles of novels, stories, and songs."[43] So Hannah felt she must fight them on their own turf. In writing these tracts, she was fighting fire with fire. These destructive ideas needed to be countered, and she wrote the tracts intentionally to compete with what was already popular.

But as with so much that Hannah did, it was the entire network of what would come to be known as the Clapham Sect that made success possible. Her wealthy friend Henry Thornton enabled these tracts to be sold for significantly less than what the other tracts sold for, and this strategy worked. Before a year had passed, two million copies sold. These Cheap Repository Tracts, as they were known, were published from March 1795 through September 1798. Hannah wrote half of the approximately one hundred and oversaw the writing of the rest. A number of them aimed specifically to awaken the middle and lower classes to the humanity of the Africans their own country was enslaving and working to death in the West Indies.

Of course it was one thing to talk of the humanity of these Africans and another to actually treat them as equals. But in 1797 when the abolitionists got involved in the issue of Sierra Leone, a West African colony established by the British Crown for freed Africans, they sent a number of African children to England, to be educated at Hannah More's schools. A number of these children also spent time at

Clapham, playing with Wilberforce's children and the children of the other abolitionists who lived there.

Trying to explain what "the Clapham Sect" was is not easy, especially inasmuch as it was not a sect. Rather, it was a network of like-minded friends, most of them evangelicals, generally led by Wilberforce, who wished not only to bring an end to the slave trade but also to end the many other social evils of that era. But it was Henry Thornton who in 1795 decided to create an environment that would foster these efforts. He realized that if many of these friends lived near each other, it would facilitate what they were trying to accomplish. They could gather in each other's homes and discuss and plan and encourage one another.

So he began expanding his own large house in Clapham, which would eventually boast thirty-six bedrooms, and he also built two more large houses adjacent. He persuaded his dear friend Wilberforce to move there with his wife and six children, and very quickly a number of their other friends followed suit. They all attended the church in Clapham, Holy Trinity, where their friend John Venn preached. Granville Sharp, Isaac Milner, Charles Simeon, Zachary Macauley, and many other notable figures of that time were a vital part of it, but none was more vital than Hannah More.

Like Wilberforce, she seemed to be involved in a hundred things at once. She was forever working to expand the reach of her Sunday schools. In 1796, she wrote of a "new parish, so surprisingly wicked and inconceivably ignorant that I feel when there as if I were queen of Botany Bay," a reference to an infamous Australian penal colony.[44] Also like Wilberforce, she continued to be attacked, not just from those on the atheistic left, who thought her a moralistic busy-body, but from those on the traditional right, who thought her efforts were undermining their way of life. "I hear with little emotion," she wrote, "such attacks on the supposed violence of my aristocratic principles; you know how much more I have had to sustain from my supposed attachment to democrats and dissenters."[45]

In 1799, seeing the vital role women were beginning to play in culture, and one that she encouraged, Hannah wrote and published *Strictures on the Modern System of Female Education*. The book sets forth a high, biblical view of women, on the one side fighting off Rousseau's misogynistic doctrine of "sensibility," which regards women as "frivolous creatures of mere emotion and sentiment," and on the other fighting off the proto-feminist Mary Wollstonecraft's notion of women's "rights.". In 1792 Wollstonecraft published her now famous book, *Vindication of the Rights of Woman*, but Hannah was in no wise enamored of the views it set out. "[T]here is something fantastic and absurd in the very title," she wrote. "How many ways there are of being ridiculous! I am sure I have as much liberty as I can make a good use of, now I am an old maid; and when I was a young one, I had, I dare say, more than was good for me."[46]

The year 1799 also marked the beginning of another painful episode for Hannah because of something that came to be known as the "the Blagdon Controversy." Blagdon was a town where in 1795 Hannah had established one of her Sunday schools. In a letter to Wilberforce from that time, she told of the early successes they were having in this particularly difficult place:

> Several of the grown-up youths had been tried at the last assizes [periodic criminal courts]; three were children of a person lately condemned to be hanged—many thieves! [A]ll ignorant, profane, and vicious beyond belief! Of this banditti we have enlisted one hundred and seventy; and when the clergyman, a hard man, who is also the magistrate, saw these creatures kneeling around us, whom he had seldom seen but to commit or punish in some way, he burst into tears.[47]

But it was this same minister who would four years later start all the trouble, violently objecting to the supposed "Methodism" in one of the schoolteachers.

The genius of Hannah was that she was able to teach "vital Christianity"—which one typically saw only in Methodist circles—but to keep everything officially under the auspices of the Church of England by working only with Anglican churches and teaming up with Church of England ministers. She knew that the desiccated tradition of the Church of England had failed all these poor people, and she knew that the evangelical Methodism of Wesley and Whitefield was what they needed to revive their interest in God—and it was what caused so many of them to change their lives for the better.

But she also knew that she must be wary of seeming to be "officially" Methodist, lest those in the Church of England think her and her schools were being merely subversive of the established order. Because of what was happening in France, anything that was not traditionally English or that meant to lift up the poor was in danger of being thought radical and "revolutionary." It was an extremely polarized time, when the slightest feint in the direction of liberty or egalitarianism was seen as a leap toward the bloody chaos across the Channel.

Because of Hannah's fame, what began as a local affair was soon fanned into a conflagration by the London papers. The "Blagdon Controversy"—in which she was over and over accused of Methodism and therefore of undermining traditional values—raged on for nearly three years and took a great toll on her, eventually causing her to have what seemed another nervous breakdown.

In 1801 Hannah thought it was time to move from her cottage at Cowslip Green to something larger. So she began building Barley Wood, the capacious estate where she lived for most of the next three decades.

As ever, the writing continued, most of it in a moralistic vein, before "moralistic" had become a pejorative. In 1805 she published *Hints Towards Forming the Character of a Young Princess*, which sets forth the idea of a monarch as a moral leader, and in 1808, she anony-mously published her only novel, *Coelebs in Search of a Wife*. The two questions that obsessed London society when it came out were "Who was the author?" and "How should one pronounce 'Coelebs'?" As with so much else she wrote, this two-volume novel was an immediate best seller. In its pages she again put forward the progressive idea of a "com-panionate marriage," based not on economic advancement or political prudence, as were most marriages in those days, but on personal com-patibility. Here again, we have the powerful advocacy of the prescient Hannah to thank for pushing forward something we now take entirely for granted.

In 1813 Hannah and her friends in the Clapham Circle would take on another vitally important initiative. It concerned a bill to send Anglican missionaries to India. Wilberforce reckoned it second in importance only to his crusade against the slave trade. He had tried and failed to pass a similar bill in 1793, when the East India Company's charter came up for renewal. Now, two decades later, when it came up for renewal again, he was ready, and he enlisted the help of everyone in the Clapham Circle to ensure success.

Wilberforce was passionate that the East India Company and England should not merely profit from the Indian people, but should try to help them, and he knew that missionaries would introduce education, the better treatment of women, and a host of other social benefits. He was most outraged at the horrific practice of suttee, then popular, in which Indian widows were burned alive on their husband's funeral pyres. That the English were profiting handsomely from their presence in India but doing nothing to end this great evil was a moral outrage. The passage of this bill would do much toward ending the practice, but the opportunity only came around once every twenty years. It was all hands on deck. For her part, Hannah wrote an anony-mous letter (signed "Philanthropos") to the *Bristol Journal*, inimitably making the case for introducing the Christian faith to India. It helped sway public opinion in this direction, and the bill passed.

But 1813 marked the beginning of a difficult time for Hannah. Her eldest sister, Mary, died. Betty would die three years later, and Sally a year later, in 1817. In 1819, Patty, the sister to whom Hannah was closest, would die. But throughout this decade and through the next, Hannah continued to write, to host a stream of visitors at Barley Wood, and to keep up a seemingly endless correspondence.

In 1821, still working to counteract the destructive irreverence of the radical literature of that time, she published *Bible Rhymes*, intended to help younger people comprehend the meaning of each of the books of the Bible. It did not sell nearly as well as her previous works, but it typified her philosophy that one must not merely rail against the darkness, but must instead light a proverbial candle by creating literary and cultural works that rival and surpass the bad.

Hannah's very last years were marked by failing health. In 1828, she moved from Barley Wood, and in 1833, at age eighty-seven, she died, just weeks after her dear friend Wilberforce. She was buried near Barley Wood, adjacent to her four sisters. But just before she died, the long effort that she and Wilberforce and their Clapham friends had worked toward finally succeeded: Parliament voted to abolish slavery throughout the British empire. One year later, innumerable African men, women, and children, whom Hannah for decades had kept before the public eye as human beings created in the image of God, would at last be freed from their chains. It is a fitting coda to her extraordinary life.

Seven years after her death, Percy Bysshe Shelley's famous essay, "In Defense of Poetry" was published. In it, as Prior points out in *Fierce Convictions*, he credited "the effects of the poetry" of Christians with ending slavery and emancipating women. The last line of his essay can serve as her fitting epitaph: "Poets are the unacknowledged legislators of the world."[48]

FOUR
Saint Maria of Paris

1891–1945

There are good reasons most people have never heard of Saint Maria of Paris, who is also known as Maria Skobtsova. For one thing, with every twist and turn of her life, her name itself changed. She began life as Elizabeth Pilenko, and was called Liza. When she married, she took her husband's name and became Elizabeth Kuz'mina-Karavaeva. Then she divorced and married again, becoming Elizabeth Skobtsova. She is generally referred to by that surname, but when that marriage was annulled, she became a nun and took a new first name: Maria. She was thenceforth known as Maria Skobtsova, although almost everyone knew her simply as "Mother Maria." Finally, in 2004, she was canonized by the Orthodox Church and officially became Saint Maria of Paris.

But even if we settle on her name, her life is a welter of contradictions. For example, she was born in Latvia but was ethnically Ukrainian. She lived her early years in Russia and then moved back to the Ukraine. Then after the Russian Revolution she moved to Paris, where she lived until she was taken to Ravensbrück, in Germany.

What she did can also be confusing. First, she was a poet who swam among the literary elites of St. Petersburg; then she managed her family's award-winning wine estate on the Black Sea—and became the mayor of the town there. When the Russian Revolution made life impossible, she moved to Paris and became a nun. Finally, even as a nun she confounds our expectations: she smoked and drank. She did not live in a monastery but considered the whole world her monastery. She married twice, divorced twice, and had three children by two different men. Yet for all of this woman's dramatically unorthodox behavior, the Orthodox Church recognizes her as a saint. Can we be blamed for being confused about this extraordinary woman?

In truth, it is precisely because of all these things that she commands our attention. Her life was messy and complicated, as most of ours are messy and complicated. By breaking every mold in which we would put her, she shows forth the beauty and the full-throated reality of the Christian life in a way that few in history have ever done.

One reason I find her compelling is because of the striking similarities between her life and that of Dietrich Bonhoeffer. Both were brilliant and grew up in an elite, intellectual atmosphere. Both eschewed "religiosity" or "pietism," and both smoked and drank. Both were profoundly enamored of the idea that Jesus was fully incarnate; and that in his humanity he connected us to God in a way that is so direct as to be shocking and life-changing—if we can only grasp it. Both wrote brilliantly and knew that their writings meant nothing if they did not live them out. Both were less interested in meeting the expectations of their own church denomination than in helping their denomination meet the expectations of God himself. Both understood it was the duty of every Christian to stand up for the Jews being persecuted by the Nazis; and both, because they did this, were murdered in concentration camps just weeks before the war ended. The parallels really are astonishing.

Finally, I wished to include this great woman because many of us know of Christian heroes from the Protestant and Catholic traditions, but few of us know of the heroes of the Orthodox tradition. I was raised in the Greek Orthodox Church, but only in later years have I come to appreciate the great treasures of Orthodoxy, and without a doubt, Maria Skobtsova—a.k.a. Mother Maria, a.k.a. Saint Maria of Paris—is one of those great treasures.

◆ ◆ ◆

Elizaveta Pilenko was born in 1891 in the city of Riga in Latvia. Her family was rooted in the Ukrainian aristocracy, so her parents were well-to-do. They were also devout Orthodox Christians, and she was raised in a pious and religious atmosphere. Little Liza was passionate about serving God from her earliest years: at seven she asked her mother when she might leave home for a convent; at eight she asked permission to journey with religious pilgrims, who were visiting monasteries and shrines; and when a new church was built in her hometown, Elizabeth scraped together every bit of her savings and made a contribution to pay for the painting of a mural of her patron saint.

Liza's family moved several times, first from Riga to Anapa on the Black Sea, where her father had inherited a large estate. When she was thirteen, her father was made director of the famed Botanical Garden near Yalta, and they moved to Crimea. But the very next year—it was the summer of 1906—tragedy struck. Liza's father died. He was forty-nine, and his death hit Liza so hard that she decided she could no longer believe in God. Her beloved father's death seemed to her such an injustice that the universe appeared meaningless to her. So in the passionate way that would mark her life, she now declared herself an atheist, saying: "If there is no justice, there is no just God. Yet if there is no just God, that means there is no God at all."[49] It is unclear whether this turn was genuine or whether she was simply angry at the God in whom she now claimed not to believe.

Soon after, Liza's mother moved the family north to the city of St. Petersburg. For the first time in her life, Liza was exposed to the poor and the uneducated, and her natural compassion caused her to want to help them. The first way she helped them was by teaching them to read. But her love for these suffering people soon found another outlet in the form of Bolshevism, which had become immensely popular at that time. As a teenager, it was "the People" for whom she would fight, in deed and in word too. She began to write poems and to meet with literary people who shared her vision for a new classless future. When she was just sixteen, she met the famous poet Alexander Blok, who would have a great influence on her.

"My spirit longed to engage in heroic feats," she wrote, "even to perish, in order to combat the injustice of the world." She wished to meet others who wanted to give their all for others, who were "daily prepared to lay down their lives for the people."[50] But there was a disconnect. It seemed she mostly met people interested in *talking* about such things—and also writing poems about them and getting together to talk about the poems.

At eighteen, she impetuously married a university student who was a Bolshevik—a member of Lenin's revolutionary Social Democrats. His name was Dimitri Kuz'mina-Karavaev, so her name now became Elizabeth Kuz'mina-Karavaeva. Years later she said that she hardly knew why she married him, but the world of revolutionary ideas in which they swam was intoxicating. Her brilliance as a poet and her connections through Blok and her husband placed her in the heart of Russia's fashionable literary elite. Meetings of the newly formed Poets Guild convened in their well-appointed apartment, attracting artists and other luminaries of the intelligentsia. Elizabeth published her first book of poems during this time, titled *Scythian Shards*, a reference to the name given by the ancient Greeks to the lands bordering the northern coast of the Black Sea.

In these heady days, God and the Russian Orthodox religion held no appeal for her. She did not see the church as alive, but as a mere tradition-laden institution that was so wedded to the culture and to the Tsarist way of life that it had become ossified, had become dead and useless. But the poor people she saw everywhere engaged her mind and heart and soul. It was these people, whom she saw as rooted to the earth and the soil—to "Mother Russia"—who were real and alive, for whom she would fight. Elizabeth longed to be rooted in what was real. All the intellectual talk felt increasingly empty to her.

Meanwhile she and her husband grew apart, separating in early 1913. Immediately thereafter Elizabeth became pregnant by another man and that October gave birth to her first child. She named the girl Gaiana, which is Greek for "earthly one."

Somehow during this time, her passion for justice and for the poor would lead her back toward the Christian faith. After all, if one was seriously interested in the people of Russia, one must be interested in the faith to which most of them looked for meaning. So in that passionate, impetuous way of hers, Elizabeth now enrolled in the Ecclesiastical Academy to study theology—the first woman ever to do so.

If there was a moment when her faith returned to her full-blown, she said it was in that moment when she prayed in front of the famous 1688 icon "Mother of God, Joy of All Who Sorrow (with Coins)" in its St. Petersburg shrine.[51] That was the real turning point. There would be many more turning points ahead, but on the issue of devotion to God, she would never again waver.

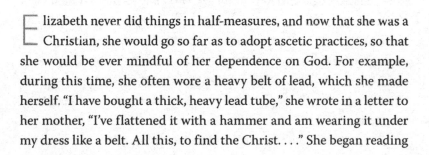

E lizabeth never did things in half-measures, and now that she was a Christian, she would go so far as to adopt ascetic practices, so that she would be ever mindful of her dependence on God. For example, during this time, she often wore a heavy belt of lead, which she made herself. "I have bought a thick, heavy lead tube," she wrote in a letter to her mother, "I've flattened it with a hammer and am wearing it under my dress like a belt. All this, to find the Christ. . . ." She began reading books about the lives of saints—to be sure most of the ones she read about outdid her in their ascetic disciplines—and she prayed, often on the cold floor, always asking God to reveal himself to her, to help her live as she should. But at last her love for the poor had found its focus. "I know their only need is Jesus."[52]

In 1914 Elizabeth left St. Petersburg, returning with her daughter Gaiana to her family roots in Anapa on the Black Sea. There she took over running the family estate, a job that required much of her energies and efforts. But even as she was engaged in this mundane work, her faith continued to grow. In her writings of the time, it's clear that she saw herself as something of a prophet, as an instrument of God in the history of Russia. She even seems to have had a sense of her eventual martyrdom. In one poem from this period, she wrote of ancient martyrs who "went forward to their torture freely/as by God's grace shall we as well."[53]

In a letter to Blok from 1916, she said that she wanted "to proclaim the simple word of God."[54] But she understood that serving God meant serving people. "[T]here is no doubt," she wrote some years later, "that the Christian is called to social work." We are "called to organize a better life for the workers, to provide for the old, to build hospitals, care for children, fight against exploitation, injustice, want, lawlessness."[1]

It was the last item on that list that needed combating in 1917, with the violence and turmoil of the Russian Revolution. Elizabeth never excluded involvement in politics as a way of serving God, so she now joined the Socialist Revolutionary Party and in February 1918 was elected deputy mayor of the town. The acting mayor resigned soon thereafter, and Elizabeth became mayor. She spent much of her energies and time protecting her people against the Bolsheviks, who were quickly gaining power. But because all Soviet Marxists applauded any challenge to Tsarist tradition, as a woman mayor she commanded a certain level of respect from them.

In April, Elizabeth traveled to Moscow as an SRP representative.

But by the time she headed home to Anapa in October, full-blown civil war had erupted across the country. Bolshevik guards, including a burly sailor named Sakharov, were stationed on her return train. When word came that enemy soldiers were moving to intercept, Sakharov decided to execute the passengers.

In a brave and brilliant move Elizabeth demanded to first send a telegram to inform Lenin's wife in Moscow of what was happening. Someone produced a form, and Sakharov told her to jot down her message. She handed Sakharov the completed form, and his confidence crumbled as he tapped out the message on the telegraph: "Tell Ulyanova I am to be immediately shot."[2] It was quite a bluff—and it worked. Believing the woman he was about to kill was a friend of Lenin's wife, Sakharov reversed course. In fact, he was so frightened that no one was executed, nor even searched. If the Bolsheviks uncovered the SRP documents in Elizabeth's possession, she would have been executed for sure.

But after arriving safely in Anapa, Elizabeth would need to marshal her courage again. The anti-Bolshevik White Army, which had taken control of the town, wasted no time in arresting her. While the Bolsheviks considered the SRP enemies for not being "Bolshevik" enough, the White Army also considered the SRP enemies for being not "anti-Bolshevik" enough. Elizabeth was caught in the middle. She didn't know what her sentence would be, but death was well within the range of possibilities. What's more, one of the main witnesses for the prosecution was the town's former mayor, who detested Elizabeth and would now have his revenge. But the judge in the trial—a onetime schoolmaster and new acquaintance named Daniel Skobtsov, five years her senior—intervened and saved her life. After the trial, the pair fell in love and married just months later.

The awful civil war between the Red Bolsheviks and the White anti-Bolsheviks raged on, but eventually the Bolsheviks again gained the upper hand in Anapa, forcing thousands to leave. Elizabeth was now well along in her pregnancy with her son Yuri, and for everyone's safety, she had to be separated for a time from her husband. In March 1920 with her mother, Sophia Pilenko, and with her daughter Gaiana, the pregnant Elizabeth boarded an overcrowded steamer bound for Tbilisi, the capital of Georgia, where Yuri was born a month later.

The following year they reunited with Daniel in Constantinople. The city was swamped with refugees so the family eventually made their way north to Belgrade, where Elizabeth gave birth to her third child, a daughter they named Anastasia. As refugees, they were often hungry and sick. Money was hard to come by, and Daniel could never find adequate work. But everyone believed the situation was temporary. As soon as the Bolsheviks were overthrown, the refugees would return. Despite these hopes, however, the years of Bolshevik rule dragged on.

In 1923 Elizabeth and her family settled in Paris, joining a growing community of Russian émigrés struggling for survival. Daniel worked part-time as a teacher, and Liza earned a few francs from sewing, making dolls, and designing stencils for silk scarves. But the many hours of close work damaged her sensitive eyes. Daniel eventually found work as a taxi driver, somewhat improving their situation, but then, during the winter of 1925–26, after years of malnourishment, the entire family came down with influenza.

Everyone recovered in time, except for their little Anastasia—whom they called Nastia. She never seemed to get better and continued to lose weight. The doctors were baffled. Finally, a new physician on the case diagnosed tubercular meningitis. Nastia was admitted immediately to the Pasteur Institute, where for nearly two months Elizabeth stayed by her four-year-old daughter's side. "I feel how all my life my soul has wandered through little, narrow alleys," she wrote at the time. "Now I want a real and cleared path."[3]

The little girl's health continued to falter until, on March 7, she died.

◆ ◆ ◆

The effects of this on the thirty-four-year-old Elizabeth were devastating and life-changing. In the weeks she watched her daughter slipping away, she had rethought everything, and now, when death came, her grief opened up a dramatic new view of the world. "Into the grave's dark maw are plunged all hopes, plans, habits, calculations, and above all, meaning, the whole meaning of life," she later wrote. "In the face of this, everything needs to be re-examined. . . . People call this a visitation of the Lord. A visitation which brings what? Grief? No, more than grief: for he suddenly reveals the true nature of things."[4]

In the death of her beloved Nastia, Elizabeth felt that she had glimpsed once and for all the eternal truth about our existence, and she didn't want ever to slip back into the quotidian concerns of life.

> I am convinced that anyone who has shared this experience of eternity, if only once; who has understood which way he is going, if only once; who has perceived the One who precedes him, if only once: such a person will find it hard to deviate from this path, to him all comforts will appear ephemeral, all treasures valueless, all companions superfluous if in their midst he fails to see the one Companion, bearing his cross.[5]

It would be the turning point of her life. She felt God was calling her to a life of ministry to the poor and outcasts among the Russian émigré population. Part of this change in her life had to do with the grim reality that after the death of Nastia, the main bond she shared with her husband, Daniel, had been taken away. Their hasty marriage came with what now seemed like insurmountable differences, and in 1927 the couple separated. Yuri stayed with his father but was free to visit his mother whenever he chose. Gaiana, then fourteen, would remain with her mother.

Elizabeth's writing now took a sharp turn. Practical questions of theology and ministry became her primary focus—and not only in words. She began traveling throughout France for the Russian Student

Christian Movement. The organization was founded in 1923 to help struggling émigrés. While despair manifested among these exiles in rampant alcoholism and suicide, Elizabeth glimpsed Christ in even the most degraded souls. She had the heart of a mother, and many of them bared their souls to her in a way they might never have been able to do with a man, and by seeing their innate dignity, she was able to help them find it again as well.

What she did from day to day and week to week varied considerably. She was often initially invited as a speaker, but once she arrived, the immediate needs of the people would arise and her plans would change. "I would find myself transformed from an official lecturer into a confessor," she said.[6] No task was too small if it meant an opportunity to extend the compassion others desperately needed. She once traveled to the Pyrenees to visit refugees who worked in the mines and lived in horrific squalor. Instead of the talk she intended to give, someone said she should scrub the floor if she really wanted to help. She promptly began doing so. Her humility warmed the atmosphere, and the repentant miners invited her to share a meal. One of the men admitted her kindness forestalled his suicide plans—but only temporarily. Elizabeth would have none of it. She bundled up his things and dragged him to the home of a family she knew. In time the man's hope was reborn.

To some extent, Elizabeth knew that God was calling her simply to share the lives of tramps and outcasts, to show them the love of Christ in a radical way and love them as a mother loves her own children. But she knew this did not mean merely accepting them as they were. To do that would be no better than judging them from on high and making them feel small and unworthy.

No, to truly see the dignity of others and to truly love them meant that love would wage war against the evil that had so terribly harmed them. To do this, she became convinced we must first see in each person a reflection of God himself and respond with the kind of humility and passion to serve that such an awesome revelation requires. As she elaborated in a landmark essay, "The Second Gospel Commandment," only once a person perceives the image of God in his brother

> will yet another mystery be revealed to him, which demands of him his most strenuous struggle, his greatest ascetic ascent. He will see how this image of God is obscured, distorted by an evil power. . . . And in the name of the image of God, darkened by the devil, in the name of love for this image of God that pierces his heart, he will want to begin a struggle with the devil, to become an instrument of God in this terrible and scorching work.[7]

As a mere instrument in the work of restoration and healing, there could be no pride in the labor. She described herself in a poem as the "sword in someone else's hand."[8] She underscored this idea of instrumentality in a slim collection of saints' lives, which she published in 1927. "Her narratives were stylized versions of ancient and already stylized tales," said her biographer, Sergei Hackel. "But she was taking stock of herself in their light."[9]

The death of little Nastia set Elizabeth on a new course, and she would soon do it again. Her growing appreciation for what it meant to give of oneself utterly to this "terrible and scorching work" of redemption was about to radicalize her life even further.

A few years after Nastia's death, an opportunity came to move her body to a better location in the cemetery. It was a hard blessing because Elizabeth's presence was legally required for the transfer. To fulfill the duty meant revisiting the death and burial of her beloved daughter in the most concrete terms. But this journey in the necropolis brought another life-changing event. "I became aware of a new and special, broad and all-embracing motherhood," she wrote. "I returned from that cemetery a different person. I saw a new road before me and

SEVEN WOMEN

a new meaning in life." What was it? "To be a mother for all, for all who need maternal care, assistance or protection."[10]

She could no longer be a mother to Nastia, but she would be a mother to everyone she encountered, a mother to the world. But what form would this life take? Elizabeth's only models for such a life were the early Christian monastics. But how could a twice-married mother of three become a nun? Surprisingly, both of her spiritual advisers were open to it. One was Metropolitan Evlogy, who was the Russian Orthodox bishop to much of the Russian diaspora. The other was Father Sergei Bulgakov, whose lectures Elizabeth attended at the Orthodox Theological Institute of Saint Sergius in Paris. In one version of the story, it was actually Evlogy who suggested the move. "I could never be a good nun," said Elizabeth. "I know," answered Evolgy. "But I would like you to be a revolutionary nun."[11]

There were preliminaries. First, her marriage would have to be annulled. This was generally permitted for monastic purposes if both parties agreed, but Daniel Skobtsov was understandably cool to the idea. He nonetheless gave his consent after further conversation with Evlogy, and the couple received an ecclesiastical divorce on March 7, 1932, six years to the day of Nastia's death. Later that month, Elizabeth, dressed all in white, was tonsured and took the monastic habit. Henceforth she would be known as Maria—named for Saint Mary of Egypt, a onetime prostitute whose life became a model of repentance.

Mother Maria began her new life by visiting some monasteries in Latvia and Estonia. But there was a business-as-usual air about these places that she found off-putting. "No one is aware that the world is on fire," she wrote.[12] Given the widening chasm between traditional monasticism and the needs of the world, Maria said there were only two possible responses: "either to deny the new needs of the time without understanding them . . . or, taking this new life into consideration . . . to create a new tradition."[13] Maria chose the second path. She would become the revolutionary nun that Metropolitan Evlogy envisioned.

Mother Maria knew the time for comfort was past and the time to hide from the world was gone. "Today," she said, "there is only monastery for a monk—the whole world. . . . Christ gave the whole world to the Church, and she has no right to renounce its spiritual edification and transfiguration."[14] Thus began a different kind of nun's life, one that would shock some and that would profoundly bless others.

Over the next decade, Maria's principal center would be the homes she established as havens for the destitute and struggling. She rather miraculously procured a desolately empty house at 9 villa de Saxe in Paris and each day providentially brought small additions of furniture and other basics. It was used principally for young Russian women who were without work, and it soon became so crowded that Maria gave up her own room and slept on a cot in the basement, next to the boiler. The large dining space became the common room, where persons of great stature would sometimes come to speak, among them Father Sergei Bulgakov. They converted an upstairs room into a chapel, where Mother Maria's many talents found expression in the icons she painted for the altar partition.

In two years, more space was needed, and the operation was moved to a house that was much larger, and in infinitely worse condition. It was located at 77 rue de Lourmel. In time, Lourmel would become legendary as a place of hospitality, grace, and Christian love. Thousands passed through its doors in the years ahead. They could come and stay as long as necessary, rest, get their bearings, and find healing for soul and body.

In the beginning, Gaiana supervised the kitchen. Mother Maria rose before the sun each morning to go to Les Halles, Paris's massive food market, to bargain for overripe fruit and other food the merchants wished to sell at bargain prices. She would then carry the haul back to Lourmel in a very large sack, and the day's cooking would begin.

Although Lourmel was the principal place of Mother Maria's ministry, she opened other homes too. There was one for single men, another for families who needed accommodation, and there was a capacious country home that served as a sanatorium for consumptives.

◆ ◆ ◆

All she did and how she behaved were without precedent in the world of nuns, and she raised both eyebrows and tempers. She often smoked cigarettes as she shuffled through Les Halles with her giant sack. She dressed shabbily, even for someone who had taken a vow of poverty. Old men's shoes and a second-hand cassock were the usual. But that was only half of it.

A young Anthony Bloom, who many years later became an Orthodox bishop in Britain and Ireland and a popular writer on prayer, was unprepared when he first encountered Mother Maria. "She was a very unusual nun in her behavior and her manners," he said in an interview.

> I was simply staggered when I saw her for the first time in monastic clothes. I was walking along the Boulevard Montparnasse and I saw, in front of a cafe, on the pavement, there was a table, on the table was a glass of beer and behind the glass was sitting a Russian nun in full monastic robes.[15]

Though a stickler at the time, Anthony later became a great admirer of hers.

Mother Maria was aware of her detractors, but she had no doubt she was doing God's will. "At the Last Judgment," she told her friend, Konstantin Mochulsky, "I shall not be asked whether I satisfactorily practiced asceticism, nor how many bows I have made before the divine altar. I will be asked whether I fed the hungry, clothed the naked, visited the sick, and the prisoner in his jail. That is all that will be asked."[16]

Still, her unorthodox ways did not sit well with some in the Russian Orthodox establishment, who made efforts to bring her vision more in line with traditional Orthodox monastic life. In 1936, for instance, a priest, Father Kiprian Kern, arrived from Yugoslavia. His "cold rigorism" caused constant strife and tension with Mother Maria.[17] Her passionate vision of Christian life was calculated to break free of such benumbing shackles, but the break wasn't easy.

Many in the Russian émigré population were also put off by her decidedly untraditional approach. After all, she seemed overly casual about ritual observances, smoked and drank, and had relationships with the most sordid of people. Anyone familiar with the Gospels will hear echoes of the criticisms leveled at Jesus by the religious leaders of his day, and there can be little doubt that Mother Maria reveled in hearing them.

She saw that those who might criticize her as being too worldly were themselves thinking in a worldly way. "The more we go out into the world," she wrote, "the more we give ourselves to the world, the less we are of the world. . . ."[18] But there was no pleasing such critics, and she knew it. "For church circles," she wrote, "we are too far to the left. For the left we are too church-minded."[19] In her radical nonreligious way of serving Christ and her fellow man, she was a picture of what Dietrich Bonhoeffer would a few years hence call "Religionless Christianity."

Maria saw the chaos and the rootlessness of the Russian émigrés as an opportunity to see God anew. "[W]e've become émigrés," she said. "What does that mean? First of all it means freedom." Comfort and convention could become chains. "[W]e must also emigrate out of this well-being," she said. As pilgrims in France, Russian Christians were free to exercise their faith as they liked. But this "weighty gift" of freedom came with obligations. She saw herself and all Christians as charged by God to live out the true faith in action and not to let the dour voices of mere traditionalism quench the fire to serve God by loving and serving others. "We cannot cultivate dead customs—only authentic spiritual fire has weight in religious life. . . . [O]ur God-given freedom calls us to activity and struggle." The struggle would be difficult, but it came with its own rewards. "[W]e will become fools [for] Christ, because we know not only the difficulty of this path but also the immense happiness of feeling God's hand upon what we do."[20]

She saw Christians as coworkers with God. Success would depend upon God's will, she said, but believers nonetheless had their divinely appointed part to play. "[E]ach of us," she said, "is faced with the demand to strain all our forces, not fearing the most difficult endeavor, in ascetic self-restraint, giving our souls for others sacrificially and lovingly, to follow in Christ's footsteps to our appointed Golgotha."[21]

She exemplified grace taken to the extreme. Some thought she took it too far. She once moved a young addict into the house. Right away the girl stole twenty-five francs from Gaiana. While there was no proof, Gaiana demanded she get the boot. Instead, Maria stashed the same amount behind a couch cushion and made a public display of finding it there. "[T]he money was not stolen, after all," she said. "It is dangerous to make an accusation without investigating," she warned.[22] The girl was undone by Maria's unwarranted kindness.

One of the greatest ironies of her life is that although she felt called by God to be a mother to the world, all three of the children she bore would die young. Nastia had died at age four. At twenty-one, Gaiana married and returned to Russia to be with her husband. Her many letters home were full of joy, but in July 1936 Maria received word of Gaiana's death from typhus. She was only twenty-two. Maria, stunned by the news, bolted into the street and didn't return until late in the day, after which she secluded herself for a month to mourn. To lose Gaiana just ten years after losing her Nastia was an earth-shattering blow. "A black night of the utmost spiritual loneliness," she described it.[23] There was no possibility of returning to Russia for herself, so Maria had to make do with a memorial service in Paris. She prayed face down on the floor the entire service. She had dreams of Gaiana and expressed her grief in more poems.

In 1937, Mother Maria was growing more restless and more radical than ever. Combatting her sorrows, she abandoned herself to service, sometimes going for a full day without food and sleep. She would occasionally disappear for days at a time, seeking out homeless sufferers wherever they were, sharing in their existence and inviting them to return to the house at 77 rue de Lourmel for a cheap meal and company. "My feeling for them all is maternal. I would like to swaddle them and rock them to sleep."[24]

◆ ◆ ◆

I n 1939 the Second World War broke out over Europe. In August, Hitler invaded Poland, and with lightning speed the Nazi juggernaut swept eastward toward Russia and westward toward France. On June 14, 1940, Paris fell to the Germans, and life changed dramatically. A mass exodus made refugees of more than two-thirds of the city's population, while those remaining lived under ever-tightening Nazi control.

The German takeover provided an unlikely opportunity for Maria and her ex-husband to reconcile. Their son Yuri lived between their homes. Working with his mother during the day, he would return at night to sleep at his father's house. The practice was too risky to continue, so Daniel recommended he temporarily stay at Lourmel until things settled down. For a brief period the three again lived together under the same roof, though mom and dad had disagreements about their boy's future. Yuri, a student at the Sorbonne, was considering ordination. Mom was for it, dad against. Little did anyone know how much was riding on this question.

Of course, the greatest and most pressing risks belonged to the Jews. Maria had Jewish friends with a farm outside of Paris. Worried the Nazis would seize the property, they transferred the title to Daniel, and he left Lourmel to manage the farm. Meanwhile, Yuri stayed with his mother and assumed a greater role in the ministry—which increasingly included resisting the Occupation.

Mother Maria and her brothers and sisters in Christ at Lourmel were not for a moment tempted to go along with Nazi rule in Paris. They knew that as Christians, they must work with the French Resistance to do all they could—and of course, this meant helping the Jews of Paris. She was one of those rare Christians who saw that the fate of the Jews and Christians, indeed all of humanity, were inextricably intertwined.

It all went back to her understanding of the idea that humanity bears the distorted image of God and the mission of Christ to restore that image. The Jews had a special historical role to play in that story. "God faces His image and likeness, His chosen people, Israel, which represents . . . the person of any people," she wrote. "Throughout its ancient history Israel, in a certain sense, was bearing God. One had to have been a person for the absolute Person to become incarnate in one."[25] So as she saw it, an attack on the Jews was an attack on personhood itself, on the image of God in all people. To defend the Jews was to defend all of humanity, all of what makes us human. But Maria's understanding was not mere theory. As the Nazis increased their persecution of the Parisian Jews, it became life-and-death reality.

In March 1942, Adolf Eichmann ordered that all Jews in occupied territories must wear the yellow star of David. The day of this decree, Mother Maria wrote an unsigned five-stanza poem that quickly spread across all of Paris. The opening and closing lines run as follows:

> *Two triangles, King David's star.*
> *No insult, this ancestral blazon.*
> *It indicates a noble way.*
> *It marks a chosen nation.*

> *May you, stamped by this seal,*
> *this star of David, by decree,*
> *in your constrained response, reveal*
> *that you are spiritually free.*[26]

It was clear that the Christians at Lourmel would not lie down in the face of the Nazi evil. The number of Jews hidden at Lourmel and Mother Maria's other houses cannot be counted. Maria and her colleagues did all they could to hide them and then to transport them to safety beyond France. The facilities were already crammed beyond capacity, but the need just grew.

In her fearlessness and defiance, she seemed to have made her peace with death. At one point, Mother Maria remarked that it was a miracle the Germans hadn't come to Lourmel. If they did, she had a plan. "If the Germans come looking for Jews," she once said, "I'll show them the icon of the Mother of God."[27] Eventually when the Nazis did come to Lourmel—to hang recruitment posters, not arrest Jews— Maria promptly tore the posters down.

There was nothing of the diplomat in her. At one point she met several times with a German pastor named Peters, who was interested in her Christian social work, but when she found out he was a proud Nazi and part of the Nazified "Deutsche Christen"[28] she challenged him: "How could you be both a Christian and a Nazi?"[29]

The year prior to the Nazi occupation, in October 1939, Father Dimitri Klepinin had come to Lourmel, replacing Father Kiprian Kern. As much as Father Kiprian and Mother Maria bumped heads and antagonized each other, Father Dimitri and she saw eye to eye. His friendship would be a profound comfort to her and to her son Yuri and the others at Lourmel. Father Dimitri was a mild-mannered and sensitive soul, but on this issue of what to do in the face of Nazi evil, he was clear and bold. He would joyfully lie to the Nazis and deceive them in any way necessary. After the Eichmann decree, many Jews came to Lourmel requesting forged baptismal certificates, and at the risk of his own life, Father Dimitri began producing them by the dozens. "I think the good Christ would give me that paper if I were in their place," he said.[30] To cover these tracks, in case the Nazis checked church rolls, he began forging the names of Jews into the congregational records of Lourmel.

On July 15–16, 1942, things took a sharp turn for the worse when the Nazis began mass arrests of the Jews. Nearly 13,000 were rounded up. Of those, 6,900 were taken to the Vélodrome d'Hiver; 4,051 were children. The enclosed sports stadium was a brief walk from Lourmel, and Mother Maria went to see what she could do to help. The guard at the entrance was French. To him Maria was any other nun—how much trouble could a nun cause? So after telling her to restrict herself to spiritual work, he let her pass.

What she saw inside was horrific. There were just ten latrines, and only a single hydrant provided water on a blazing summer day. Mother Maria did all she could to comfort those who were there and distributed the little food she was able to bring. She ministered amid this chaos for three days. Seizing an opportunity with some sympathetic garbage collectors, she helped smuggle four children out of the Vélodrome over two days in a pair of trash cans. At least these four were saved. At the end of the five days, every child in the stadium was taken from its parents and sent to Auschwitz, where—in one of the most evil acts of an evil regime—all four thousand were murdered.

After Christmas, rumors came that the Gestapo and the feared SD security force had their eyes on Maria and Father Dimitri and that arrests were likely. The pair had already been interviewed by a plainclothes SD officer named Hans Hoffmann in August and knew that he was keeping a dossier on their suspected activities. Friends advised they go underground. Daniel urged Maria to hide at the farm. She and Yuri had recently begun visiting him, and it was far enough out of town that she might escape notice. But she pushed off all concerns. "Only have faith," she said.[31]

◆ ◆ ◆

A t last Yuri decided to enter the priesthood. Metropolitan Evlogy supported the idea, but the boy's father was a different matter. Unfortunately, the persuasive bishop could not help this time. Maria decided to travel to the farm on Sunday, February 7, 1943, to convince her ex-husband the move was right for their son. As she planned it, Yuri would arrive on Monday and then talk with Daniel directly. He never arrived.

On February 8, 1943, Hoffmann and two Gestapo agents came

to Lourmel for Mother Maria. When told she was away, they began searching and seizing her files. Yuri was trying to leave to warn his mother when he was spotted by Hoffmann and searched. In his jacket pocket they found a letter written to Father Dimitri requesting a baptismal certificate. They would hold Yuri as a hostage until Maria came to see them. Many hostages of the Nazis were being shot, so the stakes were high.

The Gestapo took Father Dimitri as well and interrogated him for six hours. Hoffmann offered freedom if he agreed to stop helping Jews. "I am a Christian," he answered, "and must act as I must."[32] Hoffmann called him a Jew-lover and struck his face. Bold as Mother Maria, Father Dimitri lifted his pectoral cross and asked, "And this Jew here, do you know Him?"[33] That time he was knocked to the ground. But the Christians in Mother Maria's orbit would not compromise their faith. For them it was unthinkable. They had all made their peace with death.

Mother Maria's own mother, Sophia Pilenko, now in her eighties, was no different. Mother Maria got word of Yuri's arrest late Monday and cautiously returned to Paris on Wednesday to immediate arrest. Hoffmann taunted Sophia. "You brought your daughter up badly!" he shouted. "All she can do is help yids!" But the old woman replied, "My daughter is a genuine Christian. . . . If you were threatened by some disaster, she would help you too."[34] Mother Maria smiled and agreed. In this way they heaped hot coals on the heads of their persecutors.

Maria was first taken to the Gestapo headquarters in Paris, where Yuri and Father Dimitri were being held. Daniel tried to get help from lawyers, anyone who could secure their release, but it was useless. Together at first, the prisoners were separated later in the month. Yuri and Father Dimitri were taken to Compiègne-Royallieu, where the Nazis had established an internment camp. Mother Maria was left behind until April. Daniel tried to visit her on April 21 but only caught sight of her on a bus being transferred to Compiègne. She waved as she passed.

Briefly reunited at Compiègne, Maria saw her son for the last time.

Yuri snuck through a window to be with her. They spent a few hours together and said their good-byes at dawn. Maria told him not to fret about her. She knew that her son's faith was strong. While they were together, Yuri told his mother that his favorite prayer was the Jesus Prayer: "Lord Jesus Christ, Son of God, have mercy on me a sinner." Regardless of their circumstances, he said, this mutual prayer would hold them together.

The following morning, Maria was sealed with two hundred other women into cattle trucks to make the long journey east. They were in these trucks without sanitation or water for three days. Eventually they arrived at Ravensbrück Concentration Camp. She would spend two years there.

Yuri and Father Dimitri remained at Compiègne through 1943, making the best of circumstances by holding church, Bible study, and even some frivolity. Father Dimitri was able to write letters to his wife and told in one how he, Yuri, and two others were going to save the wine they were served with lunch and drink it together before a party planned to boost prisoner morale. It didn't do much good. On December 16, Yuri and Father Dimitri were transferred from Compiègne to Buchenwald and then moved again to Dora. Ten days after his arrival, Yuri's body erupted in boils. The Nazis had no plans to treat the condition. The twenty-four-year-old Yuri was instead dispatched on February 6, 1944. Father Dimitri joined him just days later, succumbing to pneumonia.

Mother Maria was the same beacon in Ravensbrück that she was in Paris. In the midst of horrifically depressing conditions, she organized prayer groups in the evenings. She read from the Gospels, and then everyone discussed the meaning of what they'd heard, and then they prayed together. Well-read and knowledgeable on many subjects, Maria organized discussion groups to help her fellow prisoners get their minds off the misery of the camp. After visits with her, one survivor recalled, prisoners left "radiant."[35]

Some of the Russian prisoners worked during the day in fields that were outside the camp, and when they returned they sometimes gave Mother Maria a potato or a carrot that they had smuggled back under their clothing. Mother Maria rarely ate these herself but put them in a secret place to share later with those she felt needed them more than she did. It was only in the end, when she was herself ailing, that she would indulge herself.

During her two years at Ravensbrück, Mother Maria was able to do some embroidery. The only one that survived is an extraordinary visualization of the Normandy Invasion stitched with foraged materials on a kerchief and patterned on the Bayeaux tapestry. She had bet someone that the Russians would win the war before the Allies had a chance to enact their D-day plans. But she was wrong, and she happily paid up in the form of this beautiful piece of art.

Another survivor remembered her as constantly upbeat and friendly. "She was never downcast, never," said Solange Périchon. "She allowed nothing of secondary importance to impede her contact with people."[36]

But despite her buoyant spirit, conditions in the camp deteriorated, and the overcrowding, disease, and malnutrition took their toll. In January 1945, her health was suffering, so she accepted the camp's offer of a pink card given to those who wished to be excused from the work details. Like all such offers by the Nazis, it was no offer at all. Soon all those who held such cards were transported to another camp, which was a place designed to accelerate death. The Nazis knew they were losing the war and wished to kill off as many of these prisoners as they could. Amazingly, Maria survived five weeks at that camp and then was for some reason returned to the regular camp, where she lived out her last days.

Though she was unable to stand for roll call, she traded some bread for thread so she could embroider one last icon. Survivors said she was constantly at prayer now. This embroidery would be her final litany. It depicted Mary holding Jesus, a traditional image, but in Mother Maria's rendition Mary held Christ crucified. She never had the chance to finish it.[37]

We do not know the details of her last moments. On March 30, 1945, Mother Maria Skobtsova was taken to the gas chamber at Ravensbrück. It was Good Friday. Some have said she was selected to die, but others say she deliberately took the place of another prisoner who had been chosen to die. "It is very possible that she took the place of a frantic companion," said survivor Jacqueline Péry. "It would have been entirely in keeping with her generous life. In any case she offered herself consciously to the holocaust . . . thus assisting each one of us to accept the cross. . . ." Péry added, "She radiated the peace of God."[38]

She died the next day, on Great and Holy Saturday, a paradoxical day on the church calendar when Orthodox Christians mark both Christ's Sabbath rest in the tomb from his labor on the cross *and* his violent destruction of hades and the liberation of its captives.

According to Jim Forest, writing in the introduction to Mother Maria's essential writings in English, the reason Mother Maria was not canonized by the Orthodox church until the twenty-first century was likely that she heroically and uncompromisingly challenged a church hierarchy that had allowed the church of Jesus Christ to become ossified by traditionalism and to abandon its holy and prophetic witness against the world around it.

Mother Maria remains an indictment of any form of Christianity that seeks Christ chiefly inside the walls of our churches. Like so many who have valiantly served God, she challenged the church establishment even when not wishing to do so. Her passion for God lived out in her time and place enabled others to see God anew, shorn of religious trappings. Father Michael Plekon wrote that Mother Maria's life points us to a fundamental reality . . . namely that the Christian's commitment is not primarily to a heritage, to structures of the past nor even to visions of the what the future should be. Rather, each Christian, monastic or cleric or layperson, is called to real life, life in the Church and the world as we find it, an encounter with God, oneself, and the neighbor in need.[45]

But the Orthodox Church's hesitation to canonize this great woman of God was eventually seen for what it was: a mistake. Finally in 2004, on May 1 and 2, Mother Maria would become Saint Maria of Paris. At the Saint Alexander Nevsky Cathedral in Paris, just three miles from 77 rue de Lourmel, she—along with her son Yuri and Father Dimitri Klepinin—were officially recognized as saints in the Orthodox Church by the Holy Synod of the Patriarchate of Constantinople. July 20 was established as the day each year when they would be remembered in the church calendar. Another distinction came even earlier from the Jewish people she sought to save. In 1985 Yad Vashem listed Mother Maria and Father Dimitri as Righteous Gentiles for their sacrificial efforts.[46]

Just as Dietrich Bonhoeffer prophetically challenged the Lutheran Church of Germany in his time, so Mother Maria challenged the Orthodox Church of hers. Both understood that to serve Jesus Christ with all one's heart, soul, mind, and body—that is to be the church of Jesus Christ, to be the Bride for which he will one day return.

Even so, come Lord Jesus.

FIVE

Corrie ten Boom

1892–1983

M any people know the inspiring story of Corrie ten Boom and her family, who risked their lives to rescue their Jewish neighbors during the Nazi occupation of Holland. Their saga is captured beautifully in Corrie's classic book *The Hiding Place*, as well as in the 1975 film of the same name, starring the great Julie Harris. But few people are aware of the larger story that led the family to hide Jews in their home in the first place. It was a bold and tremendously fateful decision, as we shall see.

The family's bravery didn't come out of nowhere. It grew out of a profound Christian faith of a family who had for three generations devoutly believed that the Jews were God's chosen people. Like Lutheran pastor and theologian Dietrich Bonhoeffer in Germany, they believed it was their duty as Christians to help God's chosen people when their lives were in danger, as they certainly were in Nazi-occupied Holland in the 1940s.

The same faith that led to the Ten Boom family's determination to help as many Jews as possible also led to Corrie's great ministry in the decades after the war: teaching people how to forgive even the most horrific sins committed against them.

◆ ◆ ◆

Cornelia "Corrie" ten Boom was born on April 15, 1892, in Amsterdam. She was the youngest of the four children born to her parents, Casper and Cornelia. Corrie's brother, Willem, was born in 1886; her sister, Arnolda "Nollie" was born in 1890; and Elizabeth "Betsie" was born in 1885.

Casper ten Boom was a watchmaker, just as his own father had been. The family watch shop had opened for business in 1837, in a narrow Haarlem house called the Beje (a shortened version of the street address, the Barteljorisstraat), where generations of Ten Booms had lived.

Already nearly a century before the Nazi invasion of Holland, we see the first sign that the Ten Boom family had a special commitment to the welfare of their Jewish neighbors. It happened when Corrie's grandfather Willem received a visit from the family minister, Dominee Witteveen.

"Willem," the minister had begun, "you know the Scriptures tell us to pray for the peace of Jerusalem and the blessing of the Jews."

"Yes, Dominee," Willem responded. "I have always loved God's ancient people—they gave us our Bible and our Savior."

Shortly after this, the two men formed a prayer fellowship for the express purpose of praying for the Jews. "In a divine way which is beyond human understanding," Corrie wrote, "God answered those prayers. It was in the same house, exactly one hundred years later, that Grandfather's son, my father, four of his grandchildren, and one great-grandson were arrested for helping save the lives of Jews during the German occupation of Holland."[1]

After Corrie's parents married in 1884, they moved to a house in the Jewish quarter of Amsterdam, about twelve miles from Haarlem. There Casper opened a jewelry store. He was a member of the Dutch Reformed Church, but his Jewish neighbors, sensing his openness and friendliness toward them, often invited him to take part in their Sabbaths and other holy days and study the Talmud with them. Corrie said that he was "given opportunities to understand and explain the fulfillment of the prophecies of the Old Testament in the New Testament."[2] Casper's love for the Jewish people increased during those years.

Shortly after Corrie's birth, her paternal grandfather died, so Casper and Cornelia moved the family back to Haarlem to take over the watch shop. Despite modest circumstances, the small house above the Beje was a deeply happy one, and gratitude to God that grew out of their deep faith was at the center of their happiness. Their home actually comprised two tall, narrow houses that had been turned into one. Neighbors frequently turned up for meals in the Ten Boom house, where they were welcomed enthusiastically. The conversation was lively, and family concerts often followed.

Faith was at the heart of everything for the Ten Boom's. Corrie's mother led five-year-old Corrie to belief in Jesus Christ, after which the little girl immediately began praying for the people on her street, especially for the drunks she often saw being led into jail.

Corrie's mother taught her children to have compassion for those whose minds or bodies were damaged. Her father's painstaking work repairing watches showed Corrie the importance of working hard and doing one's best. He urged his children to live out their faith and to live lives of honesty and integrity, recognizing that God's eyes were always on them.

Each day opened and closed in Bible-reading and prayer, and throughout her long life, Corrie never forgot how her father came into her room at night to tuck her in—to pray with her, touch her face, and wish her a good night. Some forty years later, while trying to sleep in a filthy concentration camp bed, she would remember the comforting feel of her father's hand on her face. Many of the experiences and Scripture lessons their parents gave Corrie and Betsie as children prepared them for what was at the time an unimaginable future.

It seemed that everyone in Haarlem knew and loved Casper ten Boom. He was known affectionately as the Grand Old Man of Haarlem. Each day after lunch it was his habit to walk through the town exchanging greetings with his friends.

Corrie's three aunts lived with the family too. They were devout in their faith as well. Corrie recalled how her Tante Anna formed a club for female servants of wealthy families, inviting them to the Beje in the evenings for sewing, embroidery, singing, and Bible lessons; and Tante Jans organized get-togethers for young women and invited soldiers to the Ten Boom home for evenings of friendly home life and Bible study.

Through the years the special family commitment to the welfare of the Jewish people continued. In fact, Corrie's brother Willem believed God was calling him to serve as a minister to the Jews. He traveled to Germany for study in the 1920s, and in 1927, just six years before the Third Reich came to power, he wrote a thesis in which he declared that (in reference to the Jewish people) the "severest pogrom in the entire history of the world could come in Germany."[3] At the time, his professors laughed at the idea, which they thought preposterous.

As the First World War came to an end, the Ten Boom family wanted to reach out to the defeated nation of Germany, where large numbers of children were suffering from malnutrition. Corrie's father contacted watchmaker colleagues all over the Netherlands, suggesting that they take in a German child or two, feed them well and get them healthy, and then return them to their families. Many agreed to do so. The Ten Boom family took in four such children.

In 1920, when Corrie was twenty-eight, she began attending a Haarlem Bible school, studying the Old and New Testaments, church history, ethics, and dogmatics. The following year Corrie lost her mother, who had suffered several strokes and become bedridden. It was around this time that Corrie, who had always been responsible for the housekeeping, began helping her father in his shop, assisting customers, keeping the books, and eventually learning how to repair watches herself. Corrie took to the family business so readily that her father decided to send her to Switzerland, so that she could learn the craft properly. She would become the first woman in the Netherlands to be licensed as a watchmaker.

Corrie's brother, Willem, and sister Nollie eventually married and had families of their own, but Corrie and Betsie remained single. In 1923, as a way of sharing their Christian faith, the sisters began forming clubs for young girls. In those days Sunday school typically ended when girls were about twelve, but Corrie and Betsie wanted to provide girls with further religious education during the critical teenage years. They began a walking club and, after many of their hikes, would take some of the girls to a youth church. The club became so popular that within a short time, Corrie and Betsie recruited dozens of other leaders to assist them. After a clubhouse was donated the sisters formed a number of clubs, some for teaching English, others for gymnastics, music, and hiking. But each of them included Bible study. As a result, many of the young girls came to faith.

Eventually, Corrie started a club for boys and girls together. Coeducation was virtually unheard of at the time, and some church leaders and many parents were shocked. But Corrie knew some of the girls in the clubs were meeting boyfriends in secret. She felt that a club, where they could meet openly and under friendly supervision, would be a healthier situation. And so it proved to be.

Corrie's zeal to share her faith seemed to know no bounds. While all the clubs continued to thrive, she began holding religious services for children with intellectual challenges. "[I]t was such a joy," she wrote, "to know that the Lord doesn't need a high IQ in a person in order to reveal Himself. In fact, people of normal or superior intelligence likewise need the help of the Holy Spirit to understand the spiritual truths, which are only spiritually discerned."[4] Corrie had also befriended a mentally disturbed woman in a hospital and visited her often, sharing her faith with her.

By the early 1930s Corrie's three aunts had died, and the population of the Beje was down to Corrie, Betsie, and their father. But the quiet did not last long. The Ten Booms soon agreed to take in seven children of missionaries, who were working abroad. The children much preferred the friendly environment of the Ten Boom home to the cold atmosphere of a boarding school.

This period was especially joyful for Corrie and Betsie. Nearly fifty years later Corrie recalled, "Our quiet, thin little three-story house was suddenly stretching its walls and echoing with the activity of [the] children. The side door swung in and out like the pendulum on one of our clocks, and it was a good sound. . . . Although Betsie and I never married, we received such love from all of our children and were able to give them so much of ours!"⁵

During these years, Corrie was constantly in prayer, asking God to help her meet the needs—particularly the financial needs—of her large family. And she taught her foster children much about God. It was not until many years later, following the war, that Corrie learned how deeply her teaching about God, and the need to forgive our enemies, had sunk into these children.

By 1940 all seven children were grown and gone, and another, darker, phase of Corrie's life was about to begin. She never forgot the night of May 14, when Adolf Hitler ordered "the first large-scale airborne attack in the history of warfare" on the citizens of Rotterdam, less than thirty miles from Haarlem.⁶ These attacks killed close to nine hundred people, mostly civilians. Thousands more were wounded, and seventy-eight thousand were rendered homeless.

That night Corrie, awakening in terror to the sounds of bombs landing and sirens screaming, learned the first of many lessons in forgiveness from her beloved sister. In addition to praying that night for their country, the injured, and the dead, Betsie was also praying "for the Germans, up there in the planes, caught in the first of the giant evil loose in Germany."[7] Corrie, hearing her sister's prayers, prayed that God would hear Betsie's prayers, because she could not bring herself to pray for the Germans. Just five days later, when the Nazis threatened Holland with another horrific air attack, the Dutch surrendered. Soon German tanks rumbled down the streets where Corrie had played as a child.

Holland suddenly became an occupied country. But the work for which God had spent fifty years preparing Corrie was about to begin.

The German occupation brought many changes to the Ten Boom family. Their telephone was cut off, their bicycles were confiscated, and everyone was issued an identity card. They needed ration cards to buy food. Throughout the country young men walking with their families on a Sunday afternoon, or merely sitting with them in church, were arrested and taken to Germany to work in factories. Many never returned.

The Nazis demanded that everyone turn in his radio. The Ten Booms had two, so they turned in one and then built a special hiding place beneath the staircase for the other. This way they could listen to news of the war from England.

Back at the watch shop, Corrie and her father now found themselves serving German soldiers. At night the family lay awake listening to dogfights between British and German planes in the skies over Haarlem.

Things gradually grew worse for Holland's Jews. Eventually they were required to wear yellow stars on their clothes, and eighty-year-old Casper, identifying with God's ancient people as he always had, decided to wear one too. Rocks were thrown at Jewish-owned businesses; anti-Semitic words were painted on synagogues; and signs were posted on stores announcing that Jews would not be served. All these things were the work of a pro-Nazi Dutch organization known as the National Socialist Bond. While some joined the NSB for more food, clothing coupons, and better jobs and housing, others did so because they truly believed in the Nazi cause.

Gradually Jewish shops were closed, and Jewish homes emptied of their inhabitants. Nobody knew where they had gone. Had they gone into hiding, or had the Gestapo taken them away?

Corrie's brother, Willem, had been bravely hiding Jews since the occupation began, both in his own home and in the homes of others. It took a terrifying incident to lead Corrie and Betsie to do the same. In November 1941 Corrie saw four German soldiers march to the store belonging to her neighbor, Mr. Weil. Moments later Mr. Weil emerged, a gun muzzle pressed to his stomach. Leaving him outside, the German soldier rejoined the others to smash everything breakable and to steal the fur coats Mr. Weil sold in his store.

Corrie and Betsie urged their friend to come into their house before the Germans could take him away. They contacted Willem, who instructed his son Kik to take Mr. Weil and his wife away to safety.

This launched Corrie's work with the underground resistance movement. But as she considered what continuing in this work would involve—lying, stealing, perhaps even killing—she had to ask herself if this was how God wanted her to behave in such circumstances. How should Christians act in the face of evil?

One evening, her mind made up, Corrie prayed, "Lord Jesus, I offer myself for Your people. In any way. Any place. Any time."[8] Since increasing numbers of Jews were being arrested on the streets, Corrie started traveling to the homes of the family's Jewish customers.

One night a knock came on the alley door. A frightened woman stood in the darkness. "My name is Kleermaker. I'm a Jew," she told Corrie. She had heard that the Ten Booms had helped another Jew. Casper ten Boom did not let her finish. "In this household, God's people are always welcome."[9]

Two nights later another knock came, and Corrie answered the door to an elderly Jewish couple. They joined Mrs. Kleermaker upstairs.

Two years into the Nazi occupation, the food shortage was becoming acute. Ration cards were not issued to Jews, so the Ten Booms used their own to purchase food for their Jewish guests. It was becoming urgently necessary to obtain more cards however they could. How else would they feed their Jewish guests—and any future guests they might receive?

A name popped into Corrie's head: Fred Koornstra, the father of a girl who attended the religious services Corrie held for the intellectually challenged. Koornstra now worked at the Food Office, where ration books were issued.

Praying that God would close her lips if Fred could not be trusted, Corrie told him they had some unexpected guests—Jewish guests. They needed ration cards. Could he help? Fred was sympathetic. But he told Corrie he could not give her extra ration cards because they were checked in too many ways. The only way to get their hands on extra cards would be to stage a robbery. He knew of a man who might cooperate in this effort. How many ration cards did Corrie need?

Corrie, intending to answer "five," instead found herself saying "one hundred." A week later Fred knocked on the Ten Booms's doors and handed them one hundred ration cards. He would continue to bring cards each week. Since even sympathetic Hollanders, due to their limited resources, were reluctant to take on extra people on their limited resources, these precious cards meant the Jews living with the Ten Booms, and those who came after them, could find safer homes farther away from the center of Haarlem.

Trust was the issue, but as writer and minister Michal Ann Goll wrote,

> In a social and political environment in which the wisest human course was to trust no one, it nevertheless was necessary on occasion for Corrie to seek help from someone who could supply a particular need. The risk was in not knowing whether the person approached would be sympathetic or would betray the operation to the Nazi

authorities. Time after time Corrie received what she called the "gift of knowledge" when these decisions were needed.[10]

There would be other problems to solve—women who went into labor, for instance. Since the Ten Booms knew so many people in Haarlem, asking for help would not be a problem, except for the ticklish fact that they did not know the political views of all their neighbors. Who would help deliver a Jewish baby in secret—and who would turn the mother in?

The only solution was to pray. They had no doubt that God was real and that he wanted them to continue doing what they were doing. They knew if they prayed he would guide them.

At a gathering of underground workers, a well-known architect suggested that Corrie allow him to design a secret room in her house, just in case the Gestapo paid an unexpected visit. He chose Corrie's bedroom at the top of the house, and within days he and his workmen had constructed a brick wall, creating a two-and-a-half-foot-wide space big enough for several people to hide in. A low, sliding panel gave access to the hiding place. The secret room contained a mattress, a bucket of water, vitamins, and hardtack. The Gestapo, the architect predicted, would never find the secret room.

Over the next few months scores of Jews passed through the Ten Boom home, staying for as little as one night or as long as several weeks. Corrie and Betsie found innovative ways to deal with all sorts of problems, such as getting their telephone line reinstalled—a great help now that Corrie was working with some eighty underground volunteers.

The sisters developed a code when talking on the telephone, which they knew might be tapped. "We have a woman's watch here that needs repairing. But I can't find a mainspring. Do you know who might have one?" This meant, "We have a Jewish woman in need of a hiding place, and we can't find one among our regular contacts."[11]

Finally the day came when the Ten Booms began taking in permanent guests—seven in all. A member of the underground installed an alarm system, and the refugees began holding regular drills to see how quickly they could make it to the hiding place at the top of the house.

Even with the shortages and the stress and strains of daily life, the Ten Booms and their guests were cheerful. Corrie and Betsie did their best to keep their guests entertained, performing little concerts in the evenings or reading Shakespeare plays aloud. Their Jewish guests also helped pass the time in the evenings with Hebrew lessons.

Eighteen months after they had begun actively helping Jews, the Beje had become "the center of an underground ring that spread to the farthest corners of Holland. Here daily came dozens of workers, reports, appeals," Corrie wrote. "We had to go on, but we knew that disaster could not be long in coming. . . ."[12]

The first blow struck at Nollie's house. Corrie's sister and the Jews hiding in her home were arrested. While the Jews were freed shortly afterward in a daring rescue operation, Nollie remained behind bars for seven weeks.

And then, on February 28, 1944, Betsie woke Corrie, who was sick with influenza. Betsie said that a man was downstairs waiting to speak with her. The man—a stranger—told Corrie his wife had been arrested, and that he needed six hundred guilders to bribe a policeman. Corrie hesitated, not liking the way the man refused to meet her eyes. But in the end, fearing a Jewish life was at stake, she told him to come back in half an hour for the money.

After sending an underground worker to the bank, Corrie went back to bed and fell asleep. Suddenly she was awakened by the sound of the ringing buzzer, running feet, and terrified voices. One by one, the "permanent guests" raced into Corrie's room and slid through the little door to the secret room.

Moments later, a man burst into Corrie's bedroom and began firing questions at her. "So you're the ringleader! Tell me now, where are you hiding the Jews."

"I don't know what you're talking about," Corrie responded.[13]

The man, a member of the Gestapo, ordered Corrie to dress and

escorted her downstairs, where her father, Betsie, and several underground workers were waiting. Other Gestapo agents were banging on
the walls with hammers, searching for secret rooms.

An agent turned his attention to Corrie, determined to find out
information. He slapped her hard across the face. "Where are the Jews?"
he demanded. "Where do you hide the ration cards?" He slapped her
again and again. "Where is your secret room?"

Corrie, about to lose consciousness from the beating, cried out,
"Lord Jesus, protect me!"

The Gestapo agent's hand stopped in mid-slap. "If you say that
name again, I'll kill you!" he shouted. But he did not slap her again.[14]

As other underground workers knocked on the shop door, the
Gestapo ordered them into the house and began interrogating them
too. Eventually Corrie, her father, brother Willem, sisters Betsie and
Nollie, along with Nollie's son, Peter, were taken to the police station,
along with thirty-five others who happened to stop by the Beje that day.

That evening, after hours of being asked for their names, addresses,
and occupations, many prisoners gathered around Casper ten Boom
to hear him pray the words from Psalm 119:114, 117: "You are my hiding place and my shield; I hope in Your word. . . . Hold me up, and I
shall be safe."

The next morning the Ten Boom family—Corrie, Betsie, Willem,
Nollie, Peter, and Casper—were marched outside and ordered onto a
bus. Two hours later they arrived in The Hague and were brought to
a building rumored to be the Gestapo headquarters in Holland. They
spent another long day answering the same questions, over and over
again, and then they were ordered into an army truck to be driven to
Scheveningen, where a brick-walled federal penitentiary awaited them.

After a long wait the women prisoners were ordered to follow a
matron down a corridor. Turning for what would be her last look at her
beloved father, Corrie burst out, "Father! God be with you!"

Casper turned to face her. "And with you, my daughters," he said.[15]

Down the corridor first Betsie, then Nollie, then Corrie were put into tiny cells. As the door opened to Corrie's cell, she saw four women already there, one on a cot, three others on straw ticking on the floor. A kind cell mate hung up her hat. This prison was to be her home for the next four months. Food was handed in through a shelf in the door, as was a sanitary bucket.

Intense boredom settled in, relieved only by Corrie's worry over her family and the fate of the little group of people hiding on the top floor of the Beje, which was now surrounded by Germans day and night.

Two weeks later the door to the cell opened, and a matron ordered Corrie out. She was led along another prison corridor and put into another cell. The matron slammed the door behind her and left. She was now in solitary confinement, with only a stinking cot and blanket to keep her company. No explanation was given. When food was shoved through the shelf in the door, she was too sick to get up. Some time later a hunk of bread was thrown in where she could reach it. In her fear, she remembered finding it difficult to pray. On April 17 she was allowed her first shower in six weeks. She was deeply grateful for small mercies.

On Hitler's birthday, all the guards attended a party. The inmates took full advantage of the sudden freedom and shouted messages to one another. Thus Corrie received a message from Betsie—"God is good"—and discovered that Nollie had been released a month previously.[16] So had her brother, Willem, and nephew Peter. Corrie was overjoyed. But what had become of her father?

A week later Corrie received a package from Nollie, filled with cookies, a sweater, a towel, and a needle and thread. There was also a message under the stamp on the envelope: "All the watches in your closet are safe."[17] Understanding the real meaning of this, Corrie burst into tears of joy.

But on May 3 there was devastating news. Nollie wrote a letter to Corrie telling her that their father, Casper ten Boom, had survived only ten days in prison.

Not long afterward Corrie was called to her first hearing. The officer treated her kindly, using every psychological tool he had to break her down and get her to admit to illegal activities. But she stood firm—and then, to her own astonishment, she began to tell him about God. The officer swiftly cut her off, but the next day, and for two additional days afterward, he had her taken out of her cell and asked her to tell him more about what the Bible taught and about her family, especially her father.

The German confessed to Corrie that he could not bear the work he did at the prison. He wanted to know how she could continue to believe in God when that same God had allowed her father to die in prison. Before she was able to answer, she was taken back to her cell. But this officer—Lieutenant Rahms—had arranged for Betsie's cell door to be opened just as Corrie was walking past it. It was a brief moment of joy.

June 6, 1944, on the beaches of Normandy, far from Corrie's prison walls, the invasion of Europe by Allied forces had begun. Within a year the terrible war would be over. But it was far from over for Corrie. Around this time, all the inmates in her prison were ordered from their cells and taken by bus to a freight yard. Weeping tears of relief and gratitude, Corrie was finally reunited with Betsie. They had not seen each other in four months. It had been their first separation in fifty-three years.

The prisoners were ordered to board a train, which jerked to a start in the early hours of the morning. Some hours later, they were ordered off in the middle of a wood and told to march for more than a mile until they reached a row of barracks. It was Camp Vught, a concentration camp. This, Corrie realized, would be their new home.

The camp staff assigned work to the prisoners: Betsie was to work sewing prison uniforms; Corrie was to make radios for German flyers. She would do this eleven long hours each day. The foreman in Corrie's barracks factory, Mr. Moorman, had served as headmaster of a Catholic school for boys before the war. One day, as he watched Corrie work on relay switches, he bent down to whisper to her, "'Dear watch lady! Can you not remember for whom you are working? These radios are for their fighter planes!' He reached over to pull a wire loose and twist tubes from their assembly. 'Now solder them back wrong. And not so fast! You're over the day's quota and it's not yet noon.'"[18]

On their lunch breaks the inmates were allowed to wander around the compound freely. Evenings meant conversation with Betsie and the sharing of camp news. Betsie, as usual, spent much time passionately sharing her faith with the women around her and praying with them too.

One day Betsie had disturbing news for Corrie. Through other prisoners, she had discovered the name of the stranger who had betrayed the Ten Booms that fateful day—and who had caused them such pain ever since. The man's name was Jan Vogel. As Corrie later wrote, "I thought of Father's final hours, alone and confused . . . of the Underground work so abruptly halted. . . . And I knew that if Jan Vogel stood in front of me now I could kill him."[19]

But Corrie was astonished at Betsie's reaction to the news. Unlike Corrie, she was completely free of anger. Finally Corrie asked, "Betsie, don't you feel anything about Jan Vogel? Doesn't it bother you?"

"Oh yes, Corrie! Terribly," Betsie replied. "I've felt for him ever since I knew—and pray for him whenever his name comes into my mind. How dreadfully he must be suffering!"[20]

Thinking of her sister's words that night as she tried to sleep, Corrie began to wonder if Betsie, in her gentle way, was reminding her that in God's eyes, she was guilty too. Didn't Jan Vogel and she both stand before an all-seeing God? And according to Jesus's standard in the New Testament, they were both guilty of murder because, Corrie wrote, "I had murdered him with my heart and with my tongue."[21] She prayed that God would forgive her, as she now forgave Jan Vogel, and asked God to bless his family.

While her work on the radios was satisfying, in its way, and the food was a marked improvement over what Corrie and Betsie had been fed in prison, there were still hours of terrible cruelty. For instance, as punishment for some slight violation of the rules by one inmate, all the prisoners were forced to rise at 4:00 a.m. or earlier and stand at attention for an hour or more.

And there was worse to come. One morning in early September 1944, the women were ordered to pack their few possessions. They were marched out of the camp down the same dirt road they had traversed ten weeks earlier, on the night they had arrived. More than one thousand women and many men were forced to board the boxcars of a freight train. Eighty women were jammed in Corrie's car before the door was slammed shut; they screamed, cried, and fainted in an upright position because of the intense press of bodies.

The women found a way to sit, but after many hours in the stationary train, the air inevitably became foul. Finally the train began to move, and for the rest of the day and for the next two days, it traveled in fits and starts as the Germans repaired damaged rail track ahead of them. The miserable passengers fought thirst and hunger and the almost unbearable stench. Then they heard frightening news: they had entered Germany. The women were forced to spend two more days and nights traveling in the filthy boxcar.

On the fourth morning of this hellish trip, the train came to a halt and the door was flung open. Their lips were cracked from thirst, and they were glad at last to relieve their thirst with buckets of water from a nearby lake. Then the women were marched off through a nearby town and into the hills.

Corrie saw a concrete wall surrounding ugly barracks, guard towers, and a smokestack. It was Ravensbrück, the notorious concentration camp for women in northern Germany. This nightmarish place would be Corrie and Betsie's new home. The women spent their first night sleeping fitfully in a field as it rained. The next day all they received to eat was a slice of black bread, some turnip soup, and a boiled potato. And after all they had endured, the women were then forced to stand at attention for the almost inconceivable period of two full days. Then the Germans began to process them, which involved ordering the

CORRIE TEN BOOM

women to throw all their possessions in a pile, strip naked, and walk before the leering eyes of the Schutzstaffel (S.S.) men on their way to the showers.

Knowing how desperately Betsie needed her vitamins, her sweater, and her Bible, Corrie swiftly cast about for a plan to keep them. She asked a guard where the toilets were. After being directed into the shower room, Corrie spied a pile of prison garb the women were being told to put on and some benches. She quickly wrapped the Bible and the vitamins in the sweater and hid them behind the benches. A few minutes later when she and Betsie returned, naked, to the shower room, Corrie put on a dress and stuffed her bundle down the front. It made quite a bulge, but somehow Corrie knew that God was watching over them.

When she emerged from the shower room, the S.S. men searched each woman thoroughly for contraband—every woman but Corrie. They were searched a second time by female guards. Again each woman was searched except Corrie. What could this be but a miracle? Corrie and Betsie were stunned and tremendously grateful to God. They had no doubt that he had done this.

Betsie and Corrie were assigned to Barracks Eight, where they were told to share a bed already occupied by three women. But because of the outrageous miracle they had just experienced, they carried a new level of faith with them. They also had their precious Bible.

The morning roll call at Ravensbrück was much more brutal than at their previous camp, especially now that the fall weather was growing colder. The women were forced to stand for hours at a time without moving. But worse than this were the terrible sounds coming from the punishment barracks next door, where prisoners screamed as the guards beat them. The smoke from the crematorium reminded them that many among them were dying every day, and as Corrie watched the smoke, she wondered when it would be her turn to die.

As the mindless suffering increased throughout the day, whenever the chance presented itself, the sisters' hidden Bible offered

361

encouragement and hope to the women living in Barracks Eight on dirty mattresses covered in lice.

In October the women were moved to different quarters: a foul-smelling barracks with overflowing toilets and no beds—just wooden structures on which they slept "stacked three high, and wedged side by side and end to end with only an occasional narrow aisle slicing through."[22] The straw atop them was rancid and swarming with fleas.

Corrie was horrified, but Betsie, as usual, responded with patience. She reminded Corrie of the Scripture they had read just that morning. "Rejoice always, pray without ceasing, in everything give thanks; for this is the will of God in Christ Jesus for you" (1 Thess. 5:16–18).

Betsie urged Corrie to join her in doing what the Bible said in that verse, even though—and perhaps especially because—it ran counter to what anyone would have wanted to do. She asked Corrie to join her in thanking God for everything in the barrack—for their Bible, for the fact that they were jammed into a building designed for four hundred people, but which now held fourteen hundred—and even to thank God for the fleas.

This was too much for Corrie. She told her sister, "Betsie, there's no way even God can make me grateful for a flea."[23] But Betsie insisted. She knew that for devout believers in Jesus, doing this was an act of purest obedience to what God said in the Bible. It was, therefore, an act of worship. What harm could come of obeying God and worshiping him? So Corrie relented and begrudgingly thanked God for the fleas.

Every day, after being roused at 4:00 a.m., Corrie, Betsie, and thousands of other prisoners were forced to walk a mile and a half to a factory to work for eleven hours, unloading large metal plates from a boxcar and wheeling them in a handcart elsewhere in the factory. It was exhausting work for women in their fifties, but nevertheless, after returning to the camp and eating a meager dinner, Betsie and Corrie held worship services under the glowing light of a single bulb.

Corrie recalled: "A single meeting might include a recital of the Magnificat in Latin by a group of Roman Catholics, a whispered hymn by some Lutherans, and a sotto voce chant by Eastern Orthodox women. . . . They were little previews of heaven, these evenings beneath the light bulb."[24] The little sermon was translated by the prisoners from Dutch into German, from German into Polish, and into Czech and Russian.

In November the factory work suddenly ceased. Had the factory been bombed? No one knew. The prisoners were now put to back-breaking work leveling the ground inside the camp. One day when Betsie was able to lift only the smallest shovelful of dirt, a guard began to make fun of her. Betsie tried to laugh along with them but only succeeded in infuriating the guard tormenting her. The guard picked up her crop and struck Betsie hard on her neck and chest.

In a blind rage, Corrie grabbed her shovel and went for the guard, but Betsie stopped her before the guard had a chance to see her. As blood began to soak her blouse, she begged her sister to keep working. Seeing Corrie stare angrily at the welt forming on her neck, Betsie said, "Don't look at it, Corrie. Look at Jesus only."[25]

Strangely, when the sisters held their worship services at night, the ever-present guards never came near them or made any effort to stop them. But soon the sisters found out why. One day Betsie asked a supervisor to come into the barracks and answer a question for her. Because of her weakened condition, Betsie had been put to work knitting socks. She had become confused about sock sizes and thought the supervisor could answer the question. But the supervisor wouldn't step through the door. "[N]either would the guards," Betsie explained to Corrie afterward. "And you know why?" Corrie had no idea. "Because of the fleas!" Betsie said.[26] Corrie now remembered how Betsie had pushed her to thank God even for the fleas, and now she suddenly could see God's hand in that prayer too. She was astonished.

God's presence began to reveal itself in another way, and it seemed nothing less than miraculous. Somehow their precious little vitamin bottle never seemed to empty. Corrie put drops on Betsie's bread each day, and Betsie insisted on sharing the drops with many others who were sick. It was impossible to see how much was left in the dark brown glass bottle. But the drops continued to fall, day after day, while fellow prisoners watched in amazement. Then one day a fellow prisoner who worked in the hospital managed to steal a large number of vitamin pills. It was not until that very evening that Corrie discovered that the vitamin bottle was at last empty. These were small mercies, but they revealed the presence of God and were deeply comforting and encouraging.

As winter progressed cold rains began to fall, and the prisoners were forced to stand in puddles during roll call. Inevitably the anemic Betsie weakened further, and one day, with a temperature of 104, she was sent to the hospital. But even there she took the opportunity to tell those around her about Jesus, of his love for them and how he wanted them to enter into a relationship with him.

Unable to stay with her sister, Corrie returned to her barracks, which over the weeks had been transformed by Betsie's loving influence. Instead of bitter cursing and fighting, the inmates now spoke gently to one another. After a friendly inmate told Corrie how she could sneak into the hospital, Corrie went to see Betsie. But because she had been indoors and not forced to work, Betsie was already better.

Three days later Betsie returned to the barracks. No doctor had ever treated her, and she was still feverish. While Betsie was no longer required to work outdoors, she was still forced to endure roll call twice each day outdoors in the December snow. Many of the women, weak and sick, died from this terrible treatment.

During one of these freezing mornings, Betsie and Corrie first envisioned what they would do after the war was over. They were watching in horror as a guard nicknamed "The Snake" sadistically beat a young, feeble-minded girl who had soiled herself while standing for roll call.

"Betsie," Corrie whispered, "what can we do for these people? Afterward, I mean. Can't we make a home for them and care for them?"

"Corrie, I pray every day that we will be allowed to do that! To show them that love is greater!"[27] Not until later did Corrie realize that while she had been thinking of the victims of the Nazis, Betsie was thinking of the Nazis themselves.

When Corrie found out that she was to be sent to work at a munitions factory, she deliberately failed an eye exam so that she might remain behind at Ravensbrück with Betsie. Corrie was assigned to knit socks with her sister. She remembered this time as a deeply joyful one. "In the sanctuary of God's fleas, Betsie and I ministered the word of God to all in the room. We sat beside deathbeds that became doorways of heaven. We watched women who had lost everything grow rich in hope."[28] They interceded for everyone in Ravensbrück.

The sisters continued to dream of the lovely, flower-filled haven they would create after the war for those who had suffered in various ways. It helped keep their minds off the horrifying reality of seeing sick women—women they knew—being helped into trucks and driven to the brick building with the huge smokestack.

How much longer could they endure this frozen hell? How much longer could the war last? One week before Christmas, when the morning siren sounded, Betsie found she could not move her arms or legs. Corrie and another inmate carried her to the hospital only to find a long line snaking out of the building with bodies of those who had died while waiting lying in the snow.

Corrie turned around and carried her sister back to the barracks. There in her filthy bed Betsie lay for the next two days. When she was awake she would mutter about the lovely home they would create for concentration camp victims and about another home in Germany to help those whose minds and hearts had been twisted by Hitler's teachings.

The next day revealed evidence that their prayers for even the most vicious guards were having an effect. As usual, the early morning siren sounded, and following the strict rules of the camp, Corrie and another inmate began to carry Betsie outside to wait in the sleet for the long roll call. But at the barracks door awaited "the Snake." She ordered that Betsie be taken back to her bunk.

Following roll call, Corrie returned to the dormitory to find "the Snake" standing beside her sister. Two orderlies were preparing to lift Betsie onto a stretcher. Corrie wondered if "the Snake" had put aside her fears of being infested by fleas and lice in order to spare Betsie from the rigors of roll call.

Outside, the orderlies took Betsie past the line of inmates waiting for care and into a ward, where she was placed on a cot under a window. All the way to the hospital, Betsie continued to babble about the work they were going to do when they were free, helping others see that "there is no pit so deep that he is not deeper still."[29] And though it made no sense to Corrie, Betsie then said that both she and Corrie would be released from prison by January 1, 1945.

A few hours later Corrie went to visit Betsie. "The Snake" was on duty, and she wrote Corrie a pass. But the hospital nurse refused to allow her into the ward. So she went to the window above Betsie's bed, and the sisters exchanged a few words with each other. Betsie's mind was still on the home they would build.

Later in the day the guards on duty refused to allow Corrie to visit Betsie. The next morning she walked to the window beneath Betsie's bed and looked in. She saw two nurses grasp the edges of a sheet, pick up the human bundle lying on the bed, and carry it away. Her dearest sister was dead.

Betsie's body, like the bodies of other women, was laid out on the floor of a stinking restroom. Fastidious Betsie had always taken such care with her appearance. But when Corrie looked down at her sister, God gave her a loving gift, another astonishing miracle. For no reason that made any sense, naturally speaking, the fifty-nine-year-old Betsie appeared youthful and radiant. As though she had grown young again, the lines of care and grief were erased from her face. This, Corrie believed, was how her sister now looked in heaven.

Three days later, on Christmas Eve, Corrie heard her name called over the loudspeaker. A guard escorted her to an administration barracks. In the street between the barracks, the Germans had erected

Christmas trees, and in a hellish tableau beneath the trees, camp personnel had dumped the bodies of dead women.

At the administration barracks Corrie stood in line behind other women. When her name was called, the officer behind the desk wrote something on a piece of paper, stamped it, and handed it to her. It read: "Certificate of Discharge."

Corrie, like Betsie, was now free. But why? She had no idea. In any event it was a fact: she was soon to be released. Years later she would discover why. The camp officials had made a clerical error. The fact was that all women of her age and older were slated to be killed a week later because of the shortage of food. Miraculously she was spared. Yet in a grotesque irony, after nearly ten months of starvation and myriad forms of torment, the camp officials would not allow Corrie to leave unless she was in good health. A camp doctor diagnosed Corrie with edema of her feet and ankles and ordered her into the hospital.

This final stop on her road to freedom was the worst of all. Trying to sleep her first night at the hospital, Corrie heard mutilated bombing victims screaming in pain. Women fell off their bunks and died where they lay. Nurses behaved viciously.

A few days later Corrie was declared fit enough to leave. It was New Year's Day. What Betsie had predicted in her delirium had come true. Corrie gave her tiny Bible to a Dutch woman, and she herself was given good clothes and food for her journey home. After she was forced to sign a document saying she had been treated well at Ravensbrück, the iron gates opened, and Corrie marched out of the camp in the company of a handful of other women who had been freed. At the little train station the camp guards left them. It was the first time since the day of her arrest that she had been free of their constant presence.

After a long wait she boarded a train and began the long, slow journey to Berlin. Along the way she stared out the window at the ruin of Germany, now just four months away from unconditional surrender to the Allies. After many confusing train changes, she was back in Holland, in the city of Groningen. She could go no farther because Allied bombing had destroyed the rails.

Not knowing where else to go, Corrie limped on painful feet to a nearby hospital. A friendly nurse fed her tea and bread and ran her a hot bath, which soothed her damaged skin. A warm, clean nightgown, clean sheets, soft pillows, gentle hands tucking her in, peace, and privacy—for Corrie, these were a foretaste of heaven itself.

After ten days at the hospital, Corrie was ready to find her way home—to her sister Nollie and brother Willem. The hospital arranged for her to ride on a food truck headed toward Haarlem. And soon, in Willem's house not far from Haarlem and in the tight embrace of her family, she was truly home.

But sad news awaited her. Willem, who had been rearrested and sent to a concentration camp for his resistance work, was dying of spinal tuberculosis. Nor was there any news of his brave son, Kik, who had been deported to Germany; it would be seven years before the family learned that he had died in the Bergen-Belsen concentration camp in 1944.

Many underground members were still hard at work. Corrie longed to go back to Haarlem to visit her surviving sister and to see the Beje. Although several families had lived in the building since the Ten Booms left, it now stood empty. Nollie and her daughters spent many hours cleaning the house for Corrie's arrival.

Inside the Beje a flood of memories of their life in this once-happy home returned to Corrie. Father and Betsie would never return, but others were now running the watch shop for them. As she resumed working behind the counter, she once again reached out to feeble-minded people, bringing them into the Beje. These precious people were among the most helpless of all Haarlem's residents—residents the Nazis had attempted to wipe out.

With the help of others a beautiful Holland home was opened for those who had been damaged by the war: those who had survived concentration camps or spent years hiding in barns and attics. Healing was linked to forgiveness, Corrie wrote. Each had something to forgive, whether it was a neighbor who had turned him in to the Nazi authorities or a vicious camp guard or a brutal soldier.

In mid-May 1945 the Allies marched into Holland, to the unspeakable joy of the Dutch people. Despite the distractions of her work, Corrie was still restless, and she desperately missed her beloved Betsie. But now she remembered Betsie's words: that they must tell others what they had learned.

Thus began more than three decades of travel around the world as a "tramp for the Lord," as Corrie described herself. She told people her story, of God's forgiveness of sins, and of the need for people to forgive those who had harmed them.

Corrie herself was put to the test in 1947 while speaking in a Munich church. At the close of the service, a balding man in a gray overcoat stepped forward to greet her. Corrie froze. She knew this man well; he'd been one of the most vicious guards at Ravensbrück, one who had mocked the women prisoners as they showered. "It came back with a rush," she wrote, "the huge room with its harsh overhead lights; the pathetic pile of dresses and shoes in the center of the floor; the shame of walking naked past this man."

And now he was pushing his hand out to shake hers, and saying:

"A fine message, Fraulein! How good it is to know that, as you say, all our sins are at the bottom of the sea!"

And I, who had spoken so glibly of forgiveness, fumbled in my pocketbook rather than take that hand. He would not remember me, of course how could he remember one prisoner among those thousands of women?

But I remembered him and the leather crop swinging from his belt. I was face to face with one of my captors, and my blood seemed to freeze.

"You mentioned Ravensbrück in your talk," he was saying. "I was a guard there. . . . But since that time," he went on, "I have become a

Christian. I know that God has forgiven me for the cruel things I did there, but I would like to hear it from your lips as well. Fraulein"—again the hand came out—"will you forgive me?"

And I stood there—I whose sins had again and again to be forgiven—and could not forgive. Betsie had died in that place—could he erase her slow terrible death simply for the asking?

The soldier stood there expectantly, waiting for Corrie to shake his hand. She "wrestled with the most difficult thing I had ever had to do. For I had to do it—I knew that. The message that God forgives has a prior condition: that we forgive those who have injured us."

Standing there before the former S.S. man, Corrie remembered that forgiveness is an act of the will—not an emotion. "Jesus, help me!" she prayed. "I can lift my hand. I can do that much. You supply the feeling." Corrie thrust out her hand.

And as I did, an incredible thing took place. The current started in my shoulder, raced down my arm, sprang into our joined hands. And then this healing warmth seemed to flood my whole being, bringing tears to my eyes.

"I forgive you, brother!" I cried. "With all my heart."

For a long moment we grasped each other's hands, the former guard and the former prisoner. I had never known God's love so intensely as I did then. But even so, I realized it was not my love. I had tried, and did not have the power. It was the power of the Holy Spirit.[30]

Another man she forgave was Jan Vogel, who had betrayed her and her family that day when he came to the Beje. After the war he was sentenced to death for collaborating with the Nazis, but when she learned of this, Corrie wrote to him, offering her forgiveness and telling him how he could receive Christ.

But her forgiveness aside, Corrie "did not want the Holocaust to be forgotten," wrote historian Lawrence Baron. "Otherwise why would she have written *The Hiding Place* and spent her ministry bearing witness to what happened to the Jews in Holland and to her family for helping them."[31]

On February 28, 1977—thirty-three years to the day of her arrest by the Gestapo—Corrie moved into a small house in Placentia, California. She was eighty-five years old, and after traveling around the world, allowing God to use her to save souls and mend hearts in some sixty countries, it was time to take life a bit slower. For some years Corrie had traveled with a companion, and her current companion, Pamela Rosewell, moved in with her. Living near Los Angeles, Corrie believed she could reach even more people, not only through writing books, but also through the making of films aimed at specific audiences. And this is what she did for the next eighteen months.

Soon, though, the first of several severe strokes hit Corrie, leaving her mute and later paralyzed. A team of caregivers looked after a deteriorating Corrie for five long, difficult years. On April 15, 1983, her ninety-first birthday, surrounded by birthday bouquets and loving friends, Corrie ten Boom went home to her Lord.

The Ten Boom house in Haarlem is now a museum. One can walk up those twisting stairs, over the spot where Corrie hid the radio, to the top floor. There, in Corrie's bedroom, is the hidden closet. The wall has been cut open so that visitors can see into it.

Reading through the many books Corrie wrote, one is struck by her great modesty—her belief that she was not as spiritual as Betsie, nor as patient as her father, nor as smart as her brother, Willem. But her own story is amazing: while in her fifties, this brave maiden lady unhesitatingly became the head of a ring of Dutch underground volunteers entrusted with the lives of her Jewish neighbors. She fulfilled the family commitment to help God's ancient people—work that led to her imprisonment at a concentration camp and to the deaths of her father, sister, brother, and nephew. That work was gratefully recognized by Israel in 1968, when it named Corrie ten Boom a Righteous Gentile and planted a tree in her honor on the Avenue of the Righteous.

SIX

Rosa Parks

1913–2005

I f you have heard of Rosa Parks, you know that this famous woman entered the history books for refusing to give up her seat on a bus. This simple act launched the now-historic yearlong Montgomery bus boycott, which in turn catapulted Martin Luther King Jr. to fame and effectively set in motion the Civil Rights movement. For this reason, Rosa Parks is rightly remembered as the "Mother of the Civil Rights Movement."

But just how did this humble, dignified woman come to be the focal point of this period in American history? And what became of her after that fateful day on that bus? This is her story.

◆ ◆ ◆

R osa McCauley was born in Tuskegee, Alabama, on February 4, 1913, to Leona Edwards McCauley, a schoolteacher, and James McCauley, a carpenter and stonemason.

For Rosa and for most blacks at that time, faith and the church were at the center of life. The church was a welcome, life-filled refuge from the bitterness of that time and place, one known for the lynching and burning of innocent blacks for their alleged crimes against white people. From her earliest years, Rosa loved the words and music of the church. Throughout her life, she attended the African Methodist Episcopal Church.

"Daily devotions played an important part in my childhood," she said. "Every day before supper, and before we went to services on Sundays, my grandmother would read the Bible to me, and my grandfather would pray. . . . I remember finding such comfort and peace while reading the Bible. Its teachings became a way of life and helped me in dealing with my day-to-day problems."[1]

But the Bible had a social mandate in its message too, one that taught Rosa that "people should stand up for rights, just as the children of Israel stood up to the Pharaoh."[2] It was not enough to pray and say that one trusted God. Sometimes trusting God meant taking action too.

During Rosa's earliest years, the economy across the South was in miserable condition, in part because a boll weevil plague had destroyed cotton plants throughout the region. So during Rosa's first years, the McCauleys lived in poverty. When she was two, her family moved to Abbeville, Alabama, to live with Rosa's paternal grandparents and other family. But the conditions were terribly overcrowded, and Leona's mother-in-law was difficult to get along with. As far as Leona was concerned, her husband's unwillingness to look after his family was the worst of it, and before long she packed Rosa off to live with her own parents in Pine Level, Alabama. Rosa saw almost nothing of her father after that.

She and her mother began attending the church at Mount Zion African Methodist Episcopal Church where her uncle preached. Life in Pine Level was easier. For one thing, there was plenty of food. On special occasions, Rosa remembered that the family feasted on ham with red-eye gravy, catfish, or rabbit, with ample sides of turnip greens, peas, and onions and a dessert of sweet potato pie.

Rosa's grandfather Edwards had been born during slavery times, and he taught her about the family history. He also taught her a lesson in self-protection against hostile whites. In 1919, when she was six, the long-dormant Ku Klux Klan became active again. "The Ku Klux Klan was riding through the black community, burning churches, beating up people, killing people," Rosa recalled. "By the time I was six, I was old enough to realize that we were not actually free."[3]

To protect his family, Grandfather Edwards told the children to wear their clothes to bed "so we would be ready to run if we had to," Rosa wrote. Nor was his double-barreled shotgun ever far from hand. Rosa vividly remembered her grandfather saying, "I don't know how long I would last if they came breaking in here, but I'm getting the first one who comes through the door." Rosa tried to stay awake as long as she could each night, hoping not to miss seeing her grandfather shoot an intruder. Mercifully no one ever attacked the family. But experiences like these, according to historian Douglas Brinkley, taught Rosa that "it wasn't enough to just 'turn a cheek' in Christian submission when one's very life was at stake."[4]

Rosa learned other hard lessons in oppression. She worked barefoot picking cotton for Moses Hudson, a local planter, for fifty cents a day, from sunup to sundown. The hot sand burned the children's feet, and when their feet were too blistered to stand on, they were made to pick cotton on their knees. If they accidentally dripped blood on the cotton, they were punished.

But there were good times too. Rosa enjoyed playing games with her little brother, Sylvester, and their friends. She was grateful she could earn some extra money by selling eggs to the neighbors. She loved wandering through Alabama's piney woods, and she even enjoyed attending school.

But racism was ever present in her life. Rosa remembered enduring insults from white children as she walked to school; they threw rocks at her and called her "nigger." But her faith sustained her, and early on she would recite specific Bible verses to herself, so that she could face her persecutors with peace and courage. Psalm 23 was one of her favorites, as was Psalm 27, whose first lines read: "The LORD is my light and my salvation; whom shall I fear? The LORD is the strength of my life; of whom shall I be afraid?"

When Rosa was eleven, she began attending the Montgomery Industrial School for Girls, also called Miss White's School. All the teachers in the school were white, as was Miss White herself, and all three hundred students were black. Students were taught cooking, sewing, housekeeping, and how to care for the sick at home, lessons that—at a time when few blacks were permitted access to hospitals—would be useful to Rosa in later years. Each day included Bible reading and prayer. But dancing, going to the movies, and wearing makeup were forbidden.

Rosa recalled that what she learned best at Miss White's School "was that I was a person with dignity and self-respect and I should not set my sights lower than anybody just because I was black. We were taught to be ambitious and to believe that we could do what we wanted in life."[5] Tragically the school was burned down by hostile whites and then closed for good when Rosa was fifteen. But she never forgot Miss White, whose dedicated efforts on behalf of her charges played a role in putting Rosa on the path to civil rights activism.

Rosa attended Booker T. Washington Junior High and completed tenth and eleventh grades at the laboratory school of the Alabama State Teachers College for Negroes. She dreamed of becoming a teacher like her mother, but when her grandmother grew ill, Rosa had to cut her education short so that she could care for her. After her grandmother's death, sixteen-year-old Rosa went to work at a textile factory, sewing men's shirts. Then her mother fell ill, and she had to leave the factory to care for her. Rosa wasn't happy about leaving either her school or the factory, but she endured these things without complaint. Every Sunday, she attended the St. Paul AME Church, which she loved.

In 1931, when she was eighteen, Rosa met her future husband, Raymond Parks, a twenty-eight-year-old barber and church sexton. He was also a charter member of the Montgomery chapter of the National Association for the Advancement of Colored People (NAACP). At first, Rosa was not eager to pursue the relationship, but Raymond, who was smitten with Rosa, was persistent. Eventually she agreed to go for a ride in his sporty red Nash. As the couple got to know each other, Rosa found herself impressed "by the fact that [Raymond] didn't seem to have that meek attitude—what we called an 'Uncle Tom' attitude— toward white people. I thought he was a very nice man, an interesting man who talked very intelligently."[6]

Under Raymond's tutelage, Rosa began to pay more attention to civil rights issues, especially the 1931 case of the Scottsboro Boys, nine black teenagers who had been accused of raping two white prostitutes. Eight of them were convicted and sentenced to death. But in a desperate effort to keep them from being executed, Raymond worked to raise money to pay for legal help. Because their work was so dangerous – police had actually murdered members of their group—Raymond refused to allow Rosa to become involved. In the end four of the young men went free, while the remaining five were given long prison terms.

Rosa could not help admiring Raymond's courage. They were married in December 1932. Raymond encouraged his wife to go back to school and earn her high school diploma, which she did when she was twenty years old, becoming one of the few blacks in Montgomery to do so. But it was still the 1930s, and Rosa's high school diploma didn't impress white Southern employers. So she earned money by sewing and working at a hospital. She later obtained a job at Maxwell Army Air Force base.

Traveling to and from the base was a daily exercise in humiliation. On the trolley at the base, Rosa could sit anywhere she chose, because President Franklin Roosevelt had prohibited segregation on military bases. If "negroes," as they were then called, could put on the uniform of the United States and risk their lives for their country, surely they were equal to the whites who were doing the same thing and shouldn't have to sit in a segregated area. But when Rosa stepped off the base trolley and climbed onto a city bus, the rules were different: she had to sit in the back.

Nor was this the only insult she and millions of other black Americans were forced to endure. In the 1930s and 1940s, blacks lived in a world of separate drinking fountains, separate restrooms, and separate elevators. Rosa, offended by this, avoided using these facilities in order to preserve her dignity, taking the stairs rather than riding the "colored" elevator and going home rather than using the "colored" restrooms.

After his work in the Scottsboro case was over, Raymond turned his attention to the issue of voting rights. At that time in Alabama, if you were black, it was nearly impossible to register to vote. Raymond and Rosa began holding meetings in their home at night to discuss strategies. But they made little progress until E. D. Nixon, a railroad porter and president of the Montgomery Branch of the NAACP, joined them. He was also president of the local branch of the Brotherhood of Sleeping Car Porters, a black railroad workers' union. Nixon worked with Arthur Madison, a black lawyer who practiced in New York. Madison explained how blacks should go about attempting to register, explaining to them that they would be asked to take a literacy test.

In 1943 Rosa decided to register to vote. Simply finding out what time city hall opened its doors was difficult, as city workers, in an effort to keep black citizens from registering, constantly changed the times and days that people could register. Finally, on her day off, Rosa went to city hall to take the test. Whites were given their certificates immediately if they passed the test, but black citizens had to wait for their certificates to arrive in the mail. Rosa never received hers. She took the test a second time and was again told she hadn't passed.

Undeterred, Rosa went back a third time, took the test, and made copies of all her answers, intending to sue the voter-registration board if it once again denied her the right to vote. This time her certificate arrived. But another hurdle stood before her: she had to pay the accumulated poll tax from the year she had turned twenty-one—something white voters did not have to do. The amount for Rosa was $16.50, no small amount of money in the 1940s. Still, she was able to vote for governor for the first time, and she voted for Jim Folsom.

◆ ◆ ◆

E ven before Rosa's birth, boycotts of segregated streetcars took place throughout the South as a result of the infamous 1896 *Plessy v. Ferguson* Supreme Court decision, which upheld state "separate but equal" laws affecting public facilities. These boycotts have largely been forgotten, but between 1900 and 1910, boycotts of segregated streetcars took place in no fewer than twenty-seven cities in the Deep South. One massive protest took place in Montgomery, where, after five weeks, the company that operated the trolleys saw its profits drop by 25 percent. The company had no choice but to give in and integrate its streetcars.

The integration was short-lived, however. Rosa was aware of this early boycott. "I thought about it sometimes when the segregated trolley passed by. It saddened me to think how we had taken one foot forward and two steps back,"[7] she recalled.

In the 1940s, bus drivers carried guns and had "police power" to rearrange the seating on the bus any way they chose. Very few people are aware of the fact that, twelve years before Rosa Parks made her historic 1955 stand against the segregated bus rule, she had another run-in with bus driver James F. Blake over an issue of segregation. Blake forced her off his bus because she had refused to obey his demand that she pay the fare at the front door and then get off the bus and reenter through the back door. This was common treatment for black riders. Rosa decided to buck this custom. "One day in the winter of 1943," she wrote,

the bus came along, and the back was crowded with black people. They were even standing on the steps leading up from the back door.

But up front there were vacant seats. . . . So I got on at the front and went through this little bunch of folks standing in the back, and I looked toward the front and saw the driver standing there and looking at me. He told me to get off the bus and go to the back door and get on. I told him I was already on the bus and didn't see the need of getting off and getting back on when people were standing in the stepwell, and how was I going to squeeze on anyway?

So he told me if I couldn't go through the back door that I would have to get off the bus. . . . I stood where I was.

He looked like he was ready to hit me. I said, "I know one thing. You better not hit me." He didn't strike me. I got off.[8]

The man had been so vile that Rosa refused to ever again board any bus he was driving, even if it meant walking home in the rain. Neither she nor the driver in their wildest dreams could have imagined that twelve years later, they would again square off against each other in a historic showdown that would change the entire country forever.

◆ ◆ ◆

Thanks to her husband's influence, Rosa was becoming more and more active in civil rights efforts. One day in 1943 she showed up at a local meeting of the NAACP when an election of officers was taking place. Rosa was the only woman there, and when she was asked to become secretary, she was too shy to refuse. Her job—unpaid—was to take the minutes of meetings, write articles, send letters and membership payments to the NAACP's national offices, answer the telephone, and deal with press releases.

Among Rosa's most important duties was keeping track of discrimination cases and violent attacks on blacks. This was work that might have embittered a lesser person. For instance, white women who accused blacks of rape received swift attention. But when a black woman was gang-raped by white men, no charges were brought—even in the case of Mrs. Recy Taylor, in which one of the rapists confessed and implicated the other five attackers. Moreover, witnesses to white-on-black violence were often too frightened to testify. Rosa recalled that the NAACP "didn't have too many successes in getting justice. It was more a matter of trying to challenge the powers that be, and to let it be known that we did not wish to continue being second-class citizens."[9]

The violence became even worse after the Second World War, in which many African Americans had nobly fought. Having served their country, they believed they deserved equal treatment. Among them was Rosa's brother, Sylvester, who became so frustrated by his treatment at the hands of racist whites in Alabama that he moved north to Detroit, Michigan.

By the late 1940s Rosa was both secretary of the Senior Branch of the Montgomery NAACP and an adviser to its Youth Council, which engaged in such tactics as checking out books from the city's library for whites instead of the poorly equipped library for blacks. Rosa also performed volunteer work at the union offices of E. D. Nixon. In 1954 Nixon introduced Rosa to someone who would become very important in her life: a white woman named Virginia Durr, who, along with her husband, was active in civil rights work. Durr promptly hired Rosa to do some sewing for her and invited her to take part in an integrated prayer group, which ended abruptly when the husbands of the white women found out about it.

The year 1954 offered a ray of hope for black Americans when the Supreme Court outlawed segregation in schools in *Brown v. the Board of Education*. "You can't imagine the rejoicing among black people, and some white people, when the Supreme Court decision came down in May 1954," Rosa wrote. "The Court had said that separate education could not be equal, and many of us saw how the same idea applied to other things, like public transportation."[10]

Rosa learned more political tactics when, in the summer of 1955, Durr suggested she attend a workshop at the Highlander Folk School in Tennessee, titled "Racial Desegregation: Implementing the Supreme

Court Decision." The school was run by whites, but it was here that Rosa not only attended workshops on desegregation, but also encountered great generosity by supportive whites, who did everything from picking her up at the bus stop to cooking her breakfast. After ten enjoyable days, it was back to segregated Montgomery and her job as an assistant tailor at the Montgomery Fair department store.

◆ ◆ ◆

Since whites were typically able to afford cars while blacks were not, far more black citizens rode Montgomery's buses than did whites. This made it all the more galling that black riders were forced to sit in the back of the bus or relinquish their seats when a white person got on. Black leaders began to attempt small changes in how blacks were treated on public transportation—such as getting buses to stop at every corner in black neighborhoods as they did in white ones. But for the most part city leaders simply paid no attention.

Around this time Rosa and others began to think about a boycott. Since blacks comprised more than 66 percent of the Montgomery bus ridership, a boycott would make quite an impact. But for a boycott to work, huge numbers of black riders would have to agree to find other ways to get to work. This was asking a lot of people who were already strapped with enough things to think about and do during a busy day.

The Montgomery NAACP also considered filing suit against the city to enforce desegregation on public transportation. For this they needed not only a strong case, but the right plaintiff. They decided it needed to be a woman, because they knew that a female would garner more sympathy than a man. And they agreed that the woman had to be someone of high moral character, so she could not be attacked for anything other than having refused to sacrifice her seat on a bus.

One young woman seemed a possibility: Claudette Colvin, whom police had arrested when she refused to give up her seat to a white rider. But fifteen-year-old Claudette was pregnant—and unmarried.

"They'd call her a bad girl, and her case wouldn't have a chance," Rosa recalled.[11] The answer to the local NAACP leaders' problem was staring them right in the face. They just didn't know it, and neither did the demure forty-two-year-old seamstress.

On the cold evening of December 1, 1955, the woman who had been taught from childhood to love her enemies, but not take any guff from them, put away her work and walked out of Montgomery Fair department store at five o'clock. Store windows proclaimed the coming holiday with toy trains, bright sweaters, and a huge Christmas tree covered with blinking electric lights. Rosa left early that evening because she had a meeting in another town, but even so, she was tired from the long hours sewing, ironing, and steampressing.

Rosa walked to the bus stop one block away. Because it was just after five, a huge crowd of people was congregated there, so Rosa decided not to get on that bus. She thought she would be better off catching the next one. She killed some time doing a little Christmas shopping at Lee's Cut-Rate Drugstore. Then back to the bus stop she went, wondering what her mother planned to cook for their dinner and thinking about that evening's NAACP Youth Council meeting.

With her mind preoccupied Rosa did not notice whose bus she was stepping onto, but when the bus driver swiveled around to stare at Rosa, she realized to her shock and dismay that it was James F. Blake, the very driver who had put her off the bus twelve years before. This time, however, the tired seamstress and the bigoted bus driver were about to make history.

Finding a vacant seat in the middle section of the bus, behind the sign reading "colored," Rosa tiredly sat down. Three other blacks were also seated in that row. In front of Rosa were several "whites only" seats.

Blake stepped on the gas, and the bus trundled on down the street. After two more stops, white passengers filled most of the seats in the front section. At the third stop, in front of the Empire Theater, the last "whites only" seats were occupied, and one white man was left standing.

Blake swiveled around and stared at Rosa. "Let me have those front seats," he ordered.

According to the law, no black person could sit in the same row as a white person—meaning all four blacks in the row Rosa occupied would have to move to accommodate one white man. Silence met the driver's command. Nobody moved. Angered, Blake tried again. "Y'all better make it light on yourselves and let me have those seats," he warned.[12]

The two women sitting across the aisle from Rosa and the man sitting next to her got up and moved to the back of the bus. But Rosa was not about to move. Instead, she simply slid over to the window seat and stared out at the Empire Theater marquee, which announced that week's film: *A Man Alone*, starring Ray Milland, a western about a man who faces down a village for a crime he did not commit.

Blake saw that one of the four had ignored his demand, and he was not going to let one small black woman make a fool of him. He got out of his seat and began walking down the aisle toward Rosa.

"I thought back to the time when I used to sit up all night and didn't sleep, and my grandfather would have his gun right by the fireplace, or if he had his one-horse wagon going anywhere, he always had his gun in the back of the wagon," Rosa said. "People always say that I didn't give up my seat because I was tired, but that isn't true. I was not tired physically, or no more tired than I usually was at the end of a working day. . . . No, the only tired I was, was tired of giving in."[13]

Rosa also thought of Dr. Martin Luther King Jr.'s words: "Some of us must bear the burden of trying to save the soul of America."[14]

Blake was now standing over Rosa. "Are you going to stand up?" he asked, urgently.

Rosa looked him straight in the eye and with great dignity responded, "No."

"Well, I'm going to have to have you arrested."

"You may do that,"[15] Rosa replied.

Blake radioed to his supervisor, who, after asking Blake if he had warned Rosa, told him to go ahead and put her off the bus. Waiting for the police to arrive, many nervous passengers got off the bus not wanting to be involved in whatever was going to happen next. Rosa was nervous herself. She wasn't thinking about possibly becoming the NAACP test case; she was wondering if the police would beat her up as well as arrest her.

Two Montgomery police officers, D. W. Mixon and F. B. Day, arrived, and Blake told them what had happened. They then boarded the bus and approached Rosa. "Why," Officer Day asked her, "did you refuse to stand up when the driver spoke to you?"

Rosa stared back at him. "Why do you all push us around?" she said.

"I don't know," Day replied, "but the law is the law, and you're under arrest."[16]

The two officers escorted Rosa off the yellow-olive bus and into their squad car. In his book, *Rosa Parks: A Life,* historian Douglas Brinkley wrote, "They did not handcuff Parks or mistreat her in any way. In fact, Parks saw them as two tired beat cops with no desire to waste their time and effort writing up reports for minor offenses."[17]

At city hall, a thirsty Rosa asked to get a drink of water at a nearby fountain. Officer Day told her to go ahead and take a drink, but Officer Mixon intervened, shouting, "You can't drink no water. It's for whites only. You have to wait till you get to the jail."[18]

"That made me angry," Rosa later wrote, and the incident made her think of the Roman soldiers who had given the thirsty Christ vinegar to drink as he hung on the cross.[19] She asked if she could use the telephone and was told she could not. More racism, she thought.

After Rosa filled out the required forms, she was taken back out to the police squad car for the trip to the city jail. By now she was chuckling to herself. As Brinkley wrote, "Who would have thought that little Rosa McCauley—whose friends teased her for being such a Goody Two-shoes in her dainty white gloves—would ever become a convicted criminal, much less a subversive worthy of police apprehension, in the eyes of the state of Alabama?"[20]

At the jail Rosa was fingerprinted and photographed. Again she asked for a drink of water and was again refused. She was then escorted upstairs to a second-floor cell. They locked her in and left. Returning moments later the female guard sympathetically asked Rosa if she would prefer sharing a cell with two other black women instead of being by herself. Rosa didn't really care one way or another, but she agreed to move. Once again she asked if she could make a telephone call to let her husband know where she was. The guard said she would check.

A while later, Rosa was allowed to call home. "I'm in jail. See if Parks will come down here and get me out," she told her mother.

"Did they beat you?" Rosa's mother asked.

"No, I wasn't beaten, but I am in jail."[21]

Overhearing his mother-in-law's side of the conversation, a horrified Raymond Parks grabbed the phone, demanding to know if his wife had been harmed. No, she replied, the police had not harmed her or even verbally abused her. Parks told her he would be at the station in a few minutes. While she waited, one of her cell mates gave her a cup of water.

Meanwhile, news of Rosa's arrest spread rapidly through the black community. E. D. Nixon attempted to discover what Rosa was being charged with and called attorney Clifford Durr, the husband of Rosa's friend Virginia. Durr was able to find out both the charges and the amount of the bail, while Raymond Parks called a white friend of his whom he knew would be able to provide the bail money.

That evening the jail matron told Rosa she was free to go. On her way out she spotted Virginia Durr, who hugged her. Clifford Durr and Nixon were there too. Rosa was given a trial date four days later. She remembered that they had left without saying much to each other. But the experience of being in jail had deeply upset Rosa. Her husband arrived in a borrowed car and took Rosa home. As her family and friends comforted her that evening, Rosa vowed never again to ride a segregated bus. But suddenly, for the very first time, something occurred to all of them. Rosa herself might make the perfect plaintiff in a test case of segregation law. She seemed tailor-made for the role. She was a churchgoing woman, decidedly dignified and decent. Nobody could say she had done anything to deserve such wretched treatment—except to be born of black parents.

Meanwhile black leaders realized this was the time to launch a boycott of the city buses. It would begin the day Rosa's trial was to take place. They printed thirty-five thousand handbills announcing the boycott during the night and dropped them off at Montgomery's black schools. "Another Negro woman has been arrested and thrown in jail because she refused to get up out of her seat on the bus for a white person to sit down," the handbill announced. "We are . . . asking every Negro to stay off the buses Monday in protest of the arrest and trial."[22]

Black ministers also got involved in the boycott effort, calling a meeting at Dexter Avenue Baptist Church on the evening after Rosa's arrest. Nixon contacted the press, hoping for front-page coverage.

At the Dexter Avenue Baptist Church meeting, Rosa described what had taken place on the bus. Most of the ministers agreed to talk about the boycott during their Sunday sermons. A local newspaper, the *Montgomery Advertiser*, reproduced the handbill on page one. But would that be enough? Getting the word out far and wide was crucial, because unless enough black citizens stayed off the buses the following day, the boycott simply wouldn't make the necessary impact.

Montgomery had eighteen black-owned cab companies, and to help people who had a long bus ride to work, they all agreed to pick up black passengers at the city's bus stops and to charge only the amount of bus fare.

When Monday arrived, vast numbers of Montgomery's black citizens stayed off the buses. They took cabs, they walked, and they carpooled. Some of them even rode mules and buggies. As for the buses, they rode around the city empty, or nearly empty, all day. The boycott was a tremendous success.

That day Rosa arrived at the courthouse dressed in a neat black dress. She was surrounded by huge crowds of people who had come to support her. Spotting Rosa, a young girl shouted joyfully, "Oh, she's so sweet. They've messed with the wrong one now."[23]

Blake, the bus driver, testified that Rosa had refused to move when he told her to, and a white woman testified, untruthfully, that Rosa had refused to take a vacant seat in the back of the bus. Rosa's attorneys, Charles Langford and Fred Gray, entered Rosa's "not guilty" plea. But they were not interested in winning this case.

"They did not intend to try to defend me against the charges," Rosa recalled. "The point of making mine a test case was to allow me to be found guilty and then to appeal the conviction to a higher court. Only in higher courts could the segregation laws actually be changed."[24]

To no one's surprise, Rosa was found guilty and ordered to pay a ten-dollar fine, plus four dollars in court costs.

That evening another meeting was held at Holt Street Baptist Church. The Reverend Ralph Abernathy, along with several other ministers, decided to form the Montgomery Improvement Association (MIA). The association elected as its first president the brilliant twenty-five-year-old minister Martin Luther King Jr.

By now, support for Rosa's brave act had swelled. The church was packed while hundreds more stood outside. The big question was, should they continue the boycott? If so, for how long? How long would white Montgomery put up with a boycott before retaliating?

King, who had received his doctorate six months earlier, rose and gave an extemporaneous speech, although the cadences and words were as lapidary as anything polished through several drafts:

> There comes a time that people get tired . . . tired of being segregated and humiliated, tired of being kicked about by the brutal feet of oppression. . . . But we come here tonight to be saved from that patience that makes us patient with anything less than freedom and justice. . . . One of the great glories of democracy is the right to

protest for right. . . . [I]f you will protest courageously and yet with dignity and Christian love, when the history books are written in future generations the historians will pause and say, "There lived a great people—a black people—who injected new meaning and dignity into the veins of civilization."[25]

Abernathy asked the assembly to vote by standing up regarding whether to continue the boycott until needed changes were made in public transportation. As Rosa wrote, "Every single person in that church was standing, and outside the crowd was cheering 'Yes!'"[26]

The next day King and other leaders presented their demands to the city commissioners and bus company representatives: more courteous treatment, hiring black drivers for black neighborhoods, and a first-come, first-served seating rule, but with blacks still riding at the back of the bus. But the commissioners and bus company would not accept any of these terms; they refused to budge. The boycott would continue.

Quite incredibly the black community was able to continue the boycott for 381 days. In all that time, no blacks in Montgomery took the buses, ever. It's difficult to imagine how they did it, but the boycott continued, despite harassment from white police officers.

Rosa's refusal to leave her seat had spawned a movement that began to get national attention. Citizens from all over America learned of the boycott and heard about all the people who had been fired from their jobs for supporting the boycott. Rosa herself was discharged from her department store job, but this freed her up to spend more time working for the MIA. Sympathizers in other states sent shoes and clothing to be distributed to people who needed them because they were no longer working—or because they were wearing out shoe leather walking long distances to and from work each day. Rosa was invited to speak publicly about her arrest and took in sewing to help pay the bills.

The white police of Montgomery bore down hard to counteract the boycott. They arrested black cab drivers for charging bus fare instead of the higher cab fare. Volunteer drivers immediately replaced them, however, and took people to work in station wagons purchased by black churches. In fact, Rosa became a dispatcher for this irregular cab service. In time thirty-four private cars and church-owned station wagons were making the rounds, taking some thirty thousand blacks to work each day. Amusingly, many white women began driving their black maids to and from their homes because they couldn't get along without them. Despite anonymous threats and an appeal from the mayor, white women continued to do this.

The boycott led to more serious repercussions—and whites became angrier and angrier, until violence broke out. Both the homes of King and Nixon were bombed, but fortunately, no one was harmed.

Meanwhile Rosa's appeal of her guilty verdict was thrown out on a technicality. But in February 1956 lawyer Fred Gray filed suit in a U.S. district court on behalf of five black women who had been treated badly on city buses. The hope was now to have all segregation on buses outlawed altogether.

The next attack on the boycott was unexpected and ludicrous. White attorneys located an old law on the books that actually outlawed boycotts. A grand jury immediately sprang into action, handing down eighty-nine indictments against King, more than twenty other ministers, leaders of the MIA, and other citizens. "I was re-indicted,"[27] Rosa recalled.

But the whole world was following every detail. The New York Times ran a picture of Rosa being fingerprinted on its front page. After the MIA paid their bail, everyone who had been arrested went home.

The only person who was actually put on trial was King. He was found guilty and was given the choice of paying a five-hundred-dollar fine or spending a year in prison doing hard labor. He decided to stay in jail and spent two weeks there before his conviction was overturned on appeal.

But these indictments and King's trial only increased the determination of Montgomery blacks to keep the boycott going. Meanwhile

Rosa continued to speak wherever she could. She was invited to speak even in New York and San Francisco and traveled there to spread the word about what was happening in Montgomery.

In June, Montgomery's black citizens were delighted when a federal district court ruled in their favor in *Browder v. Gale.* The city appealed the decision to the Supreme Court, so the boycott continued, despite baroque new efforts by whites to interfere with it—such as preventing the church-owned station wagons from getting insurance. It took the creative intervention of King to get Lloyd's of London to issue a policy that white Alabamans couldn't get canceled.

The city made one last try at breaking the boycott by claiming that those waiting for private transportation on street corners were a public nuisance. Why they hadn't been considered a public nuisance while waiting for the buses prior to the boycott was never explained. The mayor even managed to get a judge to agree with this, but in the end it was a Pyrrhic victory, because on that very same day—November 13, 1956—the U.S. Supreme Court ruled that it was unconstitutional to segregate riders on city buses. Montgomery blacks exploded with joy when they learned of it, but they still continued to stay off the buses until the city had received the court's official written order. That would take weeks. But when it finally arrived on December 20, the black citizens of Montgomery, Alabama, finally began riding the buses again.

It was a heroic 381-day effort, one that had demanded tremendous sacrifices. But as a result, they had changed the law and had begun a movement that would change America forever.

When the boycott was over, the press asked Rosa to get on a bus and sit in the front seat so they could take pictures of her, which she did. A white male reporter proudly sat behind her to make the point that the days of blacks going to the back of the bus were over.

The transition to unsegregated city buses did not go entirely smoothly. Segregation had been a part of the lives of the people of Montgomery for so long that some whites thought ending it would destroy the very order of things, would wreak havoc with everything they knew and held dear. Shots were fired at some buses, in one case hitting a pregnant woman in the legs. Shots were also fired through King's front door. One day some whites attacked a black teenager as she exited her bus. City leaders pushed back by increasing segregation in other areas of Montgomery life. Death threats against Rosa became so frequent and so frightening that she and Raymond move to Detroit in 1957, where Rosa's brother lived.

But history was moving decidedly against segregation across the country, in large part because of what Rosa had spawned in Montgomery. In other Southern cities civil rights activists, who had observed what happened in Montgomery, began their own bus boycotts.

A fter moving to a Detroit apartment with her husband and mother, Rosa continued speaking out about her experiences. During a visit to Boston, she was introduced to the president of the Hampton Institute, a black institution of higher learning in Hampton, Virginia. He offered Rosa a job as a hostess at a campus residence and guesthouse. Her job would entail managing the off-campus guests, as well as the faculty and staff who lived there. Rosa accepted the job and moved to Virginia. She enjoyed the work but missed her husband and mother, who had to remain behind in Detroit. Eventually she resigned and moved back to Detroit. She began working as a seamstress again and kept up her friendship with King, who by now had formed the Southern Christian Leadership Conference. Rosa attended SCLC conventions and put in an appearance whenever a march or demonstration took place in a Southern city.

In 1963 Rosa took part in the historic March on Washington, held to pressure the federal government to pass federal civil rights laws. "The civil-rights movement was having a big effect," Rosa recalled. "It didn't change the hearts and minds of many white Southerners, but it did make a difference to the politicians in Washington, D.C."[28]

The passage of the 1964 Civil Rights Act was a tremendous victory. It guaranteed African Americans the right to vote and outlawed segregation in all public accommodations. This law "did not solve all our problems," Rosa said. "But it gave black people some protection, and some way to get redress for unfair treatment."[29]

In Selma, Alabama, a town that still made it difficult for blacks to vote, the leaders of the SCLC staged a large demonstration. Many deliberately got themselves arrested with the idea of packing the jails. Sheriff Jim Clark and his men, angered by the demonstration, "surrounded a group of about 150 children who were demonstrating downtown. They herded them out of town like cattle, making them trot along the country roads and using electric cattle prods to force them to keep up the pace,"[30] Rosa recalled.

But this backfired dramatically. Out-of-town television reporters caught the scene on camera. As a result the entire country finally woke up to just how badly whites were treating blacks in the South. Support for their cause increased greatly, and when King announced a fifty-mile march from Selma to Montgomery, people came from all over the country to take part, black and white alike. Rosa marched in front with King and his wife, Ralph Abernathy, and other leaders. Three thousand others marched and sang behind them. Every evening at their campsite the world-famous singer Harry Belafonte performed for them.

Once the marchers arrived at Montgomery, the state capital, many whites jeered at them. One white female marcher was murdered by the Klan. Viola Liuzzo had traveled to Alabama from Detroit to take part in the march. Her crime? She had been riding in a car with a black man.

In 1965 President Lyndon Johnson signed the Voting Rights Act—another consequence of peaceful protests. This important law, according to Rosa, meant that "blacks who were denied the chance to register to vote by local officials could get registered by federal examiners."[31] She became convinced of the efficacy of large, nonviolent demonstrations and boycotts, even though she continued to believe that in some situations, as with self-defense, violence was sometimes necessary.

When Rosa was fifty-one, black attorney John Conyers ran for Congress from Michigan's First Congressional District. He asked Rosa to endorse him. He won the seat, and following his victory, she went to work for him in his Detroit office in 1965 as a receptionist and secretary. She would stay for twenty-three years.

Rosa was at home with her mother when she heard over the radio of the shooting of her old friend, Dr. Martin Luther King Jr. on April 4, 1968. She and her mother wept together, and Rosa attended her friend's funeral in Atlanta. But she did not take a bus there; instead she flew in Harry Belafonte's private plane as a guest of honor. At the King home Rosa met Robert Kennedy, the brother of President John F. Kennedy, who had been assassinated five years earlier. Rosa was saddened again when, just two months later, Robert Kennedy himself was cut down by an assassin's bullet.

During the 1970s Rosa began losing the people she loved most. Both she and her husband had been hospitalized for stomach ulcers, but now her beloved husband developed a more serious disease: throat cancer. He died in 1977 at the age of seventy-four. They had been married nearly forty-five years. Rosa's brother Sylvester also died of cancer just three months later. Then in 1979 her ninety-one-year-old mother died of cancer too.

Wishing to both memorialize her husband and help young people, Rosa founded the Rosa and Raymond Parks Institute for Self Development in 1987, which attempted to inspire Detroit young people to "pursue their education and create a promising future for themselves."[32] She also established the Rosa L. Parks Scholarship Foundation, donating her speaking fees to fund college scholarships for promising young African Americans.

This generous habit of donating her speaker's fees would cause problems later on. Rosa lived on her salary from Conyers's office, along with her husband's pension. But as Rosa began suffering from health problems, medical bills piled up, while her income fell from so much time off from her job. The resulting financial squeeze forced Rosa to accept contributions from churches.

Rosa published her autobiography, *My Story*, in 1992, and a second book, *Quiet Strength*, three years later. This second book reveals, in ways other biographies do not, how great a role Rosa's faith in God played throughout her long life and through her struggles. "As a child I learned from the Bible to trust in God and not be afraid,"[33] Rosa wrote. And "I felt the Lord would give me the strength to endure whatever I had to face. God did away with all my fear."[34]

She also wrote that during the early years of the civil rights movement, "one thing we used to keep us going was the moving words of certain hymns, many of which had been passed down from the slave days. . . . Singing gave us the feeling that—with God's help—we could overcome whatever we were facing."[35]

When she faced arrest for refusing to give up her bus seat to a white man and knew they might brutally beat her, "I knew that He was with me, and only He could get me through the next step."[36]

In 1994 Rosa wrote a third book, *Dear Mrs. Parks: A Dialogue with Today's Youth*, which reproduced some of the many letters children sent to her and the loving advice Rosa offered to them. While Rosa became weary of being asked repeatedly about a single day in her life and disliked violations of her privacy, she knew she had become a symbol, and she was grateful for the chance to travel, help a new generation of civil rights activists, and meet the likes of Eleanor Roosevelt and President Bill Clinton.

Rosa came to be called the "Mother of the Civil Rights Movement." As this iconic woman entered her seventies and eighties, towns, cities, and organizations across America heaped honors on her. Among the most important was changing the name of Cleveland Avenue in Montgomery, Alabama, to Rosa Parks Boulevard. Rosa had been riding a bus on that very avenue when she was arrested many years before. And the bus on which she made history is now in the Henry Ford Museum.

In 1990 Rosa was invited to be part of the welcoming committee for Nelson Mandela's arrival in Detroit. Recognizing her, Mandela delightedly began chanting Rosa's name and hugged her. In 1994 she traveled to Stockholm, Sweden, to accept the Rosa Parks Peace Prize. In 1996 President Clinton awarded her the Presidential Medal of Freedom; in 1999 the U.S. Congress awarded Rosa the Congressional Gold Medal. *Time* magazine named Rosa "one of the twenty most influential and iconic figures of the twentieth century."

Troy University in Montgomery, Alabama—the city where she was arrested many years before—dedicated the Rosa Parks Library and Museum in 2000. Children performed plays memorializing Rosa's refusal to give up her seat on the bus.

In 1994, when Rosa was eighty-one years old, she made headlines again when a young black man named Joseph Skipper broke into her Detroit home, demanded money, and repeatedly struck her in the face. Rosa was rushed to a hospital and treated for severe bruising. But while the nation's editorial writers expressed fury with Skipper for assaulting a national treasure, Rosa noted that he was very different from the young people she met at the Institute for Self Development. She said that she was praying for Skipper. The young man was eventually sentenced to prison.

The attack had a deep effect upon Rosa's sense of personal safety, and she decided to move to the twenty-fifth floor of a gated and guarded high-rise complex overlooking the Detroit River. There she lived out the remainder of her days.

Rosa never gave up her activism. She had engaged in Black Power events in the 1970s and had demonstrated against apartheid at the South African embassy in Washington, D.C. She had also lobbied to make Martin Luther King Jr.'s birthday a national holiday. And then in 1995 eighty-two-year-old Rosa took part in the Million Man March.

Rosa died on October 24, 2005, fifty years after her historic act, and just three years before America's first black president was elected. She was ninety-two. Her coffin was laid in honor in the Capitol rotunda—"the first woman and second African American to be granted this honor,"[37] where forty thousand people came to say farewell.

Her funeral service in Detroit was attended by former President Clinton, then-Senator Barack Obama, and many other notable people. President George W. Bush honored her with what is perhaps the greatest honor of all when he ordered that a statue of Rosa Parks be created and put on permanent display in the U.S. Capitol's Statuary Hall. The legacy of her brave stand will go on forever in the lives she touched and changed. One example we may fittingly close with is that of Condoleeza Rice, who at a service for Rosa in Montgomery boldly said, "Without Mrs. Parks, I probably would not be standing here today as Secretary of State."[38]

SEVEN
Mother Teresa

1910–1997

ast year I was in Skopje, the capital city of what is called by some
the Republic of Macedonia and by others ΓΥΚΟΜ (Former
Yugoslav Republic of Macedonia). I was there under the auspices
of East-West Ministries of Dallas to speak to that nation's parliamentary leaders about the life of one of my heroes, William Wilberforce.[1]

One day during my visit, as I was walking through the center of the
city, I was surprised to come upon a spot identified as the birthplace of
another one of my heroes, Mother Teresa. I had completely forgotten
that she was born in Skopje, and suddenly there I was standing on the
very site where she had come into the world. The house itself had been
destroyed in the great Skopje earthquake of 1963, but the dimensions
of the home were marked out on the pavement. It was incredibly tiny.
Standing there I could hardly imagine that the baby born in such a
tiny house would go on to become a saint and to inspire millions upon
millions around the world.

She certainly inspired me. When I was invited to be the speaker at the National Prayer Breakfast in Washington, DC, in 2012,[2] I immediately thought of Mother Teresa, whose speech there in 1994 was the only one many people seemed to remember. It wasn't until I had to write my own speech that I watched hers online.[3]

Mother Teresa was so short that in the video her face is mostly obscured by the microphone, but the moral authority and palpable holiness of this tiny woman is astounding, even when viewed through the less-than-grand window of a YouTube video. When she spoke about abortion, telling President Bill Clinton to "stop killing" these children, to "give them to her," it inspired me to speak of the taking of unborn life in my own speech. It was the least I could do, feeling so unequal to the high honor of following in the footsteps of this extraordinary woman of God.

In modern times, few have had the impact Mother Teresa did. Her very name represented—and still represents—holiness and compassion to many around the world. Catholics, Protestants, Muslims, Hindus, and atheists all respected and loved her. She lived out the commands of Christ: love God, and love your neighbor as yourself. And she deliberately made some of the poorest people on earth her nearest neighbors.

Some years ago, passengers on a Pan Am flight were startled by an announcement from the jet's copilot. Emerging from the cockpit, he told them that they had a special guest on board: Mother Teresa of Calcutta, founder of the Missionaries of Charity, winner of the Nobel Peace Prize, and friend to everyone from destitute leprosy victims to Pope John Paul II.

The copilot pulled off his cap. If the passengers wanted to assist in Mother Teresa's work with the poor, he said, they could put money in his cap. He then walked up and down the aisles, and when he returned to the front, he had more than six hundred dollars to present to the tiny, elderly nun.[4]

On principle, Mother Teresa always bought economy class tickets but was routinely bumped up to first class. Flight attendants—who considered it a privilege to serve her—escorted her off the plane to the airport's VIP lounge and carried her luggage for her. It was an honor simply to be near her. She was a frail treasure that needed to be guarded carefully.

My old boss Chuck Colson, who founded Prison Fellowship and BreakPoint, greatly admired Mother Teresa. In fact, he corresponded with her and kept a plaque on his desk with one of her sayings: "Faithfulness, not success." When President Ronald Reagan was asked what he told Mother Teresa at the White House in 1986, he said he had listened instead; New York mayor Ed Koch said it was impossible to say no to her when she wanted something. Mother Teresa never thought she was too important to scrub toilets at the motherhouse in India; and she so disliked spending money on plane tickets that she wrote to one airline offering to work as a flight attendant in exchange for being allowed to fly free.

Mother Teresa had a playful side to her personality. Once, when she was invited to hear Mass at the Vatican with her friend Pope John Paul II, she decided to bring a priest along to meet him. But the Vatican had not invited the priest, and showing up uninvited to see the pope in his apartments is like showing up uninvited at the White House for a little chat with the president. It simply is not done; in fact, one could get arrested for doing so, or worse. But Mother Teresa got away with it, dragging the embarrassed priest through several layers of outraged security, right into the *sanctum sanctorum* of the pope's living room.

Her impact was so great that it wasn't unusual for a few minutes' conversation with Mother Teresa to change someone's life dramatically. Mother Teresa frequently asked strangers on the street for help—such as moving heavy boxes into one of her facilities for the poor. The strangers usually agreed, and when it dawned on them who it was they had assisted, they were overjoyed.

How did Mother Teresa go about loving her neighbors, and why did she love them so richly? Perhaps her vision can be summed up in the words of Matthew 25:34–40, which she quoted often:

> Then the King will say to those on His right hand, "Come, you blessed of My Father, inherit the kingdom prepared for you from the foundation of the world: for I was hungry and you gave Me food; I was thirsty and you gave Me drink; I was a stranger and you took Me in; I was naked and you clothed Me; I was sick and you visited Me; I was in prison and you came to Me."
>
> Then the righteous will answer Him, saying, "Lord, when did we see You hungry and feed You, or thirsty and give You drink? When did we see You a stranger and take You in, or naked and clothe You? Or when did we see You sick, or in prison, and come to You?" And the King will answer and say to them, "Assuredly, I say to you, inasmuch as you did it to one of the least of these My brethren, you did it to Me."

Mother Teresa said that she saw Jesus in every man, woman, or child she met, and she treated them accordingly. She thought the biggest problem on earth was being unloved; and if, in her exhaustion, all she could offer someone was a smile, she gave it.

She wanted to show the love of Christ in all she did—in helping the malnourished child and the woman dying in the gutter. To her, all these were simply "Jesus in His distressing disguise," as she put it. Because of this she was widely considered a saint during her lifetime, long before the Vatican made it official.

◆ ◆ ◆

The girl who would become Mother Teresa of Calcutta was born Gonxha Agnes Bojaxhiu on August 26, 1910, in Skopje, at that time part of the Ottoman Empire. Agnes's parents were Dranafile (Drana) and Nikola Bojaxhiu. She had an older brother, born in 1907, and an older sister, Aga, born in 1904.

The vast majority—90 percent—of the family's neighbors were Muslims; 10 percent, like the Bojaxhiu family, were Roman Catholics. Agnes's father was a partner in a construction company, a member of the community council, and a food importer, which meant frequent travel to far-flung lands.

Agnes's father died somewhat mysteriously when she was eight years old. The family thought it possible he had been poisoned by political or business adversaries but never found out for certain. In any event the family was instantly plunged into poverty, in part because Nikola's business partner had absconded with the company's assets. To pay the bills Agnes's mother took in sewing, but Agnes recalled that even facing hard times, her mother continued to look after the needs of the poor and sick in the neighborhood.

Agnes observed her mother each week bringing food to the home of a poor woman and even cleaning her house. She also took care of another woman whose body was covered in sores, and when a poor widow died, she took the woman's children into her own family. She was the model for the young girl who would one day become Mother Teresa.

Despite the loss of her father, Agnes recalled a happy childhood. Her family had always been very devout in their faith. Her mother took Agnes and the other children to church daily, and every evening the family gathered together to pray. But they also played and sang music each night. Both prayer and music were vital parts of their daily lives. Agnes attended a convent primary school and later went to a state school. She and her sister joined the choir of Sacred Heart Church, where Agnes learned to play the mandolin.

Although she suffered from a chronic cough due to weak lungs, Agnes was popular and fun loving. She enjoyed reading and taking part in church youth group activities that included walks, concerts, and parties. She was an innate leader and organizer. Her parish priest, Father Jambrekovic, had a tremendous impact on Agnes's spiritual life.

Agnes was just twelve when she began to believe that God was calling her to the religious life. But how, she asked Father Jambrekovic, could she be absolutely certain that God wanted her to enter religious life? Joy, he responded, was the proof of the rightness of any endeavor.

Agnes was happy at home and didn't especially want to become a nun. But by the time she was eighteen, she firmly believed she was meant to "belong completely to God."[5]

Through Father Jambrekovic, Agnes learned about the mission work that the Society of Jesus was doing in India. Their inspiring letters about their work among Calcutta's poor and sick, along with their personal visits to Skopje and the enthusiasm Father Jambrekovic expressed for this work, inspired Agnes to join them.

Despite the fact she would have to leave her beloved family, Agnes chose to apply to the Sisters of Loreto, who were located in Ireland. When she told her mother what she intended to do, Drana decided to test her daughter's commitment and refused to give her consent to the plan. But Agnes stood firm. Following twenty-four hours of prayer, her mother told Agnes she could go.

On September 26, 1928, not knowing she would never again see her mother or sister, Agnes climbed aboard a train headed for Paris. There she submitted to an interview by Mother Eugene MacAvin, who ran Loreto House in Paris. She was then permitted to continue north to Dublin, where she would be entrusted to the care of Mother M. Raphael Deasy.

Agnes received her postulant's cap at Loreto Abbey in Rathfarnham, a Dublin suburb, on October 12, and spent the next six weeks learning English. She chose the name of Sister Mary Teresa of the Child Jesus, after Thérèse of Lisieux, the French Carmelite nun. Then, on December 1, she boarded a ship and set sail for India, where she would begin her lifelong service to God.

Sister Teresa's first sight of India—the city of Madras, now called Chennai—shocked her. The woman who would spend her life serving the poorest of the poor realized that she had no real idea what true poverty could look like. In a Catholic mission magazine article, she described the situation: "Many families live in the streets, along the city walls, even in places thronged with people. They are all virtually naked, wearing at best a ragged loincloth. . . . As we went along the street we chanced upon one family gathered around a dead relation, wrapped in worn red rags. . . . It was a horrifying scene. If our people could only see all this, they would stop grumbling about their own misfortunes and offer thanks to God for blessing them with such abundance."[6]

Sister Teresa and a fellow novitiate traveled to Calcutta on January 6, 1929, and a week later traveled to Darjeeling, where both formally became Loreto novices. Sister Teresa added the study of Hindi and Bengali to the English she had begun studying in Ireland. Her first job was teaching at the Loreto convent school, and she briefly assisted the nursing staff at a nearby medical station.

Another article Sister Teresa wrote for the Catholic mission magazine shows her growing concern for the deeply poor and sick. "Many have come from a distance, walking for as much as three miles," she wrote. "Their ears and feet covered in sores. They have lumps and lesions on their backs. Many stay home because they are too debilitated by tropical fever to come."[7]

"When a man brings an emaciated child to the medical station, she explains that he is afraid we will not take the child, and says, 'If you do not want him, I will throw him into the grass. The jackals will not turn up their noses at him.' My heart freezes. . . . With much pity and love I take the little one into my arms, and fold him in my apron."[8]

After her time in Darjeeling, Sister Teresa traveled to Calcutta's Loreto Convent, Entally, where she taught at two different schools— one, a boarding school for girls from broken homes or with other difficulties; the other, St. Mary's high school, where she taught geography and history to Bengali girls. Outside the walls of the convent compound, Sister Teresa also taught at St. Teresa's primary school, where her pupils were desperately poor. But while she was distressed by their poverty, she experienced great joy in teaching and loving the children, who called her *Ma*, the Bengali word for *mother*.

In 1937, at the age of twenty-seven, Sister Teresa made her final vows, pledging herself to a life of chastity, poverty, and obedience. Loreto nuns typically take on the title "Mother," and so from this point on, Agnes Bojaxhiu would be called "Mother Teresa."

In addition to her teaching duties, once a week Mother Teresa visited the poor, who lived in shacks in Calcutta's slums. Mixing with the poor, whom she called "wonderful people," reinforced what she had learned many years before at home: that one could be deeply happy despite the lack of material possessions.

The years of the Second World War brought great difficulties, including a famine that killed millions. During this time the numbers of orphans arriving at the convent increased, and the British took over the Entally compound, using it as a military hospital. Despite the danger from Japanese troops in nearby Burma, Mother Teresa refused to leave India. When the Bengali school was moved to a new location, she was promoted to headmistress. When the war ended, the sisters and their students moved back to the Entally convent.

◆ ◆ ◆

I n 1946 Mother Teresa's superiors feared she might succumb to tuberculosis because of her weak chest, so they insisted that she rest in bed several hours each day to preserve her strength—something she did with great reluctance, as she much preferred to stay busy. At the end of this period, Mother Teresa went on retreat in Darjeeling. On September 10, while traveling by train journey to the hill station, her life would change dramatically. She said that while she was riding along and praying, she heard God's call to leave the convent in which she had taught for some twenty years and go out into the streets to help the poorest of the poor. This date is now celebrated by the Missionaries of Charity as "Inspiration Day."

"The call of God to be a Missionary of Charity is the hidden treasure for me, for which I have sold all to purchase it," she later recalled. God was telling her, she said, "to leave the convent and help the poor while living among them. It was an order. To fail it would have been to break the faith."⁹

God continued to press this call on her mind and heart during the retreat, and Mother Teresa began to visualize how to implement this vision. The following month she confided in Father Van Exem and asked for his thoughts on her proposal to start a new congregation of nuns who would live among the poor.

This new congregation would take a special vow, in which they would rely entirely on God to provide for their needs, assuming, that is, anyone decided to join her in this challenging life. They would live in the same conditions in which the poor lived and would specifically seek to live out Christ's command from Matthew 25:35–36: "For I was hungry and you gave Me food; I was thirsty and you gave Me drink; I was a stranger and you took Me in; I was naked and you clothed Me; I was sick and you visited Me; I was in prison and you came to Me."

Father Van Exem suggested that Mother Teresa continue praying about this for a time, and then in January 1947 he told her to write to Archbishop Ferdinand Périer. In fact, he went to see the archbishop himself to lay out Mother Teresa's wishes. The archbishop was doubtful. After all, other orders were already helping the poor in Calcutta. The archbishop was also taken aback by Mother Teresa's desire to go out among the poor instead of letting the poor come to them. His instruction to Mother Teresa was that she wait for at least a year.

Finally in 1948 Mother Teresa was given permission to leave the convent for one year to see how she would fare living in the manner she had proposed. After that time the archbishop would decide whether she should continue. She rejoiced at the news and immediately went to a local bazaar to choose inexpensive saris for which her order would one day become famous. They were white, to represent purity, with stripes of blue, the color associated with Mary, the mother of Jesus. The saris would be worn over white habits.

On August 16 Mother Teresa left the Loreto convent to begin the work she had been praying about and envisioning for so long. She had just five rupees to her name and was leaving behind friends who would deeply miss her. She later wrote that leaving Loreto was her greatest sacrifice, "the most difficult thing I have ever done. It was much more difficult than to leave my family and country to enter religious life. Loreto, my spiritual training, my work there, meant everything to me."[10]

Mother Teresa first traveled to Patna, where the Medical Mission Sisters worked at the Holy Family Hospital, to spend three months studying the treatment for the diseases of the poor and malnourished. She knew she would need this training. When she returned to Calcutta, she began to search for an appropriate place to live and work. She was allowed to move into a little room in a building occupied by the Little Sisters of the Poor, nuns who served two hundred elderly poor in the city.

Then in December, Mother Teresa officially began what British journalist and admirer Malcolm Muggeridge called a work of "outrageous courage"—work that would occupy her time, energies, and love for the rest of her life. The first day she ventured into Calcutta's Motijhil slum and gathered together her first few children for "school" that met on a muddy patch of ground between huts. She taught the children the Bengali alphabet by drawing the letters into the mud and having the children watch and repeat the letters after her. The following day many more students came.

In her record of that time, Mother Teresa wrote, "Those who were not clean I gave a good wash in the tank. We had catechism after the first lesson in hygiene and their reading. . . . After needlework class we went to visit the sick."[11] She gave them milk at lunchtime and handed out soap as prizes. The first helper, who had once taught at St. Mary's, arrived to assist her.

Eventually, local well wishers who saw what she was doing began donating money and food, and Mother Teresa was able to rent two huts, one for her school, and the other for those who were sick and dying.

She had begun to realize that such a home was necessary in order to spare the dying from the indignity of passing away in the gutters, being gnawed on by rats. She wrote in her diary about helping an ill woman she found on the street get to the hospital. The woman was refused care because she could not pay. "She died on the street. I knew then that I must make a home for the dying, a resting place for people going to heaven. . . . We cannot let a child of God die like an animal in the gutter."[12]

Mother Teresa knew she could not stay at the Little Sisters of the Poor indefinitely; she needed to find a place to live closer to the slums in which she ministered, and where she could work in community with sisters who eventually—she hoped—would join the work. Father Van Exem found her a house owned by a lay member of the Legion of Mary. She could live in an empty room on its second floor, rent-free, and a large room on the third floor would be made available to any helpers who joined her. Inspecting Mother Teresa's small room, which then contained only a bench, a box, a chair, and an altar, the mother of the Little Sisters of the Poor dryly commented, "They cannot say that you left Loreto to become rich."[13] Nuns from Loreto eventually supplied Mother Teresa with a simple bed.

Mother Teresa began making frequent visits to local pharmacies— not to beg, but to ask, with her lovely smile, "Would you like to do something beautiful for God?" (The question would later become well known after British journalist Malcolm Muggeridge made a documentary about her titled *Something Beautiful for God*.) Of course the pharmacist would. And then she would hand him a list of medicines she needed for those she was assisting.

She was not so popular with the staffs of hospitals, who grew frustrated when they saw the nun pushing in a wheelchair, or transporting via rickshaw, or carrying in her arms various men, women, and children who were near death. The hospitals often refused to accept the would-be patients, who they knew would be unable to pay for treatment.

The work was hard, and at the beginning Mother Teresa was often lonely and sorely tempted to return to her beloved Loreto convent. On March 19, 1949, a few months after she had begun her work, one of her former students, Subashini Das, arrived at Mother Teresa's lodgings, eager to help. Eventually this young Bengali woman became an aspirant, taking the given name of her beloved teacher: Agnes. In time she became Sister Agnes. Soon another of Mother Teresa's former pupils, Magdalena Gomes, announced she wanted to join the work, and she moved in with Mother Teresa. She later became Sister Gertrude. Before long two more former students joined them. Mother Teresa's teachings about the need to care for the poor had made their mark.

The realization that serving the poor was hard work also made its mark, although what these nuns did they did with joy, knowing that it was a privilege to serve God by serving "the least of these." They worked eight hours each day, with the exception of Sundays and Thursdays. There were breaks for meals, Mass, prayer, housework, rest, and reflection. They all performed the same work Mother Teresa did: going into the slums to provide food and simple medical care, visiting the elderly, giving comfort to the abandoned, and teaching children their letters and proper hygiene. They also knocked on doors asking for money and leftover food to support the work. Many were happy to give, but not everyone was friendly or approved of the way the nuns were living, including some fellow Christians.

Eventually Mother Teresa asked Calcutta city authorities for a building for the sick and the dying. The city was well aware of the extraordinary work she was doing, and they gave her a hostel. The building was next door to a temple devoted to Kali, the fearsome and many-armed Hindu goddess of death. Pilgrims to the temple had once stayed in the building, but now it was abandoned and filthy. A delighted Mother Teresa, aided by her helpers, cleaned the place up and renamed it Nirmal Hriday, a Bengali term meaning "Place of the Immaculate Heart." There the sisters would take in the sick and the dying, wash them of the vomit and filth that often covered them, treat their wounds, feed them, and allow them a clean place to die while feeling loved and wanted and in the presence of a gentle, smiling face.

At death each person was allowed the rituals of his faith, whether Christian, Hindu, or Muslim.

Not surprisingly some of the more radical Hindus were not pleased that Christian nuns were working on the premises of a Hindu goddess and perhaps even proselytizing Hindus. So when Mother Teresa took over the building, violent protests followed. One day a Hindu leader gathered a mob of young people, armed with stones, to help him drive out Mother Teresa and her helpers. When she heard the hubbub outside, she came out the front door and courageously and calmly approached the mob. She soon learned who was leading this angry crowd and addressed him directly, inviting the Hindu leader to come inside and see for himself what the sisters were doing.

When he came out a short time later, the mob, still waiting for his instructions, asked him if they could begin what they had come to do—drive out the nuns by force. "Yes, you can," the man replied, "but only when your sisters and your mothers do what those Sisters are doing in there."[14]

During the first year of Mother Teresa's work with the poor, ten young women joined her, and by 1950 she had devised a constitution for the Missionaries of Charity—the name God had given her when she first heard her "call within a call." In the first and in every subsequent Missionaries of Charity chapel hangs a crucifix and the words "I thirst." As the journalist and historian David Aikman explained in his book *Great Souls*, "These are, of course, the real words of Christ on the cross. But to Mother Teresa they have always expressed Christ's desire, indeed His yearning, for us to love Him."[15]

Mother Teresa made it clear that the helpers—later they were called novices—were expected to be cheerful as they worked. She was determined that the members of the order would live as simply as the poor. Each morning, the nuns washed themselves and their clothing in buckets of water. They used ashes to clean their teeth, and they used the same tiny bar of soap to wash their bodies and their saris.

But with more and more helpers joining them, it became necessary to find a larger place in which to live. In 1953, after much prayer, Mother Teresa and Sister Gertrude approached Dr. Islam, a retired Muslim magistrate who had decided to move to Pakistan. His property was made up of two houses enclosing a central courtyard in the noisy heart of Calcutta. He had not mentioned his plans to anyone and was astonished when Mother Teresa brought up the possibility of buying his house. He sold it to them for far less than it was worth, and to this day it remains the motherhouse of the Missionaries of Charity. From their new home, the sisters looked out onto the streets of Calcutta, filled with pedestrians, rickshaws, and the sounds of busy traffic.

One thing that distinguished Mother Teresa as someone who truly believed in the everyday reality of God was her determination to live in complete reliance on him—meaning that she expected miracles. And there were many of them. One day the community ran out of food. Answering a knock on the door, they found a woman holding bags of rice. The woman informed them that some "inexplicable impulse" had brought her to them with the rice. It was just enough for their evening meal.[16]

Another time, in preparation for a new arrival, the sisters decided to make a mattress, which was their custom, but they ran out of cotton cloth to finish the job. When she learned of it, Mother Teresa offered to give them the fabric from her own pillow, but the sisters were reluctant to accept, feeling that she needed to have a comfortable pillow to rest on after her long day's work. But while she was insisting, there was a knock at the door. Answering it, the sisters found an Englishman standing there with a mattress under his arm. He told them that he was returning to England, and it had occurred to him that the sisters might need it. In these small ways, God assured the sisters that he was with them in their work. Each such miracle gave them tremendous encouragement.

On another occasion the sisters had no food with which to feed the seven thousand people dependent upon them over the next two days. In a "coincidence" that is simply inexplicable, the government shut down the local schools for those days and donated all the bread that would have been fed to the schoolchildren to the Missionaries of Charity.

On April 12, 1953, Mother Teresa and the first group of sisters took their final vows as Missionaries of Charity. The number of helpers continued to grow as doctors, nurses, and others volunteered their services. The sisters set up dispensaries to deal with the many diseased and malnourished people they were helping. Those in need included many Hindu refugees who had been forced out of Pakistan after the British "partition," which created the nation of Pakistan out of what had been the British India Empire.

In 1955 the Missionaries of Charity opened their first home for sick and unwanted children, Shishu Bhavan, not far from the motherhouse. It was the first of many more to come. Among the babies brought to the sisters were some who had literally been dumped in garbage cans or drains. Most of the older children who came to them suffered from tuberculosis and malnutrition.

Mother Teresa visited the children's home herself each day, taking particular interest in babies whose health was so precarious that they were likely to die soon. Wrapping the child in a blanket, she would hand him to a helper and simply instruct her to love the child until he died. She felt it absolutely central to her mission that no child should die without having experienced love. Even if tiny babies brought to them died within the hour, Mother Teresa insisted that they must die "beautifully." One of the helpers, who had been asked to love a dying baby, held the child and hummed a Brahms lullaby to him until he died that evening. Three decades later the woman still recalled how the tiny infant had pressed his little body against hers.

Of course not all the children died, and Mother Teresa taught those who regained their health at Shishu Bhavan a skill, such as typing, carpentry, or needlework, so that they would be able to get a job instead of having to beg on the streets. Others were sent to schools, and well-heeled sponsors, both in India and in other countries, paid their school fees. Families of the same faith adopted some of the children.

Mother Teresa also worked to end abortion by writing to clinics, police stations, and hospitals. The sisters made posters with this message, and young mothers began showing up day and night with babies they could not afford to keep. Childless couples were delighted to adopt many of these "unwanted" babies.

Malnourished children and the destitute dying were not the only people in whom Mother Teresa saw Christ in his "distressing disguise." In Calcutta alone, because of cramped conditions and the lack of adequate food and proper medical care, some thirty thousand people were afflicted with leprosy. Ignorance about this frightening disease made the problem worse, leading sufferers to hide it as long as possible for fear that their employers would fire them and their families reject them. So Mother Teresa opened a leper asylum in the Gobra district outside of Calcutta. When the government forced her to evacuate the patients as part of a development plan, she embarked on a fund-raising scheme, and in 1957, thanks to the generosity of wealthy Hindus and others—including the donation of an ambulance from the United States—she opened a mobile leprosy clinic.

The mobile clinic was a great improvement over Mother Teresa's original idea of building a home in which lepers could receive treatment, because patients could be treated in their own homes and, if they had a job, could continue working. Within a few months the Missionaries of Charity were treating six hundred lepers. Mother Teresa was insistent that—for the sake of their dignity—the lepers in treatment be taught skills, such as carpentry, making shoes, or sewing their own clothing, so they could be self-sufficient.

For those who would never be cured or who would never again be able to find work in the outside world, Mother Teresa built dozens of small houses and a hospital on land outside Calcutta that had been donated by the Indian government. The hospital was funded in part by raffling off a limousine given to her by Pope Paul VI following his visit to India. This home was called Shanti Nagar, meaning "The Place of Peace."

◆ ◆ ◆

Catholic canon law required ten years to elapse before the Missionaries of Charity would be allowed to open additional houses elsewhere in India. But the archbishop relaxed this rule by a year, allowing the congregation to begin expanding in 1959, nine years into the probationary period. In short order they set up houses in Delhi, Ranchi, Jhansi, and Mumbai.

In 1965 people beyond India began asking the Missionaries of Charity to come to them. Mother Teresa was asked to open a house in faraway Venezuela, which she did. On July 15 of that year, she met with Pope Paul VI, and three years later he invited Mother Teresa to open a house in Rome too.

As a child Mother Teresa had dreamed of traveling the world, and now she seemed to be on the road constantly, opening one house after another in such places as Tanzania, Ceylon, Australia, Yemen, Peru, Jordan, London, and New York.

In Western cities the needs were quite different than they were in the poverty-stricken places of the developing world. Drug and alcohol addiction were often the problems she had to deal with. In London, Mother Teresa was with a drug addict who had taken an overdose and died before her eyes. Her heart went out to alcoholics and mentally ill people, who even in wealthy countries were tragically left to fend for themselves. It was in the affluent West that Mother Teresa began to realize the extent of what she called "spiritual poverty." During a visit to London, she observed, "Here you have the Welfare State. Nobody need starve. But there is a different poverty. The poverty of the spirit, of loneliness and being unwanted."[17]

In 1968 Muggeridge became taken with Mother Teresa and decided to interview her for the BBC. This was the first time Mother Teresa was introduced to the world on a large scale. But she was nervous during the interview and gave simple answers to his polished questions. In his book, *Something Beautiful for God*, Muggeridge said that the "verdict on the Mother Teresa interview was that, technically, it was barely usable, and there was for a while some doubt as to whether it was good enough for showing at all except late at night."

In the end, the program aired on a Sunday evening. "[T]he response," he wrote, "was greater than I have known to any comparable programme, both in mail and in contributions of money for Mother Teresa's work. All of them said approximately the same thing—this woman spoke to me as no one ever has, and I feel I must help her."[18] When the program aired again not long afterward, the response was greater yet, with twenty thousand pounds pouring in for the little nun with the simple answers.

Muggeridge traveled to Calcutta in 1969, hoping to persuade Mother Teresa to allow him to film her and her sisters at work among the poor. She reluctantly agreed. Part of the filming was to be done in the Home for the Dying. The resulting film contained an unexpected and luminous miracle. As Muggeridge explained:

This Home for the Dying is dimly lit by small windows high up in the walls, and Ken [the cameraman] was adamant that filming was quite impossible there. We had only one small light with us, and to get the place adequately lighted in the time at our disposal was quite impossible. It was decided that, nonetheless, Ken should have a go, but by way of insurance he took, as well, some film in an outside courtyard where some of the inmates were sitting in the sun. In the processed film, the part taken inside was bathed in a particularly beautiful soft light, whereas the part taken outside was rather dim and confused.

How to account for this? Ken has all along insisted that, technically speaking, the result is impossible. To prove the point, on his next filming expedition—to the Middle East—he used some of the same stock in a similarly poor light, with completely negative results. He offers no explanation. . . . I myself am absolutely convinced that the technically unaccountable light is, in fact, the Kindly Light

Newman refers to in his well-known exquisite hymn. . . . Mother Teresa's Home for the Dying is overflowing with love, as one senses immediately on entering it. This love is luminous, like the halos artists have seen and made visible round the heads of the saints.[19]

Mother Teresa had a tremendous impact on this lifelong skeptic, who became a Christian in his sixties and a Catholic when he was seventy-nine, largely through Mother Teresa's influence. Her effect on him is clear in a passage in *Something Beautiful for God.* Muggeridge wrote that he dropped her off one morning at a Calcutta train station, and "when the train began to move, and I walked away, I felt as though I were leaving behind me all the beauty and all the joy in the universe."[20]

◆ ◆ ◆

M other Teresa's increasing fame brought criticism from those who thought they knew more about helping the poor than she did. They wondered why she did not attack the institutional structures that caused poverty. Why did she not reorganize the Missionaries of Charity in such a way that more people could be helped? Why did she not condemn dictators? Couldn't governments, with all their vast resources, do a better job helping the poor than a congregation of nuns? To all these critics Mother Teresa responded that God required her to do small things with great love; that while government welfare programs exist for quite admirable purposes, "Christian love is for a person."[21]

"I do not add up," she noted. "I only subtract from the total number of poor or dying. With children one dollar saves a life. . . . So we use ourselves to save what we can. . . . Every small act of love for the unwanted and the poor is important to Jesus."[22]

Others criticized Mother Teresa for not being more willing to witness to the teachings of the Church, not realizing the fine line Mother Teresa had to walk as a Christian missionary in a Hindu country. As well, she preferred to let the work itself do the witnessing. As she frequently told her sisters, quoting the words of Jesus: "Let them see your good works and glorify your father who is in heaven."[23]

The Missionaries of Charity continued to grow, even during a time when vocations for other religious orders were decreasing. It seemed there was something strangely compelling about the call to great poverty and a hard life aiding the poorest of the poor. In the 1980s and '90s, the Missionaries of Charity were able to open houses even in Communist and formerly Communist nations.

In 1963, because there were some things that could be better accomplished by men than women, a new branch of the congregation, the Missionary Brothers of Charities, was begun. A few years later the International Association of Co-Workers of Mother Teresa came into being, allowing thousands of laypeople around the globe to join the work. The Missionaries of Charity Contemplative Sisters was founded in 1977, and the Missionaries of Charity Contemplative Brothers was begun three years later. In 1984 the Missionaries of Charity Fathers joined the work.

◆ ◆ ◆

As the years passed, Mother Teresa received recognition and awards, which she always accepted on behalf of those she served. Documentaries were made of her life and work, and the famous—including sports stars, film celebrities, and Princess Diana—began to beat a path to her door to meet this woman many considered a living saint and to ask her blessing. Mother Teresa treated them just as she treated Calcutta's poor, with warmth and compassion. And she reminded one and all that taking care of the poor and hungry was nothing heroic or extraordinary. She referred to it as "a simple duty for you and for me."[24]

In 1979 one of the world's greatest honors was bestowed on Mother Teresa when she was awarded the Nobel Peace Prize. She decided that she would travel to Oslo, Norway, to accept the prize in person. But in her typical fashion, even in this highly secular nation Mother Teresa did not hesitate to proclaim her faith to the gathering of well-dressed guests, which included Norway's royal family. Jesus, she announced, "died on the cross to show that greater love, and He died for you and for me and for that leper and for that man dying of hunger and that naked person lying in the street. . . . And we read that in the Gospel very clearly: 'love as I have loved you; as I love you; as the Father has loved me, I love you.'"

She spoke of the spiritual poverty of wealthy nations where aging relatives are pushed into nursing homes, relatives who suffer emotional pain because they are seldom visited. She spoke of parents who were too busy working to pay attention to their children. And then she took direct aim at the violence of abortion in a country that had not only legalized it but also provided state funds to pay for what she regarded as nothing less than the murder of a human child:

> The greatest destroyer of peace today. Because if a mother can kill
> her own child—what is left for me to kill you and you kill me—there
> is nothing between. . . . Today, millions of unborn children are being
> killed—and we say nothing . . . nobody speaks of the millions of little
> ones who have been conceived with the same life as you and I. . . . We
> allow it. To me, the nations who have legalized abortion, they are the
> poorest nations. They are afraid of the little one! They are afraid of
> the unborn child, and the child must die because they don't want to
> feed one more child, to educate one more child.

She reminded her unsmiling audience of the humanity of the unborn baby:

> It was that unborn child that recognized the presence of Jesus when
> Mary came to visit Elizabeth, her cousin. As we read in the gospel,
> the moment Mary came into the house, the little one in the womb
> of his mother leaped with joy, recognizing the Prince of Peace. And

so today, let us here make a strong resolution: We are going to save every little child, every unborn child, give them a chance to be born.

We are fighting abortion with adoption. And the good God has blessed the work so beautifully. . . . We have saved thousands of children, and thousands of children have found a home where they are loved and wanted . . . and so today, I ask you: Let us all pray that we have the courage to stand by the unborn child.[25]

One can only imagine the reaction of the sophisticates on the Nobel committee, who had intended to grandly bestow one of the world's highest honors on this little nun for her good work among the poor, and who in the crowning apex of the ceremony found themselves being soundly rebuked for their embrace of a great moral evil.

Mother Teresa reprised this peroration fifteen years later, when she was invited to be the guest speaker at the National Prayer Breakfast in Washington, DC. Addressing President Bill Clinton and Hillary Clinton, Vice President Al Gore and Tipper Gore, members of the U.S. House and Senate, religious leaders, and the very court that had put their legal imprimatur on the violent act that had taken the lives of millions of unborn American babies, Mother Teresa said: "But I feel that the greatest destroyer of peace today is abortion, because Jesus said, if you receive a little child you receive me. So every abortion is the denial of receiving Jesus—is the neglect of receiving Jesus."[26]

What many news outlets left out of their coverage of her speech was the fact that, at this point, the audience burst into sustained applause. If you watch the speech on YouTube, you may see the cameras pulling back during the seemingly unending applause to reveal the Clintons and the Gores, well-known for their strong defense of abortion rights, stiff and uncomfortable on either side of Mother Teresa, refusing to applaud what she had just said and surely wishing they were somewhere else.

◆ ◆ ◆

| n 1975 the Missionaries of Charity celebrated its Silver Jubilee. These twenty-five years had been "joyful and hard," Mother Teresa wrote in a letter to those who had shared in the work. "We have worked together for Jesus and with Jesus. . . . Let us thank God for all gifts and promise [that] we will make our Society something beautiful for God."[27]

In January 1985 she traveled to China, visiting a Beijing home for the elderly and a factory where handicapped workers were employed. That year she also became aware of the AIDS epidemic in America and of how its victims were often abandoned by friends and family and left to die miserable deaths alone. While some Christians may have privately considered that these mostly homosexual men were reaping the consequences of their own behavior and thus deserved little sympathy, Mother Teresa, observing their suffering, saw Jesus in yet another "distressing disguise." She opened New York's first hospice for AIDS victims in Greenwich Village.

In 1990 Mother Teresa turned eighty and resigned, with considerable relief, as superior general of the Missionaries of Charity. It was something she had wanted to do for some years. She had many health problems caused by exhaustion, flare-ups of malaria, and failing vision, and she had suffered various injuries. She had a stroke in her midsixties and in 1981 had learned she had a serious heart condition, something she insisted be kept secret. In 1989 an external pacemaker had been fitted; it was later replaced with an internal one.

In a letter to all those involved in the work of the Missionaries of Charity, Mother Teresa offered her prayers, love, and gratitude "for all you have been and have done all these forty years to share in the joy of loving each other and the Poorest of the Poor. . . . Beautiful are the ways of God if we allow him to use us as he wants."[28]

But her resignation, which had been announced by Pope John Paul II, was dramatically short-lived. When she was once again reelected by the Missionaries of Charity General Council to lead the congregation, Mother Teresa accepted it as God's will. Now stooped with age, she continued to travel on behalf of the poorest of the poor and to attend the professions of Missionaries of Charity sisters making first or final vows.

In 1997, Mother Teresa was finally allowed to step down as superior general for the Missionaries of Charity. Elected to take her place was Sister Nirmala, a Hindu convert.

On August 26, Mother Teresa celebrated her eighty-seventh birthday at the motherhouse in Calcutta. Time was running out for this passionate servant of Jesus. A few days later, on August 31, her friend, thirty-six-year-old Princess Diana, died in a car crash in Paris. Shocking as it was, this became the focus of the whole world's attention for several weeks. Mother Teresa told the press she would pray for the princess, who, she said, had a special love for the world's poor. But on September 5, while the world was still in the midst of mourning Princess Diana's untimely death, Mother Teresa—thousands of miles from the funeral frenzy in London—quietly passed away, or went home to God, as she would have put it.

India, mourning the loss of a woman loved by the world, gave Mother Teresa a state funeral. Her body lay in state at St. Thomas's Church, visited by hundreds of thousands of mourners, from the very poor to those occupying high places in the world, including the duchess of Kent, representing Queen Elizabeth; Hillary Clinton, representing the United States; and Bernadette Chirac, representing her husband, Jacques Chirac, the president of France. All wanted to bid farewell to the woman who, for many of them, had been the personification of love. Pope John Paul II sent a message to be read at her funeral, urging others to continue the work Mother Teresa had begun.

This work, at the time of her death, amounted to a tremendous achievement. The woman who had heard God's voice on a train some fifty years before had left behind a huge legacy: four thousand sisters serving Jesus around the world, more than four hundred brothers, plus the many Missionaries of Charity Fathers, Lay Missionaries of Charity, and other volunteers, all carrying on the work to which she had devoted her life.

Mother Teresa was laid to rest at the motherhouse in Calcutta, surrounded by the sounds of the city—trams and traffic, rickshaw bells, and passing parades—which had served as background music to her magnificent work for decades. In October 2003 she was beatified by Pope John Paul II.

In the years following Mother Teresa's death, some of her private letters to her spiritual adviser, Father Van Exem, and Archbishop Ferdinand Périer, were published. Some of their contents surprised those who had come to know and love her. As CNN put it, "The world is discovering a new Mother Teresa—one at times fraught with painful feelings of abandonment by God."[29]

Among the fascinating details: Mother Teresa had always stated that on Inspiration Day, she had not had a vision. But her writings revealed what she had obviously felt unable to share publicly during her lifetime—that for several months she experienced a period of union with God during which she heard a series of interior locutions in which Jesus called her to carry him into the "holes" of the poor, to bring the light of faith to those living in darkness, and so bring joy to the suffering heart of Jesus. . . . She also "saw" a series of progressively intensifying scenes of an immense crowd of all kinds of people in great sorrow and suffering, eventually covered in darkness. Most surprising of all was Mother Teresa's admission that she "no longer felt the proximity of God in the same way that she had for that privileged period in 1946 and 1947." She experienced "spiritual dryness, the profound pain of God's apparent absence despite her great thirst for him, and a lack of sensible consolation."[30]

And yet, many who knew her well—who witnessed her joy, her smile, and her work—would have been puzzled by her revelations.

"It is clear that Mother Teresa's inner (and outer) world was a place in which the brilliance of God's light and the bleakness of man's darkness met and mingled—from which her victorious light only shone the brighter," wrote biographer Father Joseph Langford. "What emerged from that inner struggle was a light in no way lessened by her bearing the cloak of humanity's pain, but a light all the more resplendent, and all the more approachable . . . a light entirely accessible to the poorest, beckoning to God's brightness all who share in the common human struggle."[31]

Those who made the decision to publish her words had done so in order to increase not only the world's understanding of Mother Teresa but also the true meaning of holiness.

◆ ◆ ◆

Mother Teresa was considered a saint because she was seen to personify an ideal: to love God, and to love one's neighbor. And yet, what she did was so simple that each one of us can do it—in fact, must do it, if we are to obey the command of Christ: to feed the hungry, care for the sick, invite the stranger in, clothe the naked, visit those in prison, and quench the thirst of those who simply need a cup of water.

It was constant prayer that gave Mother Teresa the strength to keep going and caused her to produce such tremendous fruit. And it is prayer that must undergird all efforts to obey God, because as Mother Teresa of Calcutta would be the first to say, obedience is not always easy. In fact, without God's help, it is impossible.

As Langford put it, Mother Teresa plunged, "for love's sake, into the dark homes and hearts of the poor. May her gentle, guiding light born of the heart of the Almighty be yours: A light that flies not from darkness—but ever towards it."[32]

Notes

INTRODUCTION

1. Eric Metaxas, *Bonhoeffer: Pastor, Martyr, Prophet, Spy* (Nashville: Thomas Nelson, 2010).
2. Eric Metaxas, *Amazing Grace: William Wilberforce and the Heroic Campaign to End Slavery* (New York: Harper San Francisco, 2007).
3. Eric Metaxas, *Seven Men and the Secret to Their Greatness* (Nashville: Thomas Nelson, 2013).
4. For more information, please visit www.socratesinthecity.com.
5. Alice von Hildebrand, *The Privilege of Being a Woman* (Ypsilanti, MI: Veritas Press, 2002).
6. Alice von Hildebrand, *Man and Woman: A Divine Invention* (Ave Maria, FL: Sapientia Press of Ave Maria University, 2010).
7. For a link to that interview, visit www.socratesinthecity.com.

CHAPTER ONE: JOAN OF ARC

1. *The Passion of Joan of Arc* was directed by Carl Theodor Dreyer and stars Renée Maria Falconetti. The 1928 silent film is based on the transcript of her trial in 1431 and is a widely acclaimed work of cinema.

2. Patricia Moynagh, "Beyond Just War: Joan of Arc and Fighting Without Malice," July 2014, http://web.isanet.org/Web/Conferences/ FLACSO-ISA%20BuenosAires%202014/Archive/22fa5cfc-9c9c-4241-a910–6e8bfe9ff74f.pdf.

3. Mark Twain, *Joan of Arc* (San Francisco: Ignatius Press, 2007), 92.

4. Regine Pernoud and Marie-Véronique Clin, *Joan of Arc: Her Story*, ed. Bonnie Wheeler, trans. and rev. Jeremy du Quesnay Adams (New York: St. Martin's Press, 1999), 23.

5. Hilaire Belloc, *Joan of Arc* (Charlotte, NC: Neumann Press, 1997), Kindle edition location 255.

6. Ibid.

7. Ibid., Kindle edition location 305.

8. Ibid., Kindle edition location 358.

9. Ibid., Kindle edition location 367.

10. Pernoud and Clin, *Joan of Arc*, 31.

11. Belloc, *Joan of Arc*, Kindle edition location 404.

12. Peggy McCracken.

13. Kelly DeVries, *Joan of Arc: A Military Leader* (Stroud, Gloucester: The History Press, 2011), 63.

14. Ibid., 64.

15. Pernoud and Clin, *Joan of Arc*, 37–38.

16. Ibid., 39.

17. Walter Adams, "April 29—Joan Arrives to Orleans and Crossly Scolds Dunois, the Bastard of Orleans," *Le Royaume des Ste. Jehanne et Ste. Thérèse*, http://joanandtherese.com/2010/07/31/april-29-joan-arrives-to-orleans-and-crossly-scolds-dunois-the-bastard-of-orleans.

18. Walter Adams, "May 5—Feast of the Ascension–Joan Refuses Battle in Honor of the Holy Day–but Sends a Final Ultimatum," *Le Royaume des Ste. Jehanne et Ste. Thérèse*, http://joanandtherese.com/2010/07/31/may-5-feast-of-the-ascension-joan-refuses-battle-in-honor-of-the-holy-day-but-sends-a-final-ultimatum.

19. Pernoud and Clin, *Joan of Arc*, 43.

20. Ibid., 44.

21. Ibid., 45.

22. Walter Adams, "May 6—Joan's Bravery in the Face of Confusion at Iles-aux-Toiles Provokes an Ill-Fated English Attack," *Le Royaume des Ste. Jehanne et Ste. Thérèse*, http://joanandtherese.com/2010/07/31/may-6-joans-bravery-in-the-face-of-confusion-at-iles-aux-toiles-provokes-an-ill-fated-english-attack.

23. Belloc, *Joan of Arc*, Kindle edition location 582.

24. Ibid., Kindle edition location 594.

25. Ibid.

26. Ibid., Kindle edition location 623.

27. Pernoud and Clin, *Joan of Arc*, 58.

28. Belloc, *Joan of Arc*, Kindle edition location 653.

29. Ibid., Kindle edition location 653.

30. DeVries, *Joan of Arc*, 133.

31. Belloc, *Joan of Arc*, Kindle edition location 786.

32. "Joan of Arc's Letter to the citizens of Rheims (August 5, 1429)," *Joan of Arc Archive*, http://archive.joan-of-arc.org/joanofarc_letter_aug_5_1429.html.

33. Pernoud and Clin, *Joan of Arc*, 89.

34. Ibid., 87.

35. Ibid.

36. Ibid., 96.

37. Belloc, *Joan of Arc*, Kindle edition location 993.

38. "Third Public Examination," *Saint Joan of Arc Center*, www.stjoan-center.com/Trials/sec03.html.

39. Belloc, *Joan of Arc*, Kindle edition location 1007.

40. Pernoud and Clin, *Joan of Arc*, 129.

41. Penelope Duckworth, "Saint Martha and Saint Joan: Proposals for the Commemoration of Two Women Who Shaped the History of Their Times," Episcopal Women's Caucus, www.episcopalwomenscaucus.org/ruach/GeneralConvention2006_vol26_3/06SaintMartha.html.

42. "Deliberations Held on May 9th, 12th and 19th and the Final Session and Sentence and Recantation," St. Joan of Arc Center, www.stjoan-center.com/Trials/sec20.html.

43. Pernoud and Clin, *Joan of Arc*, 130–131.

44. Ibid., 131.

45. Steven Kanehl, *I Was Born for This: Devoted to God Whatever the Cost* (Mustang, OK: Tate Publishing, 2008).

46. Pernoud and Clin, *Joan of Arc*, 132.
47. Robert R. Edgar, Neil J. Hackett, and George F. Jewsbury, *Civilization Past and Present* (New York: Longman, 2005), 2:435.
48. Steven R. Kanehl , "Jehanne la Pucelle: A Mini Biography," *Saint Joan of Arc Center*, www.stjoan-center.com/time_line/part10.html.
49. Pernoud and Clin, *Joan of Arc*, 133.
50. Belloc, *Joan of Arc*, Kindle edition location 1062.
51. Pernoud and Clin, *Joan of Arc*, 135.
52. Ibid., 136.
53. Allen Williamson, "Biography of Joan of Arc," *Saint Joan of Arc Center*, http://archive.joan-of-arc.org/joanofarc_short_biography.html.
54. "Joan of Arc, French National Heroe: A Theology for Mankind's Liberation," http://dbr-radio.com/joan-of-arc-theology.html.

CHAPTER TWO: SUSANNA WESLEY

1. Eric Metaxas, *Amazing Grace: William Wilberforce and the Heroic Campaign to End Slavery* (New York: Harper San Francisco, 2007), 168.
2. Such events give us some background in understanding why the Founding Fathers of the United States gave religious liberty such a prominent position, making it "the first freedom" by putting it first in the Bill of Rights.
3. Arnold A. Dallimore, *Susanna Wesley: The Mother of John and Charles Wesley* (Grand Rapids: Baker Book House, 1993), 14.
4. John. A. Newton, "Samuel Annesley (1620–1696)," *Proceedings of the Wesley Historical Society*, Sept. 1985, 45:39, www.biblicalstudies.org.uk/pdf/whs/45–2.pdf.
5. Susanna Wesley, *The Complete Writings*, ed. Charles Wallace, Jr. (Oxford: Oxford University Press, 1997), 99.
6. Luke Tyerman, *The Life and Times of the Rev. Samuel Wesley, M.A., Rector of Epworth, and Father of the Revs. John and Charles Wesley, the Founders of the Methodists* (London: Simpkin, Marshall & Co.), 251.
7. Wesley, *The Complete Writings*, 35–36.
8. Ibid., 37.
9. Ibid., 210.
10. John Kirk, *The Mother of the Wesleys*, vol. 1 (Cincinnati: Poe and Hitchcock, 1865), 161 (Available through Theclassics.us.).
11. Ibid., 151.

12. Dallimore, *Susanna Wesley*, 57–58.
13. Kathy McReynolds, *Susanna Wesley* (Ada, MI: Bethany House, 1998), 75.
14. Ibid., 76.
15. Ibid., 82.
16. Ibid., 76.
17. John Wesley, *The Journal of John Wesley*, vol. 1 (London: J. Kershaw, 1827), 371.
18. Ibid., 371–372.
19. E. V. Lucas, ed., *Her Infinite Variety: A Feminine Portrait Gallery* (University of California Libraries, 1908), 184.
20. Adam Clarke, *Memoirs of the Wesley Family* (London: J. & T. Clarke, 1823), 104. (Available through Ulan Press.)
21. Dallimore, *Susanna Wesley*, 67.
22. Clarke, *Memoirs of the Wesley Family*, 94.
23. Wesley, *The Complete Writings*, 65–66.
24. Dallimore, *Susanna Wesley*, 101.
25. John Wesley, *The Works of the Reverend John Wesley, a.m.*, vol. 3 (New York: J. Emory and B. Waugh, 1831), 265. (Available through Ulan Press.)
26. John Wesley, *The Works of the Rev. John Wesley, vol. 1* (London: The Confernece-Office, 1809), 39.
27. Susanna Wesley, *The Prayers of Susanna Wesley*, ed. W. L. Doughty (Grand Rapids: Zondervan, 1984), vii.
28. Ibid., 17.
29. Ibid., 19.
30. Ibid., 40.
31. Ibid., 3.
32. Ibid.
33. Dallimore, *Susanna Wesley*, 81.
34. McReynolds, *Susanna Wesley*, 54.
35. Ibid.
36. Mary Beth Crain, *Haunted Christmas: Yuletide Ghosts and Other Spooky Holiday Happenings* (Guilford, CT: Globe Pequot Press, 2010), 113–114.
37. Eliza Clarke, *Susanna Wesley*, Classic Reprint Series (London: Forgotten Books, 2012), 121.

38. John Fletcher Hurst, *John Wesley the Methodist* (New York: Eaton & Mains; Cincinnati: Jennings & Pye, 1903), 46.
39. Clarke, *Susanna Wesley*, 125.
40. Dallimore, *Susanna Wesley*, 91.
41. Ibid., 93.
42. Clarke, *Susanna Wesley*, 63–64.
43. Dallimore, *Susanna Wesley*, 132.
44. Ibid., 102.
45. Arthur Quiller-Couch, *Hetty Wesley* (London and New York: Harper and Brothers, 1903), 35–36.
46. Dallimore, *Susanna Wesley*, 113.
47. Ibid., 117.
48. "John Wesley and His Wife (part 2)," *Church History Blog*, https://lexloiz.wordpress.com/2010/03/19/john-wesley-and-his-wife-part-2/.
49. Dallimore, *Susanna Wesley*, 148.
50. "John Wesley the Methodist, Chapter VII—The New Birth," *Wesley Center Online*, http://wesley.nnu.edu/john-wesley/john-wesley-the-methodist/chapter-vii-the-new-birth/.
51. Christian Classics Ethereal Library, Sermons on Several Occasions, Sermon 128 "Free Grace."
52. Clarke, *Susanna Wesley*, 47.
53. Ibid., 191–192.
54. Dallimore, *Susanna Wesley*, 162.
55. Ibid., 165.
56. Clarke, *Susanna Wesley*, 208.

CHAPTER THREE: HANNAH MORE

1. Sharp, in addition to being a biblical scholar and legal beagle of the first order, came from a renowned musical family that played their music while on barges floating in the Thames. He could reportedly play two flutes at once and sometimes signed documents "G#."
2. Isaac Milner is known mainly for leading Wilberforce to faith in their chaise journey through the snowy Alps, but he was also a polymath who was the Lucasian professor at Cambridge, a lifelong academic chair held by Isaac Newton and Stephen Hawking. Milner was also physically gigantic and was a storytelling raconteur in the mold of the great Dr. Johnson.
3. Hannah More, *The Complete Works* (New York: Derby and Jackson, 1857), 1:355.

4. William Roberts, *Memoirs of the Life and Correspondence of Mrs. Hannah More* (New York: Harper and Brothers, 1834), 1:138.

5. Roberts, *Memoirs*, 1:45.

6. William Forbes, *An Account of the Life and Writings of James Beatie* (New York: Brisban and Brannan, 1807), 377.

7. Roberts, *Memoirs*, 1:146.

8. Caddell would also in 1797 publish Wilberforce's book, *A Practical View of the Prevailing Religious System of Professed Christians in the Higher and Middle Classes of This Country Contrasted With Real Christianity.*

9. Roberts, *Memoirs*, 1:77.

10. More, *Complete Works*, 1:545.

11. Samuel Johnson, *The Lives of the Most Eminent English Poets* (London: T. Longman et al, 1794), 2:247.

12. Karen Swallow Prior, *Fierce Convictions* (Nashville: Thomas Nelson, 2014), 86.

13. Ibid., 107.

14. Roberts, *Memoirs*, 1:138.

15. Ibid., 1:111.

16. Ibid., 1:291.

17. Henry Thompson, *The Life of Hannah More* (Philadelphia: E.L. Carey and A. Hart, 1838), 1:86.

18. Roberts, *Memoirs*, 1:50.

19. Prior, *Fierce Convictions*, 98.

20. John Ker Spittal, *Contemporary Criticisms of Dr. Samuel Johnson, His Works, and His Biographers* (London: John Murray, 1923), 207.

21. Prior, *Fierce Convictions*, 115.

22. Roberts, *Memoirs*, 1:281.

23. Ibid., 1:266.

24. John Pollock, *Wilberforce* (London: Constable, 1977), 64.

25. Roberts, *Memoirs*, 1:421.

26. More, *Complete Works*, 1:58.

27. Prior, *Fierce Convictions*, 141.

28. Thompson, *Life*, 1:116.

29. Roberts, *Memoirs*, 1:339.

30. Ibid., 1:339.

31. Ibid., 1:477.

32. More, *Complete Works*, 1:275.
33. Roberts, *Memoirs*, 1:455.
34. Ibid., 1:472.
35. Ibid., 1:474.
36. Ibid., 1:427.
37. Ibid., 1:346.
38. Percy Bysshe Shelley, *Essays, Letters from Abroad, Translations and Fragments* (Philadelphia: Lea and Blanchard, 1840), 1:62.

CHAPTER FOUR: SAINT MARIA OF PARIS
1. Sergei Hackel, *Pearl of Great Price* (Crestwood, NY: St. Vladimir's Seminary Press, 1965), 76.
2. Ibid., 78–79.
3. The chapel housing this icon was struck by lightning in 1888. The poor box fell to the floor and broke open, scattering its coins. Everything burned. Only the icon survived untouched, but for twelve half-kopek coins fused to its surface.
4. T. Stratton Smith, *The Rebel Nun* (Springfield, IL: Templegate, 1965), 61.
5. Hackel, *Pearl of Great Price*, 95.
6. Maria Skobstova, *Mother Maria Skobtsova: Essential Writings*, trans. Richard Pevear and Larissa Volokhonsky (Maryknoll, NY: Orbis Books, 2003), 16.
7. Ibid., 54.
8. Smith, *The Rebel Nun*, 74.
9. Ibid., 109.
10. Hackel, *Pearl of Great Price*, 5.
11. Ibid., 6.
12. Ibid., 11.
13. Skobstova, *Mother Maria Skobtsova*, 57.
14. Hackel, *Pearl of Great Price*, 15.
15. Ibid., 15.
16. Ibid., 16.
17. Smith, *The Rebel Nun*, 115.
18. Hackel, *Pearl of Great Price*, 23.
19. Skobtsova, *Mother Maria Skobtsova*, 93.
20. Ibid., 95.

21. "Metropolitan Anthony's [Sourozh Diocese, London] Memories of Mother Maria," Orthodox Christian Laity, August 19, 2002, http://archive.ocl.org/?id=12426.

22. Smith, *The Rebel Nun*, 135.

23. Hélène Arjakovsky-Klepinine, *Dimitri's Cross* (Ben Lomond, Conciliar Press, 2008), 102.

24. Skobtsova, *Mother Maria Skobtsova*, 78.

25. Ibid., 31.

26. Ibid., 109, 113, 114–115.

27. Ibid., 60.

28. Smith, *The Rebel Nun*, 122.

29. Ibid., 129.

30. Hackel, *Pearl of Great Price*, 52.

31. Grigori Benevitch, "The Saving of the Jews: The Case of Mother Maria (Scobtsova)," *Occasional Papers on Religion in Eastern Europe*, 2000, 20:1:1, http://digitalcommons.georgefox.edu/ree/vol20/iss1/1.

32. Hackel, *Pearl of Great Price*, 113.

33. Ibid., 115.

34. This group, calling themselves "German Christians," were committed Nazis who tried to reconcile National Socialist and anti-Semitic ideology with what they called "Positive Christianity." Bonhoeffer and his colleagues in the Confessing Church were their chief enemies.

35. Hackel, *Pearl of Great Price*, 108.

36. Smith, *The Rebel Nun*, 171.

37. Ibid., 209.

38. Ibid., 218.

39. Arjakovsky-Klepinine, *Dimitri's Cross*, 128.

40. Hackel, *Pearl of Great Price*, 122.

41. Ibid., 137.

42. Ibid., 130–131.

43. While the original was lost, survivors recalled its details and a reproduction was later made.

44. Hackel, *Pearl of Great Price*, 148.

45. Michael Plekon, *Living Icons* (South Bend, IN: University of Notre Dame Press, 2002), 80.

46. "The Righteous Among The Nations," http://db.yadvashem.org/righteous/family.html?language=en&itemId=4044235.

CHAPTER FIVE: CORRIE TEN BOOM

1. Corrie ten Boom, with C.C. Carlson, *In My Father's House: The Years Before the Hiding Place* (Old Tappan, NJ: Revell Company, 1976), 11–12.
2. Ibid., 16.
3. Corrie ten Boom, with Elizabeth and John Sherrill, *The Hiding Place*. (Washington Depot, CT: Chosen Books, 1971), 15.
4. Ten Boom, *In My Father's House*, 47.
5. Ibid., 133, 137.
6. Ibid., 145–146.
7. Ten Boom, *Hiding Place*, 49.
8. Ibid., 58.
9. Ibid., 61.
10. Michal Ann Goll, *Women on the Frontlines* (Shippensburg, PA: Destiny Image, 1999), 119.
11. Ten Boom, *Hiding Place*, 76–77.
12. Ibid., 83.
13. Ibid., 96.
14. Ibid.
15. Ibid., 105.
16. Ibid., 114.
17. Ibid., 115.
18. Ibid., 132.
19. Ibid., 133.
20. Ibid.
21. Ibid.
22. Ibid., 145.
23. Ibid., 146.
24. Ibid., 148.
25. Ibid., 150.
26. Ibid., 153.
27. Ibid., 154.
28. Ibid., 234.
29. Ibid., 159.
30. Corrie ten Boom, with Jamie Buckingham, *Tramp for the Lord*. (London: Hodder & Stoughton, 1975), 217–218.

31. Lawrence Baron, "Supersessionism without Contempt: The Holocaust Evangelism of Corrie ten Boom," in *Christian Responses to the Holocaust: Moral and Ethical Issues*, ed. Donald J. Dietrich (Syracuse, NY: Syracuse University Press, 2003), 127.

CHAPTER SIX: ROSA PARKS

1. Rosa Parks, *Quiet Strength: The Faith, the Hope, and the Heart of a Woman Who Changed a Nation* (Grand Rapids, MI: Zondervan, 1994), 54.
2. Douglas Brinkley, *Rosa Parks: A Life* (New York: A Penguin Life, 2000), 15.
3. Ibid., 24.
4. Ibid., 25.
5. Ibid., 35.
6. Ibid., 38.
7. Ibid., 32.
8. "Rosa Parks and the Montgomery Bus Boycott," www.africanafrican.com/folder11/world%20history1/black%20history/Rosa%20Parks.pdf.
9. 145 Cong. Rec. S3837 (daily ed. April 19, 1999) (statement of Sen. Abraham), www.gpo.gov/fdsys/pkg/CREC-1999–04–19/html/CREC-1999–04–19-pt1-PgS3837.htm.
10. Rosa Parks, *My Story* (New York: Dial Books, 1992), 100.
11. Ibid., 112.
12. Jennifer Rosenberg, "Rosa Parks Refuses to Give Up Her Bus Seat," *About.com 20th Century History*, http://history1900s.about.com/od/1950s/qt/RosaParks.htm.
13. Brinkley, *Rosa Parks*, 109.
14. Ibid.
15. Ibid., 107.
16. Ibid., 108.
17. Ibid., 109.
18. Ibid., 110.
19. Parks, *My Story*, 118.
20. Brinkley, *Rosa Parks*, 110.
21. Bettye Collier-Thomas and V. P. Franklin, *Sisters in the Struggle, African-American Women in the Civil Rights–Black Power Movement* (New York: New York University Press, 2001), 63.

22. "Overview," *The Montgomery Bus Boycott: They Changed the World,* www.montgomeryboycott.com/overview/.
23. Parks, *My Story,* 133.
24. Collier-Thomas and Franklin, *Sisters in the Struggle,* 68.
25. Juan Williams, *Eyes on the Prize: America's Civil Rights Years, 1954–1965* (New York: Viking, 1987), 76.
26. Parks, *My Story,* 140.
27. Ibid., 148.
28. Ibid., 166–167.
29. Ibid., 167.
30. Ibid., 168.
31. Ibid., 173.
32. Parks, *Quiet Strength,* 75.
33. Ibid., 16.
34. Ibid., 17.
35. Ibid., 58–59.
36. Ibid., 23.
37. Jeanne Theoharis, *The Rebellious Life of Mrs. Rosa Parks* (Boston: Beacon Press, 2013), vii.
38. Ibid.

CHAPTER SEVEN: MOTHER TERESA

1. My book about Wilberforce has been translated into Albanian, spoken by most people in the Republic of Macedonia.
2. My account of this experience can be found in *No Pressure, Mr. President: The Power of True Belief in a Time of Crisis* (Nashville: Thomas Nelson, 2012).
3. "Mother Teresa at National Prayer Breakfast," www.youtube.com/watch?v=OXn-wf5ylgo.
4. Leo-M. Maasburg, *Mother Teresa of Calcutta: A Personal Portrait* (San Francisco: Ignatius Press, 2011).
5. Kathryn Spink, *Mother Teresa: A Complete Authorized Biography* (New York: HarperOne, 2011), 8.
6. Amy Ruth, *Mother Teresa* (Minneapolis, MN: Learner Publications, 1999), 35.
7. Robert E. Barron, *The Priority of Christ: Toward a Post-Liberal Catholicism* (Grand Rapids: Brazos Press, 2007), 332.

8. Christie R. Ritter, *Mother Teresa: Humanitarian and Advocate for the Poor* (Edina, MI: ABDO, 2011), 32.

9. Spink, *Mother Teresa*, 22.

10. James Martin, *My Life with the Saints* (Chicago: Loyola Press, 2006), 166.

11. Spink, *Mother Teresa*, 35.

12. Ibid., 36.

13. Ibid., 38.

14. Maasburg, *Mother Teresa of Calcutta*, 158.

15. David Aikman, *Great Souls: Six Who Changed the Century* (Nashville: Word, 1998), 221.

16. Spink, *Mother Teresa*, 49.

17. Ibid., 86.

18. Malcolm Muggeridge, *Something Beautiful for God: Mother Teresa of Calcutta* (New York: Harper & Row, 1971), 30–31.

19. Ibid., 41–44.

20. Ibid., 17.

21. Ibid., 28.

22. Spink, *Mother Teresa*, 87.

23. Ibid., 125.

24. Ibid., 179.

25. "Mother Teresa—Nobel Lecture," *Nobelprize.org.* Nobel Media AB 201, www.nobelprize.org/nobel_prizes/peace/laureates/1979/teresa-lecture.html.

26. www.motherteresa.org/Centenary/English/Holinessisnot_MT.html.

27. Spink, *Mother Teresa*, 148.

28. Ibid., 225.

29. "Doubts, Exorcism Shine Spotlight on Mother Teresa," CNN.com/World, Sept. 7, 2001, http://edition.cnn.com/2001/WORLD/asiapcf/south/09/07/mother.teresa/.

30. Ibid., 300.

31. Joseph Langford, *Mother Teresa's Secret Fire: The Encounter that Changed Her Life and How It Can Transform Your Own* (Huntington, IN: Our Sunday Visitor Publishing Division, 2008), 31.

32. Ibid., epigraph.

Acknowledgments
For Seven Men

Previously, whenever someone asked me who helped research my books—especially the Wilberforce and Bonhoeffer biographies—I usually laughed, saying how much I wished that had been possible, but making clear that no one had helped, that I had done every jot of research and had written every tittle myself. My process was something like juggling while riding a unicycle. One did it alone or one didn't do it at all. This book, however, happily marks at least a one-volume departure from the standard juggling and unicycling. For the first time I am happy to have had help, most notably from my friend Anne Morse—especially on the Washington, Liddell, and Robinson chapters—and from our *BreakPoint* colleague Gina Dalfonzo, who helped with the Wojtyla chapter. I also must here acknowledge another *BreakPoint* colleague, my dear friend Roberto Rivera, who in 1998 tipped me off to Jackie Robinson's faith—and Branch Rickey's—and alerted me to the definitive Arnold Rampersad biography. Finally, I wish to acknowledge and thank my dear friend Markus Spieker, whose encouragement to write a book along these lines has finally borne fruit. May it continue to do so.

— Eric Metaxas
New York City
November 2012

Acknowledgments
For Seven Women

I am first of all grateful to all the women who after reading my *Seven Men* book encouraged me to write this book. And I am deeply grateful to all those people who helped me write it. I am most grateful to my friend Anne Morse for helping me research a number of the chapters and for writing the initial drafts of those chapters. Thanks also to Karen Swallow Prior for writing *Fierce Convictions*, without which my knowledge of Hannah More could not be what it is. Finally, I am grateful to Joel Miller for encouraging me to write this book for Thomas Nelson, and for educating me about the existence of the extraordinary Maria Skobtsova, without whom this book might well have included a chapter on Shirley "Cha-cha" Muldowney, Totie Fields, or Moms Mabley. *Soli Deo Gloria.*

About the Author

E ric Metaxas is the #1 *New York Times* bestselling author of *Bonhoeffer, Martin Luther, Amazing Grace,* and *Miracles.* His books have been translated into more than twenty-five languages. His writing has appeared in *The Wall Street Journal, The New York Times,* and *The New Yorker,* and Metaxas has appeared as a cultural commentator on CNN, the Fox News Channel, and MSNBC. He is the host of *The Eric Metaxas Show,* a nationally syndicated daily radio show. Metaxas is also the founder and host of Socrates in the City, the acclaimed series of conversations on "life, God, and other small topics," featuring Malcolm Gladwell, Dick Cavett, and Rabbi Lord Jonathan Sacks, among many others. He is a senior fellow and lecturer at large at the King's College in New York City, where he lives with his wife and daughter.

www.ericmetaxas.com